TRUCKING COUNTRY

POLITICS AND SOCIETY IN
TWENTIETH-CENTURY AMERICA

Series Editors
William Chafe, Gary Gerstle, Linda Gordon, and Julian Zelizer

A list of titles in this series appears at the back of the book

TRUCKING COUNTRY

THE ROAD TO AMERICA'S
WAL-MART ECONOMY

Shane Hamilton

Princeton University Press
Princeton and Oxford

Library of Congress Cataloging-in-Publication Data
Hamilton, Shane, 1976–
Trucking country : the road to America's Wal-Mart economy / Shane Hamilton.
p. cm. — (Politics and society in twentieth-century America)
Originally presented as the author's thesis (doctoral)—Massachusetts Institute of Technology.
Includes bibliographical references and index.
ISBN 978-0-691-13582-3
1. Truck drivers—United States—History.   2. United States—Rural conditions.
3. United States—Economic conditions—20th century.   I. Title.
HD8039.M7952U529 2008
303.48'32—dc22   2008009874

British Library Cataloging-in-Publication Data is available

For Chloe

CONTENTS

ILLUSTRATIONS AND TABLES

ACKNOWLEDGMENTS

Writing a book, like driving a big rig, involves many solitary hours of work, and I am grateful for this opportunity to thank colleagues and friends who have shared ideas and camaraderie with me on this long haul. At the Massachusetts Institute of Technology, Deborah K. Fitzgerald taught me how to reframe and rethink rural history. Her warmth and generosity are unparalleled and remain inspiring. Meg Jacobs made this book possible in countless ways, and above all encouraged me to tackle the biggest questions in American political economy. Merritt Roe Smith's work on technology, culture, and capitalism drew me to MIT—even before I discovered that we share a passion for classic country music. I am indebted to many friends and teachers in Cambridge, especially the Atomic Harvesters, Lizabeth Cohen, David Kaiser, Dave Lucsko, Leo Marx, Harriet Ritvo, Jennifer Leigh Smith, William J. Turkel, and Anya Zilberstein. Undergraduate mentors at the University of Wisconsin-Madison convinced me I could make a career out of studying rural culture and political economy, particularly James Baughman, Paul Boyer, Colleen Dunlavy, and Stanley Schultz.

Generous readers helped me transform an unwieldy dissertation into a book. Julian Zelizer carefully read multiple drafts, and his uncanny ability to extract clarity out of chaos has been invaluable. Nelson Lichtenstein graciously offered crucial insights, critiques, and encouragement at every stage of revision. An anonymous reader for Princeton University Press provided extraordinarily thoughtful suggestions, as did the editors of the Politics and Society in Twentieth-Century America series. Incisive comments from William Childs, James Cobb, Mark Rose, and Edmund Russell led to substantial improvements. I am also grateful for the feedback and friendship of my colleagues at the University of Georgia—especially Ben Ehlers, Peter Hoffer, Allan Kulikoff, Ari Levine, Stephen Mihm, Bethany Moreton, Claudio Saunt, William Stueck, Paul Sutter, and Pamela Voekel. Thanks are also due to individuals who have read and shared wisdom on various portions of this project over the years, including Hal Barron, Paul Burnett, William Cronon, Deb Fink, Walter Freidman, Grace Hale, Thomas Hughes, Joan Jensen, Jon Lauck, David Nye, Jeffrey Sklansky, John Staudenmaier, and Richard Tedlow. Brigitta van Rheinberg and Clara Platter at Princeton University Press deserve innumerable thanks for guiding me through the revision and production process.

It is fitting that a book about trucking culture required me to spend many days (far more than six) on the road. A Dissertation Improvement Grant from the National Science Foundation and research funds provided by the University of Georgia Alumni Research Foundation and the Willson Center for the Humanities and Arts made those travels possible. At a crucial juncture in the writing process, the Royal Institute of Technology in Stockholm provided me with a chance to view U.S. history from an outsider's angle. Predoctoral fellowships from the Dibner Institute for the History of Science and Technology, the Smithsonian Institution's National Museum of American History, and the Miller Center of Public Affairs at the University of Virginia gave me time and space to do research. These travels allowed me to share ideas and company with great scholars and wonderful people, including Brian Balogh, Bernard Carlson, Alex Checkovich, Pete Daniel, Sara Gregg, Derek Hoff, Arne Kaiser, Chris Loss, and Sidney Milkis.

The archivists who suffered my endless requests for dusty boxes deserve special thanks. Harry Miller at the Wisconsin Historical Society, Joe Schwartz at the National Archives, Dawn Oberg at the Country Music Hall of Fame, the staff of the Smithsonian Institution Archives Center, Bill Johnson at the American Truck Historical Society, and Olga Montgomery at the Finney County Historical Society pointed me to sources I never could have found on my own. Ty and Earl Brookover, Ken Greff, Kevin Patterson, Lawrence Pilgrim, and Robert Vandivier welcomed me and my tape recorder into their lives, while many other truckers shared their working knowledge with me anonymously. I only hope I have done their stories justice.

Although I grew up in rural Wisconsin, I knew I would never be a farmer as nearly every member of every previous generation on both sides of my ancestral tree had been. My family's support allowed me to take the trip "back East" to write about the people and places I can never leave behind. My parents struggled to make a living in a world of limited opportunities, and I know how proud both would have been to see this book in print. My mother's wisdom, work ethic, and refusal to surrender despite unceasing adversity offer daily inspiration as I strive to honor her memory. My sisters, Shamane and Sheri, have been extraordinary role models and I can never thank them enough for the sacrifices they have made on my behalf. Jay, Laura, Nancy, Elliot, Max, Carol, and Mort deserve special thanks for warmly welcoming a country boy into their family.

Chloe Wigston Smith has worked nearly as hard on this book as I have. I dedicate this book to her, because she has read every word I have written, sharpened my thoughts on gender and culture, and patiently listened as I tried to formulate words and thoughts as elegantly as she does. I could not have completed this book if Chloe had not completed me.

INTRODUCTION

Armed with bricks, knives, and shotguns, angry bands of truck drivers roamed the nation's highways in the summer of 1979, shattering windshields and slashing fellow truckers' tires. Governors of nine states summoned National Guard troops as escalating violence caused one death and dozens of injuries. Though most remained peaceful, as many as 75,000 truckers blockaded interstates, encircled fuel pumps, parked their rigs at home, or otherwise tried to shut down the nation's highway transportation system. Many refused to haul milk, meat, fruit, and vegetables, provoking panic buying sprees in suburban supermarkets. Midwestern meatpacking factories laid off workers and produce rotted in California fields. The protest ostensibly erupted in response to rapidly rising fuel prices in the wake of the Iranian Revolution. But for Mike Parkhurst, self-proclaimed instigator of the shutdown and editor of *Overdrive* magazine ("Voice of the American Trucker"), much more than the cost of diesel fuel was at stake. The tens of thousands of truckers who joined his Independent Truckers Association, Parkhurst declared, were angered not by a global energy crisis but by a crisis of U.S. capitalism.[1]

"If the mood of America is for a rebirth of free enterprise," Parkhurst had informed Congress three years before the shutdowns, "there is no nobler cause than that of the independent trucker." Beholden neither to union leaders nor to corporate employers, the independent truck driver was celebrated in popular culture as the last American cowboy. But the truck driver was not in fact the king of the open road, according to Parkhurst. Government regulations in place since the early years of the New Deal discouraged competition in the freight trucking industry, ensnaring the truck-driving man in the grip of federal bureaucrats and the Teamsters Union. Consigned to hauling "unregulated" commodities—particularly farm and food products—that brought low returns for sweated labor, the independent trucker was locked out of the more lucrative regulated freight market. In the context of rising fuel prices, the fact that regulated trucking firms dominated general freight trucking put a squeeze on the hard-working trucker who refused to give part of his paycheck to the Teamsters. "Are the independent truckers to remain forever hostages [to] Teamster domination and apathetic lawmakers?" Parkhurst demanded of a congressional committee in late 1979. "Is this system [of trucking regulation] truly serving the cause of freedom so many soldiers have died for in so many wars?"

Setting unionized truckers free and allowing independents to join in the fray for all freight, not just farm products, would revive a culture of economic liberty, benefiting U.S. consumers who were not yet "aware of the giant rip-off of their pocketbooks and their dinner plates because . . . there is not enough free enterprise, not enough competition in the transportation industry." The drivers who refused to haul food and freight in the summer of 1979, Parkhurst insisted, were the ground troops in a larger battle to overthrow New Deal economic liberalism. America's independent truckers were fighting, in the name of personal freedom and low consumer prices, to dismantle government regulations, unleash free enterprise, and deliver a fatal blow to organized labor.[2]

Mike Parkhurst had reason to see independent truck drivers as a militant vanguard of the free-market revolution that characterized the Nixon, Ford, Carter, and Reagan years. As I argue in the following chapters, such a revolution had long been quietly underway on America's rural highways, where independent truckers, encouraged by agribusinesses and farm policymakers, challenged the regulatory structures and labor policies of New Deal political economy from the outset. A special breed of trucker was born in the 1920s and 1930s, as industrialized agriculture forced many farmers off the land and onto the roads to seek a living. These rural truckers developed a culture of fierce independence, encouraged by farm-friendly policies that shielded them from federal regulations and discouraged unionization. By the 1960s, these "wildcat" rural truckers had upended the nation's railroad-based farm economy. Agribusiness and factory farmers relied on nonunion rural truckers to deliver cheap food to suburban supermarket shoppers, enabling the affluence of postwar consumerism while fostering a broad transformation of U.S. economic culture and politics. Through the 1930s and 1940s, urban workers and consumers had called upon labor unions and the federal government to contest the power of industrial agriculture in the food marketplace. By the late 1960s, however, working- and middle-class consumers accepted agribusiness's ability to decimate organized labor and defy government regulation in the countryside in exchange for low food prices. Long-haul trucking allowed agribusinesses to simultaneously provide the good life to U.S. consumers while resisting liberal efforts to administer private enterprise in the name of worker prosperity and consumer purchasing power. The "mood for free enterprise" that enraptured Mike Parkhurst and the nation in the 1970s had been coalescing for decades on the nation's rural highways, bringing in its wake a low-price food economy unhindered by union or government interference.

In making this argument, I offer a firm rebuttal to social commentators who see modern conservatism as a devil's bargain between culturally conservative working-class Americans and economic conservatives in the modern Republican Party. In *What's the Matter with Kansas?*, for instance, Thomas Frank lambastes working-class rural Kansans for betraying their economic interests by voting against Democrats, perceived as "latte-drinking, sushi-eating, Volvo-driving" liberals, in favor of tax-slashing, deregulating "grandstanding Christers." The idea of a middle-American, working-class "backlash" against liberal East Coast elites has dominated journalistic and historical analyses of modern conservatism since the 1960s. In this vein, it might seem that the thousands of truck drivers who revolted against government regulation of trucking in the 1970s were archetypal members of Richard Nixon's "silent majority," politically primed by their disgust with civil rights and anti-Vietnam protestors to accept not only Nixon's attempts to dismantle the New Deal but also Ronald Reagan's flag-waving message of budget-cutting, union-busting, and deregulation in the election of 1980. But the truckers who demanded the end of government intervention in the nation's transport economy in 1979 were not reacting to a perceived breakdown of social mores and "law and order." Nor did the protesting truckers see the main threat to the white working man's liberty as affirmative action or mandatory busing or welfare. From their perspective, the problem was the entire set of government policies imposed by Republicans and Democrats alike—bureaucratic red tape, cozy relations with corrupt Teamsters officials, the fifty-five mile-per-hour speed limit—that seemed to infringe upon individual economic freedoms in an era of stagnating wages and inflated prices. Pocketbook politics, not cultural conservatism, framed truckers' disdain for liberalism in the 1970s. Importantly many of the independent truckers who took part in the protests of 1979 earned their living hauling the nation's farm and food products—which meant that they already worked in an economic environment that had been unregulated since the mid-1930s. The taste of freedom provided by the "open road," contrasted with the apparent failure of the federal state and the Teamsters to protect job security and incomes in the 1970s, drove these truckers to demand an overthrow of economic liberalism within trucking. The anarchic libertarianism of Parkhurst and his followers was not a revolt against cultural liberalism, East Coast elitism, or even the Democratic Party. Instead it was a rejection of a central tenet of New Deal economic liberalism: the idea that the government could and should manage the economy to maintain business stability, worker prosperity, and consumer purchasing power.[3]

Conservatives may or may not have "won the heart of America," as Thomas Frank's subtitle declares, but if they did, it was not by hoodwinking rural Americans into rejecting their own economic interests. Instead rural Americans' ideas regarding state intervention in the economy helped shape the broader conservative ideologies of the late twentieth century. Unlike the Populist movement that spurred the economic interventionism of the Progressive era and the New Deal, however, the neopopulism expressed by the country-bred truckers of the 1970s marked the triumph of a radically antistatist capitalist ideology embraced by farmers, workers, consumers, and politicians alike.[4] Truckers were key to this broad transformation of U.S. political culture, not only because they expressed their new-found libertarian politics so dramatically in the summer of 1979, but because their work as truck drivers helped to construct a new economic order in the post–World War II U.S. countryside. Though often referred to in scholarly discourse as "postindustrial" or "post-Fordist" capitalism, the economic culture that emerged in America in the final quarter of the twentieth century involved much more than a turn away from industrial mass production.[5] It involved a categorical embrace of free-market ideology by workers, consumers, and politicians who, since the height of the New Deal in the late 1930s, had called upon labor unions and a powerful central government to strike a balance between private economic gain and equality of economic opportunity.[6] Those who accepted this post–New Deal "free enterprise" vision did so for material as much as ideological reasons. New forms of business enterprise emerged in the postwar period to use technologies of efficient mass distribution, rather than of mass production, to provide "luxuries for the masses" while slashing labor costs and defying government antitrust provisions.

The retail firm Wal-Mart provides the most familiar example of the new capitalist culture of the late twentieth century. Founded in 1962 in a small Arkansas town, Wal-Mart began spreading throughout the rural and then suburban United States. While selling cut-rate merchandise and promoting a "family atmosphere" for both shoppers and employees, the firm held worker wages to a minimum in a virulently antiunion workplace. By the mid-1990s the company employed more workers and sold more consumer goods and groceries than any other U.S. firm—and, revealingly, operated one of the world's largest and most efficient trucking fleets. With its fearsome market power, technological sophistication, and low-wage, low-price business model, Wal-Mart set the pace for the fanatically deregulatory and antiunion capitalism that emerged in the last quarter of the twentieth century. In an economy increasingly driven by distribution and retailing rather than manufacturing, union membership collapsed while corporations shipped jobs across state and national boundaries at will. Keynesian economic ideas lost traction as workers' wages stagnated. Free-market ideology reigned, as consumers expected to pay "always low" prices for the necessities and comforts of suburban life, while aggressive wage-cutting corporations obliterated competitors in a lightly regulated economic environment.[7]

But decades before Wal-Mart began selling discount hosiery in rural Arkansas, it was agribusiness—industrial processors and marketers of farm and food products—that first forged the template for the low-price, low-wage economy of the late twentieth century. And like Sam Walton's retail empire, the agribusiness assault on economic liberalism sprouted in rural soil. By relying on long-haul trucking to craft a low-price food economy on America's rural highways, agribusinesses cultivated the antistatist, antiunion ideologies that made post–New Deal capitalism palatable not only to Mike Parkhurst's anarcho-populist followers, but to the broad swath of the American populace who came to demand "always low prices" at the supermarket. Historians have not integrated the transformation of the rural economy into postwar U.S. political and social history. The supermarket, for instance, serves as a proxy for the postwar age of affluence, evoking images of the "modern housewife" meekly purchasing a plastic-wrapped prepriced T-bone, rather than resolutely demanding a bargain from the neighborhood butcher.[8] But the supermarket, I argue, was a central cause, rather than symptom, of the economic conservatism of the postwar era. In the account that follows, I look back to the factory farm that raised the grain and the steer, to the rural factory where the steer became a T-bone, and to the superhighway on which refrigerated trucks sped packaged meat to the suburban supermarket. I show how agribusinesses crafted a business model that promoted low consumer prices, low wages, and minimal government regulation as inherent social benefits. As more Americans gained access to the low-cost foods lining supermarket shelves in the 1950s and 1960s, the importance of government regulators and labor unions as guarantors of working- and middle-class consumer purchasing power diminished. The most mundane of technologies—highways, refrigerated trailers, and diesel engines, none of which were particularly revolutionary in and of themselves—allowed agribusinesses to materially undermine the New Deal-era political integration of state power, organized labor, and mass consumption within the food economy. In building the infrastructure of this "post-industrial" economy on the highways of rural America, agribusinesses set the stage for the uncompromising free-market ideology that took root in the United States in the last quarter of the twentieth century. Decades before the rise of the religious right, conservative business leaders won over America's stomach, not its heart.

Although consumers at the end of the century treated the price of food as a product of private decisions in the marketplace—a choice, say, between organic and conventional or between Whole Foods and Wal-Mart—the price of food was among the most politically charged economic issues of the first half of the twentieth century. As chapter 1 shows, American farmers initiated one of the most significant New Deal interventions in the economy. Suffering from an economic crisis that began a decade before the stock market crash of 1929, farmers renounced laissez-faire ideology and turned to the federal government to intervene in the food marketplace on their behalf. One of the first pieces of New Deal legislation, the Agricultural Adjustment Act, drastically expanded the power of the federal government in an effort to boost farm prices. The relationship between rural Americans and the New Deal state quickly emerged in the 1930s as a central battleground over the goals of economic liberalism. Farm policies enacted at the outset of the New Deal put the federal government in the business of boosting farmers' incomes, but did so by increasing the market power of factory farmers and food processors at the expense of small farmers, organized urban workers, and consumers who demanded reasonably priced food. At a time when food costs dominated the daily economic concerns of every American who purchased milk, meat, bread, and produce for their families, consumers had reason to believe that neither the free market nor federal farm policies operated in their best interest. In the milk and meat industries, for instance, a handful of agribusiness firms relied on railroad transportation to control the production, marketing, and pricing of food products that Americans considered essential to the nation's health and industrial productivity. Since the turn of the century, urban consumers had attacked the firms that made up the so-called Beef Trust and Milk Trust for unfairly manipulating the marketplace. Their complaints took on new urgency under the administration of Franklin D. Roosevelt, which explicitly courted working- and middle-class consumers, along with farmers and industrial workers, as members of an emerging Democratic electoral coalition. Consumers and labor representatives demanded strong government intervention in the food marketplace, recognizing that New Deal farm policies primarily benefited corporate agriculture despite rhetorical claims of saving the small family farm. Organized consumers and laborers, backed by liberal New Dealers, mounted a bold but unsuccessful attempt to construct new government agencies, revise agricultural policies, and revive antitrust laws to check the power of factory farmers and industrial food processors to profit at the expense of consumers.

This conflict over the proper degree of state power in the farm economy is a consistent theme of subsequent chapters, which trace the political efforts of public figures and private enterprises to solve the "farm problem." In chapters 2 through 7, I approach agricultural policy as a central conflict within U.S. political culture, with implications not only for the structure of the U.S. farm economy but for urban workers and consumers as well. Both during and after the New Deal, liberals struggled unsuccessfully to use state power to contest, rather than subsidize, the market power of industrial agriculture. Through the 1930s and 1940s, liberal farm policymakers such as Jerome Frank, Henry A.

Wallace, and Charles Brannan devised plans intended to balance the interests of small farmers, urban workers, and consumers with those of corporate agriculture. All of these attempts to overturn the regressive features of New Deal farm policies failed. Even at the end of the century, the 1996 "Freedom to Farm Act," although intended by fiscal conservatives to cancel the mailing of government checks to corporate farmers, led to an immediate redoubling of subsidies under the guise of "market transition payments." The old New Deal-era joke still applied long after progressive New Dealism had died: the best way for a commercial farmer to boost his or her income was to get another mailbox. Political historians have tried to explain the continuation of regressive farm policies as a function of federalism, agrarian ideology, interest group politics, and institutional capacity. Certainly all of these factors shaped farm policy in its early years. The farm programs emerged from a Congress dominated in the 1930s by representatives of rural districts with political power disproportionate to their population. Emotionally tinged agrarian rhetoric, which upheld the family farm as the nation's moral and political backbone, helped commercial farmers to cultivate ties to the congressional "farm bloc" and to bureaucrats in the essentially autonomous Department of Agriculture. But while all of these factors help explain why New Deal farm policies were not as progressive as they might have been, none explain why the policies lasted so long even when conservatives as well as liberals decried them as unfair exercises of state power.[9] Only by tracing the technological transformation of the farm and food economy during the mid-twentieth century, I contend, can we solve this puzzle of political history.[10] Trucks, as the next six chapters demonstrate, were inherently political technologies, used by agribusinesses to craft "free market" solutions to the farm problem while ironically allowing regressive New Deal farm policies to outlive the labor, consumer, and regulatory programs of the New Deal.[11]

The emergence of long-haul trucking in the 1930s, as chapter 2 discusses, provided factory farmers and their political allies with a tool that would ultimately undermine New Deal liberalism in the farm and food economy. As long-haul trucking became a viable alternative to railroads for the transportation of farm and food products, farm-friendly congressmen amended New Deal transportation policies in ways that ensured the vast majority of farm and food products would soon travel not on unionized railcars but in tractor-trailers driven by nonunionized, self-employed rural truckers. Shielded from government regulatory oversight, long-haul country trucking was a relatively easy business to get into, and appealed particularly to white rural men who sought a way to escape the tenuous life of a small farmer while maintaining a sense of economic independence. Though Teamsters president Daniel Tobin derided these over-the-road country truckers as "gypsies" and "trash," social-conscience film director Raoul Walsh dramatized the "wildcat" trucker's challenge to corporate power in the 1940 movie *They Drive by Night*. Minimal government regulation combined with a country culture of masculine independence, however, discouraged unionization and encouraged rampant rate-cutting in farm trucking. Chaotic country trucking drove down transportation costs in ways that at first threatened the economic power of corporate food processors, but would later provide "free market" solutions to the New Deal-era farm problem and consolidate the strength of agribusiness. Even so, technological change did not lead inevitably to the entrenchment of corporate power. In fact, liberal New Dealers, including Secretary of Agriculture Henry A. Wallace, correctly recognized that trucking posed a significant challenge to industries such as the Big Four meatpackers whose monopoly power rested largely in their control of railroad distribution.

As long-haul trucking matured in the 1940s, U.S. entry into World War II set the context for organized consumers, workers, and allied policymakers to mount the twentieth century's strongest political challenge to agribusiness. As chapter 3 explains, Democratic political figures during and after the war redoubled their efforts to balance the economic interests of urban workers and consumers against those of factory farmers and corporate food processors. The Office of Price Administration provided consumers with unprecedented state power to prevent meatpackers from taking advantage of wartime inflationary pressures to reap windfall profits. After the war, Secretary of Agriculture Charles Brannan attempted to replace farm subsidies with food subsidies to unite the interests of small farmers and urban consumers under the umbrella of the Democratic Party. Despite widespread support from liberal groups such as the National Farmers Union, the Americans for Democratic Action, and organized labor, Brannan's effort to reanimate New Dealism in the farm and food economy suffered an ignominious defeat. At the same time, an expanding trucking industry provided new opportunities for monopolistic food marketers and commercial farmers to consolidate their political and economic strength. Through subtle manipulations of state power, bureaucrats deep in the bowels of the Department of Agriculture fended off the efforts of the Interstate Commerce Commission to regulate rural trucking, while simultaneously confronting the growing power of the Teamsters Union. Rural "asphalt cowboys," unimpeded by union organizers or government regulators, began piloting ever larger tractor-trailers down federally funded highways. Railroads lost business as trucking firms became the primary movers of the nation's farm products and foodstuffs, setting the stage for a "free market" revolution in the postwar countryside. Because transportation costs composed the greatest share of the consumer's food dollar (second only to labor costs), the expansion of nonunionized rural trucking promised to achieve some of the goals of the Brannan Plan—namely higher farm prices without dramatic increases in consumer food costs—without the need for a progressive revision of agricultural policy.

Chapter 4 scrutinizes the intersection of country culture and industrial agribusiness on the postwar superhighway. As the industrialization of U.S. agriculture intensified in the 1950s and 1960s, small farmers vacated the land in record numbers. Would-be farmers increasingly turned to trucking in order to sustain a masculine culture of economic independence. The rural work culture of the independent trucker inspired an onslaught of popular paeans to the "knights of the road," from the 1954 honky-tonk nugget "Truck Driving Man" to the 1963 country music chart-topper "Six Days on the Road." Actual owner-operators may or may not have appreciated the popular interest in their work—or references to "little white pills"—but they were certainly aware that the nature of their work placed them somewhere between the "king of the open road" and the modern-day "sharecropper" upon whose back the industrial machinery of modern agribusiness rode. Even so, owner-operators took enough pride in their "independent" status to stoutly refuse the efforts of the increasingly powerful Teamsters Union to organize them. As modern interstate highways penetrated deep into the countryside, rural unregulated truckers—rather than unionized truckers or railroaders—increasingly hauled the products of factory farms and food processors to the new supermarkets of booming suburbia. Within this changing economic context, the virulently anti–New Deal Secretary of Agriculture Ezra Taft Benson launched a full-scale assault on economic liberalism in the farm and food economy. Decrying New Dealism as counterproductive, Benson sought to use state power to craft a new rural economy driven by marketing of processed foods like frozen concentrated orange juice rather than by subsidized commodity crop production. While touting the benefits of "free enterprise" and the "freedom to farm," Benson generously provided government funds and technological research to help corporate food processors and supermarket chains modernize their distribution systems to provide such "luxuries for the masses" as frozen peas and TV dinners. Benson's assistant secretary of agriculture, John H. Davis, coined the word "agribusiness" to describe the new technological and political reality of this marketing-driven farm economy. Transportation and distribution grew in importance in this agribusiness economy devoted to expanding consumer abundance through mass marketing, especially as Benson's Department of Agriculture worked assiduously to undermine the power of unionized transportation firms within the farm and food economy.

Agribusiness, relying on both the technology and the country culture of trucking, triumphantly beat back all New Deal-era challenges to its corporate power in the 1950s and 1960s, as I argue in two case studies in chapters 5 and 6. By delivering the good life via superhighway to cost-conscious supermarket shoppers, agribusinesses convinced U.S. consumers that "free enterprise" could serve their interests more effectively than could labor unions or government regulators. Anticipating a strategy used by Wal-Mart in later decades, the meatpackers I describe in chapter 5 relied on long-haul trucking to fundamentally restructure the beef industry by driving down both worker wages and consumer prices. The Big Four meatpackers, despite nagging antitrust concerns, had paid strong wages to large, unionized workforces in the urban Midwest since the union drives of the mid-1930s. In the 1950s and 1960s, however, a new breed of upstart meatpackers relied on highways and "asphalt cowboys" to replace factories built in nineteenth-century railroad cities like Chicago and St. Louis. In the "Old West" cowboy country of Kansas, Colorado, and Texarhoma, the meatpackers built a new West—replete with industrially fed steers and hyperefficient slaughterhouses staffed by underpaid rural and immigrant workers. By the early 1970s, a few of these upstart packers relied on long-haul refrigerated trucking to construct a beef empire that would have surprised even Upton Sinclair. Despite the reconstruction of a meatpacking "Jungle," the new beef industry satisfied consumer demands for cheap beef while flouting government antitrust laws. Rural truckers, hostile to labor unions, provided the labor needed to make this new marketing-driven beef empire run, but their antipathy to economic liberalism was born of economic necessity, not an ideological betrayal of the Populist and Progressive politics of their midwestern forbears.

Long-haul trucking, as I show in chapter 6, offered a different sort of political power to milk dealers. Milk bottlers, like the big meatpackers, had long come under attack for abusing their monopoly power to drive up the price of "nature's perfect food." Unlike the "Beef Trust," however, milk dealers and large dairy farmers had cultivated tight relationships with sympathetic government administrators since the onset of the New Deal. But in the 1950s and 1960s, milk bottlers sought to break their dependence on the heavy hand of government regulation. Ironically this turn to "free enterprise" occurred even as milk dealers increasingly relied on government-funded research into trucking technology—research explicitly encouraged by Ezra Taft Benson as part of his effort to repeal the New Deal in agriculture. Milk dealers began relying on nonunionized truckers to gather milk in enormous refrigerated tanks from industrialized dairy "super co-ops," forcing thousands of small farmers out of business. Long-haul truckers also began transporting cartons of milk directly to supermarkets, bypassing the doorstep bottle delivery system that for decades had paid good wages to urban Teamster milkmen. Teamsters and small farmers—whose insistence on a "fair price" for milk had long allowed them to confront the economic power of organized commercial dairymen and milk dealers—publicly protested the highly monopolistic "free market" milk economy that emerged in the 1960s. Their efforts to blockade supermarket aisles and dump milk on the side of highways, however, gained little sympathy from consumers who demanded low priced jugs of milk in an era of rising food prices. Meanwhile the rural Wisconsin truck drivers whose work made the new milk infrastructure possible mounted protests of their own in the 1960s, calling for better working conditions and higher pay—not as organized workers, but as small business owners. Although rural milk haulers drew on Progressive-era midwestern antimonopoly language, they firmly repudiated the Teamsters Union, setting a precedent for the neopopulist trucker revolts of the 1970s.

The final chapter explains how these triumphs of corporate power in the farm and food economy spearheaded a broader transformation of U.S. political culture in the 1970s. For the first time in a generation, antistatist economic ideologies became politically palatable to many working- and middle-class Americans who had previously looked to the government to protect their economic interests. Once consumers had accepted cheap beef, milk, and frozen orange juice—basic items of the postwar U.S. standard of living—little stood in the way of the widespread acceptance of a new political economy dedicated to "always low" prices at any social cost. This broad acceptance of laissez-faire ideology was exemplified by the deregulation movement of the 1970s. Figures across the political spectrum successfully pressed President Carter to end government economic regulation of basic industries, including the airlines, railroads, natural gas, and trucking—all in the name of lower consumer prices. Although trucking deregulation advocates drew upon the neoliberal economic theories of Milton Friedman and like-minded economists at the University of Chicago, they also saw material evidence for their free-market theories in the historical record: agribusiness had triumphantly relied on "deregulated" trucking to boost profits, slash wages, and drive down consumer prices since the mid-1930s. Independent truckers bore the brunt of the economic risks entailed by this deregulatory structure, but according to country music producers and Hollywood filmmakers in the 1970s, it seemed as if the life of a trucker was nothing but a hedonistic joyride populated by truckstop waitresses and the freedom of "the open road." More sober analysts of the trucking economy, including consumer advocates such as Ralph Nader and neoliberal economists, agreed that government and labor intervention in the trucking industry was little more than a "giant rip-off of [consumers'] pocketbooks and their dinner plates," as *Overdrive* editor Mike Parkhurst put it. The anarchic neopopulism expressed by Mike Parkhurst's followers in the massive trucker shutdowns of 1979 may have infuriated automobile drivers who could not pass interstate roadblocks, but the truckers' demands for an injection of "free enterprise" into the nation's economy had a broad appeal to consumers as well as post–New Deal Democrats such as Senator Edward M. Kennedy of Massachusetts, who agreed with the truckers that deregulation and union-busting would provide effective solutions to the era's economic woes. The antiauthoritarian, antistatist, and antiunion rural trucking culture that spawned the Hollywood hits *Smokey and the Bandit* and *Convoy* had serious implications for the nation's political economy.

Every truck stop in the nation sells belt buckles that proudly declare: "Independent Truckers Move America." In the following pages I reveal the motto's deeper meaning, showing how agribusiness relied upon independent truckers to shift U.S. capitalism into overdrive, introducing lean and mean business strategies and cultivating a culture of economic conservatism welcomed by both rural producers and suburban consumers. On country stretches of asphalt, in rural food factories, and in supermarket warehouses and shopping aisles, agribusinesses sowed the seeds of the antistatist market populism that defined late twentieth-century capitalism. Though it may seem surprising to link the country culture of trucking to the collapse of economic liberalism in America's post–World War II consumer economy, we might do well to pay heed to the words of country musician Del Reeves. As he twanged in his 1968 jukebox hit, "looking at the world through a windshield" helps put "everything in a little bit different light."

CHAPTER ONE

Food and Power in the New Deal, 1933–42

"The city-dweller or poet who regards the cow as a symbol of bucolic serenity," declared U.S. Circuit Court judge Jerome Frank in 1941, "is indeed naïve." Presiding over an acrimonious legal battle involving the price of milk, Frank noted that the liquid gently coaxed from a cow's udder might be "indispensable to human health," but it was also responsible for "provoking as much human strife and nastiness as strong alcoholic beverages." Frank had witnessed such nastiness firsthand as a member of the "Brains Trust" in Franklin Roosevelt's New Deal administration. As legal counsel for the Agricultural Adjustment Administration (AAA), Frank spent much of his time shaping federal milk policies, attempting to hammer out compromises among dairy farmers, milk bottlers, deliverymen organized in labor unions, and urban consumers. Earning himself a reputation as a "brilliant wild man" and a "potent left-winger" for his work on behalf of small black and white farmers, Frank worked to craft agricultural policies that would also benefit urban workers and consumers, even if those benefits came at the expense of large farmers and food processors. Frank's prolabor and proconsumer efforts at the AAA put him at odds with the first administrator of the agency, George N. Peek, who pegged Frank as an intellectual city-boy and tried unsuccessfully to have him fired. Peek's successor, Chester C. Davis, likewise saw Frank's politics as counter to the USDA's core constituency of commercial farmers, and in February of 1935 "purged" Frank and dozens of his like-minded colleagues from the AAA. Milk politics alone did not doom Frank's career as an economic liberal within the Department of Agriculture, but his efforts to frame farm policy as an issue of concern to all Americans highlighted one of the central tensions within the New Deal.[1]

The bitter fights surrounding the price of milk during Frank's brief tenure in the AAA represented a broader political struggle over farm and food policies during the early years of the New Deal. In response to the Great Depression, organized farmers, consumers, businessmen, and laborers all renounced laissez-faire ideology and demanded government intervention in the food economy. The New Deal policies erected in response to these conflicting demands engendered prolonged debates over the proper role of the state in regulating and administering the economy. Of particular concern was the decades-old dilemma of monopoly power in an age of mass produced and mass consumed food. Should the government break up monopolies such as the widely reviled "Milk Trust" or the "Big Four" meatpackers to protect the interests of small farmers and urban consumers? Or would action against these efficient businesses, which employed thousands of workers, actually do more harm than good in an economy reeling from underconsumption in the city and overproduction on the farm? The answers to these questions would dictate the future of New Deal economic liberalism, since government intervention in the food economy inherently affected every U.S. producer, consumer, and worker. Neither conservatives nor liberals could readily justify "free enterprise" in the farm economy at a time of worldwide economic crisis—yet neither could they agree on how the state could effectively intervene to benefit the greatest number of Americans.

From the beginning of Franklin Roosevelt's term in office until the entry of the United States into World War II, antimonopoly and agrarian rhetoric clashed with the reality of farm policies that benefited large-scale farmers and powerful food processors at the expense of smaller farmers, urban workers, and consumers. Beset by conflicting demands from all of these groups, liberal New Dealers such as Jerome Frank and Secretary of Agriculture Henry A. Wallace struggled to balance the concerns of workers, consumers, and small farmers with the interests of corporate agriculture. Their efforts, though only partially successful, made government regulation of private farming and food processing enterprises a central but deeply controversial aspect of New Deal political economy. As later chapters show, the expansion of long-haul trucking transformed the nature of this political question, as powerful agribusinesses relied on unregulated trucking to develop "free market" solutions to the New Deal-era farm problem. To understand that transformation, however, we must first understand the roots of the farm problem and its implications for the political economy of the New Deal in an era of railroad-based transportation. Despite the economic liberalism that animated the New Deal in a time of depression, the material reality of a transportation infrastructure forged during the Gilded Age required significant compromises—particularly the acceptance of a certain degree of monopoly power within the farm and food economy.

THE GREAT DEPRESSION AND THE FARM PROBLEM

The onset of the Great Depression in 1929 put farm prices and food costs front and center in U.S. politics, but the issue had deeper historical roots. The "farm problem" first became politically salient during the Populist movements of the 1880s and 1890s. Southern tenant farmers pressed by the credit squeeze of the crop lien system, along with northern plains farmers struggling to adjust to globalizing wheat markets, called for a strong federal government to countervail the power of the nation's "money interests"—landlords, banks, and especially railroads. Although the Populists failed to elect their presidential candidates in the 1892 and 1896 elections, they successfully put the farm problem on the nation's political agenda. Progressive reformers of the early twentieth century adapted many of the Populists' ideas as new legislation and policies, from the strengthening of the Interstate Commerce Commission to the establishment of rural producers' cooperatives to improve the leverage of farmers in agricultural markets. These policy efforts had some success in mitigating the farm problem, but even more important was the rising global demand for U.S. farm products that drove up prices in the 1910s. The period leading up to and through World War I witnessed a "golden age of agriculture" that significantly defused political agitation by farmers.[2]

The farm problem returned to the nation's political consciousness with a vengeance in the 1920s. Huge surpluses created by production for World War I led to a postwar drop in farm prices and an agricultural depression. Congressmen from rural states in the South and West reacted by forming a "farm bloc" devoted to increasing farmer's incomes, either by limiting agricultural production, by dumping surpluses on foreign markets, or by guaranteeing farmers a "parity" price for their crops. Attempts to pass legislation such as the McNary-Haugen Bill foundered in the 1920s, however, as farm representatives from different regions of the country could not reach consensus on the proper mechanism for assuring steady farm incomes. But when the Great Depression struck in 1929, desperate farmers called urgently upon the federal government for relief. Herbert Hoover's Farm Board attempted to implement the least statist proposals of the McNary-Haugen era—particularly voluntary marketing associations to shore up farm prices—but with little success. Most farmers, as individual business owners, refused to cooperatively reduce their production to increase prices. The agricultural depression continued. As farm prices and credit structures collapsed, sending even formerly prosperous U.S. farmers deeply into debt, laissez-faire ideology lost its hold in the countryside, paving the way for heavy government intervention in the depressed rural economy.[3]

One of the Roosevelt administration's first acts was to sign into law the Agricultural Adjustment Act of 1933. The legislation sought to shore up farmers' incomes through both price supports and production controls, making centralized economic planning the cornerstone of New Deal farm policy. Price supports were meant to guarantee stability in the agricultural marketplace, with the visible hand of government creating what Secretary of Agriculture Henry A. Wallace called an "ever-normal granary" through federal purchases of surplus crops. Production controls, meanwhile, would force farmers to reduce the amount of acreage planted to crops through an unprecedented extension of government power. These policies—which combined government subsidization with planned scarcity—helped raise farm incomes for many commercial farmers, but at the cost of forcing thousands of small farmers, tenants, and sharecroppers off the land. Even as the AAA sought to limit farmers' production, the scientific bureaus of the USDA continued to push farmers to use pesticides, fertilizers, hybrid crops, and tractors to boost yields. Encouraged by economists such as M. L. Wilson, who helped formulate the AAA production control policies, the USDA's technological and scientific efforts from the late nineteenth century into the 1930s focused on creating giant industrial farms where commodities could be produced factory-style. New Deal farm policies reaped rewards for the Democratic Party by securing solid political support from large commercial farmers, but also pushed many small, "inefficient" farmers out of the market. The AAA consequently offended conservatives as an affront to free enterprise while liberals decried the programs for harming the most vulnerable members of rural society. As we shall see, this tension between large and small farmers, and between conservatives and liberals, would shape farm policy debates for several decades after the economic crisis of the Great Depression.[4]

The farm problem, however, was not just a problem for farmers. The price of milk, meat, bread, and produce impacted every U.S. family trying to put food on the table during a devastating depression. The AAA's focus on taming overproduction put farm policies at odds with other New Deal economic reforms, since raising farm prices increased the cost of food for urban industrial laborers and consumers, who were also members of the emerging Democratic coalition. Even as agricultural policymakers formulated plans for slashing production of midwestern wheat crops in the spring of 1933, unemployed factory workers queued up in breadlines in the nation's largest cities. In the summer of 1933 bakers began charging eight to ten cents for loaves of bread that had previously cost five cents. Consumers around the country blamed farm policies for inflating the price of bread and flooded the offices of President Roosevelt and Secretary of Agriculture Henry A. Wallace with letters demanding change. In the fall of 1933 and spring of 1934, the farm program came under heated attacks when Wallace ordered six million hogs culled and one-quarter of the southern cotton crop plowed under to increase market prices. Critics of the New Deal ridiculed the Roosevelt administration for destroying food and fiber when millions of Americans were starving and poorly clothed. The federal government appeared to be subsidizing powerful farmers and rural landlords at city dwellers' expense.[5]

In an effort to stave off a full-scale revolt against New Deal farm policy, Wallace appointed veteran trustbuster Frederic C. Howe to the office of AAA Consumers' Counsel in June 1933. An ally of Jerome Frank, Rexford Tugwell, and other urban liberals in the AAA who hoped to transform the entire agricultural economy rather than merely raise farm prices, Howe gained the authority to investigate consumer complaints against food processors, distributors, and retailers. Although Howe's actions had no direct impact on New Deal farm policies, his office energized a growing consumer movement. By publishing the *Consumers' Guide,* a master list of food prices in the nation's major cities, Howe hoped to "awaken public sentiment and put its power behind the drive to get more money for the farmer without gouging the consumer." Howe worked assiduously to prevent profiteering in the food economy—so assiduously, in fact, that he was included in the "great purge" of liberals from the AAA in 1935. Although Secretary of Agriculture Wallace sympathized with and encouraged Howe's antitrust harangues, AAA administrator George N. Peek believed that consumer purchasing power was outside the ambit of the farm program. As Peek put it, the AAA was part of the Department of Agriculture, not the "Department of Everything."[6]

The split between agrarians and urban-industrial reformers within the Department of Agriculture in the early years of the New Deal was due in part to the divergent personal histories of the individual policymakers involved. Agrarian reformers—represented by farm leaders George N. Peek and Henry A. Wallace, economists M. L. Wilson and Howard R. Tolley, and sociologist Carl C. Taylor—were all born in the rural Midwest, had been educated at midwestern land-grant schools, and either began their early careers working as farm businessmen (Peek and Wallace) or as agricultural economists or rural sociologists in the USDA/land-grant college complex (Wilson, Tolley, Taylor). Wallace, for instance, was the grandson of Henry Wallace—the founder of the influential farm journal *Wallace's Farmer*—and the son of Henry Cantwell Wallace, who served as secretary of agriculture under Presidents Harding and Coolidge. Before becoming Franklin Roosevelt's first secretary of agriculture, Henry A. Wallace attended Iowa State College, wrote scientific articles and political editorials for *Wallace's Farmer,* and in 1914 founded the hybrid seed corn company that later became Pioneer Hi-Bred. Wallace was no conservative—he firmly believed the federal government could and should intervene in the agricultural economy to nurture a Jeffersonian republic of landed farmers, and furthermore believed the government should play an active role in diffusing scientific knowledge to those farmers. Wallace's politics were forged, however, in the rural Midwest, where white family farmers did not encounter the same racial tensions and extremes of poverty and wealth that plagued the farmscapes of the South and West and the industrial cores of the nation's largest cities. The urban-industrial reformers who joined the New Deal Department of Agriculture, by contrast, formed their political consciousnesses in more cosmopolitan spheres far removed from heartland agriculture. Rexford G. Tugwell, Jerome Frank, and Frederic C. Howe were all born in the urbanized Northeast, attended prestigious private colleges, and spent their early careers practicing law or teaching in Ivy League universities. Jerome Frank, for instance, was born in New York City in 1889 to German-Jewish immigrants who later moved to Chicago. At the age of sixteen Frank entered the University of Chicago, where he studied political science before entering the Law School, from which he graduated with the highest grades in that school's history. After spending several years on Wall Street practicing corporate law, Frank met Felix Frankfurter, an influential Harvard legal theorist who, like Frank, sympathized with the politically and economically disempowered members of U.S. society. Frankfurter, a personal friend of Franklin Roosevelt, encouraged Frank to join the Department of Agriculture in 1933 as Rexford Tugwell's top legal aide. Frank took the job, and brought with him a host of like-minded cosmopolitan reformers, including a young Alger Hiss, Thurman Arnold, and Adlai Stevenson.[7]

Both the agrarians and the urban-industrial reformers denounced laissez-faire capitalism in the rural economy, but their political philosophies had little else in common. Agrarian reformers such as Wallace concentrated their concerns on the perceived plight of the white-owned, family-run, commercially oriented midwestern farm, which they understood to be the moral, political, and economic "backbone" of the nation. Antitrust actions against railroads and meatpackers and government stabilization of commercial farmers' incomes formed the core of these agrarians' political-economic philosophies. Urban-industrial reformers such as Tugwell and Frank, however, saw agricultural policymaking as part of a broader political package that could bring European-inspired progressive social reforms. Firmly planted in the intellectual Progressive political tradition of labor scholar John Commons, trustbuster Louis Brandeis, and legal realist Felix Frankfurter, the urban-industrial reformers within the AAA expected New Deal farm policy to help urban consumers lower their food costs, provide tools for African American and poor white landless farmers to rise up the "agricultural ladder" to land ownership, and foment European-style social democracy in labor organization as well as farm policy. For these urban-industrial reformers, the example of 1930s Swedish farm politics provided at least as much inspiration as the U.S. agrarian movements of the nineteenth century. In Sweden in 1933, the Social Democrats cemented a decades-long hold on political power by allying their core constituency of urban industrial laborers with farm interests in the Agrarian Party. Under the leadership of agrarian Per Edvin Sköld, the Social Democrats declared that Swedish farmers and workers suffered similar exploitation under capitalism and so had to unite as producers to attain mutually beneficial political power. The Swedish approach held little appeal, however, for U.S. agrarians such as George N. Peek, the first head of the AAA. Peek denounced Frank and his colleagues as a "plague of young lawyers" who had their "hair ablaze" with radical ideas about "collectivist agriculture"—ideas that animated the early New Deal but also ensured the intellectual city boys would have short careers within the tradition-bound USDA.[8]

The divisive nature of New Deal farm policies also reflected broader conflicts within rural U.S. society and politics in the 1930s. In the American South, cotton and tobacco production dominated a landscape in which landless farmers struggled to climb out of persistent indebtedness under the crop lien system established in the wake of the Civil War. Groups such as the Communist-led Share Croppers' Union (formed in Alabama in 1931) and the Socialist-led Southern Tenant Farmers Union (formed in 1934) sought to unite black and white tenant farmers in a mass revolt against racial and economic oppression in the cotton belt. Southern tenant and sharecropper farmers understood that the AAA's production controls and price supports were unlikely to benefit them. They were soon proven correct. Planter elites took the vast majority of government price-support payments for themselves, while using the AAA's acreage-reduction provisions to evict tenants from the land. Despite organizing a massive 1935 cotton-pickers' strike, the Southern Tenant Farmers Union collapsed in 1939. The group faced not only terroristic reprisals from white southern elites but also internal divisions, as the group's Socialist leaders sought collectivist agriculture while rank-and-file members wanted private land ownership. Radical organizations such as the STFU, furthermore, may have gained some sympathy from left-leaning agricultural policymakers such as Gardner Jackson within the AAA, but tenants' pleas for land redistribution held little sway in Congress, even before the 1935 "purge" in which Jackson was included.[9]

With southern Democrats in the driver's seat of the congressional farm bloc, commercially oriented farm organizations did not need mass strikes to gain the ear of farm policy legislators. The most powerful farm organization, the American Farm Bureau Federation, was formally founded as a national group in 1919. The Farm Bureau united local and state farm educational institutions that had been founded during the Country Life Movement of the early twentieth century, when agricultural reformers such as Cornell horticulturalist Liberty Hyde Bailey aimed to enlighten supposedly benighted U.S. farmers in the science of farm productivity and farm management. With the 1914 passage of the Smith-Lever Act, nearly every county in the nation would soon have a federally funded county agent serving under the Federal Extension Service. These county extension agents, tasked with propagating the technical knowledge forged in the nation's land-grant agricultural colleges, formed tight relationships with local farm bureau agents—relationships so tight that critics would decry the "Farm Bureau-Extension Axis" for making the county agent a "tool for politicians." By the 1930s the Farm Bureau was the nation's largest farm organization by far, maintaining an active lobbying presence in Washington and an "umbilical attachment" to farm policymakers at every level of governance. The Farm Bureau exerted more pressure than any other group on New Deal farm policy, but its power was diluted somewhat by internal divisions. As a national organization, the Farm Bureau tried to simultaneously represent southern cotton planters, northern grain growers, and western cattle raisers—farmers whose views on issues such as tariffs, production controls, and price supports were often in direct opposition. A host of other farm organizations, furthermore, added to the cacophony of voices heard in the halls of Congress. The National Farmers Union, founded in 1902, took root primarily among northern plains grain farmers in the 1910s by promoting European-style cooperatives dedicated to strengthening farmers' access to credit and markets. Although commercially oriented and ill-disposed toward organizing mass revolts of black or white landless farmers, the Farmers Union claimed to represent the interests of small family farmers. Throughout the twentieth century the Farmers Union would criticize the Farm Bureau's leaders as big businessmen intent upon using farm policy and federally funded science and technology to drive common farmers off the land.[10]

The tensions within 1930s farm politics revealed more than a clash of personalities in the AAA and differences among interest group lobbyists, however. Debates over interventionist farm programs revealed contradictions inherent to the political economy of the New Deal. Conservative critics of the New Deal predictably decried the farm program as a decisive step toward state socialism, even though congressional conservatives from southern and western states had written the enabling legislation of the AAA in consultation with the conservative American Farm Bureau Federation. For many Democrats though, the far more troubling concern was not right-wing attacks but the farm program's potential to split apart the emerging New Deal coalition. While both liberal and conservative farm policymakers framed the agricultural depression as a result of overproduction, urban labor and consumer advocates pointed instead to the need to boost consumer purchasing power. Even labor- and consumer-friendly agricultural policymakers could not agree on how best to reconcile policies aimed at raising farmer's incomes with urban Americans' demands for affordable foodstuffs. Some liberal New Dealers, including Frederic Howe and Henry A. Wallace, advocated antitrust action against meatpackers to restore competition to the food economy. Others, such as Jerome Frank, called instead for the government to cooperate with monopolistic meatpackers and milk distributors to achieve efficiencies in the mass production and mass distribution of food. The only thing all could agree upon was that the federal government could and should play an active role in managing the farm economy.

These conflicts over the "problem of monopoly" were not confined to farm politics. Concerns over corporate power led to acute disputes over every major aspect of New Deal economic reform, from labor policy to antitrust action to regional planning initiatives. In labor policy, for instance, the 1933 passage of the National Industrial Recovery Act (NIRA) provided workers with an unprecedented state-guaranteed right to organize their own unions under section 7(a), while simultaneously providing business leaders with the tools to create legal cartels under "codes of fair competition." The National Recovery Administration (NRA) quickly proved a dismal failure in stabilizing U.S. business, even before the Supreme Court declared the NIRA unconstitutional in 1935. Section 7(a) nonetheless provided impetus to the labor movement's efforts to tie collective bargaining to economic recovery. New Deal labor advocates such as William Leiserson declared that a "living wage" for U.S. workers would raise consumer buying power, overcoming the problem of "underconsumption" that economists such as Paul H. Douglas, business leaders such as Edward A. Filene, and liberal politicians such as Robert F. Wagner (D-NY) understood as the underlying cause of the Great Depression. "Purchasing power" became a rallying cry after 1933 for workers who looked to the federal government to provide economic security. In 1935 Congress passed the Wagner Act, guaranteeing workers the right to organize their own unions and collectively bargain with employers. Recalcitrant corporate leaders refused to acknowledge a new era of labor empowerment, however, so workers had to wage their own fights for industrial democracy, and often relied on radical Communists to lead the battles. After a successful 1937 sit-down strike by militant General Motors employees, millions of inspired employees joined new industry-wide unions, many under the umbrella of the Congress of Industrial Organizations (CIO), which promoted racial harmony as essential for mass unionism's success. Millions more joined the older, craft-based American Federation of Labor (AFL), where racial and gender exclusion based on white male workers' assumption of superiority hammered cracks in the façade of working-class cohesion. By the end of the 1930s, New Dealism had inspired a massive upswing in organized labor's power on the shop floor and in the political sphere. New Dealism also cemented the resolve of liberals within the Democratic Party to boost purchasing power, even if that required redistribution of business profits into workers' pockets.[11]

The laissez-faire approach to labor relations was officially dead after 1935, as New Deal economic liberals announced that capitalism could not survive without government intervention to assure a modicum of social justice and economic fairness. Deep, unresolved tensions remained within the New Deal labor universe, however. Corporate executives, conservative labor leaders, and southern Democrats in Congress remained hostile to the perceived radicalism of the militant CIO. White male workers in both the AFL and the CIO struggled to maintain their assumed prerogatives of masculinity and whiteness, while millions of southern and western workers of all races and genders remained unorganized. And although the politics of "purchasing power" could serve to boost labor's claims to primacy within the New Deal coalition, it also held the potential to generate a political backlash among middle-class consumers and small business owners whose economic interests seemed threatened by state-backed labor power. All of these conflicts were built into the New Deal order from the outset, and as we shall see, would dog the ideas and practices of economic liberalism through the mid-twentieth century.[12]

New Deal economic liberalism also had contradictory roots and implications in the arena of government-business relations. The "problem of monopoly" took center stage in the early years of the New Deal. Trustbusters both inside and outside the federal government—including Roosevelt advisor Thomas G. "the Cork" Corcoran, Harvard law professor Felix Frankfurter, and Democratic Senator Joseph O'Mahoney of Wyoming—drew on Populist and Progressive-era rhetoric to call for curbs on corporate power. Economist Gardiner Means's concept of "administered prices" resonated with this crowd, who sensed that modern corporations set prices according to their firms' needs rather than in the public interest. Yet the exigencies of business bankruptcies in 1933 led the Roosevelt administration to downplay the problem of monopoly in its first effort to revive the industrial economy. The NRA, seeking to revive "business confidence," allowed businesses to self-regulate their prices and wages through cartels that were exempt from antitrust laws. Business self-regulation failed to end the Depression, however, as the NRA "codes of fair competition," even when businesses chose to comply with them, did little to stimulate production or boost consumption. By the time the Supreme Court killed the NRA with its 1935 *Schechter Poultry* v. *United States* decision, most New Dealers agreed that self-regulation was not a viable path to economic recovery. Meanwhile populist figures such as Senator Huey P. Long (D-LA) and Detroit "radio priest" Father Charles Coughlin attacked the New Deal for failing to rein in corporate power, pushing President Roosevelt to reconsider antimonopoly policies. After denouncing "economic royalists" for transforming private enterprise into "privileged enterprise" in his 1936 acceptance speech for renomination on the Democratic presidential ticket, Roosevelt cultivated closer ties to trustbusting New Deal advisors. One of the principal drafters of the "economic royalists" speech, Thomas Corcoran, became Roosevelt's right-hand-man on economic affairs. Corcoran's friend, Secretary of Interior Harold Ickes, delivered a blistering radio speech in December 1937 warning of the threat of a "big-business Fascist America—an enslaved America." In 1938, Thurman Arnold, as the new head of the Antitrust Division of the Department of Justice, stepped up enforcement of existing antitrust laws; by 1940 Arnold had initiated 93 prosecutions and 215 investigations of economic concentration. Senator Joseph O'Mahoney, as chair of the Temporary National Economic Committee, carried out sweeping investigations of monopolistic practices in dozens of important industries from 1938 to 1941. The antimonopoly fervor of the late 1930s would fade, however, as the nation entered World War II, when the need to mobilize an "arsenal of democracy" made the bigness of big business a national asset rather than a liability.[13]

Despite shifting antimonopoly politics, however, by the end of the 1930s New Dealers had fundamentally transformed the government's power to regulate and administer the nation's economy in the name of "the public interest." Besides strengthening the power of older agencies such as the Interstate Commerce Commission, the Federal Trade Commission, and the Antitrust Division, New Dealers erected powerful new regulatory bodies such as the Securities and Exchange Commission, the Federal Communications Commission, and the Civil Aeronautics Authority. But if New Deal economic liberals forged a consensus regarding the need for government intervention in private enterprise, deep contradictions remained. Large corporations such as General Motors or Ford might have deserved censure for making private enterprise into "privileged enterprise," but they also effectively used techniques of mass production to make consumer goods such as automobiles affordable to the nation's masses. After the labor movement's successes in the mid-1930s, furthermore, such giant corporations provided good wages and secure employment to millions of organized American workers. Federal antitrust action, meanwhile, was often more effective as a means of courting popular approval of the New Deal rather than actually serving "the public interest." The chain-store food and clothing stores that dominated U.S. retailing in the 1930s, for instance, underwent constant antitrust investigations and anti-chain legislation through the decade, and yet probably did more to keep consumers' expenses for necessities in check than any government agency during the Depression. Although the New Deal cemented the role of the federal government in regulating and administering the nation's economy, contradictory ideologies and definitions of "the public interest" posed inherent challenges to economic liberalism even at its highest tide.[14]

Despite the contradictions, the New Deal brought unprecedented intervention in the agricultural economy, transformations in labor relations, and upended the nineteenth-century laissez-faire tradition of government-business relations. By setting the United States on a liberal political-economic course in response to the global crisis of capitalism of the 1920s and 1930s, New Dealers raised the stakes of ideological and political conflict over the proper relationship between a democratic federal government and capitalistic private enterprise. By delving further into the nature of the "farm problem" of the 1920s and 1930s, however, we can see that the battles waged among farmers, consumers, business leaders, and policymakers over the shape of New Deal economic liberalism were not simply the product of long-standing ideological divides or of predictable interest-group politics. The intractability of the farm problem in the 1930s was, in important ways, a product of the material structure of the farm and food economy—namely the centrality of the railroad in U.S. food distribution. In an era when most urbanites did not raise or process their own crops or livestock, transportation technology was an essential factor in determining the prices farmers received for their commodities, the wages workers earned in food industries, the profits to be had by food manufacturers and distributors, and ultimately the prices that consumers paid for foodstuffs. Transportation technology did not act as a force outside of human society to determine the shape of political and economic conflict, but the technological structure of a rail-bound nation established the framework within which such conflicts took place during the New Deal era. A close look at the milk and beef industries, both of which involved intense political struggles over monopoly power within the food economy of the 1930s, reveals the extent to which the politics of the farm problem—and by extension, labor, consumer, and business politics—were inextricable from the nation's reliance on railroad technology.

The "Fair Price" of Milk

In the early twentieth century, Progressive reformers convinced city dwellers that cow's milk was necessary for human health. This was news to many urban consumers, who had for several decades considered cow's milk to be a "baby-killer," produced by diseased animals fed on distillery wastes (or worse). The introduction of refrigerated rail transportation in the 1890s, however, along with pasteurization and sanitary glass bottles, helped dairy farmers and enterprising milk dealers transform the feared "baby-killer" into "nature's perfect food" in the early twentieth century. Consumers who had previously shunned cow's milk began to demand high-quality milk, delivered year-round, at prices that working families could afford. Milk dealers such as Borden and National Dairy Products offered to meet these needs by pasteurizing, bottling, and delivering milk to consumer doorsteps for a profit. To do so, however, bottlers had to make significant capital investments in processing and distribution technologies, and expected to capture market share proportionate to their investments. Dealers also had to pay premium prices to dairymen to enable farmers to invest in disease-free cattle herds, quality feed, and clean barns. Furthermore the extreme perishability of milk, especially in the days before most consumers owned refrigerators, required daily delivery services by milkmen— teamsters who, along with coal and ice wagon drivers, had developed craft unions that were among the most successful in the country in gaining wage concessions from employers. As long as consumers felt they were paying a fair price for a quality product, and as long as farmers, bottlers, and teamsters believed the profits to be gained were fairly divvied up, milk might not have caused animosity. But conflicting interpretations of what constituted a "fair price"—conflicts that were at their heart based on the geographical structure of dairying in an age of railroad transport—meant that milk production and marketing was one of the most deeply politicized economic concerns of the first half of the twentieth century.[15]

The cost of transporting this highly seasonal and highly perishable product structured much of the conflict within the milk economy of the early twentieth century. Transportation costs were first defined as the key factor in milk pricing by Johann Heinrich von Thünen in his 1826 essay *The Isolated State.* Von Thünen, a Prussian gentleman farmer seeking to understand what made some farms more profitable than others, imagined a city surrounded by perfectly flat and uniformly fertile farmland. What a farmer decided to raise at any particular location in this imaginary world, predicted von Thünen, would depend on two variables: the price city consumers were willing to pay for a particular food and the cost of transporting those foods to market. A farmer located close to a city would profit most by producing fruits, vegetables, and fresh milk, considering that consumers were willing to pay a premium for these highly perishable foods, thereby offsetting the high costs of daily transportation. Farther away from the city, where land rents were lower, a farmer could make better profits producing grains, meat, and manufactured dairy products like cheese and butter. Although they brought lower prices in the market, these less perishable commodities had sufficiently lower transportation costs to make up the difference.[16]

Von Thünen's abstract model, which imagined farmers located in a series of concentric "rings" surrounding cities, has been criticized by geographers and historians as unrepresentative of a world in which cities are not isolated in the center of featureless plains. Nonetheless von Thünen's theory was remarkably accurate in predicting the geographical outlines of city milksheds that developed in the United States in the late nineteenth and early twentieth centuries. This was because railroad transportation was the only effective means of delivering fluid milk to the nation's expanding cities. Railroad transportation costs were directly tied to a farmer's distance from the city, enforcing compliance with von Thünen's rings. The rates charged by railroads for delivering milk to cities increased with distance, making shipment of fluid milk from beyond approximately 100 miles prohibitively expensive for outer-ring farmers (see figure 1.1). As a general rule, dairy farmers close to major cities such as Chicago and New York City, who benefited from lower transportation costs, could invest capital in the equipment and quality herds necessary for sanitary milk. Farmers located farther from the city, however, faced high transportation charges that prevented them from culling tuberculosis-prone cattle from their herds—these farmers needed all the milk they could get. Farmers deeper in the dairy hinterlands of northern Wisconsin and upstate New York thus focused on producing lower-quality milk suitable only for butter and cheese manufacturers located in rural districts. Through the 1910s and 1920s, local and state officials cemented this geographical division by imposing strict railroad rate structures and public health codes that ensured that dairy farmers in the inner ring would produce tuberculosis-free milk for drinking, while outer-ring farmers would only produce milk for eating as cheese or butter.[17]

Cows, however, remained unwilling to cooperate with the rhythms or politics of industrial society. Before the widespread adoption of growth hormones that made the dairy cow amenable to industrial production in the latter half of the twentieth century, cows tended to produce far more milk during the spring than in other seasons. During spring, cows ate the juiciest grasses and produced great quantities of milk in expectation of feeding their calves. Milk dealers trying to supply consumers with year-round milk consequently had to pay farmers to overproduce in the spring in order to have a sufficient supply later in the year. This surplus milk could, of course, be turned into Euro-American society's oldest convenience foods—cheese and butter—except that farmers who lived farther away from cities, and were consequently shut out of urban milk markets by transportation costs and health regulations, already produced milk for cheese and butter. These more distant dairy farmers did not need the expensive equipment, the spotless barns, and the tuberculosis-free cows required to meet the health standards that city officials demanded for

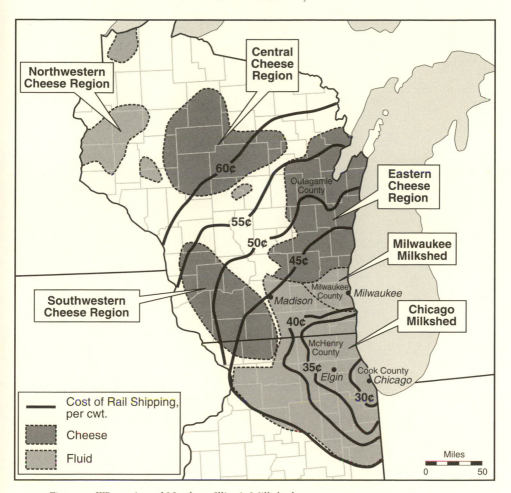

Figure 1.1. Wisconsin and Northern Illinois Milksheds, 1932.
The cost of shipping milk by railroad established a radial geography of milk production. Fluid milk producers clustered close to metropolitan centers, while cheese and butter producers remained in the "outer rings" (*Sources*: Wisconsin Cartographers' Guild, *Wisconsin's Past and Present: A Historical Atlas* [Madison: University of Wisconsin Press, 1998], 48; H. A. Ross, *The Marketing of Milk in the Chicago Dairy District* [Urbana: University of Illinois Agricultural Experiment Station, 1925], 470).

fluid milk supplies. Nonetheless these distant farmers had to accept a lower price for their milk than city milk producers, and consequently suffered when the spring surpluses of city farmers flooded cheese markets and drove down prices. Dairymen located close to cities likewise resented more distant farmers who tried to evade public health regulators and sell lower-quality milk to city

dwellers at cut-rate prices. Furthermore some farmers located somewhere between cheese and fluid milk dairymen tried to get the highest price possible for
their milk by selling either to cheese factories or to city milk dealers, depending on the season. Milk dealers, for their part, relied on this market instability
to force down the price they had to pay the rest of the year to inner-ring farmers. The cow's refusal to produce evenly throughout the year, coupled with the
inherent geographical tension between the fluid milk and the manufactured
milk markets, led to constant power struggles among farmers—struggles that
would shape the elaborate milk politics of the 1930s.[18]

Events of the early 1930s transformed these related issues of seasonal surpluses and geographical tensions into a contentious issue of New Deal-era political economy—the so-called milk problem. Sustained droughts ravaged pastures in the Midwest and Northeast, reducing the average milk production per
cow by 9 percent between 1929 and 1933. In order to regain their production
levels, dairy farmers increased their herd sizes—primarily by choosing not to
kill or sell off low-yielding cows. When pastures began to improve, farmers
consequently faced unprecedented surpluses produced by extraordinarily populous dairy herds. Meanwhile consumers hit hard by the Depression spent less
money on dairy products—especially cheese and butter, which lower-income
Americans tended to cut back on during hard times, when they chose substi-
tutes such as oleomargarine. Oversupply and slack demand drove down the
prices farmers received for their milk by 51 percent between 1929 and 1933.
Cheese and butter farmers saw their incomes drop rapidly, with the wholesale
price for butterfat dropping by 58 percent in the same period. In early 1933,
with the combination of low prices and large surpluses raising the stakes of
competition in dairying, the longstanding division between inner-ring and
outer-ring farmers predicted by Johann von Thünen set the stage for desperate action.[19]

Impoverished farmers began violently demanding higher prices for their milk
in 1933, paving the way for massive government intervention in the nation's
milk markets. Farmers in New York, Illinois, Michigan, and elsewhere withheld their milk from market, often dramatically dumping it on the road, in
efforts to drive up the price dealers paid for their milk. One of the first and
most spirited milk strikes occurred in Wisconsin in February 1933, when a
group of several thousand farmers organized the Wisconsin Cooperative Milk
Pool. The leader of the Milk Pool was Walter M. Singler, a "firebrand" who
traveled around the state wearing a red blazer, cowboy hat, goatee, and spats
while whipping farmers' rallies into a frenzy with tirades against the Milwaukee and Chicago "Milk Trusts." Singler, in concert with Milo Reno of the
Iowa-based Farmers Holiday Association, called upon farmers to withhold

their products from market, forcing buyers to offer a "fair price plus profit." On February 15, 1933, Singler told his followers that a statewide strike would be necessary to achieve this. Singler first proposed a five-day "peaceful strike," but his lieutenant in the Milk Pool, A. H. Christman, recommended "literally knock[ing milk dealers] over the head with a club." Within days, Milwaukee area farmers took up Christman's call to arms, withholding their milk from market and "swarming over the roads of Outagamie County [north of Milwaukee], dumping truckload after truckload of milk and roughing up [truck] drivers." Farmers blocked roads with heavy timbers, threatening milk factories with dynamite and diesel fuel in their storage vats. Sheriffs hastily deputized locals to escort milk trucks to town with shotguns and tear gas to prevent a "milk famine" in Milwaukee.[20]

The violence of the Milk Pool strike dramatized one of the key conflicts at the heart of the "milk problem"—the division between outer-ring cheese farmers and inner-ring fluid milk farmers. The inner-ring farmers who provided milk for the urban markets of Milwaukee and Chicago were already organized into two strong cooperative associations, the Milwaukee Cooperative Milk Producers and the Pure Milk Association, which maintained exclusive contracts with city milk dealers and thus held no animus toward companies like Borden or National Dairy Products—the members of the so-called Milk Trust. The inner-ring farmers who belonged to the Milwaukee Milk Producers and the Pure Milk Association tended to be larger, relatively prosperous farmers who "despised" farmers who were "[Milk] Pool-minded." One such prosperous dairy farmer remembered in an oral history that members of the Milwaukee Milk Producers were "pretty well satisfied" with milk prices in the 1930s while Milk Pool members tended to be "the farmers that didn't run a good operation." In less subtle words, there was a recognized class division between well-off inner-ring milk farmers and poorer upstate cheese dairymen.[21]

The Milk Pool strike of 1933 set the stage for federal regulation of the nation's milksheds. Organized dairy farmers and city milk dealers in Chicago sought an opportunity to prevent a recurrence of the strike by regulating upstate cheese farmers out of the city milk market. The Agricultural Adjustment Act provided the tools to do so. The day after President Roosevelt signed the act, representatives of the Pure Milk Association and their allies, the large milk dealers of Chicago, petitioned Secretary of Agriculture Henry A. Wallace to begin administering milk prices in the Chicago milkshed. Wallace responded by establishing a Dairy Section of the AAA, headed by economist Clyde L. King, and by calling a series of regional hearings to negotiate an agreement among the dairy farmers and milk distributors of the Chicago milkshed. From that agreement would emerge a system of milk marketing orders that, for the next thirty years, would invoke federal government power to uphold the milk monopoly of inner-ring dairy farmers and urban milk dealers. Although the railroad-based "Milk Trust" predated the New Deal, policies erected during the earliest days of the New Deal effectively cemented the power of this inner-ring milk coalition—at least until trucking technology upended the economic geography of milk distribution in the 1960s.[22]

The marketing orders that emerged in 1933 drove a federally administered regulatory wedge between outer-ring cheese dairymen and inner-ring fluid milk farmers. Government administrators, cooperating with milk dealers and organized inner-ring dairymen, would prevent future outbreaks like the Milk Pool strike by establishing a firm price difference between milk used to manufacture cheese or butter and milk sold to city consumers in bottles. The federal system stabilized milk prices by preventing farmers in either the outer or inner rings from dumping their seasonal surpluses on each others' markets. Inner-ring farmers enjoyed protection from the intrusions of outer-ring farmers on their markets, and vice versa. Milk dealers agreed to cooperate in the milk marketing agreements even though it meant they would be forced to buy from inner-ring farmers at higher prices, because the system guaranteed them a reliable source of disease-free milk at government-stabilized prices. The first federal milk marketing agreement went into effect in Chicago in 1933, and although it quickly broke down due to lack of enforcement, it was copied in cities around the country including Boston, Indianapolis, Detroit, New York, and Philadelphia, and was soon reinstituted in Chicago. After Congress passed the 1937 Agricultural Marketing Act, bolstering the constitutionality and enforceability of the marketing orders, USDA administration of prices in the nation's milksheds became a permanent policy for dealing with the "milk problem."[23]

The marketing orders initiated by Chicago's inner-ring dairy farmers and corporate milk dealers, however, ignored the interests of two very important groups—organized urban milk deliverymen and city consumers. The USDA's single-minded focus on dividing farmers into abstract geographical rings did not address the wage demands of urban labor unions. This was no small matter, since Teamsters controlled the house-to-house distribution of milk in the presupermarket era. In the negotiations that established the Chicago order, the issue of Teamster wages had been thoroughly discussed. In particular, Jerome Frank, the general counsel for the AAA during the drafting of the orders, advocated adherence to section 7(a) of the 1933 National Industrial Recovery Act to include workers' demands for decent pay as an integral component of the marketing order system. Milk dealers in Chicago originally agreed to maintain high wages for organized deliverymen in that city—less out of sympathy for the labor movement than out of pragmatic fear of the powerful

Teamsters locals in Chicago, who threatened to derail the negotiations. Over the previous two decades, Chicago's Teamsters had proven willing to use anything from fists to dynamite to protect their economic interests; for milk dealers, paying decent wages to drivers was a matter of survival. Jerome Frank nonetheless rightly feared that if the Chicago marketing order did not include a written guarantee of the right of dairy employees to bargain collectively, milk deliverymen in other cities might suffer. Urban teamsters who had not developed the strength of the Chicago deliverymen might suffer wage cuts, Frank argued, if milk dealers used the pretense of the orders to pass onto labor the higher costs of their federally administered milk supplies. An urban liberal who viewed the AAA as a means of achieving a European-style social welfare state rather than as a mere tool for raising farmers' incomes, Frank would be included in the famous "purge" of liberals from the USDA in 1935. Without Frank, the USDA would administer all of its future milk marketing orders with little effort to appease organized labor—an oversight that would remain unresolved until the 1960s, when milk dealers would rely on highway transportation to make the Teamsters obsolete in the milk economy.[24]

Consumers, like the Teamsters, called for government policies that benefited not only corporate food processors but also average Americans during the 1930s and 1940s. The federal milk marketing orders, consumers protested, were undisguised attempts by the Milk Trust to increase the retail price of milk and boost their own profits. Before the milk orders, chain grocery stores such as the Great Atlantic and Pacific Tea Company and independent "cash-and-carry" stores began competing directly with milk dealers such as Borden and National Dairy Products. At a time when the cost of home delivery accounted for over a third of the price of a bottle of milk, while dealer profits took five cents and payments to farmers took forty cents of every consumer dollar spent on delivered milk, eliminating home delivery provided the simplest means for milk retailers to cut milk prices without harming profit structures or infuriating organized inner-ring dairymen. By not delivering directly to consumers' doorsteps, Chicago's chain stores and cash-and-carry outfits were able to sell a quart of milk for only nine cents in 1932—two cents less than the home-delivered price. Chicago's milk dealers, having written the nation's first milk marketing order on their own terms in 1933, sought government support to eliminate this competition by requiring all retailers sell milk at the price of a home-delivered quart. In pushing for a minimum price for store-bought milk, dealers claimed that chain stores were able to sell their milk cheaply only by using it as a "loss leader" and by "sweating their labor." Upon the advent of the milk marketing order, store milk prices rose from nine cents to eleven cents per quart. When the USDA called a hearing in Chicago in November of 1933 to assess the system's strengths and weaknesses, consumer representatives lodged bitter complaints against this minimum retail price. The most succinct protest came from one Sylvia Schmidt, who saw price fixing as an unfair tax on consumers: "People who want the privilege of having their milk delivered should pay for that privilege and people who are willing to take the inconvenience of getting their milk [from a store] should be allowed the difference in price." Chicago resident Rose Fourier agreed, noting that "consumers are quite angry" at being "compelled by the Government" to pay higher prices for milk from powerful dealers such as Borden. Robert S. Marx, representing the Kroger Grocery chain, pointed out that his company was "forced to charge the consumer for a [home] delivery service that we don't give him, that he does not want, that he cannot afford to pay for."[25]

Chicago consumers' protests against the injustice of the minimum retail price convinced the USDA to eliminate the policy from future iterations of its milk marketing orders. However, the primary goal of the Dairy Section of the AAA was to stabilize farmers' prices, and under the leadership of Clyde L. King, the USDA believed this could best be achieved by cooperating with the largest milk dealers. This meant that when milk dealers in cities throughout the country petitioned their city or state milk control boards to set minimum retail prices for milk, the USDA made no effort to stop the de facto reinstitution of price-fixing arrangements. In 1939, *Fortune* magazine surveyed 129 cities and found that half of them had retail price-fixing laws, forcing the average chain store to sell a quart of milk at four cents over cost, even though most chains believed one cent would be a reasonable margin. Consequently most consumers had little choice but to pay an extra three or four cents for the "convenience" of having their milk delivered to their doorsteps. The milk marketing order system, dedicated to boosting the incomes of organized inner-ring dairy farmers, made no room for lower-cost distribution methods, thus entrenching the economic power of monopolistic milk dealers—at least until supermarkets began using long-haul trucks to circumvent the power of milk dealers in the 1950s.[26]

The federal milk policies of the New Deal era did not effectively solve the milk problem, because the milk marketing orders did not take into account the interests of either workers or consumers. While organized inner-ring dairy farmers and urban milk dealers gained the support of USDA administrators, workers and consumers were forced to take the problem of a "fair price" for milk into their own hands. The late 1930s saw numerous strikes by organized Teamster milk delivery drivers in Chicago, Milwaukee, Detroit, New York, and Cleveland—all asking for, and gaining, a greater portion of the milk dollar. Milk dealers such as Borden remained dependent on the Teamsters to deliver milk from the processing plant to consumer doorsteps, and so generally responded to drivers' wage demands by increasing the price of milk to consumers. With federal administrators encouraging dairy farmers, milk bottlers, and Teamsters to increase the price of milk, consumers cried foul. Given the New Deal's focus on the problem of strengthening consumer "purchasing power" to overcome the Depression, consumers demanded federal investigations into the assumed price predations of the Milk Trust.[27] Consumer outrage at the prices charged by national dairy chains like Borden and National Dairy Products culminated in 1939 with vitriolic antimonopoly hearings before the Senate's Temporary National Economic Committee, chaired by Wyoming senator and inveterate trustbuster Joseph O'Mahoney. The following exchange between O'Mahoney and Frederic C. Howe, former Consumers' Counsel of the AAA, captures the gist of the hearings, which resulted in antitrust actions against the national dairy distributors:

> O'MAHONEY: Is it your conclusion, after all your studies, that distributors maintain the price of milk at an excessively high figure which is not warranted by the cost of production?
> HOWE: It is.[28]

The USDA's efforts to stabilize the dairy industry satisfied only a powerful minority of those affected by the price of milk—that is, organized inner-ring farmers and city milk dealers. Consumers, Teamsters, and outer-ring farmers shut out from the federal milk marketing orders all continued through the early 1940s to agitate for a "fair price" for milk. Despite massive government intervention in local milk economies, the milk problem remained fundamentally unsolved by New Deal policies.

In 1942 journalist Wesley McCune, a liberal sympathetic both to the demands of organized farmers and organized labor, sought to understand "Why Milk Costs So Much?" He found a ready answer: USDA milk marketing orders, having been hijacked by inner-ring dairy farmers and their corporate allies in the milk bottling industry, had resulted in "a plain conspiracy to raise prices."[29] But the milk marketing orders did not emerge primarily from nefarious collusions between agricultural policymakers and corporate milk dealers. Instead agricultural policymakers within the AAA Dairy Section intended the orders to realize and reify the geographical theories of Johann von Thünen— to use the power of the federal administrative state to enforce an economic division between outer-ring and inner-ring dairy farmers to stabilize farm incomes. Consumers and Teamsters had no reason to accept the federal milk marketing orders, however, since von Thünen's model sought only to predict how to maximize farmers' profits in relation to transportation costs. Within the theoretical space of von Thünen's concentric rings, there was no room for real-world political and economic contests among consumers, workers, farmers, businessmen, and government officials. These endemic conflicts over the fair price of milk would continue to plague economic liberals seeking to resolve the milk problem through the end of World War II. As we shall see in later chapters, it was not until truckers began hauling most milk in refrigerated trucks that the milk problem would cease to animate consumer and worker attacks on regressive New Deal farm policies.

Beef and the Problem of Monopoly

As in the case of milk, the cost of transporting beef from farmer to consumer played a fundamental role in the farm and food politics of the New Deal era. The refrigerated railcar, introduced in the 1870s, provided a means of sending relatively inexpensive dressed beef from the cattle-producing regions of the Midwest to the beef-consuming Northeast. However, the rapid perishability of fresh beef required a distribution system of unprecedented scale and technological integration that laid the foundations for what came to be known as the "Beef Trust." From the 1870s until the 1950s, a handful of giant firms dominated every aspect of converting western cattle into eastern steaks and roasts, from buying and selling in stockyards to slaughtering the animals and distributing carcasses to retail butchers. During the height of New Deal economic liberalism, the "Big Four" meatpackers drew repeated attacks from farmers, consumers, small businessmen, and politicians who demanded an overthrow of monopoly power in the meat industry. But as in the milk industry, the structure of the railroad-based beef economy prevented New Dealers from satisfying the diverse demands of all interested parties. In contrast to milk, however, the federal government made little effort to intervene directly in the beef economy.

The rise of monopoly power in meatpacking was tied to the industry's reliance on an extensive system of refrigerated railcars to distribute their product to the masses. Uncured beef begins to rot immediately after slaughter, so achieving a tasty steak in the nineteenth century required that a cow be kept alive until just before it was distributed to consumers. No form of transportation was speedy enough to allow a mid-nineteenth-century meatpacker to mass-slaughter western cattle and deliver the beef to eastern consumers in edible form at a reasonable price. Furthermore the cow is a long-legged beast with about 45 percent of its weight taken up by inedible hide, bones, gristle, entrails, horns, and hooves. Carrying such a low proportion of saleable meat, the bulky beef steer did not make for transport economics efficient enough to justify long-distance shipping, especially since cattle were apt to die or be injured in railroad cars and needed repeated watering and resting on a lengthy trip. As a consequence, the slaughter and distribution of beef in urban centers was a highly atomistic, small-scale industry carried on mainly by neighborhood butchers who slaughtered cattle only as needed. The development of the refrigerated railroad car made mass distribution possible for the first time in the 1880s and set the stage for the monopoly power that would define beefpacking until the 1950s. Gustavus Swift, the key figure in this technological revolution, was determined to find a way to ship dressed beef rather than the entire steer to eastern consumers, thereby eliminating the cost of transporting the inedible parts of the animal. Building on the work of earlier inventors and entrepreneurs, Swift hired engineer Andrew Chase, who perfected the refrigerated railcar in 1878, using an innovative combination of insulation and ventilation to provide cool, dry air that kept beef carcasses fresh between Chicago and New York. By 1884, Swift was the largest shipper of dressed beef in the country, though he soon faced competition from giant Chicago meatpackers George Hammond, Nelson Morris, and Philip Armour. With the deployment of the refrigerated railcar, beef slaughter began a geographical shift from the small butcher shops of the East to the enormous meatpacking factories of Chicago.[30]

Dressed beef was cheap for consumers, but came at the cost of economic concentration of the industry. The reduced costs of shipping dressed beef allowed the Chicago packers to sell meat profitably in New York at prices 5 to 10 percent lower than local slaughterers. The mass distribution of dressed beef was no simple task, however. Enormous capital investments in technology were essential if the dressed beef packers were to achieve the low prices needed to overcome resistance to the new product. Eastern consumers distrusted dressed beef from Chicago, delivered over a thousand miles by an unseen butcher and touched by an unknown number of railroad men. Only a very low price could trump the presumed risk of food poisoning. Eastern butchers, meanwhile, saw a direct threat to their livelihood, and generally refused to carry dressed beef in their meat markets. Railroads were also uncooperative. In their effort to increase traffic volume in the West during the 1860s and 1870s, railroads had made large investments in livestock cars and urban stockyards. Dressed beef would make this equipment obsolete while taking half of their western routes' most lucrative cargo. Facing such resistance, the Chicago packers constructed their own infrastructure to bypass the wholesale butchers and railroads. Swift erected hundreds of "branch houses," or cold storage stations, in eastern cities and towns. Branch houses received carloads of dressed beef, then immediately distributed the meat to local retailers before spoilage set in—all without the need for wholesale butchers. To circumvent the railroads that refused to provide refrigerated railcars, Swift and his competitors built their own. Swift also found an ally in the Canadian Grand Trunk Railroad, which unlike the New York Central or the Pennsylvania Railroad had no significant investments in the livestock business, to send its dressed beef to New York. With an enormous, tightly integrated technological system, the dressed beef packers achieved economies of scale that made inexpensive meat both a widely accepted food and a highly profitable line for the packers. In short, the introduction of the refrigerated railcar sowed the seeds of monopoly in beefpacking.[31]

From the beginnings of dressed beef in the 1880s to World War I, a handful of Chicago meatpackers sought to dominate the entire trade. These firms, led by Swift and Armour and known as the "Big Five"—and after 1923, the "Big Four"—used capital and technology to maintain a tight grip on the nation's meat business.[32] With their branch houses, the Big Five dominated the wholesale distribution of beef in both large and small cities located on railroad lines throughout the heavily populated areas of the Northeast and Mid-Atlantic. Independent meatpackers were almost entirely shut out from the branch house system. The Big Five also owned most of the railroad car routes connecting packing houses to distant branch houses—in 1918, the Big Five owned 90 percent of such routes, making it nearly impossible for smaller packers to market their product over a long distance. By maintaining this stranglehold on the infrastructure of distribution, the Big Five achieved control of 73 percent of the nation's interstate meat trade by 1916. Significantly most of the profits gained by the big packers through their monopoly power were immediately reinvested in their distribution systems—building more branch houses and refrigerator cars—in order to gain economies of scale and increase their control over marketing. Dressed beef marketing was inherently big business.[33]

The capital investments required for nationwide mass distribution compelled the packers to slaughter unprecedented numbers of cattle to achieve economies of scale in mass production. With its giant Union Stock Yard, built in 1865, Chicago gained a reliable source of cattle from the grasslands of the West. To further assure reliable supplies, the Big Five invested in stockyards in other major cattle markets such as Kansas City, St. Louis, and Omaha. When the Federal Trade Commission investigated the Big Five's monopoly power in 1917, officials discovered that the firms owned a majority of shares in twenty-two of the fifty largest stockyards, with more than eight of every ten cattle passing through yards in which the big packers held an interest. The Big Five located their slaughtering plants strategically in the railroad centers that connected the marketing channels of the populated East with the livestock production areas of the West. Their control of stockyards allowed a relatively small number of cattle buyers to have a disproportionate control over the prices offered to livestock sellers. Economists call this situation—in which a few buyers control a market with many sellers—a monopsony. The Big Five quickly established monopsony power over livestock buying, complementing their monopoly power in beef marketing. Livestock sellers repeatedly complained that packer buyers at the major urban stockyards manipulated the price of cattle through illicit and arbitrary means. For instance, a Kansas livestock feeder in 1918 received a call from the yards in St. Joseph, Missouri, to ship as many cattle as possible for immediate slaughter. Sorting and loading a large cattle shipment took time, so the livestock feeder only managed to send four railcars on the first day, for which he received $14.85 per hundredweight. The next day he shipped the remaining 33 carloads, but received only $13.00 per hundredweight for the same quality of cattle—a price drop of $20 per head that made him regret the shipment.[34]

In popular discourse, the moniker "Beef Trust" represented all that was despised about this combination of monopoly and monopsony power. In a best-selling 1905 book, journalist Charles Edward Russell famously labeled the meatpackers the "Greatest Trust in the World" for their "great brute strength." Even though dressed beef was generally cheap beef, the apparent ability of the Beef Trust to set prices based on their costs rather than according to the laws of supply and demand led consumers in cities throughout the country to blame the trust for any rise in price. Organizations such as the Ladies' Anti-Beef Trust Association, formed in New York in 1902 to protest a 50-percent rise in meat prices, pointed an accusing finger at "the Trust" for "taking meat from the bones of your women and children." Many consumers felt they simply could not trust the Beef Trust, located hundreds or thousands of miles away from the neighborhood meat shop. This was most famously illustrated by the public response to Upton Sinclair's 1906 exposé of the Chicago meatpackers in his novel *The Jungle*. Intending to illustrate the plight of immigrant workers in the packinghouses, Sinclair instead disgusted his middle-class readers with images of rats scampering about the kill floors below vats of adulterated sausages. The book consequently helped lead to the 1906 passage of the Pure Food and Drug Act and the Meat Inspection Act, but did not inspire the socialist political movement Sinclair had hoped for; as he later quipped, "I aimed at the public's heart and by accident I hit it in the stomach." Nonetheless Sinclair's work added to the growing consumer displeasure with the distant, unseen meatpackers and their power to affect daily food choices in nearly every city in the United States.[35]

Antitrust sentiment thus united both livestock raisers and urban consumers in their animus toward the Beef Trust, which reached the height of its unpopularity during World War I. Consumer concern over the soaring cost of living dominated the domestic politics of the war, with inflated food prices inflicting painful sacrifices for working- and middle-class consumers. Under pressure from both outraged consumers and from organized cattlemen, President Woodrow Wilson directed the Federal Trade Commission (FTC) to investigate the profits of the packing industry in 1917. The FTC report on the meatpacking industry, published in five thick volumes from 1918 to 1920, confirmed the worst suspicions of both consumers and cattlemen. The Big Five had garnered substantial profits during the war, averaging a 4.6 percent return on each dollar invested, or 350 percent more than prewar earnings. The FTC recommended sweeping government action to restore competition to cattle buying and beef marketing—outright public ownership of railroad livestock and refrigerator cars, terminal stockyards, and branch houses. Congress opted not to undertake this potentially expensive populist solution, so instead the Justice Department began antitrust proceedings against the Big Five in 1919. Facing both popular anger and the strongest government threat to date, the meatpackers capitulated in 1920, signing a Consent Decree. Under this agreement, the packers would not be prosecuted for violations of antitrust laws if they divested of their holdings in terminal stockyards, pulled out of the retail meat business, and agreed not to conspire to restrain interstate trade. Over the next several decades, however, the Consent Decree proved toothless. The big packers continued to expand their ownership of refrigerated railcars and branch houses in an effort to maintain market share. Despite the Consent Decree's prohibition of mergers, the packers continued to absorb their competitors; in 1923, the Big Five became the Big Four when Armour bought out Morris. The packers also proved loath to dispose of their holdings in the public stockyards that provided them with their cattle supplies; by 1925, they had only sloughed one-quarter of their yards.[36]

The packers' defiance pushed livestock producers to petition Congress for additional regulations, putting the USDA rather than the Federal Trade Commission in the driver's seat of antitrust policy for the rest of the century. Seeking to bolster public confidence in the federal government's ability to restrain the Beef Trust, Congress passed the Packers and Stockyards Act of 1921. Congress intended the act to supplement the Consent Decree by conferring broad antitrust powers to the secretary of agriculture. The intent of the act was further clarified in 1922 when the Supreme Court affirmed its constitutionality, with Chief Justice William Howard Taft arguing that the "chief evil feared is the monopoly of the packers, enabling them unduly and arbitrarily to lower prices to the shipper who sells, and unduly and arbitrarily to increase the price to the consumer who buys." In practice, however, the Packers and Stockyards Administration proved rather friendly to both the packers and the stockyards.

Secretary of Agriculture Henry C. Wallace (the father of New Dealer Henry A. Wallace) publicly declared in 1922 that his department would "not assume that men are rascals until they have been proved to be such. We take it for granted that the various people who are under the supervision of this law will be glad to co-operate with us." The problem of monopoly had become a significant state concern, but had not yet produced any effective state action.[37]

During the Great Depression, however, the meatpackers' monopoly power took on added urgency, provoking farmers and consumers to push for anti-trust action against the Big Four packers. While farmers received disastrously low prices for their cattle in the early 1930s, consumers found prices of fresh beef increasingly out of reach. The prices of sirloin steak and round steak, for instance, increased 5 percent between June and July of 1933. From August 1933 to August 1935, the average price of sirloin increased by more than a third, with round steak up 40 percent. At a time when up to one-quarter of the workforce was unemployed, such price rises forced many families to buy less meat. Between 1929 and 1935 per capita meat consumption dropped from eighty-five pounds to seventy-seven pounds, and with lowered consumption farmers suffered from lower cattle prices. Purchasing less meat was one form of resistance to high prices, but in a nation where beef had been transformed from a luxury to a prerogative of the American way of life, many consumers sought more active political solutions. In 1935, activists in New York, Detroit, and Boston organized extensive meat boycotts. Picketing housewives shut down butcher shops, demanded lower prices, and called for thorough investigations of the Beef Trust. The Women's Auxiliary of the United Auto Workers mounted further protests against beef prices in 1937–38 in a nationwide campaign known as "No Meat Weeks." Livestock raisers generally sympathized with consumers' outrage, since high retail prices reduced demand. An Iowa cattle feeder, bewildered by rock-bottom cattle prices at a time when consumers could not afford to buy beef, wrote Secretary of Agriculture Henry A. Wallace in 1933 to offer his take on the problem: "I do not blame any one but the packing industry."[38]

Faced with the protests of both cattle raisers and consumers, Henry A. Wallace came under constant pressure in the 1930s to use his antitrust power to deal with the Big Four's apparent control of meat pricing. Ironically the first approach of New Deal agricultural policymakers was to consider relaxing antitrust efforts rather than strengthening them. With the milk marketing agreements as a model, agricultural policymakers gave significant thought to creating a legalized monopoly in beef marketing, providing the big packers with immunity from antitrust actions in exchange for a guarantee of higher prices to farmers and reduced prices for consumers. Economists believed this might be possible to achieve, considering that the big packers would have incentives to increase capital investments in their operations without fear of state intervention, thereby achieving greater economies of scale that would benefit farmers and consumers while still allowing a "reasonable profit" for the packers. Perhaps the most surprising advocate of this approach in 1933 was the liberal Jerome Frank, legal counsel for the AAA who was also active in crafting the milk marketing agreements. Writing to fellow liberals at the AAA—Rexford Tugwell, Mordecai Ezekiel, and Frederic C. Howe—Frank recommended in June of 1933 that the entire concept of antitrust be reexamined. Rather than consider the profit structures of the big meatpackers, Frank suggested a more appropriate strategy was to "restrict our attention to precisely computable *savings* affected by [economies of scale] and require that some portion of these savings be given to the farmer and some to the consuming public." For a year, the USDA actively courted the meatpackers' opinions on this approach through private negotiations led by Frank.[39]

Unsurprisingly the packers proved quite receptive to the idea. Frederick H. Prince, a majority stockholder in the Armour company and the Chicago Union Stock Yard, argued that "the most complete monopoly power that could possibly be granted" was necessary to achieve the New Deal goals of "fair profit on manufacturing" (a central tenet of the National Industrial Recovery Act) while still maintaining high farm prices (the main goal of the Agricultural Adjustment Act). Prince drafted a detailed proposal for this "most complete monopoly," to be known as the Union Purchasing and Distributing Company. This company was to be owned by the Big Four packers and would "do all of the purchasing for the packers, fix the price to be paid for all commodities purchased, and have complete control of all shipments. . . . The company is also to fix the prices to be charged for all products sold." According to Prince, retail prices of meat would plummet with the savings in transportation and distribution costs achieved by shared facilities.[40]

Yet Prince's dream of a state-sanctioned megatrust would never come to fruition—at least not until the firm IBP relied on long-haul trucking to erect such a monopoly in the late 1960s. During the New Deal era, such blatant approval of big business in the beef economy held no traction within policymaking circles. Mordecai Ezekiel, Henry Wallace's top economic advisor, called the proposed plan "a blank check of tremendous magnitude . . . made out to the packers, and payable by farmers and consumers." The proposed agreement, Ezekiel angrily wrote to Assistant Secretary of Agriculture Rexford Tugwell, would give the packers "unlimited monopoly power to fix prices" and would lead to a "national scandal" for the USDA. In response to such criticism, Jerome Frank redrafted the proposed agreement in August 1933 to authorize the secretary of agriculture to examine packers' books to insure that their profits remained reasonable. The packers, however, resisted what they called "fishing expeditions" into their company records. Gustavus Swift wrote Wallace in January 1934 to argue that his company made only "moderate profit," most of which went to the company's 55,000 stockholders—"a collection of small people." Reducing profits, Swift asserted, would not only be unfair to the "small people" but would have only an insignificant impact on either farmers' prices or consumers' costs. By May 1934, it was clear that the meatpackers and the USDA's liberal economists would never reconcile their conflicting interpretations of monopoly power. The agreement was scrapped when the packers flatly refused to provide Wallace with unlimited access to their books. Whereas Henry C. Wallace had been able to court the cooperation of monopolistic beefpackers in the 1920s, the packers recognized his son Henry A. Wallace as a potentially dangerous liberal.[41]

Meanwhile consumer activists and livestock raisers pressured Wallace's Department of Agriculture to confront the Beef Trust. The implication that New Deal agricultural programs were promoting inflated meat costs for urban workers at a time of economic crisis would not easily dissipate. Secretary Wallace received hundreds of letters from citizens demanding USDA investigations of the meatpackers throughout the 1930s. For instance, Massachusetts Governor Charles F. Hurley reported in 1937 that his state's Labor and Industries Department had found retail meat prices to be "exorbitant," and requested a formal investigation into the matter by the USDA. Wallace replied that drought-induced feed shortages were the primary cause of high meat prices, and besides, the Packers and Stockyards Act did not grant the USDA "authority or power to regulate or supervise the activities of retail meat dealers." Though a liberal and an agrarian antimonopolist, Wallace feared the power of the meatpackers. Even so, the Packers and Stockyards Act gave Wallace the power to order meatpackers to cease and desist from price-fixing and other collusive behavior. In the spring of 1934, as the proposed meatpacker marketing agreement fell apart, Wallace initiated hearings to investigate eleven major packing firms for colluding to set retail prices and control competition. In 1936 Wallace formally ordered the packers to end such practices, but by then the packers had voluntarily stopped the illicit activities. Wallace was further humiliated in 1938 when Swift retaliated by filing a lawsuit in federal court charging the Department of Agriculture with overstepping its authority under the Packers and Stockyards Act.[42]

Although this lawsuit went nowhere, it symbolized the uncertain status of the USDA as a trustbuster. Even when the Department of Agriculture had widespread political backing from both consumers and farmers as well as an internal commitment to enforce antitrust provisions, its efforts were always one step behind the evasive packers. This left only the Federal Trade Commission and the Justice Department to cajole the packers into observing the antitrust provisions of the toothless 1920 Consent Decree. Like the Department of Agriculture, these federal agencies found effective action difficult to achieve in the 1930s, even after the Supreme Court ordered the packers to comply fully with the terms of the original Consent Decree in 1932. The packers maintained the two key elements of monopoly power in meat marketing, because the Consent Decree allowed the packers to retain their fleets of refrigerated railcars and their branch houses. Political figures, though strongly supported by farmers and consumers during the New Deal, could not easily surmount the tremendous economic strength that the Big Four had achieved through technological means in the railroad era. As in the case of milk, the nation's transportation system was not the cause of the political problem of monopoly in the beef industry, but the railroads' centralized structure made New Deal antitrust efforts extraordinarily difficult to administer with lasting effect.[43]

The New Deal inaugurated an era of unprecedented government intervention in the nation's farm and food economy, decisively replacing the laissez-faire politics of previous decades. New Deal farm policies, however, did not resolve longstanding conflicts among farmers, consumers, urban workers, and food processors over whose economic interests those policies should serve. Despite the efforts of liberals such as Jerome Frank to make New Deal farm policies into tools for boosting consumer and worker economic power, the production controls, marketing agreements, and half-hearted antimonopoly efforts of Henry A. Wallace's Department of Agriculture succeeded only in securing the incomes of commercial farmers and the monopoly power of corporate food processors. Through World War II and for several years afterward, as chapter 3 will show, liberals would make a renewed and somewhat more successful effort to use state power to rein in corporate power in the farm and food economy. But as the next chapter demonstrates, the arrival of long-haul trucking in the Depression-era countryside threw the entire farm and food economy into a turmoil that set liberals and conservatives into pitched battles over the nature of New Deal political economy. The outcome of those battles, which cemented the "deregulatory" nature of rural trucking, shaped the rural assault on economic liberalism that stretched out over the next forty-five years. Encouraged by "free market," farm-friendly transportation policies, truckers in the 1930s would challenge monopoly power in the farm economy. In later years, however, a new generation of truckers would help to not only overthrow the Milk Trust and the Beef Trust, but would also spark a widespread repudiation of New Deal economic liberalism.

CHAPTER TWO

Chaos, Control, and Country Trucking, 1933–42

The irresistible dream of being an "independent" trucker was the central dramatic theme of the first major trucking film, *They Drive by Night,* released by Warner Brothers in 1940. Joe and Paul Fabrini, played by George Raft and Humphrey Bogart, are two "wildcat" truckers seeking a living hauling farm produce in California's Imperial Valley. Driving a straight truck ("no speedway special") purchased on credit, the Fabrinis struggle to find enough loads of apples and melons to keep the finance company from repossessing their machine. The prospects are grim; the brothers rely on a San Francisco produce broker to send loads their way, but the cigar-smoking fat-cat is in cahoots with the finance company, and seems as dedicated to having the Fabrinis lose their truck as he is to having them deliver his produce. But for Joe, the chance to be his own man is the fuel that keeps him going. When confronted by another driver who works for a trucking company and brags of receiving a steady paycheck "every Saturday," Joe retorts, "Yeah, but you get ordered around every *other* day." The company driver questions Joe's independence, pointing out that "you ain't workin' for you, you're workin' for the finance company." But Joe will have none of it; he is sure that with enough hard work he can turn the tables on the capitalists: "I'm on my own, anyway. You know if a guy can get together two or three big rigs there's a fortune in this business." Wildcat trucking is a gamble, as Joe fully realizes, but the psychological dividends of self-assured manhood make the risk worth taking.[1]

The movie quickly became a popular and critical success (and incidentally propelled Humphrey Bogart to stardom), reinforcing the idea that the independent truck driver represented a manly challenge to concentrated corporate power. But *They Drive by Night* also reveals the close relationship between the "wildcat" trucker and the agricultural economy of the Depression era. Joe's only entry into trucking is to haul farm products rather than manufactured goods. This was also the case for the thousands of real-life independent truck drivers who first took the wheel of a big rig in the 1920s and 1930s. The same farm crisis that forced many farmers to look to the federal government to ease the pain of a collapsed rural economy inspired many others to hit the highways hauling farm and food products. Trucking became an appealing rural occupation for young men with an agrarian attraction to "independent" work and few prospects on the farm. Railroad managers and urban truckers organized in the growing Teamsters Union derided these upstart farm-boy truckers as "gypsies" who brought only disorder to the transportation industry, and sought to control that competitive chaos through New Deal regulatory policies that cartelized the freight trucking industry. Some agricultural policymakers, however, including members of the congressional farm bloc and Secretary of Agriculture Henry A. Wallace, recognized that independent truckers might undermine the monopoly power of railroad-based food processors within the farm and food economy. Under Wallace's watch, Congress and the Department of Agriculture devised regulatory policies in the mid-1930s that ensured country trucking would remain, for the next four decades, far more chaotic than the tightly controlled and unionized freight trucking and railroad industries. The real-life independent truckers upon whom the Fabrini characters were based helped to upend the railroad-based food economy of the early twentieth century. Whether increasing reliance on truck transportation would lead to increased market power for corporate agribusinesses, or would help liberal reformers achieve a new solution to the pressing farm problem, however, remained an open question during the New Deal era.

The Farm Crisis and the Rural Trucker

The 1920s and 1930s witnessed a wrenching transformation of rural life, as U.S. farmers suffered bruising market conditions even as they became more deeply integrated into the nation's industrial economy. Long-haul trucking became an industry of national import within the context of this farm crisis. Through the early twentieth century, poorly maintained rural dirt roads forced many farmers to maintain a localistic worldview. In the 1920s, however, paved highways and the Ford Model T penetrated the countryside, enveloping farmers in a national culture of mass consumption and mass production. Recognizing the political significance of rural highways, the Department of Agriculture oversaw rural roadbuilding in an effort to help farmers transport crops and livestock to market. Farmers began investing in small trucks to haul their products to city markets and railroad depots, seeking to gain the economic advantages of marketing their products on their own terms rather than on the terms of the railroad. With the deepening of the farm crisis in the 1930s, many farm boys looked to truck driving as a full-time profession—as a way to get off the farm while staying true to their country roots. The culture of early trucking that emerged from this agrarian context carried an element of chaos into the political economy of the New Deal. While urban liberals sought to use state power to stabilize industry through economic regulations and support of labor unions, the "flexibility" of trucks driven by fiercely independent truckers undermined those efforts in the rural countryside.

The Department of Agriculture's Bureau of Public Roads, from its inception in 1918 until the late 1940s, coordinated the construction of an extensive network of paved rural highways to serve farm interests. Until the late 1910s, rural road building remained the province of counties, who relied on farmers to maintain the roads abutting their property voluntarily, in lieu of taxation. Farmers resisted construction of paved stone and macadam roads, seeing them benefiting "eastern bicycle fellers or one-hoss lawyers with patent leather boots" (as declared in 1893 at an Iowa farmer's convention), or, later, city slickers who frightened horses as they sped through the countryside in their "devil wagons." But farmers' mistrust of urban outsiders and resistance to paved roads evaporated in the 1920s. Henry Ford's inexpensive Model T could be used to haul farm products to the railhead, take the kids to town for a moving picture while adults bought supplies, and provide an all-purpose engine for operating washing machines and hay elevators on the farm. Farmers who had previously used dirt roads to maintain local communities began using paved roads to expand their marketing range for farm products and as paths out of the isolation of rural life and into the national consumer culture. When a farm woman was asked by a bewildered sociologist in the 1920s why her family had purchased a Ford instead of indoor plumbing, she declared: "You can't go to town in a bathtub!"[2]

In response to farmers' new demands for paved roads, the USDA's Bureau of Public Roads worked with state governments to get farmers "out of the mud" after World War I. The task of coordinating the construction of a nationwide network of rural highways fell to the Bureau of Public Roads, headed by "Chief" Thomas H. MacDonald, who required states to build those roads according to exacting engineering standards. After 1919, the states relied heavily on gasoline taxes to fund this construction, along with federal matching monies that came with the passage of the 1921 Federal-Aid Road Act, which mandated that 40 percent of the federal funds be used to construct farm-to-market roads. Rural roads expanded rapidly in the 1920s under this arrangement. Between 1921 and 1930, state rural highway systems increased from 203,000 miles to 324,000 miles.[3]

Even as rural roads improved, engineers and manufacturers worked to convert the truck from an urban delivery vehicle based on the horse-and-wagon into a rural road machine. In the 1910s, few trucks were capable of traveling outside of cities, not only because rural roads were inadequate, but because early trucks were designed and built to operate in cities, delivering goods such as coal, ice, milk, and mail. In 1919, the U.S. Army Transport Corps sponsored a transcontinental convoy of trucks, hoping to demonstrate the possibilities of long-haul trucking in the countryside. The trip took two months, however, demonstrating the continued superiority of railroads for long-distance freight shipment. The commercialization of the pneumatic balloon tire in 1923, however, helped change that. Pneumatic balloon tires allowed manufacturers to build larger trucks that could travel at high speeds with less vibration than the solid rubber tires they replaced, causing less damage to truck bodies and roadbeds. Roy Fruehauf's 1914 decision to turn his Detroit wagon-building shop into a factory for producing custom-designed truck trailers helped make it possible for trucks of the 1930s to pull three times the weight allowed by straight-truck designs. Truck manufacturers such as Ford, General Motors, and International Harvester, along with specialized firms such as Mack, White, and Kenworth, increasingly built trucks that resembled neither horse-drawn wagons nor passenger cars. Enclosed cabs, sleeper compartments, hydraulic brakes, "fifth wheels" to allow attachment of separate trailers, and a host of other developments made trucks by the 1930s capable of traveling relatively long distances outside of cities. Even so, the vast majority of trucks in use in 1930 were used for short hauls, primarily by the Post Office, grocers, general contractors, bakeries, dairies, oil and gasoline stations, and meat-packing firms making urban deliveries. Furthermore most such trucks were relatively small by post–World War II standards, generally with less than 1½ ton capacities.[4]

In the 1920s and 1930s, rural truckers began driving Model Ts, Diamond Reos, and other trucks along the expanding rural highway network, posing a considerable challenge to railroad transportation of farm commodities. This competition was most marked in the transportation of perishable agricultural goods such as milk, livestock, poultry, and produce. For example, in 1913 only 91,000 hogs arrived by truck at an Indianapolis livestock market; by 1929 over 1,350,000 did so. In 1932, trucks accounted for 80 percent of fruits and vegetables shipped in southwestern Michigan. Railroad managers worried that trucks would soon take over short-haul traffic. The fear was well-founded, considering that truck transportation of highly perishable commodities often "skimmed" the most profitable classes of freight from the railroads. In order to subsidize the very long and expensive hauls that allowed railroads to build up their overall volume, the rails generally charged very high rates on short-haul perishables. Trucks traveling only short distances, however, could easily undercut the rates quoted by the rails, as well as provide faster, point-to-point service. In 1933, a group of railroad executives asked the federal government to be allowed to abandon unprofitable short branch lines and replace them with rail-owned truck lines.[5]

Most worrisome to the railroads was the rise of the rural owner-operator trucker, the wildcat farm product hauler who inspired the film *They Drive by Night*. Farm boys were common recruits for the growing trucking industry in the 1930s. In one of the first comprehensive government surveys of the industry, the Federal Coordinator of Transportation noted in 1936 that over-the-road truck drivers were mostly "farm boys and young men from country villages" who were willing to work unconscionably long hours at low pay just to be working at all. But their work ethic was not the only reason many farm boys became truckers. As Secretary of Agriculture Henry A. Wallace noted in testimony before the Interstate Commerce Commission in 1934, the price of gasoline and tires dropped sharply in the early 1930s, making it possible for farmers located near good roads to ship more cheaply by truck than by rail. Furthermore trucking, as "a business comparatively easy to enter," attracted both unemployed rural men and farmers who, "faced with lower returns from production, have been willing to spend more of their time in marketing their products." The emergence of long-haul trucking came at a time when thousands of young rural men were forced to look for off-farm work. With an agricultural depression that began in the early 1920s, as well as an increasingly mechanized agriculture requiring fewer farm workers, many young rural men had to make an uncomfortable choice. Staying on the farm most likely would entail years of debt and uncertain prospects. Moving to the city to take a factory job might provide economic security, but it might also entail a painful separation from one's rural roots, particularly if those roots were southern and the factory city was northern. For southern whites in particular, the psychological toll of leaving the countryside for better economic opportunities in northern cities could lead to years of longing for the "old home place."[6]

For many rural men in the interwar period, trucking offered a chance to remain in the country while, at least theoretically, becoming the owners of small businesses rather than factory "hands" deprived of their independence. As the data in table 2.1 suggest, a significant portion of the trucker population in 1940 had recent farm backgrounds. Of those individuals who reported their occupation as truck drivers in the 1940 census—including not only over-the-road truckers but also urban local delivery drivers—14 percent had lived on a farm in 1935. It seems reasonable to assume that a greater proportion, especially in the over-the-road sector of trucking, had lived on a farm in earlier years, although unfortunately such data are not available. Importantly fully 20 percent of truck drivers who were self-employed had resided on a farm five years

TABLE 2.1

Farm Backgrounds of Truck Drivers, 1940

	All Drivers	*Owners*	*White*	*Black*
Lived on Farm in 1935	14%	20%	15%	8%

Source: IPUMS 1940.

earlier. Being from a farm, then, made a truck driver more likely or more able to own his own truck than the average driver. A disproportionate number of these truckers with farm backgrounds were white; white truckers in 1940 were almost twice as likely as African American truckers to have lived on a farm in 1935. Black drivers in the 1930s and 1940s, whether former farmers or not, faced discrimination from loan providers that prevented them from becoming owner-operator truckers. Such discrimination, along with the less subtle forms of racial hostility in the trucking industry discussed below, set a pattern of disproportionate whiteness within the owner-operator sector of the trucking industry that would continue over the next several decades (see table B.2 in the appendix).[7]

For many white rural men, however, trucking often provided a more secure route to business ownership than farming in the 1930s. Many others found that buying a truck to haul farm products could provide the cash needed to keep a family farm afloat. Trucking at the time had relatively low barriers to entry. An individual needed only a truck to start in the business, and truck manufacturers readily extended seemingly generous credit terms—at least to whites—to encourage new recruits. Farmers bought 26 percent of the nation's total truck production in 1936, contributing to a record-breaking year of sales for truck manufacturers. Mack's sales grew by 118 percent that year. Approximately 150,000 individuals bought or leased a truck in the 1920s and 1930s and began hauling any loads they could find to try to pay off the loan. Those loads were often farm products. As figure 2.1 illustrates, the tight correlation between agriculture and owner-operator trucking that emerged in the 1920s and 1930s set a distinct geographical pattern through the mid-twentieth century. Owner-operator truckers, relative to the overall labor force, tended to be concentrated most heavily in midwestern states such as Iowa, Nebraska, Kansas, and Missouri, where family farms and mixed livestock-grain operations dominated the rural landscape. In the more impoverished rural regions of the cotton-dependent deep South, where land tenure was less secure and credit less available for either whites or African Americans to purchase trucks, owner-operator truckers comprised a very low proportion of the total labor force. Owner-operator con-

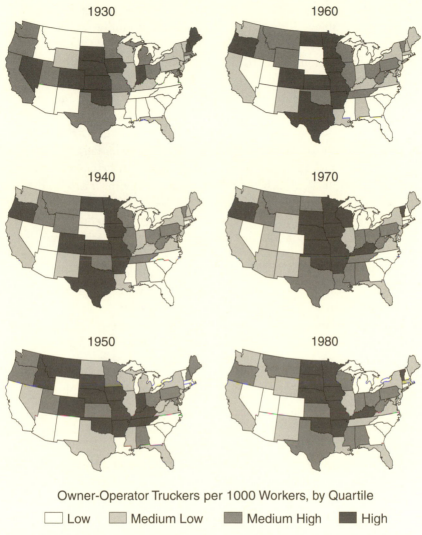

1930

1960

1940

1970

1950

1980

Owner-Operator Truckers per 1000 Workers, by Quartile

☐ Low ▨ Medium Low ▨ Medium High ■ High

Figure 2.1. Owner-Operator Truckers Relative to Total Labor Force, 1930–80.
Owner-operator truckers consistently formed high proportions of the overall labor force in midwestern farm states through the entire period of study. In the South, owner-operator truck drivers were less well represented until nonunion trucking firms sprouted there in the 1960s and 1970s. States with urban-industrial manufacturing economies tended to fall in the middle ranks in terms of owner-operators within the total work force (*Source*: IPUMS 1930–80).

centration tended to lie somewhere between these two poles in states such as California and Illinois that maintained strong manufacturing industries along with high levels of agricultural production.[8]

The rural backgrounds of early truckers would shape the politics of long-haul trucking over the next four decades, as former or would-be farmers brought an intense individualism to their work that challenged the labor and regulatory structures of New Deal economic liberalism. Trucking appealed to rural men in this period as a relatively easy way to leave farming, yet avoid the dependence of industrial wage-work. R. E. "Blick" Blickenstaff, for example, founded Ideal Truck Lines of Norton, Kansas, in August 1933, after a summer of drought left him with such stunted corn that he "left the tractor at the end of a row of that corn and headed for town," Blickenstaff later recalled. "I could see the need for a truck and since it looked like the thing to do at the time, I started in this trucking business. I always planned to go back to the farm if things got better, or after it rained. It didn't rain to any extent for seven years, and by that time I had a nice business going." Stories abound of farm boys turning one Depression-era truck into a giant postwar trucking empire. J. B. Hunt, whose name was emblazoned on over 46,000 tractor-trailers by 2005, was born to Arkansas sharecroppers but escaped the farm by hauling rice and chicken feed in the 1940s. Arno Dalby, who founded T.I.M.E. Freight, Inc.—one of the nation's largest trucking firms by the 1960s—started with a $200 loan from his farmer father in 1927, buying a used Ford Model T truck to haul cotton for a Texas ginning mill. Paul Merrill was raised on a farm in Cumberland County, Maine. He bought his first truck, a used 1922 four-cylinder Reo, in 1929. By 1975 his Merrill Transport Company had become the largest trucking firm in Maine, with $9 million in gross sales.[9]

But for each driver who became a big businessman and had his name recorded in the trade literature, thousands of anonymous drivers struggled to become economically independent in the 1930s and 1940s. Many of the men who were able to scrape together enough money for a down payment on a truck in this period were simply desperate for work and had little business experience. They were often unfamiliar with the concept of depreciation, for instance, and rarely kept careful track of expenses. "Such men were not really entrepreneurs," noted economist Samuel E. Hill in a 1942 report on work conditions in New England trucking. "They were, in essence, workers who had hired tools with which to manufacture and sell the product of their own labor." Although they did not fit the economist's definition of "entrepreneur," the men who purchased beat-up Fords, Reos, and Dodges in the 1930s contributed to a central tenet of trucking culture—the belief that with enough hard work, it was possible to gain economic security as an independent small business owner.[10]

Even when truckers realized that relatively few made "a fortune in this business," as Joe Fabrini imagined in *They Drive by Night,* the feeling of owning a stake in one's financial future mattered deeply. When a *Christian Science Monitor* reporter asked Burly Lockwood in 1947 why men like him had become truckers, the answer came readily, if in a "slow Iowa drawl": "We're our own bosses; most of us own our own businesses. There's a lot of responsibility, but it's all our own—nobody else's." Or as H. A. Strayer of Greeley, Colorado, put it two decades later: "What do I like most about trucking? Independence, I suppose. I've been in trucking 28 years for myself and it's made a good living for my family, wife, and son. I like it fine." This intense attachment to the "independence" of country trucking was not only a product of masculine rural culture, however. It was also closely tied to the farm politics of the New Deal era, and established a social basis for the deregulatory, antiunion politics that would define rural trucking over the next four and a half decades.[11]

Monopoly Power and Agrarian Power

While rural owner-operators saw themselves as "independent" truckers, railroad executives, operators of urban trucking firms, and leaders of the Teamsters Union took to calling them "gypsies," "wildcatters," and "fly-by-nighters." Trucking in the early 1930s was undeniably chaotic, characterized by intense, cut-throat competition between small and large truckers, as well as between trucking firms and railroads. Small trucking firms rose quickly in the 1920s and 1930s due to the low capital costs of entry, but often fell just as rapidly as inexperienced truckers failed to calculate their actual operating costs. Freight truckers, railroaders, organized labor, and government transportation experts pushed Congress to control that chaos by regulating the emerging trucking industry. With the 1935 passage of the Motor Carrier Act, large trucking firms used the increased regulatory power of the New Deal federal government to successfully promote their own desires for cartelization. The Motor Carrier Act initiated forty-five years of remarkably tight regulation of the freight trucking industry. The legislation also contributed to the rise of the Teamsters Union as one of the most powerful labor organizations in U.S. history. But as we shall see, farm interests made sure that the business and labor stability achieved under the Motor Carrier Act would not apply to agricultural trucking. The chaos of pre–New Deal unregulated trucking would continue to reign on rural highways, setting the stage for the deregulatory politics of the post–World War II era.[12]

Jack Keeshin was one of the most energetic promoters of federal regulation as a way to minimize competition in the trucking industry.[13] In 1917 Keeshin operated one truck, hauling Fig Newtons from Chicago to South Bend. By

1932, he had transformed his Keeshin Southwest Motor Company into one of the nation's largest trucking firms, with a fleet of 250 machines serving shippers such as the Great Atlantic and Pacific Tea Company. In November of 1932 he and two other commercial fleet owners created the American Highway Freight Association to lobby for federal legislation to clamp down on "gypsy" truckers. "It was a 'dog-eat-dog' business," Keeshin later remembered, "and would so continue unless [federal] regulations were introduced." Keeshin's desire for government oversight was not at first shared by other large truckers, however, who preferred self-regulation. The opportunity to self-regulate came with the 1933 establishment of the National Recovery Administration (NRA) as a mechanism for industry trade groups to write "codes of fair competition" meant to foment industrial recovery. President Roosevelt and liberal Democrats such as Robert Wagner intended the NRA to serve labor as much as business interests by guaranteeing stable wages and employment in exchange for exemption from antitrust laws. The codes that emerged from the experiment instead provided highly competitive industries an opportunity to cartelize by creating state-sanctioned price-fixing arrangements.[14]

Cartelization was exactly the intent behind the formation of the American Trucking Associations, Inc. This group primarily represented trucking firm owners who preferred self-regulation to government intervention, but in September 1933 it absorbed Keeshin's proregulation group and would soon become the nation's leading proponent of tight federal regulation of commercial trucking. Although the American Trucking Associations presented a unified voice to the NRA negotiator assigned to the trucking industry, drafting the NRA trucking code proved exceedingly difficult. Trucking firms were most interested in the NRA's power to prevent destructive price competition, but the NRA negotiator also insisted on equalizing drivers' working conditions and wage rates across the industry, a provision that trucking firms bitterly resisted and only ruefully accepted. The code that emerged from the negotiations was signed into law by President Roosevelt in February 1934. As with many of the NRA codes, however, the difficulties of maintaining self-regulation in a highly competitive industry quickly became apparent. Although 300,000 firms signed on to the code, at least 75,000 refused to abide by its rules; many firms continued to cut wages and slash rates in defiance of the agreements. The NRA found enforcement impossible in an industry in which individual trucking companies had every incentive to shirk the code's provisions to gain a competitive edge on those who followed the rules. By the fall of 1934, even before the Supreme Court declared the NRA's enabling legislation unconstitutional, the NRA trucking code had clearly failed. Most of the ATA's members abandoned their faith in self-regulation and turned toward Jack Keeshin's view that only strong federal regulation could control the chaos of trucking. They would find a sympathetic ally in Joseph B. Eastman.[15]

Eastman, a member of the Interstate Commerce Commission since 1919, was a Progressive public servant in the mold of Louis D. Brandeis. Like Brandeis, Eastman sought to serve the "public interest" by using the regulatory power of the state to create efficiency in transportation. In June of 1933 President Roosevelt appointed Eastman to the new post of Federal Coordinator of Transportation. With the goal of bringing the efficiency of big business to the world of small-time trucking, Joseph Eastman pulled together a coalition of interest groups to convince Congress to pass the Motor Carrier Act of 1935. Achieving efficiency in transportation, Eastman believed, could not "be attained or even approached without public regulation." As he told the Senate Committee on Interstate Commerce in 1935, the rapid rise of the trucking industry created intense competition between trucks and railroads, leading to "an oversupply of transportation facilities" that harmed the interests of railroad investors, shippers, and truck drivers alike. Eastman understood that federal regulation might encourage large trucking firms to raise freight rates without fear of antitrust prosecution, but argued that cartelization was not contrary to the public interest. Large-scale business would bring efficiency, argued Eastman, pointing to the example of Ford Motor Company's use of vertical integration to drive down the costs of production and make automobiles affordable to the masses. "Gradually there will be a development of larger operations," admitted Eastman, but those larger trucking companies would "be more economical when well organized." Just as economic concentration in the meatpacking and automobile industries had led to economies of scale and lower prices for consumers, Eastman predicted that consolidation of the trucking industry would lead to lower freight rates for shippers.[16]

After the Motor Carrier Act became law in the summer of 1935, the U.S. highway transportation market was defined more by government policy than by purely economic motives. Operators of a new trucking firm suddenly needed much more than just a truck and trailer to start in business. They needed to gain operating authority as well, which the ICC granted only after lengthy and expensive proceedings meant to discourage competition. In order to engage in interstate commerce, a trucking firm had to apply to the ICC for a certificate of "public convenience and necessity," which was only awarded if the firm's attorneys convinced ICC administrators that the geographical areas to be served were not adequately served by existing railroad or trucking routes. Certificated trucking firms also had to publish their freight rates, which the ICC closely administered to prevent price-cutting. Although the ICC "grandfathered" in all existing trucking firms in the first year after passage of the Motor Carrier

Act, over the next forty-five years these regulations created significant barriers to entry. Large firms such as Yellow Freight, Pacific Intermountain Express, Roadway, and Consolidated Freightways would be among the primary beneficiaries of this regulatory regime. Although even these large firms never enjoyed a true monopoly in trucking, they were able to swallow up smaller firms to gain ICC operating authorities in order to consolidate their control over key markets without fear of significant competition. The American Trucking Associations, founded primarily to promote self-regulation of the highway freight industry under the NRA, became the nation's leading proponent of ICC regulation for the next forty-five years, recognizing that government-mandated limits to free-market competition in trucking could be profitable. The ATA hired a permanent cadre of researchers and lobbyists to keep members of Congress aware that, even if ICC regulations allowed for cartelization of trucking, the benefits of carrier financial stability, operating efficiency, and reliability of service for shippers outweighed any potential concerns about monopoly power. As the ATA's self-published history recalled the advent of the regulatory regime in 1935: "An industry that was born as a struggling, often unwanted infant has become a mature, responsible adult."[17]

The International Brotherhood of Teamsters (IBT) benefited greatly from this new cartelized regulatory structure. Before the passage of the Motor Carrier Act, the Teamsters Union was a weak federation of craft-based locals of wagon and truck drivers—deliverers of milk, bread, coal, and ice. In the first thirty-odd years after its establishment in 1899, the Teamsters Union remained tied to local hauling within specific urban areas. Daniel Tobin, Teamsters president from 1907 to 1952, called over-the-road drivers—who trucked goods between cities rather than within them—"trash" unworthy of membership in his union in 1934. But with the passage of the 1935 Motor Carrier Act, Teamsters leaders such as Farrell Dobbs in Minneapolis, Dave Beck in Seattle, and James R. Hoffa in Detroit gained a powerful tool for organizing truck drivers across entire regions. Because the legislation limited competition in geographical areas and required all regulated carriers to publish their rates, each regulated trucking firm had an incentive to charge the same rates as every other firm. If one trucking firm contracted with the Teamsters and raised its rates to accommodate increased wage demands, other firms had little incentive to resist unionization since they could just as easily increase their rates. Without competition from other trucking firms over specific geographical routes, the higher rates that attended unionization had little impact on individual regulated freight trucking firms. The Motor Carrier Act in effect created what political scientists call a "free rider effect," allowing the Teamsters to monopolize the labor market in freight trucking as an unintended consequence of regulated carriers' efforts to limit competition in the transportation market. Although Congress had not intended to use regulatory reform to boost worker wages and improve working conditions in the trucking industry, the Motor Carrier Act empowered the Teamsters Union to do so.[18]

The Motor Carrier Act did not automatically boost Teamster power, however, as trucking firm managers initially resisted unionization at every step. Teamster organizers had to fight, and fight hard, to gain union recognition in the 1930s. Farrell Dobbs, a Trotskyite based in Minneapolis, developed one of the union's most important organizing strategies—"leapfrogging." After witnessing two exceptionally violent but effective citywide strikes by Minneapolis drivers in the spring and summer of 1934, Dobbs declared that the over-the-road trucker was not in fact "trash," but instead could help the Teamsters carry "the message of unionism wherever he goes." By refusing to deliver loads to plants outside of Minneapolis that remained unorganized—that is, by using secondary boycotts—over-the-road truck drivers could force even nontrucking firms to recognize the union. By 1937 Dobbs had created the Central States Drivers Council, which united thirteen Teamster locals in the Dakotas, Minnesota, Wisconsin, and upper Michigan with the express purpose of using established centers of Teamster power to "leapfrog" throughout the region, bringing in their wake uniform labor contracts that standardized wages and working conditions for truck drivers across hundreds of firms. Dobbs's Communist politics would set him at odds with Daniel Tobin at IBT headquarters, but his regionwide organizing strategy dramatically boosted the union's membership rolls and inspired a number of local Teamster organizers, especially James R. Hoffa and Dave Beck.[19]

Hoffa, born in Indiana in 1913, was no Trotskyite. Visions of working-class solidarity held little sway for a man who saw the world in social-Darwinist terms as an individualistic struggle for survival in a vicious economic jungle. Hoffa's coal-worker father had died when Jimmy was seven years old, and the young Hoffa remembered the challenges his mother and three siblings faced in surviving the hard times of the 1920s and 1930s. Hoffa's first experience organizing workers "out of a need for self-preservation" occurred in a Kroger grocery warehouse in Detroit in 1931, when Hoffa and other workers in the produce section of the warehouse demanded an end to their "miserable" working conditions. Later fired by Kroger for his rebelliousness, Hoffa joined Teamsters Local 299 in Detroit as an organizer in 1934—the same year that Minneapolis truck drivers demonstrated the possibilities of Teamster power. Hoffa met with Farrell Dobbs and adopted his leapfrogging strategy but not his Trotskyism. Throughout the 1930s Hoffa used secondary boycotts, fists, and collusive "sweetheart" relationships with trucking firm managers such as Jack Keeshin to expand the reach of Local 299's power in the Midwest and simultaneously establish himself as a man widely admired within the IBT's ranks.[20]

On the West Coast, meanwhile, Dave Beck adopted the leapfrog strategy to establish the Western Conference of Teamsters in 1937. Beck, like Hoffa, saw boosting union membership and worker wages as more pressing than any political ideology, so forged cozy relationships with compliant business owners and, when necessary, waged violent organizing campaigns against more recalcitrant firms. But to an even greater extent than either Dobbs or Hoffa, Beck realized that the Teamsters could transcend its localism and become one of the nation's largest unions through aggressive enrollment not only of over-the-road truckers but also of nondrivers in industries that relied on highway shipments. The regulations put in place by the 1935 Motor Carrier Act significantly helped Beck's efforts, since the ICC's oversight of geographical competition meant that interstate trucking firms could not reroute their drivers around Beck's strategically placed roadblocks. Beck's successful organization of much of the West Coast from Seattle to Los Angeles, combined with the efforts of Dobbs, Hoffa, and lesser leaders throughout the nation, made the Teamsters into a force to be reckoned with by the end of the 1930s. By 1939 the IBT counted more than 400,000 members, a 433 percent increase since 1933.[21]

But even as the 1935 Motor Carrier Act provided Teamsters and large trucking companies with the power to stabilize profits and wages in trucking, Congress made a significant exception for agricultural trucking. A clause in the Motor Carrier Act that came to be known as the "agricultural exemption"— Section 203(b)—allowed truckers hauling certain farm products to do so at any rate they wished to charge, over any geographical route, and without an expensive certificate of authority. From the beginning of the regulatory drive, farm groups such as the National Grange lobbied Congress to allow farmers and farm cooperatives to truck their products to market without ICC oversight. After all, farmers who had come to rely upon paved rural roads and Model Ts to deliver a few cans of milk or a load of produce to city markets were hardly in the same league as Jack Keeshin. Farm lobbyists pushed hard to assure that farm trucking would remain forever unregulated. During the NRA code hearings, the National Cooperative Milk Producers Association declared that the NRA trucking code would create "a gigantic trucking trust." Every major farm group in the nation flooded farm bloc congressmen and Secretary of Agriculture Henry A. Wallace with telegrams demanding the NRA code be stopped. Wallace, steeped in the antimonopoly sentiment of his midwestern forebears, asked his friend Donald Murphy, editor of the influential farm journal *Wallace's Farmer and Iowa Homestead,* to "sound a warning, privately or publicly, as you see fit, on the perils of the [NRA] trucking code." Wallace coordinated a strategy to present Congress with evidence that trucking had "mitigated the effect of the depression on farmers" by allowing them to bypass middlemen, such as country elevators and produce commission merchants, whose services had been necessary in a railroad-based agricultural economy but unnecessarily cut into farmers' incomes in a highway-based economy. Dredging up antimonopoly sentiments that had run strong in the rural United States since the Populist movements of the late nineteenth century, farm interests demanded that Congress not cave in to the ATA's demands for state-sanctioned cartelization.[22]

Farm opposition to trucking regulation continued during the congressional hearings on the Motor Carrier Act. The National Grange, in particular, fought Joseph Eastman's efforts to "perpetuate the transportation monopoly which will be dominated by the railroads." Testifying before the Senate in 1935, the national representative of the Grange noted that trucking regulation "would result in serious handicaps to the farmer, the stockmen, and the horticulturists" by allowing trucking companies to peg their rates to those of the railroads, creating an upward pressure on all freight rates for farm goods, whether traveling by rail or road. Farm opposition to Eastman's bill strengthened during testimony in the House. Organizations from the Grange to the American National Livestock Association declared the legislation an effort by railroads to "consolidate in one vast system all the transportation facilities of the country." Only unregulated trucking, farm lobbyists argued, could help farmers escape the tentacles of the steel-railed octopus.[23]

Joseph Eastman, for his part, felt the farm organizations misunderstood the proposed legislation. Eastman informed Wallace that farmers hauling their own products to market in their own trucks would not fall under the ambit of the ICC, since they were "private carriers . . . not subject to the proposed regulation." Attempting to assuage farm interests, Eastman amended his original proposal to specifically exempt truckers hauling "unprocessed agricultural commodities" from the ICC's regulations. As Eastman saw it, such phrasing would allow any farmer or farm cooperative to haul products such as milk to a dairy or livestock to a meatpacker (from farm to "first market") without need for ICC authority. But Congressmen from farm states feared this was not enough. As Representative Walter Pierce (D-OR), noted during debates on the Motor Carrier Act, "many members [representing agricultural states] will lose their seats on this very issue." Bowing to the pressure from farm lobbyists, Congress went Eastman one step further and wrote into the Motor Carrier Act a clause exempting all "agricultural commodities (not including manufactured products thereof)." With this phrasing, any trucker who hauled agricultural goods that were not "manufactured" was exempt from ICC regulation, whether he was a farmer or not. Without this amendment, the Motor Carrier Act would never have become law under a Congress beholden to agricultural interests. Congress declined to state exactly what an unmanufactured commodity was, but debates on the bill implied the phrasing was meant to include such minimally processed products as pasteurized milk and ginned cotton. This was a firm rebuke of Eastman's efforts to limit exempt hauling solely to private farm-to-first-market transportation, considering that the "first market" for raw milk was a pasteurization plant.[24]

The agricultural exemption provided more than just a minor loophole allowing farmers to haul a few cans of milk to the processing plant in the back of a Model T. In fact, the agricultural exemption implicitly challenged the core values of economic liberalism. Other New Deal policies instituted during the heady days of 1935, including the National Labor Relations Act and the Social Security Act, sought to use state power to boost wages, stabilize the economy, and provide an economic safety net to the citizenry. The agricultural exemption of the Motor Carrier Act, however, shielded rural trucking firms from federal regulation and foiled the efforts of the Teamsters Union to organize rural truckers. In this, the agricultural exemption shared much with the provisions of the National Labor Relations Act and the Social Security Act, as well as the National Fair Labor Standards Act of 1938, that prevented farm workers from being fully integrated into the urban-industrial New Deal order. Along with the compromises built into the Agricultural Adjustment Act and the doomed optimism of the Resettlement Administration (later the Farm Security Administration), liberal New Dealers gained relatively little in the way of policy tools for helping landless farmers or rural wage workers.[25] But the agricultural exemption embedded in the Motor Carrier Act would have far-reaching impacts not only on rural workers but on the entire structure of the U.S. farm and food economy. Over the next several decades, agribusinesses would rely on sympathetic congressmen and USDA bureaucrats to transform the chaotic nature of unregulated trucking into a "free market" solution to the New Deal-era farm problem. This radically antistatist and antiunion agenda would not become clear until after World War II, however. In many agricultural industries of the late 1930s, the exemption primarily served its intended function: it helped individual farmers to haul products such as milk and livestock to market more cheaply than they could via railroad or regulated trucks. But as the politics of trucking in the milk and beef industries of the 1930s demonstrated, even truckers hauling just a few loads of milk or several head of cattle to market posed significant challenges to the Gilded Age status quo in the railroad-based farm and food economy.

DISORDERLY MILK MARKETS AND DIRECT BEEF MARKETING

Dairy and cattle farmers, who had long felt abused by the railroad monopoly on long-distance transportation of milk and livestock, were among the earliest adopters of truck technology. In choosing to drive their milk or cattle to market in the back of a Model T or to have a neighbor with a larger trailer-truck do the job for them, such farmers took advantage of the chaos of unregulated farm trucking to achieve better farm prices during the Depression. In practice, the agricultural exemption for farm truckers reflected deep tensions within the political economy of the New Deal. Efficiency-minded Progressives such as Joseph Eastman saw the decentralized, dispersed nature of trucking as contradictory to the New Deal aims of industrial and labor stability during the Depression. Farmers and farm-minded liberals such as Secretary of Agriculture Wallace, however, saw in trucks a possible solution to the age-old monopoly problem in the farm and food economy. By driving their goods directly to market rather than to the railhead, dairy and beef farmers expected to gain economic power at the expense of the long-despised railroads. Reflecting this political tension during the 1930s, the impacts of trucking technology within agriculture were mixed. In the dairy economy, the threat that unregulated farm truckers posed to the stability of the industry led to a redoubling of New Deal efforts to control milk markets through deeply intrusive administrative machinery. In the beef economy, however, the unregulated nature of country trucking provided a key resource for challenging the monopoly power of the Big Four meatpackers without the need to resort to the heavy hand of government economic intervention. In both cases, farmers' adoption of trucking technology during the 1930s set the stage for "free-market" assaults on economic liberalism in later decades.

In the early 1920s, enterprising dairy farmers began loading pickups with milk to haul to local processing plants. Dairy farmers had long been accustomed to transporting their own milk in cans via wagon to a country collecting depot, from which railroads would assemble larger tanks of milk for delivery into the city (see figure 2.2). Most early milk truckers were dairy farmers who saw a chance to replace their horse-and-wagon with a modified Model T or some other small truck, and then bypass the railroad milk collecting system by gathering their own and their neighbors' milk cans for direct delivery to a processing plant. In those days of heavy milk cans and poor roads, haulers rarely traveled more than fifty miles a day, stopping at fewer than two dozen neighboring farms. More often than not, a motorized truck was little or no improvement over a horse-drawn wagon, because both were liable to get stuck in rutted, muddy rural roads. But in the 1930s, as roads improved and pneumatic

Figure 2.2. Milk Hauler Unloading Cans at Receiving Station.
A farmer in the early 1930s drove his own truck filled with milk cans to a local dairy plant's receiving station. The backbreaking task of lifting milk cans remained a daily feature of dairying until the introduction of bulk tanks in the 1950s (*Source*: Wisconsin Historical Society, WHi 31171).

tires made higher motor-truck speeds possible, hauling became bigger business. Drivers often bought a larger truck or two, sometimes equipped with a tank to allow cans to be unloaded directly on the patron's farm. Allison Pickering of Trempealeau County, Wisconsin, for instance, traded in his trusty Ford Model T in 1927 for a larger Chevrolet capable of hauling three times as much milk. With larger equipment, drivers began expanding their routes into the seventy-five-mile range. In doing so, dairy truckers posed a significant challenge to the status quo of the railroad-based milk economy, threatening to take valuable freight away from railroads while also destabilizing agreements between urban milk dealers and inner-ring dairy farmers.[26]

Economist John D. Black clearly recognized this threat. Born in a dairy region of southern Wisconsin in 1883, Black was one of the most influential agricultural economists of the twentieth century. He received his Ph.D. at the University of Wisconsin in 1918, taught at the University of Minnesota until 1927, then moved to Harvard University to teach until his death in 1960. Although he never took a permanent government position, many of his students became members of the Roosevelt and later administrations, and Black frequently served as an influential consultant on farm policy boards. Furthermore the Agricultural Adjustment Act, with its focus on production controls, owed much to Black's work in refining his friend and fellow economist M. L. Wilson's concept of domestic allotments (the primary mechanism used to control levels of farm production under the AAA). Firmly committed to the use of New Deal-style production controls rather than Hoover-era voluntary marketing agreements to stabilize farm incomes, Black was a somewhat unlikely candidate to be tapped by Edwin G. Nourse of the Brookings Institution in 1934 to assess the early results of the AAA's milk marketing program. Convinced of the importance of the project, however, Black was determined to ascertain whether the milk marketing orders should be treated as only emergency measures or as permanent solutions to the milk problem. In *The Dairy Industry and the AAA,* published in 1935, Black offered both a comprehensive history of the orders and a sustained argument for the system's continuation into the indefinite future. Most important, Black defined the milk problem not as an issue of class tension but of geographical conflict.[27]

The essence of the milk problem, according to Black, was disorder—and trucks were the cause. More specifically, Black saw the price wars and milk strikes of the early 1930s as undesirable "disturbances" of Johann von Thünen's geographical model, as dairymen located far from city centers used trucks to defy the geographical dictates of railroad-based milk shipping. Before New Deal regulation of milk economies was introduced in 1933, the government agency with the most power to achieve order in milk marketing was the Interstate

Commerce Commission. After a set of ICC rulings in 1916–17, railroads developed a uniform rate schedule based on the distance of a dairy farm from its urban market. Rate regulations effectively drove up the cost of shipping milk from a hinterland farm into a city market. Upstate farmers were prevented from shipping milk to high-priced city markets, and instead had to settle for the lower prices offered by butter and cheese manufacturers. Railroads and federal regulations limited geographical and seasonal competition within the milk economy, minimizing opportunities for upstate dairy farmers to ship their less sanitary but more cheaply produced milk to lucrative urban markets. Truckers hauling tanks of milk, however, did not have to comply with ICC rate regulations. Paid by milk distributors to bring milk from farms to processing stations, milk truckers were mainly interested in filling their tanks quickly. By traveling on a highway straight out from the city, collecting from farms along the way, a trucker could fill his tank more rapidly than by traveling circumferentially within a city's milkshed where roads could be unreliable. According to Black, trucking technology thus produced an "evil effect." Truckers interested only in filling their tanks quickly recruited outer-ring farmers, who had been accustomed to producing milk for cheese and butter markets, into what was supposed to be the city fluid milk market—at least according to von Thünen's geographical theories. When upstate farmers used trucks to defy the prohibitive costs of shipping their milk by rail into city markets, they drove down the price of milk for all farmers, hurting themselves as well as their competitors. This, according to Black, led to "serious economic waste" and propagated economic unrest in dairy country—the same kind of unrest that had led to the violent milk strikes of the early 1930s discussed in chapter 1. Black saw an "urgent . . . need for introducing order into the business of transporting milk from the farm to the city, especially by truck."[28]

With the agricultural exemption of the 1935 Motor Carrier Act, however, milk truckers would never be subject to federal economic or geographical regulation. Unregulated truckers, unlike railroads, had no incentive to obey the geographical dictates of Johann von Thünen's concentric rings, and so posed a potentially serious threat to the monopoly power of inner-ring dairy farmers and urban milk dealers in cities like Chicago and Milwaukee. Neither the inner-ring dairymen nor federal administrators could control the "evil effect" of chaotic milk trucking, so the only option remaining was the use of the AAA's strong federal power to erect artificial price differentials between fluid milk and manufactured milk (i.e., milk used for butter and cheese production). According to John Black, strong federal intervention by the AAA was essential to create "proper [price] differentials between different [dairy] products and different areas," thus subduing "the confusion" that had emerged with the expansion of unregulated milk trucking. In effect, the AAA milk marketing orders of 1933 and onward achieved, by fiat, the "orderly marketing" that the tightly controlled railroad rate schedules of earlier decades had failed to maintain under the challenge of highway-based milk transportation during the economic crisis of the Depression. But using federal power to revert to railroad-based price structures meant that monopoly conditions would continue to characterize the urban milk market. Price regulations that served to guarantee inner-ring milk farmers and city milk dealers a higher price for their product while shutting outer-ring farmers out of the urban milk markets—much as the railroad rate schedules had done in the 1910s and 1920s—became the USDA's primary method for preventing disputes over the price of milk. When Congress passed the Agricultural Marketing Act in 1937, shoring up the constitutionality of milk marketing orders, the federal administration of milk markets became a permanent feature of agricultural policy. Despite continuing challenges from consumers, workers, and policymakers who saw the USDA's milk marketing orders as state-sanctioned monopolies, the system remained intact for decades to come.[29]

While trucking did not fundamentally change the cartelized structure of milk distribution in the 1930s, the impact of unregulated trucking within the cattle industry of the 1930s proved more problematic for the Big Four meatpackers. Whereas inner-ring dairy farmers and monopolistic milk dealers teamed up with government administrators to limit the chaotic impacts of unregulated trucking on their business, beef raisers turned to independent truckers to launch a subtle attack on the monopoly power of the Big Four packers in the New Deal-era beef economy. Cattlemen who generally refused to call upon the federal government for help in boosting their marketing power turned instead to unregulated trucking as a tool for challenging the packers' control over live cattle prices. Cattle raisers began using trucks in the 1930s to circumvent the monopsony power that the packers had forged in the central stockyards located at key railroad junctions in cities such as Chicago, St. Louis, Omaha, and Kansas City. Trucks and highways presented cattle farmers with opportunities to decide when and where they would market their cattle in ways that they had never been able to do in a railroad-based beef economy. In doing so, livestock farmers initiated a decades-long transformation of the economic geography of cattle marketing that would ultimately spell the end of the Big Four's monopoly power.

Trucks became powerful political technologies in cattle country in the 1930s partly because of widespread distrust of government power among beef producers. Unlike organized inner-ring dairy farmers, livestock raisers were almost universally opposed to using government power to gain higher farm prices. Even though dust and depressed prices dominated livestock raising in the early 1930s, cattlemen denounced efforts to impose government regulations on livestock marketing akin to the milk orders or to introduce planned production controls under the AAA. This did not mean they were opposed to government help. Ranchers appreciated federal land subsidies, generous credit terms, tariffs on imported livestock, and efforts to eradicate tick fever, foot-and-mouth disease, and wolves. Still cattle raisers organized in the American National Cattlemen's Association bitterly resisted any federal efforts to coordinate or control livestock production in the twentieth century.[30] This antipathy toward government interference in beef production was not purely a product of political ideology, however. Antistatism in cattle country emerged from two material factors of livestock production. First, the vast majority of cattlemen in the United States from the late nineteenth century until the 1960s were not ranchers on vast tracts of the western and southern plains. Most cattle producers were instead Corn Belt producers, sited on relatively small plots of land, who generally fed less than 200 head of cattle as part of a mixed farming operation. Corn Belt cattle feeders would buy young "stocker" cattle from ranchers on grasslands farther west, then confine them in small feedlots to eat corn until they reached a profitable weight. These grain-fed "finished" steers generally brought good prices from certain customers, especially managers of upper-crust hotels, who readily paid extra for the highly marbled, tender corn-fed beef. But even if cattle prices were not high, feeding one's own grain to one's own cattle provided an effective economic safety net. The cattle provided a "home market" for grains when prices dropped too low to justify the cost of shipping to grain elevators, and besides, feeder cattle provided piles of rich manure to fertilize fields. This was a crucial factor shaping both the political economy and the geography of livestock feeding through most of the twentieth century. Midwestern cattlemen relied on fluctuations in the prices of grains and cattle in order to make their profits. In such an ecologically intricate and economically uncertain game of supply-and-demand, cattlemen had material reasons to believe that federal government regulations or subsidies would do more harm than good.[31]

The second material factor contributing to antistatism in beef production was the "cattle cycle." The biology and ecology of beef cattle production created continuous boom-and-bust cycles that posed (and continue to pose) fundamental challenges to any state efforts to stabilize prices over the long run. The biology of the beef cow has defied most efforts to significantly speed up the process of turning a newborn calf into a steer ready for fattening; the process has generally taken at least two years, often several more. The ecology of cattle raising requires much of this time to be spent on large expanses of grassland. Cattle ranchers must invest in giant plots of range land that serve no economic purpose other than providing grass for herbivorous meat animals. As a consequence, all ranchers attempt to fill their land with as many cattle as they can until disastrous price drops—such as those that occurred during 1933 and 1934—force them to cull their herds. But because several years lapse before a rancher's decision to reduce production results in fewer fattened cattle, price changes consistently lag behind changes in cattle supplies. The result is an iterative cattle cycle of 10 to 12 years, in which the first 6 to 7 years see livestock raisers expanding production as prices rise, then 4 to 5 years of declining production when prices fall due to oversupply. The cattle cycle was a permanent feature of beef production throughout the twentieth century. *Successful Farming,* noting the regularity of the phenomenon up to 1975, advised its readers to "buy a 10-year calendar." Regulating such lengthy price cycles would require a degree of foreknowledge beyond the capacity of most government bureaucrats; and in any case, politicians' terms of office tend to be several years shorter than cattle cycles.[32]

Given the ecological and economic basis of antistatism in cattle country, livestock raisers suffering from the economic crunch of the 1930s found trucks to be more effective for boosting incomes than government antitrust policies, price supports, production controls, or marketing agreements. Farmers first began using trucks to haul livestock to markets in the 1920s. Much like dairy farmers, midwestern cattle raisers began loading up their own or their neighbors' animals on pickup trucks and driving them to the nearest market. They could rarely travel more than fifty miles in those days of dirt roads. Farmers fortunate enough to be located within fifty miles of a market such as Chicago, St. Paul, or St. Louis, however, could avoid rail shipping costs and boost profits by taking animals to market only on days when prices were high. Using trucks, farmers could counteract the monopsony power of cattle buyers by simply refusing to sell until the price was right. At first, many terminal stockyards proved resistant to trucked-in livestock. Because yards often had tight financial relationships with railroad companies as well as significant investments in railheads and unloading platforms, they charged sellers of trucked-in livestock higher yardage and commission fees. The meatpackers and stockyard managers realized that their economic power was based in their control of railroad transportation and wielded their power to prevent livestock truckers from offering too much competition to the rails.[33]

Secretary of Agriculture Henry A. Wallace entered the fray in 1935, realizing the potential power of trucking to shift the balance of power in cattle marketing without the need for heavy-handed government antitrust action. The giant Union Stock Yard at Chicago offered a ready target. When Chicago petitioned Wallace to be allowed to raise its fees from 40 cents to 50 cents per head of cattle trucked in, Wallace denied the application, noting that it would place "an undue burden on the shippers of livestock arriving by truck." After denying the petition, Wallace drove the point home by ordering an investigation of trucking rates at the Chicago yards. Chicago quickly learned its lesson, as stockyards deeper in cattle supply areas—especially Omaha and Kansas City—began building improved truck unloading facilities in the mid-1930s to draw livestock producers away from Chicago to their facilities. In 1936, trucks hauled 55 percent of cattle shipped to public stock yards. The proportion of cattle moving to public stockyards via truck rather than rail steadily increased over the next few decades. In 1939 three of every five cattle arrived by truck; in 1949, nearly three-quarters did so, and by 1960, nine of ten cattle came to public stockyards in truck trailers. The railroads and central stockyards that had formed the basis of the Big Four's monopsony power became increasingly irrelevant in an age of unregulated highway transportation.[34]

Even as truckers challenged the railroads' domination of cattle marketing in cities like Chicago, a more fundamental shift in cattle marketing power relations came with the advent of "direct" or "country" buying in the 1930s. Rather than ship livestock all the way to urban stockyards to be sold by a commission merchant, farmers found that they could reduce shipping costs by selling their stock at smaller yards in the countryside. Packer buyers came to these yards to buy directly from the farmers rather than through commissioners. At first, direct buying posed only a small threat to the business of the big urban stockyards. In 1933, only 17 percent of cattle were direct marketed. As early as 1934, however, stockyard managers foresaw that direct buying might render their urban facilities obsolete. The American Stock Yards Association, which represented the fifty largest central markets in the country, proposed to Secretary of Agriculture Wallace that a code of fair competition be drawn up under the auspices of the National Recovery Administration to prevent packers from buying livestock outside the traditional marketing channels. The stockyards claimed that direct buying "seriously depresses the price of livestock." Most of the farmers who testified at the hearings, however, thought otherwise. A livestock feeder from northwest Iowa swore that "when the packer came along to purchase livestock from the farmer for cash it was to the farmer's great advantage." No longer did the farmer have to pay shipping costs or extortionate yardage fees, and he was furthermore guaranteed an instant cash payment. A cattle feeder from eastern Iowa agreed, denouncing the urban stockyard companies as "autocratic and dictatorial" and blaming the Chicago Union Stock Yard in particular for "greatly overcharging in feeding charges." Producers' protests, along with a deep-seated antimonopoly agrarianism, led Wallace to offer no support to the proposed NRA code, and it was never enacted.[35]

Over time Wallace and his advisors became increasingly convinced that direct buying offered a politically painless solution to the problem of monopsony in cattle buying. Livestock raisers continued to put their cattle on trucks and send them to country buying stations in the 1930s, prompting agricultural economist Albert G. Black (a former student of John D. Black, but unrelated) to state in 1938 that "a movement such as direct marketing must have tremendous popular appeal to livestock producers and to livestock processors, otherwise it would hardly have grown as rapidly as it has." The rise of hundreds of country buying stations and local auction markets created an increasingly decentralized marketing structure, allowing a farmer to load cattle on a truck trailer and sell his stock at a place and time of his choosing. This produced a new economic geography in cattle marketing. Although the number of meatpacking firms buying slaughter cattle still remained relatively small, the number of possible points of sale multiplied dramatically, thereby limiting the ability of the meatpacker buyers to collusively set prices. The despised Beef Trust was quickly losing its power to control cattle pricing.[36]

The convenience and flexibility of livestock trucking led farmers to abandon the rail-based terminal market system. Oscar Mayer, a leading independent meatpacker, argued at the 1934 NRA livestock code hearings that the shift to country buying was not only beneficial for farmers, but was the product of technological change, the "result of good roads, motor transportation and radio." Though his determinism was a bit strong—after all, the choice to ship by truck rather than train was made within a very specific political and economic context—Mayer was quite right to note the possibilities opened up by these three technologies. Radio allowed the farmers to maximize the power of trucking, because farmers would listen to early morning livestock market reports to decide whether they could get a good price that day at the local auction or cattle buying station. As Ernest Kellenberger, a cattle feeder from Algona, Iowa, would recall thirty years later, it was very convenient to "turn my radio on early in the morning and back the old truck up to the chute and put the cattle on and take them [to market], if the [price] seem[ed] desirable." Producers with access to trucks could exercise more freedom in choosing when and where to market their livestock. Most notably, farmers could haul their animals to either a country market or to an urban market, and if the price was not right that day, either take the cattle to another market with higher prices or simply take them home. This had been impossible in the days when railroads controlled cattle shipments according to their strict schedules, and when big packers and their stockyard allies monitored the daily prices at all major markets via telegraph. By the beginning of World War II, trucking brought cattlemen a newfound power in the livestock marketplace. Without having to flex much state muscle, Henry A. Wallace's Department of Agriculture had helped cattle farmers to surmount the decades-old political problem of monopsony in livestock marketing, setting the stage for a post–World War II "free-market" solution to the nagging problem of monopoly power on the retail end of the U.S. beef economy.[37]

Farmers, agribusinesses, and farm policymakers all recognized in the 1930s that trucking posed a significant challenge to the existing rail-based economic order. For deeply antistatist agrarians in midwestern cattle country who had a sympathetic secretary of agriculture in Henry A. Wallace, unregulated trucking provided powerful "free market" solutions to complex problems of political economy. For organized dairy farmers and milk bottlers, however, trucks posed serious threats to the monopoly power they had achieved under New Deal economic regulations. Meanwhile urban freight truckers, railroad firms, and the Teamsters Union all saw "fly-by-night" country truckers as destabilizing influences in the industrial economy. The politics of trucking, then, contributed to broader disagreements in the mid-1930s over the proper role of the state in regulating free enterprise. After 1935, even as New Deal liberals introduced new social welfare, labor, and consumer-friendly policies, the future of regressive farm policies and chaos-inducing transportation policies remained uncertain. With the onset of World War II, as the next chapter discusses, economic liberalism took firm root in farm and food politics, as organized labor and urban consumers called upon the federal government to contest the power of factory farmers and agribusinesses. Many farmers and agricultural policymakers, however, continued to seek "free market" solutions to the New Deal-era farm problem. The technologies and politics of long-haul trucking became deeply embedded in these disputes during and immediately after the war, ultimately undermining New Deal economic liberalism through technological means.

CHAPTER THREE

Food Fights in War and Peace, 1942–52

Charles F. Brannan was trained as a lawyer and dressed like a banker, but as secretary of agriculture from 1948 through 1952, he engineered one of the century's most vigorous attacks on corporate power in the farm and food economy. Brannan embodied the spirit of New Deal economic liberalism, having arrived in Washington in 1935 as an attorney for the Department of Agriculture's Resettlement Administration and later serving as a regional director of the Farm Security Administration—two left-leaning agencies reviled by conservatives for attempting to boost the economic and political power of poor white and black farmers. After his appointment by President Truman as secretary of agriculture in 1948, Brannan spearheaded an ill-fated effort to recast New Deal farm policy and solve the "farm problem" by supporting the interests of small farmers and urban consumers, intending to unite both under the banner of the Democratic Party. Republicans and southern Democrats in Congress, however, smeared the plan as costly and "socialistic" in its effort to redistribute farm wealth at the expense of organized commercial farmers. The Brannan Plan marked the high tide of economic liberalism in farm and food politics, and its spectacular failure underscored the resurgence of economic conservatism in post–World War II U.S. politics. But even as Brannan failed to reconstruct New Deal-era farm price supports and acreage controls, his Department of Agriculture set in motion a technological transformation on U.S. highways that would long outlast his legacy as a liberal reformer.[1]

During Brannan's tenure at the helm of the USDA, bureaucrats and agricultural economists subtly transformed food and farm politics by turning away from efforts to control agricultural production and toward efforts to streamline the marketing of food products in an era of abundance. As part of a broader effort to raise farm prices without unduly raising consumer food costs, Brannan's Department of Agriculture began expanding the agricultural exemption for rural truckers. Intending to allow farmers to use unregulated long-haul trucking to ship products to market at the lowest possible costs, Department of Agriculture bureaucrats and agricultural economists pursued seemingly liberal policies in regards to food transportation. In administrative, legislative, and judicial battles against the Interstate Commerce Commission's regulatory power, the USDA expanded opportunities for independent truckers to haul farm and food products free of regulatory oversight. These actions, little noticed at the time, ensured that the majority of farm and food products would soon travel from farm to table via nonunionized, unregulated trucking firms. In so doing, Brannan's Department of Agriculture ironically helped to undermine the material basis for economic liberalism within food politics in ways that even the most vocal conservative Republicans and southern Democrats in Congress could not hope to do. Agribusinesses and their political allies would soon look to the new trucking technology of the postwar period as a tool for entrenching their market power, particularly by limiting the role of organized labor within the marketing structures of the farm and food economy. By the time the ardent anti–New Dealer Ezra Taft Benson was appointed secretary of agriculture in 1953, Charles Brannan's Department of Agriculture had already set in motion a new form of technological machinery that would unintentionally undermine consumer-labor liberalism within the farm and food economy.

The Farm Problem at War

Although Charles F. Brannan surprised Congress and the press in the spring of 1949 by announcing his agricultural plan with little forewarning, his proposal was a product of the long-standing debate over farm and food policies that dominated domestic politics during and immediately after World War II. The rapid rise in demand for U.S. farm products by soldiers overseas and civilians at home boosted farm prices more effectively than any New Deal policies had. But if the farmer's side of the farm problem was solved by wartime demand, urban consumers and labor leaders had reason to fear rampant inflation in food prices; during World War I, food costs had soared while meatpackers, milk dealers, and other food processors raked in record profits. In an effort to prevent a recurrence of such inflation and presumed "profiteering" during World War II, the Roosevelt administration erected the Office of Price Administration (OPA). Through an elaborate system of price controls and rationing, the OPA enabled and encouraged consumers to challenge the economic power of large farmers and corporate food processors. In the all-important beef and milk industries, the wartime emergency and a sense of patriotic duty led to a redoubling of government efforts to regulate and administer private enterprise. The results were mixed. Through the Office of Price Administration, economic liberals achieved remarkable results in the beef economy, holding prices relatively steady for urban consumers while allowing rural livestock producers and independent meatpackers to reap economic rewards at the expense of larger meatpackers. In the milk industry, however, consumer prices rose steadily throughout the war, as government policymakers beholden to organized farm interests continued to strengthen the hands of inner-ring dairy farmers and city milk bottlers at the expense of smaller farmers and unionized milk delivery-men. While federal policymakers effectively quelled the farm problem during the war, the end of the war would unleash a renewed political conflict over farm and food policies. Ultimately legislative and administrative politics would take a backseat to technological efforts to solve the farm problem.

The onset of the war brought the price of beef to the forefront of food politics. As the United States emerged from the Great Depression, consumers anxious to spend dollars earned in a revived industrial economy demanded plenty of beef for their tables. High demand for beef as well as other foods—from sugar to bread to milk—raised significant concerns about monopolistic food processors fleecing the U.S. consumer. As detailed in the first chapter, the long-standing problem of monopoly in beef production encouraged New Deal liberals such as Secretary of Agriculture Henry A. Wallace to respond sympathetically to farmers' and consumers' demands for reining in the Beef Trust during the Depression. Despite Wallace's populist rhetoric, however, the Department of Agriculture's Packers and Stockyards Division had made only limited efforts during the 1930s to pursue antitrust actions against the Big Four; the packers continued to effectively control the price of meat and live cattle through the 1930s. The exigencies of the war, however, brought into being the most vigorous and extensive federal government intrusion into the meat marketplace of the twentieth century: the Office of Price Administration.

Established to prevent runaway inflation like that experienced during World War I, the OPA proved surprisingly successful at holding meat prices steady through World War II. While meat prices had risen by 60 percent during World War I, prices only rose about 30 percent under the watch of the OPA. This was remarkable, insofar as the armed forces purchased enormous quantities of meat for soldiers even as good-paying wartime jobs allowed consumers to put meat back on the domestic table. Producers could barely keep up with the demand. The OPA's success in dampening inflation relied on extensive and deep intrusions into the workings of the nation's economy—price controls and rationing—enforced by thousands of committed staff members and volunteers at the community level. The OPA's efforts to check corporate power in the food economy began in April 1942, when President Roosevelt signed into action the General Maximum Price Regulation, which empowered the OPA to freeze retail and wholesale prices throughout the economy. Even with "General Max" in place, however, meat prices quickly climbed upward, forcing Congress to strengthen price controls on meat in December of the same year, when beef ceiling prices were pegged at actual dollars-and-cents levels based on federally mandated USDA grades. With these federal grades replacing packers' in-house grading and branding systems, consumers could check printed price lists to know whether they were being charged above-ceiling prices for a particular cut of meat—such as USDA Choice or Prime. Even so, prices continued to climb, so Congress allowed the OPA to ration meat in March 1943. Rationing helped keep prices in line by limiting consumer demand for meat. This combination of price controls, grading, and rationing was popular with consumers—especially the twenty million housewives who signed pledges during the war declaring that they would "pay no more than top legal prices" for meat and other goods. Butchers, grocers, and meatpackers, however, deeply resented the government's refusal to allow private enterprise to reap windfall profits during a time of swelling demand for beef. Administrators and propagandists for the OPA nonetheless countered that keeping the price of beef in check was a patriotic duty. Arming millions of housewives with detailed price lists that allowed them to catch "profiteers" and "chiselers" in the act of inflating prices was a form of "democracy in action," according to OPA administrator Chester A. Bowles. For most of the war, the Big Four meatpackers were forced to accept the fact that the federal government had thrown its full weight behind the long-standing efforts of urban workers and consumers to prevent monopolistic food processors from abusing their market power.[2]

Meanwhile farmers in cattle country also benefited from state action—or more properly, state inaction—during the war. Importantly the prices of livestock were not as effectively controlled as were retail and wholesale meat prices, providing livestock raisers an unprecedented opportunity to recoup losses incurred during the Depression. Powerful lobbyists from the Farm Bureau and livestock organizations descended on Congress during the deliberations establishing the OPA, convincing farm bloc representatives to create price ceilings for cattle that would fluctuate with the cost of living. As a result, the price of live cattle—which was administered by the Department of Agriculture rather than the independent OPA—was allowed to creep upward during the war. With record-high numbers of cattle available for slaughter in May 1942, it appeared to *Business Week* that livestock producers would "be in the money up to their saddle horns" throughout the war. Indeed without strict price controls on livestock, cattlemen benefited handsomely from rising prices during the war. Whereas cattle sold for $9 per pound in 1941, cattle brought $12.50 per pound by 1943. Cattle raisers who had received $1.7 billion in cash income in 1941 earned $3.3 billion by 1945. Even though feed costs also rose during the war, cattlemen nonetheless received prices for their animals of 115 percent of parity by January 1944, meaning that livestock raisers cleared 15 percent more on their operations in that month than they did during the "golden years" of U.S. agriculture from 1910 to 1914. As far as livestock producers were concerned, the problem of monopoly in beefpacking was not really a problem during the war, although, as we shall see below, the end of the war brought the issue squarely back into farm politics.[3]

Lax control of cattle prices also provided a unique opportunity for independent meatpackers to challenge the monopoly power of the Big Four. With the price of live cattle essentially uncontrolled, illicit entrepreneurs had a tremendous incentive to buy cattle at prices well above the legal prices offered by the major packers, then sell carcasses at above-ceiling prices to black market dealers. These "fly-by-night" operators developed a number of ingenious methods for avoiding price controls and rationing quotas. For instance, each slaughterer was allowed by law to slaughter fifty cattle for his own personal use. Quite often, these animals would make their way to retailers who would pay an artificially inflated price by "hiring" an employee of the slaughterer to receive the extra cash. Smaller meatpackers and wholesalers found it much easier than the Big Four packers to engage in such illicit practices, because small packers, unlike their larger competitors, were not subject to federal inspection by the USDA's Packers and Stockyards Division. Staff members of the OPA realized early on that such black market operations threatened the entire meat price control program, and demanded the USDA determine how many non-federally inspected plants were in operation and begin tracking their production. The USDA never compiled reliable data on these "fly-by-night" packers, although later estimates put the volume of slaughter by such independent packers at one-half of wartime meat production. The lack of enforcement of price controls on cattle, combined with the federally mandated grading system for meat, benefited small, independent meatpackers at the expense of the Big Four packers in ways that the anemic antitrust actions of the 1920s and 1930s had failed to do.[4]

While the OPA directly confronted monopoly power in the meat industry, the dairy industry provided a different sort of challenge, as USDA administrators worked to assure that wartime price controls would not undermine the monopoly power of urban milk dealers. As discussed in chapter 1, the economic crisis of the 1930s spurred the creation of federally administered milk marketing orders—state-sanctioned monopolies aimed at driving up prices for the coalition of dairy farmers located near cities and urban dealers who delivered the milk to consumers' doorsteps. U.S. entry into World War II did not fundamentally change this Depression-era solution to the "milk problem." Wartime purchases of dairy products, both for military and consumer uses, brought higher prices to all dairy farmers, whether inner- or outer-ring. Consumer and Teamster efforts to gain a stronger voice in determining a "fair price" for milk were forestalled by wartime policies designed to maintain existing arrangements in the milk industry. The OPA instituted price controls that might have provided consumers with a state-supported voice in directing milk pricing policies, but milk rationing was never instituted due to heavy opposition from organized milk lobbyists. As a result, the OPA did little to challenge the USDA's inflationary system of milk marketing orders. Furthermore actions by the National War Labor Board and the Office of Defense Transportation limited Teamster efforts to gain power in the milk industry. Federal price control and labor policies prevented direct attacks on the milk marketing orders, but set the stage for consumers and Teamsters to put pressure on the USDA to rearrange the milk marketing structure in the postwar period.

Like beef producers, U.S. dairy farmers prospered during the war. Inner-ring fluid milk farmers achieved their best sales in over a decade as urban consumers' incomes rose due to wartime employment. Per capita consumption of milk in 1941 reached 162 quarts; a year later consumption was up to 172 quarts, and in 1943 the average American ingested 186 quarts of milk. At the same time, the U.S. armed forces supplied their training camps and military bases with generous quantities of milk to strengthen soldiers' bones. This domestic demand for bottled milk was further supplemented by extraordinary overseas demand for cheese, butter, and evaporated milk. In 1942, for instance, the British imported the equivalent of more than 2 billion quarts of manufactured milk products under lend-lease arrangements. Rising demand for fluid and manufactured milk meant that both inner-ring and outer-ring dairy farmers gained their highest prices in decades, effectively preventing an outbreak of the intraregional tensions that had spurred such violent Depression-era episodes as the Wisconsin Cooperative Milk Pool strike. By the end of 1941, even before the United States had fully mobilized for war, milk had reached 106 percent of parity price—indicating that dairy farmers were making even more money than they had during the prosperous years of 1910–14. Under such conditions, dairy farmers had little reason to contest the federal milk marketing order system as an abuse of state power.[5]

Consumers, on the other hand, continued to mistrust the marketing orders. The creation of the Office of Price Administration gave consumers a potential tool to contest the power of the inner-ring milk coalition during the war. When Congress passed the Emergency Price Control Act of 1942, it not only gave the OPA independent status and enforcement powers, but created an opportunity for consumers' interests to be directly represented in the politics of administering prices. Most importantly, the OPA could have replaced the USDA's milk marketing order system as the primary agency responsible for stabilizing milk prices. During the Depression, the need to raise farm prices to boost rural purchasing power justified a marketing order system that favored inner-ring dairymen and city milk dealers, but during wartime, the pressing concern was inflation—and milk marketing orders were inherently and intentionally inflationary policies. As journalist Wesley McCune pointed out in May 1942, "milk prices are higher than they have been in twenty-one years." Milk marketing orders, according to McCune, were "a plain conspiracy to raise prices." But even though the OPA instituted price ceilings on fluid milk beginning in May 1942, the federal milk marketing orders survived the war stronger than ever, and consumers' interests in a "fair price" for milk continued to take second place to the interests of the inner-ring dairy coalition. This was because, unlike in the beef industry, the OPA was never able to institute effective rationing on milk.[6]

Price ceilings without concomitant rationing cannot stabilize consumer prices. Ceilings cause producers to limit production, leading to shortages that in turn create incentives to sell at higher prices on the black market in the absence of rationing. Understanding this, city milk dealers and fluid milk farmers actively opposed OPA efforts to institute rationing, hoping to throw a wrench into the agency's efforts to hold the line on retail prices. The milk industry's opposition to the OPA succeeded because food rationing during World War II was administered by the War Food Administration—an agency of the USDA, headed by Secretary of Agriculture Claude Wickard. Under pressure from the inner-ring milk coalition, the War Food Administration determined early on that any OPA actions in the milk economy "should interfere as little as possible with existing distribution practices." Wickard insisted in 1943 that because of milk's high degree of perishability, it moved only in localized markets, and would therefore be "extremely complex" to ration on a nationwide scale. This was certainly true, although whether rationing would have required more administrative machinery than marketing orders is debatable. Even so, for the USDA to favor the interests of consumers over those of farmers would have required a radical break with its own institutional history while also infuriating the congressional farm bloc. Fluid milk would not be rationed during the war.[7]

Without effective rationing of milk, the OPA found itself forced throughout the war to allow price rises to inner-ring dairy farmers to prevent shortages. This in turn led to price rises for consumers. The rise in demand by both civilians and the military put a "squeeze" on milk dealers who could not sell milk above OPA ceilings, yet had to pay farmers high enough prices to encourage sufficient production to meet local demand. For instance, between October and December 1942, milk dealers in Milwaukee increased the price they paid to area farmers from $2.63 per hundredweight to $3.00. Too many local farmers had begun diverting their milk to the Chicago market where a hundredweight of fluid milk brought $3.22, thereby offsetting the higher cost of transportation that normally precluded them from selling on that market. Milwaukee's milk dealers petitioned the OPA to allow a retail price increase, arguing that without it "the milk supply for the Milwaukee area will be seriously curtailed," because they would be forced to deliver milk to consumers at a loss. In this case, the OPA granted an increase that pushed the retail price of milk in Milwaukee up to 13 cents per quart in February 1943. Similar increases were granted in the Chicago and New York markets. The OPA originally intended these increases to be temporary, but dealers continued to argue that they were "unable to absorb the further cost increases" of raw milk through the spring and summer of 1943. By November, the maximum retail price of home-delivered milk in Chicago had reached 16 ½ cents.[8]

These constant price increases might have led the OPA to force the War Food Administration to institute rationing to rein in demand, but such action was forestalled when the two agencies reached a compromise. In August 1943 the War Food Administration established dealer quotas in cities facing milk shortages, thereby limiting the amount of fluid milk that dealers could sell in any given month—in other words, rationing. The quotas were pegged to dealers' sales in June 1943, however. June was the month of heaviest production, when cows spent their days masticating juicy grasses and producing their highest volumes of fluid milk. The quotas, then, had little actual effect in dampening sales of milk through the rest of the year. Nonetheless, the quota system appeased the OPA, allowing the War Food Administration to proceed with an alternate strategy to put a lid on rising retail prices. This alternate strategy involved using subsidies to encourage dairy farmers to produce more milk. OPA administrators understood that subsidy payments would do nothing to rein in the rising cost of milk, merely putting the cost increase on the federal government's tab rather than on the consumer's. Without effective rationing to dampen demand, however, the OPA was forced to side with the War Food Administration in October 1943, helping convince Congress to enact the subsidy program. With subsidies and price controls in place, retail prices stabilized—but consumers had not gained the OPA-backed power to participate directly in the politics of milk pricing.[9]

A further difference between the wartime politics of beef and milk pricing was the importance of organized labor within the milk delivery economy. The wartime emergency, however, limited the power of Teamster milk deliverymen to shape federal milk policies. The establishment of the National War Labor

Board in January 1942 created a means for organized milkmen and other unions to gain incremental wage increases, pegged to the rising cost of living as determined by the "Little Steel" formula beginning in July of that year. These concessions to organized labor came in exchange for a "no-strike" pledge that the nation's trade unions had signed immediately after Pearl Harbor. For organized milkmen, the wartime labor truce meant that arguments over the "fair price" of milk would be carried out in calm hearings before a tripartite board composed of representatives for Labor, Industry, and the Public. As John S. Picago, the Teamsters organizer in the Chicago milk market, informed his compatriots at the Mid-States Dairy Conference in 1943, "the days of shouting and yelling for wage raises are definitely over." Milkmen gained the support of the federal government in achieving wage increases, but those wage increases were tied to changes in the overall economy rather than to the price of milk in the drivers' local economies.[10]

The need to conserve rubber and gasoline during the war further constrained the Teamsters' power to participate directly in the politics of milk pricing. Urban milk delivery at the time relied almost entirely on trucks rather than horse-drawn wagons with steel-rimmed wheels. As a consequence, the milk industry was one of the nation's largest users of gasoline and rubber, essential wartime commodities. The Office of Defense Transportation (ODT), established in December 1941 to coordinate and conserve the nation's transportation resources, called on John L. Rogers of the Interstate Commerce Commission to work with the milk industry to reduce its rubber usage. The International Association of Milk Dealers, the main lobby group of urban milk dealers, petitioned Rogers with a plan that dealers had been hoping to institute long before Pearl Harbor: every-other-day delivery. The concept was as simple as it sounds—milkmen would deliver two days' worth of milk to customers on alternating days, allowing milk dealers to consolidate delivery routes, conserve gasoline, and reduce tire wear. Rogers agreed that every-other-day delivery would reduce milk truck mileage as requested by the ODT, but he understood that such a plan would require "cooperative action by management and labor." That cooperation would be hard to come by, because the Teamsters knew that every-other-day delivery threatened to cut their milk driver membership in half. Daniel Tobin, president of the Teamsters, further realized that instituting every-other-day delivery during the war might extend into the postwar period and limit the enrollment of new drivers. Tobin dictated an immediate response to John Rogers upon learning of the every-other-day delivery plan, making a thinly veiled threat to break the no-strike pledge: "It may be [that the] fifty percent of the [milk]men who are laid off, without wages, may prevail on the other fifty percent to cease work [but] it isn't humanly possible for [Teamster] officials to prevent men from striking if they feel aggrieved." The situation came to a head in April 1942, when the ODT issued General Order Number 6, calling on milk dealers to reduce monthly mileage in deliveries by 25 percent, although without dictating any specific method for achieving the reduction. Desperate to prevent dealers from pushing forward with their plans for alternate-day deliveries, the Teamsters passed a resolution at the Mid-West Dairy Conference in May stating their desire to comply with General Order Number 6, but through "joint cooperation between management and Labor within the industry itself." Teamster locals hoped to preserve their power within local milk markets to bargain directly with dealers, rather than have the conditions of work dictated by federal policy.[11]

The Teamsters failed to come up with an alternative, however, and the ODT quickly vetted the dealers' plan to comply with General Order Number 6 by consolidating routes in May 1942. Teamster locals in New York and Chicago announced their intention to strike if necessary to prevent implementation of the plan. In November 1942 the National War Labor Board mediated a compromise. The milk dealers would be allowed to begin the shift to every-other-day deliveries, but could not lay off currently employed milk drivers. Dealers were furthermore encouraged to work with the Teamsters to try alternate methods for reducing mileage, such as eliminating special deliveries to unscheduled stops, making deliveries only during daylight hours, and using horse-drawn wagons whenever possible. But when these alternative methods did not reduce milk delivery mileage by the necessary 25 percent, the ODT issued an amended order in May 1943, prohibiting more than four home deliveries per week. New York's Teamsters immediately objected and refused to comply. Once again the issue came before the National War Labor Board; this time, the board ruled that the Teamsters had to allow the dealers to institute every-other-day delivery, but dealers were to maintain full employment of deliverymen. By June 1943, the Teamsters had grudgingly accepted the shift to every-other-day delivery. The federal government negotiated a truce between labor and management in the milk industry, guaranteeing full employment and limited wage increases for the nation's milkmen, but at the cost of constraining Teamster power within local milk economies.[12]

Federal price control and labor relations policies during the war thus served the interests of the inner-ring milk coalition. Fluid milk farmers and city milk dealers continued to benefit most from the milk marketing orders. Outer-ring cheese dairymen, consumers, and labor were all precluded from having much power to shape the administering of a "fair price" for milk. In contrast to the wartime state's direct challenge of the economic power of large meatpackers under the Office of Price Administration, the fluid milk industry emerged from the war with its monopoly power essentially intact. The end of the war, however, would unleash renewed debates over the proper role of the state in regulating and administering the farm and food economy—and both beef and milk would serve as central issues of concern.

THE FARM PROBLEM RETURNS

At war's end, a key question haunted agricultural politics: What should the role of the state be, vis-à-vis private enterprise, in dealing with the problem of maintaining high prices for farmers without unduly raising consumer food prices? The OPA provided a model for doing so through highly interventionist state policies, administered by economic experts and supported by price-conscious consumers. But although the OPA remained popular with consumers for some time after the war ended, powerful agricultural interests—meatpackers in particular—worked assiduously to make "free enterprise" rather than centralized price administration the basis of the nation's food economy. The resulting defeat of the OPA in 1946 did not signal the end of economic liberalism within farm and food politics, however, as Charles F. Brannan and other dedicated New Dealers plotted postwar strategies for tapping into farmers', consumers', and workers' unwillingness to swallow the laissez-faire vision promoted by corporate food processors. In the years between the end of World War II and the Korean War, small farmers, urban consumers, and unionized workers in food industries perceived that New Deal-era farm policies continued to support the most powerful interests in the food economy at the expense of average Americans. In response, Truman's secretary of agriculture, Charles Brannan, charted a new course for economic liberalism within the farm and food economy. In concert with influential agricultural economists and farm bloc congressmen, Brannan redefined the postwar farm problem not as an issue of preventing overproduction, but of encouraging abundance to confront "underconsumption." Within this context, Brannan proposed a plan in the spring of 1949 that, had it gone into effect, might have fundamentally restructured farm and food politics along liberal lines. The Brannan Plan, although supported by influential Democratic politicians and consumer and labor organizations, nonetheless suffered an ignominious defeat at the hands of farm bloc congressmen in 1950. Never again would liberals make such a concerted effort to rewrite New Deal-era farm policies, while agribusinesses continued to deploy technological means for undermining economic liberalism within farm and food policy.

The price of beef engendered the most important postwar attack on economic liberalism in the food economy, as meatpackers and cattlemen launched

an all-out assault on the OPA. The Big Four meatpackers had chafed under
the OPA throughout the war, blaming price controls for allowing independent ("fly-by-night") packers to make ill-gotten inroads into their business. In
1944 the big packers convinced the OPA that price controls without effective
livestock price ceilings were putting them in a "squeeze" that would force them
to cut back production. Packers predicted dire meat shortages for U.S. consumers. In January of 1945, the OPA responded by instituting enforceable
price ceilings on live cattle. Packers could now be charged with price violations
for paying too much for their livestock. Packers were also given a direct subsidy, which would be withheld if the OPA determined the packer was overpay-
ing for cattle. Even so, the ceilings on live cattle proved nearly impossible to
enforce; small packers could earn far more from selling overpriced carcasses on
the black market than they could by taking the government subsidy. OPA administrator Paul Porter realized in March 1946 that packers who complied
with the cattle ceiling prices were finding it difficult to get a sufficient supply
of animals, making them "extremely antagonistic" to the continuation of price
regulations. This antagonism would lead the meatpackers to organize a "strike,"
refusing to ship meat to stores in the summer and fall of 1946 until the OPA
was killed. If U.S. consumers wanted meat, they were going to have to do so
in a marketplace unhampered by price controls.[13]

Livestock raisers and their allies in the congressional farm bloc aided the
meatpackers in their efforts to break the OPA in 1946. The Farm Bureau
mounted a strong campaign against livestock price ceilings, arguing that only
increased production, rather than government price controls, could achieve
lasting reductions in consumer prices. Truman's first secretary of agriculture,
Clinton Anderson, agreed with this logic, and so refused to help the OPA enforce the livestock ceilings once they were instituted in 1945. Anderson had no
patience for economic liberalism when it challenged the prerogatives of powerful commercial farmers organized in the Farm Bureau. With the OPA's enabling legislation set to expire on July 1, 1946, Congress began debating whether
to renew price controls. Both live cattle and dressed beef costs were poised to
skyrocket in a decontrolled economy, so labor- and consumer-friendly Democrats redoubled their efforts to keep the OPA in action through the postwar re-
conversion period. President Truman vetoed a weak OPA extension bill in June,
demanding that Congress pass a tough measure to keep inflation in check, but
farm interests pushed to make sure that any legislative extension of OPA
would be self-defeating. In July 1946, Congress passed the Price Control Extension Act to keep the OPA running for another year, but included an all-
important clause giving Secretary Anderson the power to raise live cattle ceilings independently of the OPA. Without this clause, few members of the

congressional farm bloc would have been willing to allow the OPA to continue. Republican August H. Andresen of Minnesota, for instance, announced on the House floor that extension of the OPA would make "meat . . . disappear from legitimate channels of distribution" unless the secretary of agriculture had the power to "save the country from collapse and chaos [by making] up his mind to let farmers and industry produce food for the people at reasonable prices." With the proviso that the secretary of agriculture could contest OPA ceilings on livestock, the price control extension bill passed the House relatively easily, with 210 yeas and 142 nays. Support from farm bloc Democrats representing rural regions proved essential, as 49 Democrats from rural congressional districts voted for the bill, despite the strong opposition of farm lobbyists to any price controls whatsoever. Democratic senators representing farm states likewise approved of the compromise, with 29 Democratic farm state senators voting for the price control extension, allowing the bill to pass with 53 yes and 26 no votes. President Truman felt compelled to sign the bill to check rampant inflation, but blasted Congress for passing watered-down legislation, announcing his hope that "the Price Administrator and the Secretary of Agriculture will work closely together to maintain unified policies."[14]

Truman's hope proved short-lived, as Secretary of Agriculture Anderson soon raised the ceiling prices on livestock in August. The Department of Agriculture thus directly undermined the OPA's efforts to keep consumer beef prices low. Unsatisfied with even this significant weakening of the OPA's strength in the beef economy, cattlemen saw an opportunity to permanently destroy all price controls by staging an unofficial "strike" in coordination with the meatpackers' efforts to create a meat shortage in October 1946. One Iowa cattle feeder wrote to Secretary Anderson that he had once been an "ardent supporter of OPA" but felt that it had lost "popular support," and thus had also lost his. He would keep his cattle on feed and out of sales channels until all government interference in the cattle market was removed.[15]

With both meatpackers and livestock raisers on "strike," the OPA was doomed as angry consumers demanded pot roasts, whatever the price. President Truman cancelled all price controls and rationing in mid-October, but was widely ridiculed for "bungling" the entire program. The so-called beefsteak elections of November 1946 would help Republicans gain control of Congress for the first time since 1928, as conservative candidates used the slogan "Had Enough?" to tap into a widespread sense of discontent with the failures of economic liberals to maintain an abundant and reasonably priced supply of red meat. The once-despised Beef Trust, aided by farm bloc congressmen and rural cattle raisers, successfully deflected consumers' anger away from monopoly power and toward the Democratic-led federal government.[16]

But if the big packers successfully courted consumer opinion at the end of the war, skyrocketing meat prices over the next few years would soon bring the Beef Trust back into disrepute. The packers' main argument against the OPA had been that price controls created an unfair "squeeze" situation that prevented them from producing enough meat to satisfy consumer demand at low prices. But for two years after the end of controls, meat prices skyrocketed. In 1947 the mayor of New York declared that "housewives in this city" saw prices rising from 6 to 16 cents per pound, a "shocking" development that belied the packers' promise of "plenty of meat at reasonable prices." Consumer activists organized meat boycotts in 1947 and 1948, blaming the Beef Trust for taking unreasonable profits; some even called for a return to price controls to check spiraling meat costs. The Justice Department filed a new antitrust suit against the Big Four packers in 1948. Even though meatpackers had won the battle against OPA, economic liberalism remained animated within the beef economy.[17]

Postwar developments in the milk economy also highlighted the continuing strength of liberal economic ideas in food politics. As in the case of the meat industry, the price of milk shot up rapidly after the initial dismantling of the OPA in July of 1946. The Bureau of Labor Statistics announced that milk prices rose by an average of two and a half cents nationwide after price controls were removed, with increases up to four cents occurring in certain cities. Consumers became ever more voluble about expensive milk driving up the cost of living, causing accused "milk trusters" such as National Dairy Products to take out advertising campaigns defending themselves as making "far less profit than the public thinks." The Teamsters, meanwhile, began a concerted strike campaign in 1945 and 1946 to bounce back from the restraints imposed during wartime. Daily deliveries did not return, however, partly because many milkmen had found that every-other-day delivery brought them higher commissions from customers who ordered greater volumes of milk. Nonetheless the new round of strikes succeeded in gaining milk drivers hefty wage increases in renegotiated contracts, allowing milkmen to join in the general success enjoyed by organized labor immediately after the war. Meanwhile, outer-ring dairy farmers began a decades-long effort to break the monopoly of inner-ring farmers and urban milk dealers on city fluid milk markets, as rural cooperatives began calling on their farmer members to increase their production of fluid milk, hoping to use sheer volume of production to force their way into city milk markets. Although the New Deal-era milk marketing order system would remain in place for the rest of the century, consumers, Teamsters, and small farmers made spirited efforts in the immediate postwar years to contest the monopoly power of the inner-ring milk coalition. The effects of this unrest, however, would not become clear until later decades (as discussed in chapter 6).[18]

Along with these deep conflicts over monopoly power in the food economy, the return of the decades-old problem of farm surpluses gave new energy to economic liberalism at war's end. The heightened demand for U.S. farm products during the war had placed the surplus problem on the back burner for a time, because the surpluses that dogged farmers during the 1920s and 1930s were absorbed by domestic and overseas consumption. But as the war wound to a close, U.S. farm production had increased by 33 percent over the prewar average in the years 1935 to 1939. Faced with significant manpower shortages, U.S. farmers had adopted a host of technological and scientific methods for boosting production, including tractors, combines, fertilizers, hybrid seeds, and chemical pesticides. Agricultural policymakers in Congress and the USDA sincerely feared that the wartime ramp-up in domestic farm production would lead to massive overproduction in peacetime, sparking a return to economic depression in the countryside. But with famines and droughts besetting war-ravaged Europe and millions of U.S. families anxious to spend money on bettering their lifestyles after years of deprivation, demand and prices for U.S. farm products continued strong through 1946. But fears of overproduction continued to haunt agricultural policymakers through 1947. In the spring of that year, the House Agriculture Committee began holding extensive hearings in search of new, long-range approaches to the surplus problem. In 1947 the National Planning Association gathered together a group of agricultural economists, farm organization leaders, and labor and consumer representatives to discuss the future of farm politics in the postwar United States. The results of the meeting, published under the title *Dare Farmers Risk Abundance?*, concluded that farmers were hard-wired to keep producing ever more food and fiber, no matter how strongly government administrators worked to limit production to keep prices high. With farmers demanding government guarantees of high farm prices, consumers and workers demanding reasonable meat and milk prices, and corporate processors declaring outright war on state intervention in the food economy, the stage was set for a tenacious reconsideration of New Deal-era farm policies. The lead role would be played by Charles F. Brannan.[19]

Brannan spearheaded the most determined effort to reinvigorate economic liberalism within the postwar farm and food economy. The son of a Quaker electrical engineer, Brannan was born in 1903 in Denver, Colorado. His personal background and political philosophy reflected a western version of New Deal progressivism, in tune both with the "Brains Trust" urban-industrial reformers such as Jerome Frank and with midwestern agrarian reformers such as

Henry A. Wallace. Rather than studying agricultural economics or rural sociology as did most farm leaders of the time, Brannan earned his law degree from
the University of Colorado in 1929. He entered government service as an attorney for Rexford Tugwell's Resettlement Administration in 1935 after practicing private mining and irrigation law. From 1937 to the onset of the war,
Brannan worked as a regional attorney for the USDA, helping farmers create
cooperative irrigation districts in the arid West. For most of the war he served
as regional director of the ill-fated successor to the Resettlement Administration, the Farm Security Administration, where he worked to provide loans to
boost the earning power of needy western farmers. In 1944 President Roosevelt
appointed Brannan as assistant secretary of agriculture under Claude Wickard,
in which post Brannan oversaw flood control programs, irrigation projects,
and management of grazing and timber lands. In short, Brannan was a committed New Deal bureaucrat, steeped in Progressive-era ideas about natural
resource management and cooperative agrarianism, who firmly believed the
Department of Agriculture could and should exercise federal power to help
not only large-scale commercial farmers but also smaller farmers struggling to
make ends meet in challenging economic and ecological environments.[20]

Brannan's bureaucratic expertise, combined with his earnest desire to craft
farm policy that served ordinary farmers, would place him at the center of the
most crucial farm policy debate in the immediate postwar years. In December
1946, Secretary of Agriculture Anderson appointed Brannan to lead a Department of Agriculture policy committee focused on providing a long-term solution to the surplus problem. The committee's recommendations, presented
before the House Agriculture Committee in April 1947 by Secretary Anderson,
offered a subtle but significant rebuke of New Deal farm policy. Rather than
using state power to plan scarcity in the farm economy through production
controls and expensive price supports, Brannan's committee announced, Congress should write legislation that would encourage farmers to produce abun-
dantly. The committee did not offer much in the way of specific methods for
encouraging abundance rather than discouraging surpluses, suggesting only
that price supports be made more flexible to allow for adjustments to changes
in supply and demand for specific farm commodities. Partly because of the
committee's optimistic philosophy of abundance, and partly because of the
vagueness of the proposal, everyone from the Farm Bureau to President Truman to conservatives in Congress lauded the work. Unfortunately when it came
to the messy business of hashing out specific changes in farm policy, differences in opinion among cotton farmers, grain growers, livestock raisers, the
conservative Farm Bureau, and the liberal Farmers Union prevented Congress
from making any substantive changes in the farm program. With the passage

of the compromise Hope-Aiken Act of 1948, U.S. farm policy continued essentially on the same course that had been set in 1933, with only the slightest revisions of the price support system that had originally been enacted only as an emergency response to the Great Depression. Nonetheless Charles Brannan's attempt to rewrite farm policy in terms of abundance rather than scarcity remained squarely in the center of domestic food politics as the election of 1948 neared.[21]

The election of 1948 provided the impetus for Brannan to chart a new course for economic liberalism within farm politics. Clinton Anderson resigned from Truman's cabinet in order to run for the Senate, opening up the post of secretary of agriculture. Truman, as part of a broader effort to convince voters of his liberal credentials and to convince farmers to remain loyal to the party of Roosevelt, appointed Brannan to the slot. The decision proved essential to Truman's surprise victory in the election, as Brannan campaigned with gusto throughout farm regions, viciously attacking the "Do-Nothing Congress" for threatening U.S. farm prosperity. Implying—rather ingenuously—that Republicans would dismantle the price support system if Thomas Dewey defeated Truman in the presidential race, Brannan helped to rake in votes from farmers unprepared to give up their economic safety net. But Truman's victory in the election was also heavily dependent on the support he received from organized consumers and organized labor. This meant that if Truman were to hold together the Democratic coalition, the new secretary of agriculture would somehow have to appease consumers and workers justifiably concerned about rapidly rising food prices. Brannan rose to the challenge in April 1949 by proposing the most sweeping revision of farm policy since 1933.[22]

The Brannan Plan sought to remake farm policy to simultaneously serve the interests of small farmers and urban consumers rather than factory farmers and corporate food processors. New Deal farm policies had driven many small farmers off the land, especially southern tenants and sharecroppers, by directing price supports and acreage reduction payments primarily to large commercial farmers. As a liberal who had become attuned to the plight of small farmers during his stints in the Resettlement Administration and the Farm Security Administration, Brannan proposed to guarantee farm *incomes* rather than crop or livestock prices. Benefits would be paid out on a graduated scale, with large farmers receiving proportionately less government assistance. Tied to this was a proposal to rein in food prices. Here Brannan focused on the booming demand for meat and milk products, foods that had become central to working- and middle-class diets and were widely acknowledged as markers of a rising U.S. standard of living. The spiraling costs for these foods could be tamed, Brannan announced, by encouraging farmers to produce more meat and milk to meet growing demand. Rather than use the heavy hand of the federal government to prevent grain, cotton, and tobacco producers from planting on all their land, the Department of Agriculture would establish incentives for these farmers to move out of staple commodity production and into high-value perishable food production. To sweeten the pot for urbanites, Brannan suggested offering subsidies to consumers. Subsidized prices for beef and milk would encourage city dwellers to buy more of these high-value products, boosting farm incomes while enriching consumer's diets. The Brannan Plan firmly repudiated New Deal-era efforts to plan scarcity, but it was nonetheless a dramatic statement of economic equality. A powerful federal government would intervene even more deeply in the farm and food economy than it had during the Great Depression and World War II. But rather than trying to plan scarcity through production and price controls, the government would encourage abundance. As a matter of political economy, the plan may have been overly optimistic. As a political effort to cement farmers and consumers in the Democratic coalition, however, Brannan's plan seemed to be a masterstroke that would ensure the Democratic Party of near-permanent dominance in an era of pocketbook politics. Linking the interests of middle-class consumers, working-class laborers, and middling farmers might have sustained and extended the worker-consumer purchasing power coalition forged during Franklin Roosevelt's New Deal. Its failure, however, would symbolize the triumph of a "consumer's republic" in which consumers' demands for low-priced goods would be politically delinked from the politics of economic equity that had dominated New Deal liberalism.[23]

The plan would always be associated with Brannan, but it drew on ideas that had been floating in agricultural policy circles for several years. In a broad sense, Brannan's plan meshed well with the increasing acceptance of Keynesian theories among agricultural and other economists, since the plan was predicated on using government policy to boost consumption and therefore economic growth. Furthermore the essential outlines of Brannan's plan had been implemented in Sweden in 1947 under that country's New Agricultural Price Policy, which set farm prices in relation to urban wage rates. Administered via a Food Commission on which representatives of farmers, consumers, and industry shared votes regarding farm pricing policies, the Swedish Parliament sought to simultaneously boost farm incomes, assure industrial workers an adequate and nutritious diet, and unite rural and urban Swedish voters in the Social Democratic Party. The Swedish approach to postwar farm and food policy undergirded that country's commitment to economic liberalism until the early 1990s, when environmental and free-trade concerns cracked a half-century's consensus on the value of Swedish farm subsidies. Closer to home, the Brannan Plan drew on the ideas of Theodore W. Schultz and John D. Black, the two most influential U.S. agricultural economists at the time. Schultz, a University of Chicago economist, had proposed in 1945 what he called "forward pricing" for farm products, meaning that the government should work not to discourage farmers from producing more commodities but should instead use pricing policies to encourage farmers to produce commodities for which demand was rising—a concept that lay at the heart of the Swedish New Agricultural Price Policy. Black, often called away from his desk in the Harvard economics department to testify before Congress on matters of farm policy, declared in 1945 that the time had come to move away from a "production-adjustment program" to a "consumption-adjustment program." Rather than pay farmers to overproduce commodities such as wheat and cotton, the government should encourage farmers to raise and feed more livestock; this, coupled with consumer subsidies for meat products, would "go a very long way toward getting rid of our agricultural surplus." Thus, when Brannan told a joint hearing of the House and Senate Agriculture Committees that his plan contained "no revolutionary ideas," he had reason to believe that Congress would agree. He could not have been more wrong.[24]

The Brannan Plan failed. At a time when the Truman administration was ratcheting up the Cold War with the Soviet Union through rhetoric dividing the world into good and evil—with the former represented by free markets and representative democracy and the latter represented by command economies and totalitarianism—conservatives in and out of Congress painted the Brannan Plan as the most significant step toward state socialism since the Tennessee Valley Authority. Republican senator George Aiken of Vermont predicted a "controlled economy with a vengeance," while other farm bloc Republicans estimated that the program would cost taxpayers up to $8 billion annually. The Farm Bureau and the Grange quickly announced their opposition to the plan; Farm Bureau president Allan B. Kline told Congress that the proposal advocated "Government control of all land and livestock production" and would stiff taxpayers with a "staggering" bill. Farmers around the country flooded Brannan's office with letters, decrying his "communistic agriculture plan" as a rebuke of "free enterprise." Even consumers wrote to Brannan to express their fear that the new farm program would lead to "totalitarianism." A woman from Watervliet, New York, informed Brannan that "we consumers have been waiting for a break in the high cost of living," but begged the secretary of agriculture to "heed the handwriting on the wall and let Nature take its course in the problem of supply and demand. . . . Government shouldn't mess in and try to play God."[25]

Brannan responded to the attacks with relish, presenting his case before the

U.S. public with the hearty support of President Truman, the Farmers Union, consumer organizations, organized labor, and the Americans for Democratic Action. Brannan's efforts were to no avail; southern Democrats united with Republicans in Congress to table the plan in 1949 and then, after Republicans nearly retook control of Congress in the 1950 elections, to bury it forever. Despite strong support from liberal politicians and many constituents, Brannan had failed to vet his plan with farm bloc congressmen and powerful farm organizations, forestalling the possibility of productive compromise in crafting legislation. Avid support from the Farmers Union could not easily overcome the power wielded by conservative members of the congressional farm bloc such as Jamie L. Whitten (D-MS)—a member of the House Appropriations Committee from 1941 to 1995 who became known as the "permanent secretary of agriculture" for using his influence over the congressional purse to resist changes to existing farm policies.[26] Brannan might have broken down congressional intransigence through an orchestrated public relations campaign, but Brannan's technocratic approach to policymaking prevented him from clearly communicating to consumers how his plan would actually lower food costs rather than simply shift food costs to taxpayers. Persia Campbell of the National Association of Consumers offered friendly advice, suggesting he make a "clear simple statement" to an "'average' urban audience" rather than discussing the complexities of price supports and production payments to farm audiences already familiar with the terminology—advice that Brannan failed to heed. U.S. entry into the Korean War put the final nail in the coffin. Under wartime conditions, the surplus problem once again evaporated as farm incomes soared. Farm Bureau leaders slandered Brannan's plan as unpatriotic at a time when cotton and grain were in high demand. An infuriated Brannan sent an open six-page letter to Farm Bureau president Allan B. Kline decrying his "wholly unfair attacks" and blaming the organization for killing a plan that would have boosted farm incomes while lowering consumer food costs. But neither Kline nor conservatives in Congress were solely to blame for the defeat. Brannan had introduced an extraordinarily complex policy proposal without securing the support of the farmers and consumers who were intended to benefit from the plan.[27]

Even with the death of Brannan's plan, economic liberalism remained viable within farm and food politics in the early 1950s. Spiraling food costs during the Korean War, especially for beef, led consumer organizations and liberal politicians to call for a renewal of price controls under the Office of Price Stabilization (OPS). Memories of the disastrous defeat of the OPA by meatpackers and cattlemen, however, led Congress to insert a clause requiring a "reasonable margin of profit" for these producers under the OPS. Furthermore the

OPS set price ceilings without instituting rationing. Having seen the OPA go from a broadly supported to a broadly despised program due to artificial beef shortages, Congress wanted to hold retail beef prices steady without having cattlemen derail the program by withholding animals, or by having consumers lose confidence because they could not buy a roast without resorting to the black market. Demand for beef continued to rise during the war, however, fueled especially by army purchases. Without livestock ceilings, the price of cattle rose to a record high of 152 percent of parity. With the price of beef rapidly rising, President Truman faced pressure from consumers and liberal Democrats to make the OPS succeed in controlling meat prices, but he faced a House Agriculture Committee that refused to cooperate. Without rationing, beef remained plentifully available during the war, but the impressive supply came at a price; the only beef cuts that did not become more expensive during 1951 were luxury cuts such as T-bones and porterhouse steaks. Fears of inflation continued to figure high in the political consciousness of working- and middle-class consumers. With food prices rising, New Deal-era farm programs aimed at boosting farm prices came under increasing attack. A 1951 editorial in the *New York Times* expressed a common sentiment, attacking the agricultural price support system as a drag on the entire economy: "Food is the No. 1 item in the wage-earner's budget. If the price keeps rising, how can wages and the rest of the economy be stabilized?" The farm problem remained unsolved, threatening to tear apart the Democratic coalition as farmers and consumers continued to make conflicting demands on the federal government. But if Brannan's plan to resolve this conflict through new legislation had failed, bureaucrats within his Department of Agriculture gave new impetus to the technological revolution on U.S. highways that would reframe the debate over the farm problem. During Brannan's tenure in office, trucks would become increasingly powerful political tools, providing the basis for the next secretary of agriculture, Ezra Taft Benson, to transform the farm problem into an industrial problem.[28]

The Technological Fix

The National Planning Association met in 1949 to consider, once again, the question *Must We Have Food Surpluses?* The assembled gathering of economists, farm leaders, and consumer representatives agreed that maintaining a healthy economy required that farmers receive reasonable returns on their investments through rising farm prices. To do so without driving up the cost of living for U.S. consumers, however, required a new approach to the farm problem: "increased efficiency in marketing to . . . cut costs of distribution."

Whereas agricultural policymakers had always focused on rationalizing the *production* of food, now they should also, according to the agricultural experts of the National Planning Association, use technology to rationalize the *consumption* of food. The recommendations of the National Planning Association bolstered a new direction in agricultural policy already being put in place by Congress and the USDA in the mid-1940s. In 1943, economist F. L. Thomsen of the USDA's Bureau of Agricultural Economics (BAE) addressed a national gathering of agricultural policymakers, calling for a technological solution to the farm problem: "For a century, the leaders of farmer and consumer groups have been shouting from the rostrums . . . for a more efficient marketing system. It is now time to do something about it." That "something" turned out to be the Agricultural Research and Marketing Act of 1946 (RMA), which ordered the USDA's economists and engineers to devise technologies to streamline the marketing of U.S. agricultural products. The RMA provided funding for the Department of Agriculture to embark on a decades-long project to construct new marketing machinery in the U.S. countryside to support the postwar consumer-driven economy. The rise of long-haul trucking, particularly of unregulated, nonunionized transportation, would prove crucial to this new food economy in which supermarkets, factory farmers, and monopolistic food processors would dictate the terms of food pricing rather than government price supports and acreage controls.[29]

The main sponsor of the Research and Marketing Act was Representative Clifford R. Hope of Kansas. Hope described the legislation's intent to Congress in July of 1946: "The [Research and Marketing Act] is based upon the idea of abundant production and efficient distribution and utilization of food and other farm products." Efficient food distribution, Hope argued, required technologies for lowering or eliminating labor costs, along with technical research into the economics of mass consumption. With the optimism suggested by his surname, Congressman Hope believed that more machines and smarter marketing experts would solve the farm problem that decades worth of political haggling over production controls and price supports had never solved. Furthermore the new technological solution would come with the avowed acceptance of an economic philosophy of abundance, rather than scarcity—a dramatic political statement in a country seeking to pull itself out of the lengthy trials of depression and war. Much as the Brannan Plan would later do, the RMA proposed a method for forging a consensus on agricultural policy, transcending partisan divisions and uniting the interests of food producers and consumers.[30]

Hope's appraisal of the power of technology to transcend decades-old political conflicts drew on a wider current of technological optimism in postwar

U.S. culture. Despite the worrisome devastation wrought by atomic weapons in Hiroshima and Nagasaki, U.S. journalists in the immediate postwar years touted atomic energy as "a blessing that will make it possible for the human race to create a close approach to an earthly paradise." Predictions of inexpensive nuclear-powered automobiles, ultraproductive atomic agriculture, and "power too cheap to meter" proliferated in popular culture in 1946, despite scientists' repeated warnings that atomic energy could not so easily be harnessed to create a consumer economy of unquestioned abundance. The plastics industry boomed after the war as entrepreneurs and chemical corporations manufactured everything from fishing rods to furniture out of inexpensive hydrocarbon compounds. Tens of thousands of visitors attended the first National Plastics Exposition in New York in April 1946, where one exhibitor declared that "the public are certainly steamed up on plastics." Mass production techniques promised a world of affordable suburban homes after 1947, when Levitt and Sons began constructing the first Levittown on Long Island, using gang construction and prefabricated home parts to erect the nation's then-largest private housing development. As technological fixes, each of these solutions proved effective in fueling the postwar consumer-driven economic boom, but did little to resolve deeper political and social conflicts. Atomic utopians could not forever downplay the destructive potential of nuclear power, particularly after the Soviet Union tested its first nuclear weapon in 1949 and the United States ratcheted up the arms race with its 1952 test of the hydrogen bomb. Plastics offered a vibrant and colorful sheen to a consumer society nonetheless beset by continuing class tensions and lurking anxieties about the ephemeral nature of material abundance. Levittowns and other sprawling suburbs provided good housing at affordable prices, but did nothing to confront racial residential segregation based on white homeowners' self-fulfilling prophecies that property values would decline in integrated neighborhoods. William Levitt explained away his firm's implicit support of white flight and restrictive race-based housing covenants, declaring that his firm could "solve a housing problem, or we can try to solve a racial problem, but we cannot combine the two."[31] The technological optimism of U.S. postwar culture illustrates the historical truism that technological fixes, whether premised on utopian fantasies or upon pragmatic politics, tend to produce simplistic, reductionist "solutions" to complex social problems. Even when "successful," a technological fix more often displaces, rather than resolves, the source of conflict—generally by empowering technocrats and technical experts to approach political conflicts in engineers' terms rather than in the messy public sphere of democratic debate.[32]

In considering the Research and Marketing Act of 1946, however, Congress seemed assured that technological research would resolve the persistent farm problem. With over $30 million in funding in the first five years after the RMA's passage, agricultural engineers and economists eagerly embarked on thousands of projects aimed at streamlining the marketing of agricultural products. Researchers studied everything from transforming corn into automobile fuel to developing dehydro-frozen food to investigating the possibilities of transporting grain by airplane. The majority of studies, however, focused on down-to-earth questions of how to help farmers and food processors get their products to market more cheaply. An efficient marketing machine would be a system that moved food from farms to consumers with the smallest number of intermediary firms—whether food processors, wholesalers, or retailers—paying workers' wages and taking profits along the way. Agricultural economists working with food industries under the RMA focused on decreasing the cost of food distribution to raise the farmer's share of the consumer's dollar. Much of this research involved improved packaging techniques, warehousing and retailing methods, and reducing the need for skilled labor in the food marketing chain. The cost of transportation, however, attracted the most sustained attention from USDA economists. Although the cost of labor contributed the largest share of the price spread of food between the farmer and the consumer, transportation had always followed close behind labor in costs incurred in the marketing of agricultural goods and food products. Unlike workers, though, transportation technologies could be reengineered with less need for political delicacy in an era of strong labor unions.[33]

Unregulated trucking offered a particularly attractive means for driving down the cost of moving food from farmers to consumers. "Independent" nonunionized truck drivers, operating outside the regulatory umbrella of the Interstate Commerce Commission, could lower the labor costs of transporting farm and food products. It is impossible to know exactly how many unregulated truck drivers or trucking firms there were in the late 1940s (or in later decades for that matter), but available evidence suggests that independent, unregulated trucking expanded dramatically after the war. The average size of trucks on the road grew, as veterans and other entrepreneurs scraped together cash and loans to buy new and larger trucks—straight trucks with tonnage capacities twice as high as trucks of the 1930s, as well as much larger tractors with separate semi-trailers suitable for long hauls. The number of registered trucks on the nation's highways increased by 35 percent between 1945 and 1947, while the number of new trucks manufactured in the same time period increased by 45 percent. Some of those new trucks must have been purchased by the approximately 130,000 truck drivers who were self-employed in 1950. Whether these individuals bought old or new trucks, many postwar trucking entrepre-

TABLE 3.1

Income Comparisons of Agricultural and Industrial Truck Drivers by
Employment Status, 1950

	Agricultural		Industrial	
	Self-Employed	Employees	Self-Employed	Employees
Median Income	$1,350	$2,250	$1,450	$2,550

Source: IPUMS 1950.

neurs started out in business by hauling farm products, as the exemption
clause of the 1935 Motor Carrier Act made farm hauling a much easier market
to enter than industrial hauling. Trucking farm produce provided opportunities for young men "on the make" to start up a small business—a fact dramatized in the 1949 film *Thieves' Highway,* in which war veteran Nico Garcos
(played by Richard Conte) uses his savings to buy a truck and a load of California produce hoping to make a quick buck. Just as Joe Fabrini's character had
discovered in the 1940 film *They Drive by Night,* however, Nico Garcos soon
realizes that produce hauling is a rough business with no guarantee of economic success. The price to be paid for the independence of self-employment
was not a Hollywood fiction, however, especially in the agricultural trucking
industry. As table 3.1 illustrates, the median income of self-employed truckers
in 1950 paled in comparison to that of drivers who worked for wages, while
drivers working in agricultural fields earned 7 to 13 percent less than their industrial counterparts. Self-employed farm haulers earned the least of any category of trucker. The highly competitive nature of unregulated "exempt" rural
trucking opened up opportunities for "independent" self-employment on the
highways, yet kept driver incomes comparatively low.[34]

Transportation specialists within the Department of Agriculture consequently recognized that the agricultural exemption clause of the 1935 Motor
Carrier Act provided a powerful tool for driving down farm transportation
costs. For more than a decade after the end of World War II, bureaucrats
within the USDA worked to expand the agricultural exemption, explicitly intending to spur the growth of the unregulated, nonunionized country trucking industry. The bureaucrats in question owed their positions to Section 201
of the 1938 Agricultural Adjustment Act, which empowered the secretary of
agriculture to contest any actions of the Interstate Commerce Commission
that might increase freight rates for farmers. The secretary of agriculture at the
time, agrarian antimonopolist Henry A. Wallace, created a special branch
within the USDA to administer this authority, which Wallace intended to use

to force railroads to keep their rates low for farm products. Headed by economist Charles B. Bowling from 1938 to 1955, the Transportation Rates and Services Division of the Agricultural Marketing Service claimed to have saved
farmers over $1 billion during the war by preventing "profiteering" by railroad
executives. But after 1945, Bowling's office shifted its focus away from attacking railroads and toward encouraging the growth of the nonregulated trucking
industry. Several years before the term "deregulation" entered the nation's political vocabulary—railroad executives began touting the concept in 1949—
Bowling and his staff of lawyers and economists began pursuing de facto
deregulation by expanding the agricultural exemption clause of the Motor
Carrier Act.[35]

The most important opportunity for doing so came in 1947. Norman E.
Harwood, the owner and driver of a single tractor-trailer, petitioned the ICC
for authority to transport washed salad packaged in cellophane bags to grocers
in the upper Midwest. In hearing the petition, ICC commissioners determined that placing the salad in cellophane bags constituted a process of manufacturing, and so required Harwood to be certified as a regulated trucker
rather than an exempt hauler. Charles B. Bowling and his staff of economists
and lawyers in the Transportation Rates Division immediately recognized the
implications of this decision. If packaged salad was a manufactured product,
the ICC could expand its oversight to include truckers hauling any packaged
or minimally processed agricultural product. This would effectively limit the
agricultural exemption to very few commodities, meaning that most shippers
of food products would be required to use the higher-priced services of regulated, unionized transportation firms. In July 1948, economist Donald Leavens
of the USDA's Transportation Rates division asked the ICC to reconsider the
case, developing in the meantime a plan "to obtain the maximum exemption
for agricultural commodities." Determined to "show that the exempt carrier
provides a more flexible and adequate service to the farm community than
does the regula[ted] carrier," Leavens and his colleagues at the USDA decided
to "line up witnesses" from farm groups to challenge the ICC's interpretation
of washed salad as a manufactured commodity.[36]

A year's worth of hearings before the ICC ensued, pitting the antimonopoly
forces of the USDA against the promonopoly forces of the Teamsters and regulated trucking firms. The USDA's legal team argued that Congress had intended the exemption to apply to "not only those agricultural commodities
which are marketable in their natural state but those on which labor has been
performed or mechanical skill applied, without materially affecting the natural state of the articles." This was a disingenuous argument, making it seem as
if Congress had known in 1935 that trucking of agricultural products would

someday be performed not by individual farmers driving small trucks but by for-hire truckers in big tractor-trailer rigs. During the hearings, Brannan's Department of Agriculture indicated its intention to contest the issue before the Supreme Court if the ICC did not rule in a manner that would expand the exemption to cover haulers of such items as washed, packaged salad. Under such pressure, the ICC overturned the *Harwood* decision in 1949, but opened up a new set of hearings to lay out a clear policy for interpreting the agricultural exemption clause. In 1951 the ICC issued its findings in a case known as *Determinations,* which declared that in all future petitions from motor carriers seeking certificates to transport agricultural commodities, the ICC would interpret a "manufactured" commodity as one that was no longer in its "natural state." *Determinations* set out a list of commodities that the ICC would consider "natural," including, for instance, peeled apples and unshelled nuts; "manufactured" commodities included such goods as smoked, canned, or cooked chickens. Even *Determinations,* however, opened up a window for the USDA to contest the ICC's interpretation of the exemption clause. The ruling defined pasteurized and vitamin-enriched milk, for instance, as being in a "natural state," while milled grain was not. The upshot was that the ICC could not set down a firm and common-sense definition of "agricultural commodities (not including manufactured products thereof)" that would prevent the USDA from contesting a ruling that limited the exemption's coverage in any particular trucking firm's application for authority. USDA economists and bureaucrats, deeply steeped in the premises of industrial agriculture, were unlikely to accept the ICC's contention that highly processed foods were somehow "unnatural."[37]

The fight over the agricultural exemption, however, was not fundamentally about whether a bag of washed salad or a bottle of pasteurized milk was or was not "natural" or "manufactured." The USDA was instead engaged in a roundabout attack on unionized, cartelized transportation firms. By expanding the agricultural exemption to allow more "independent" truckers to haul farm and food products, the USDA's legal team was directly challenging the rise of Teamster power in the trucking industry. During World War II, the International Brotherhood of Teamsters had solidified its power in freight trucking, benefiting from the establishment of a Trucking Commission under the National War Labor Board during World War II. The Trucking Commission fostered a cooperative atmosphere between trucking firms and the union to achieve uniform wage rates and working conditions among large trucking firms. Throughout the war, the IBT demanded few, if any, fundamental changes in the wage structures or conditions of employment in the trucking industry, accepting in return occasional cost-of-living wage increases and, more importantly, a state-granted monopoly on the trucking labor market.[38] Following the war, the Teamsters continued to expand their membership, making impressive gains in the early 1950s. The Teamsters had little luck, however, organizing trucking firms hauling exempt agricultural commodities. There were several reasons for this. First, most exempt haulers were small businesses, most often operating only one or two trucks. Drivers at such firms tended to maintain a sense of independence as small businessmen rather than wage workers, and so were hostile to labor unions. Furthermore exempt trucking firms were generally dispersed throughout rural areas, forestalling the Teamsters from using the "leapfrog" organizing strategy that had proven so successful in urban contexts in the late 1930s. Third, because exempt trucking firms did not have to file their rates with the ICC, the pressures to compete with other firms on price were much more intense than in the regulated freight industry. Whereas regulated carriers had little incentive to resist unionization or increased wage demands in a sheltered economic environment, the highly competitive nature of the exempt trucking sector provided rural haulers every incentive to resist unionization. When the USDA and the ICC fought over what exactly should count as a "manufactured" agricultural commodity, the USDA was effectively pushing to keep the Teamsters from organizing agricultural trucking firms and thereby driving up the cost of labor involved in transporting food from farms to consumers.[39]

An example of this strategy was a lengthy debate, beginning in 1948, between the USDA and the ICC over a practice known as "trip-leasing." This practice allowed exempt haulers, who did not have ICC authority to transport manufactured freight, to temporarily lease their equipment to a regulated carrier in order to obtain a "backhaul" (a load that would bring the trucker home and defray the cost of fuel). For example, an unregulated trucker might haul exempt Florida oranges north to Atlanta, but upon arrival be unable to find a load of agricultural commodities that would take him home. An expensive return trip hauling an empty trailer—"deadheading"—would result. By leasing his equipment out for the trip to a larger certificated carrier, the trucker could gain temporary ICC authority to haul a load of regulated freight back to Florida. Regulated trucking firms gained flexibility through such arrangements. The ICC, however, saw trip-leasing as a direct challenge to its regulatory authority, while the Teamsters noted that trip-leasing allowed regulated firms to contract with independent truckers and avoid paying union-scale wages. In 1951, Teamster representatives testified before the ICC that trip-leasing amounted to sweated labor, forcing workers to drive "from 16 to 76 hours without adequate rest." Owners of many regulated trucking firms disagreed, however, arguing that limits to trip-leasing infringed on the rights of management to choose between leased and purchased equipment. Beset by contradictory demands from such powerful interest groups, ICC commissioners issued a compromise ruling in 1951, allowing trip-leasing to continue, but requiring all trip-lease contracts to last for a minimum of thirty days.[40]

Department of Agriculture leaders rallied the troops to overturn the ICC's ruling. Attorney Earl W. Love, arguing on behalf of the secretary of agriculture in the 1951 hearings before ICC examiners, declared that trip-leasing provided one of the only ways for exempt truckers to stay in business without drastically increasing their rates. Under pressure from the Farm Bureau and the National Grange as well as agricultural shipping associations, the solicitor general's office of the Department of Agriculture declared the ICC's thirty-day requirement to be a backhanded attack on the agricultural exemption clause of the Motor Carrier Act, and took the issue all the way to the Supreme Court. On behalf of the secretary of agriculture, attorney Neil Brooks argued before the Supreme Court in 1952 that the ICC had overstepped its authority. The Court, however, sided with the ICC in its decision of January 1953, finding that the commission had the authority to limit the "evils that had grown up in [trip-leasing] practice." Undaunted, Assistant Secretary of Agriculture John H. Davis called upon farm organizations such as the Farm Bureau and the National Grange to lobby Congress for a law that would moot the Supreme Court's decision. After hearing testimony from farm organizations who protested that the ICC intended to put exempt truckers out of business, Congress amended the Interstate Commerce Act in 1953 to prevent the ICC from limiting trip-leasing. The ICC refused to abandon efforts to tighten its grip on "gypsy" truckers, however, and amended the order in 1955 to allow trip-leasing by agricultural haulers, but only for a return trip to a point from which the original exempt haul had started. Farm lobbyists from the Grange to the Farm Bureau to the Farmers Union—groups normally at odds over farm policy matters— called in unison upon Congress to once again rebuke the ICC, with the full support of Ezra Taft Benson's Department of Agriculture. As Benson informed the Senate, U.S. farmers and food consumers relied upon "the flexibility and economic advantages derived from [owner-operator truckers'] freedom to lease for single return trips." The result in August of 1956 was the passage of Public Law 957, which clearly and firmly exempted agricultural haulers from trip-leasing limitations. Nearly a decade after the ICC had first attempted to clamp down on trip-leasing, USDA bureaucrats in both Democratic and Republican administrations had used every judicial, administrative, and legislative weapon at their command to prevent any restrictions on the agricultural exemption clause of the 1935 Motor Carrier Act. In 1956, just as in 1935, the "independent" exempt trucker owed his status to the political machinations of federal agricultural bureaucrats.[41]

What the ICC interpreted as the chaotic nature of unregulated trucking was viewed by the USDA as essential for allowing not only farmers, but all industries engaged in agribusiness, to keep their transportation costs low. Agricultural economist Ralph Dewey summed up the department's attitude toward exempt trucking in 1954: "The truly competitive, small-scale carriers should be regulated only as to abuses that cannot be corrected through free competition," meaning that agricultural truckers should be subject only to safety regulations, with all other issues dictated by the market. Notably agricultural economists in the land-grant college complex and within the halls of the Department of Agriculture came to this consensus on unregulated trucking well before President Eisenhower's secretary of commerce, Sinclair Weeks, began his ill-fated push for partial deregulation of transportation in April 1955.[42] This "free market" approach to truck transportation began during Charles Brannan's tenure as the secretary of agriculture, but as we shall see in the next chapter, it would be Ezra Taft Benson who would push an even more ambitious deregulatory agenda, seeking to expand the agricultural exemption to cover heavily processed items such as frozen chickens and frozen orange juice as well as raw agricultural commodities. As part of his broader attack on the vestiges of economic liberalism in U.S. farm and food politics, Ezra Taft Benson would encourage the expansion of unregulated, nonunionized rural trucking as an effective tool for boosting the market power of corporate food processors and factory farmers without alienating middle-class consumers. Charles Brannan had failed to unite the interests of farmers and consumers by revising farm policy in 1949, but within a decade Ezra Taft Benson would succeed in doing so—not by repealing New Deal farm policies, but instead by urging the consolidation of economically concentrated agribusiness through technological change. As the next three chapters show, the expansion of long-haul trucking and of a fiercely independent nonunionized trucker culture underwrote the triumph of agribusiness during Benson's tenure as head of the USDA.

CHAPTER FOUR

Trucking Culture and Politics in the Agribusiness Era, 1953–61

Robert Vandivier's first experience as a truck driver came before he was tall enough to see over the steering wheel, hauling skim milk and grain to feed the livestock on his parents' southern Indiana farm during the Depression. After serving briefly in World War II, he was on the verge of making a down payment on a farm when a local trucker advertised a sale on several used trucks. Without any knowledge of the livestock hauling business, Vandivier soon found himself running a ten-truck operation, hauling sheep, hogs, and cattle from the Midwest to New Jersey and West Virginia. Lawrence Pilgrim, born on a farm in northern Georgia in the late 1930s, followed a southern version of the same path. After the war, as pine thickets and Jesse Jewell's chicken processing plants replaced depleted cotton fields, Pilgrim decided to follow his father and older brother into the trucking industry—though at the age of sixteen he had to forge his driver's license to be able to haul chicken feed throughout the South and dressed chickens as far north as Detroit. The unregulated nature of most agricultural trucking allowed young men like Vandivier and Pilgrim to enter the business relatively easily—and buying a truck to haul livestock or grain seemed a surer bet than buying a farm during an era of industrialized agriculture. Both of these men watched as the rural landscapes into which they had been born became industrial landscapes after World War II and both chose to become truckers to maintain a sense of rural identity and manly independence in an era when agribusiness limited the possibilities of doing so as farmers. Even so, both men refused to romanticize their work as "asphalt cowboys." As Vandivier put it, the main thing cowboys and truckers shared was a culture of hard, lonesome work that neither "should have got into." Like the range-riding cowboy of old, the truck driving man of the 1950s and 1960s was "independent" only in the sense that his work did not take place within the four walls of an office or factory; the work was nonetheless fully integrated into the machinery of industrial capitalism.[1]

Many would-be farmers who became "kings of the open road" in this period recognized that they could be considered modern-day "sharecroppers" upon whose backs the industrial machinery of capitalist agribusiness rode. Rural truckers of the 1950s and 1960s often worked as drivers for small, unregulated trucking firms, specializing in hauling agricultural products and foodstuffs from factory farms to the supermarkets springing up across the suburban land-scape. By hauling the products of a mass-production agricultural economy to the warehouses and retail stores of a mass-consumption food economy, rural truckers unintentionally contributed to a material undermining of economic liberalism within U.S. farm and food politics. Under the guiding hand of Presi-dent Eisenhower's secretary of agriculture, Ezra Taft Benson, the Department of Agriculture relied upon the "flexibility" of rural truckers to make a full-scale assault on economic liberalism within the farm and food economy. Through close cooperation with agribusiness firms—such as the frozen food packers, beefpackers, and milk dealers discussed in this chapter and the following two chapters—Benson's USDA encouraged private firms to use highway transpor-tation to engineer attacks on labor unions and small farmers as part of his efforts to repeal the New Deal in agriculture. Without actually overturning any New Deal farm policies, Benson upheld the "free market" and modern technology as the solution to the decades-old farm problem. The expansion of long-haul trucking and new warehousing methods allowed agribusinesses such as frozen food packers to triumphantly claim they could construct a "classless society" of satisfied supermarket consumers. By producing "luxuries for the masses"— from frozen orange juice to TV dinners—food processors in the agribusiness era overturned liberal efforts to administer private enterprise in the name of farm prosperity and consumer purchasing power. In their stead, agribusinesses constructed a new geography of food production and consumption that em-bodied conservative ideologies of "free enterprise."

TRUCKING IN THE RURAL INDUSTRIAL LANDSCAPE

The expansion of long-haul trucking in the countryside came at a key moment in rural U.S. history, as industrialized agriculture made the practice of farming increasingly peripheral to the economic and social lives of most rural people. Over the long twentieth century, and with especial rapidity following the end of World War II, a set of wrenching economic and social changes redefined rural life in the United States. The size, scale, and sophistication of the aver-age farming operation increased dramatically after World War II, leading to a rapid decline in the number of people who made their living directly from the land. The number of farms in the United States decreased by 32 percent be-tween 1945 and 1960, while the average farm size increased by approximately 34 percent. At the same time, the proportion of the U.S. population living on farms declined by half from 1945 to 1960. Fossil fuel-powered tractors and combines replaced oat-powered mules and horses, while also lessening farmers' reliance on human labor; the number of unpaid family members and hired hands working on farms decreased by 29 percent between 1945 and 1960. For those Americans who continued to eke out a living on the farm, off-farm employment became essential to the household economy; nonfarm jobs contributed 26 percent of the total farm income of the nation in 1945, but by 1960, nonfarm sources accounted for 38 percent of the farm population's income. Such grim prospects for U.S. farmers—which only grew dimmer over the years—help explain why trucking would seem such an attractive option for so many young men entering adulthood in 1950s rural America.[2]

Dry statistics mask the role of powerful government and business agents in fomenting the depopulation and industrialization of the postwar countryside, as if the process were the product of inevitable technological forces or of the "logic" of industrial capitalism. In one of the great ironies of twentieth-century U.S. history, the "farm problem" that so bedeviled agricultural policymakers from the 1920s through the 1960s was in large part a product of federal government policies. Since the 1862 founding of the Department of Agriculture as a cabinet-level federal agency, government researchers had guided "progressive" farmers to adopt ever more industrial-style techniques and machines to intensify and expand their operations. Federally funded agricultural scientists, engineers, and extension agents, along with bankers, land-grant university researchers, and agromachinery and agrochemical companies, urged farmers to rely on tractors, mechanical cotton pickers, grain combines, hybrid seeds, pesticides, and inorganic fertilizers to transform their mixed farming operations into giant monocropped fields. The state of Iowa, which in 1920 had produced everything from apricots to pigs to watermelons for on-farm consumption and off-farm sale, had by the 1960s become an enormous corn and soybean factory producing grain and hogs primarily for out-of-state markets. This "rationalization" of American agriculture produced anything but rational results after World War II, as would-be farmers were forced to seek off-farm employment while agricultural policymakers were forced to wrestle with declining farm incomes at a time of unprecedented prosperity for the nation as a whole. The growth of long-haul trucking played a key role in both of these struggles. Trucking offered nonfarm jobs to rural men, while simultaneously contributing to a shift in agricultural politics toward abundant marketing of farm products rather than planned scarcity as in the New Deal era.[3]

For rural men seeking off-farm employment in the 1950s and 1960s, trucking provided a career that would allow them to stay close to home. Census data (see table B.1 in appendix B) show that truck drivers in the postwar period were more likely than the average worker to live outside of major metropolitan areas. In 1960, for example, nearly a third of truck drivers lived in nonmetro-politan areas, compared to only a quarter of all workers. Regions in which agri-business dominated the economy generally had high concentrations of truck drivers, especially owner-operator truckers—a point graphically demonstrated in figure 2.1 (see chapter 2). In Kansas in 1950, for instance, the trucking indus-try provided the second-highest number of jobs in the state, behind only agri-culture. In a state with two major manufacturing industries—aeronautics and meatpacking—this was a remarkable fact. Part of the reason for the availabil-ity of driving jobs in agricultural states like Kansas was the fact that farmers became increasingly dependent on trucking rather than railroads for shipping goods to market. In the era of agribusiness, as farm owners used tractors and other machines to do work themselves that had previously been done by hired hands and family members, farm owners had less time to do their own truck-ing. Farm-to-market hauling became a full-time occupation in its own right, as farmers who had once used pickups to haul their goods to market came to rely upon for-hire truckers with larger tractor-trailers to do their hauling. An-other key factor was the social process by which many drivers entered the trucking industry in the postwar period. Although formal driver-training schools existed from the earliest days of long-haul trucking, a significant per-centage of drivers in the postwar years learned to drive from a relative or friend. Two sociological studies from the late 1960s found that approximately one of every three drivers was related to another driver who had convinced and trained him to enter the occupation. Fathers who had left the farm to become truckers in the 1930s, moreover, commonly brought their sons into trucking after the war. Friends and neighbors also recruited individuals into trucking. Richard Gingerich, who grew up on a farm near Kouts, Indiana, in the 1950s, remembers spending his early teenage years doing odd jobs around local livestock yards to help out his parents who were "having a tough time finan-cially." When invited to ride along with livestock truckers, Gingerich would enthusiastically accept—especially because the drivers would let young Gin-gerich take the wheel "with orders to 'wake me up when you approach the east gate [the border checkpoint between Indiana and Ohio].'" After graduating from high school in 1965, Gingerich's informal driving experience helped him to be hired "on the spot" by a local fertilizer and grain trucking firm, a job that would allow him to save up enough money to buy his own tractor-trailer in due course.[4]

Perhaps most importantly, rural men were able to enter the unregulated farm hauling market much more easily than they could enter the regulated freight hauling market. As detailed in previous chapters, the Department of Agricul-ture had worked since 1935 to make sure that agricultural truckers would re-

main exempt from Interstate Commerce Commission regulations that re-
stricted entry into the freight trucking industry. Although rural men could
become owner-operator farm truckers without having to file papers with government regulators, they were also forced to accept more economic uncertainty than their unionized counterparts in the regulated freight trucking industry. The distance between nonunion and union drivers widened during the
1950s, as the Teamsters achieved unprecedented power within the urban freight
trucking industry. With their dominance in regulated freight trucking established by the end of World War II, the Teamsters were able to refuse deliveries
or pickups at the docks of businesses that had not yet signed up with the
union, allowing the union to pad its rolls with plant and warehouse workers.
This was particularly the case after Dave Beck replaced Daniel Tobin as president of the IBT in 1952. Beck, unlike Tobin, had no qualms about boosting
the union's membership by organizing nondrivers. As one of Beck's colleagues
told a reporter in 1953, "Dave will take anybody he can get his hands on, then
he'll find some kind of justification for it. A 'teamster' to him is anybody who
sleeps on a bed with movable casters." By 1957, the Teamsters claimed the
largest membership of any union in the nation, with 1.5 million members, of
which half a million were truck drivers. Those half-million organized truck
drivers, employed primarily by regulated common-carrier trucking firms,
earned very good wages. In 1957, the average annual pay of a Teamster driver
was $6,886, significantly better than the average annual earnings of $4,242 for
workers in manufacturing or the $5,214 of workers in construction. Along with
high wages, Teamsters enjoyed seniority rights, health and pension benefits,
and job security. The benefits of union membership, however, rarely extended
very far outside of urban centers.[5]

Most rural trucking firms remained small and nonunionized throughout
the postwar period. In Kansas in 1962, for instance, 95 percent of the state's
trucking companies had fewer than five employees each. Such small rural firms
proved consistently difficult for the Teamsters to organize, as exemplified by a
failed effort in the summer of 1960 by a Teamster recruiter to organize Hanefeld Trucking, a cattle-hauling firm in central Wisconsin. Hanefeld employed
twelve drivers, making it the largest—yes, the largest—cattle-hauling firm in the
state at the time. Though union organizers assured drivers that "only through
the Teamsters Union can you make this job a decent one," the Hanefeld brothers who owned the firm threatened to cease operations if the workers organized. Only six of the drivers voted to accept Teamster representation, with the
other six drivers and four additional employees—dispatchers and office staff—
opting out. Certainly the antiunion hostility of the Hanefeld brothers drew on
a rural antipathy toward labor organizations, but more important was the fact

that such a firm—which hauled live cattle, officially considered "agricultural commodities (not including manufactured products thereof)" according to the Motor Carrier Act of 1935—did not have to publish its rates with the ICC. As an exempt agricultural trucking firm, Hanefeld had little incentive to welcome the Teamsters. If such a firm drew up a union contract with its workers, it would almost assuredly go out of business as nonunionized owner-operators rushed in to capture their market with cut-rate freight charges. The "independent" rural truck driver was thus as much a creature of federal transportation policies as of cultural resistance to urban union organizers, much as the "independent" yeoman farmer had always been a creature of agrarian politics that privileged white male land owners as the backbone of U.S. democracy.[6]

Even for drivers who owned their own rigs, the appropriate occupational analogy was often the sharecropper rather than the yeoman farmer. After interviewing a group of long-haul truckers in Livingston, Alabama, in 1953, Alfred Maund wrote in the *Nation* magazine that the typical owner-operator "is apparently no better off than a share-cropper, being held in similar peonage by his employer." In order to purchase a truck and trailer, truckers often relied on installment loans provided by the trucking firm to whom they contracted their labor. In return, owner-operators received a specified share of the revenue for each load. The typical contract, however, did not guarantee a minimum number of loads for the driver. During slow business periods, it was all too easy for an owner-operator to miss a payment on his loan, sending "his" truck and trailer directly to the firm. Even obtaining the pink slip on a rig rarely propelled a driver into the managerial class. As the Bureau of Labor Statistics pointed out in its 1959 guide to careers, "Promotional opportunities in [truck driving] are limited," no matter whether drivers owned their trucks or worked for wages. Still the "sharecropper" analogy is remarkably apt, for it highlights rural working-class men's deep attachment to self-directed work and their intense desire to own their own property. Agricultural sharecropping, for all its oppressive features, provided an important sense of autonomy to both black and white landless farmers in the post–Civil War South. The system of sharecropping emerged in the postbellum period as a way for cash-poor but land-rich plantation owners to secure a steady workforce of free laborers; in order to do so without paying cash wages, plantation owners had to negotiate with freed blacks and poor whites who found the self-directed work of cropping on shares to be socially empowering if not necessarily economically remunerative. Similarly the post–World War II truck drivers whom journalist Alfred Maund labeled "sharecroppers" had reason to believe that leasing a truck from a larger trucking firm was preferable to wage work. Even when the firms captured most of the profits while drivers shed most of the sweat, the lease provided a potential ticket to business ownership in one's own right.[7]

The "sharecropper" analogy also opens a window onto the racial hierarchy of trucking culture in the mid-twentieth century. Much as the crop-lien system of agricultural sharecropping tended to reinforce economic discrimination against African American farmers by creating perpetual cycles of debt, the racially inscribed provision of truck leases, loans, and hauling contracts tended to benefit white truckers disproportionately to blacks. As the census data in table B.2 (see appendix B) illustrate, white truckers were far more likely than black truckers to be self-employed. Although black drivers made up 12 percent of the trucking labor force as of 1950, only 5 percent of owner-operator truckers were African American. By contrast, at a time when whites comprised 88 percent of all truckers, 94 percent of self-employed truckers were white. This racial disparity in truck ownership resulted from numerous factors. One was that the most common route for a wage worker to become a truck owner was to save up one's earnings until a down payment could be made on a truck. Unfortunately rampant discrimination within the for-hire trucking industry and within the Teamsters Union generally kept black drivers' take-home pay dispiritingly low in comparison to their white counterparts. As the data on income in table B.2 illustrate, white truck drivers earned median incomes more than one and a half times greater than black drivers in 1950, and in 1960 the income gap was even wider. Furthermore even if an African American truck driver managed to save up enough money for a down payment on a truck, he would likely face daily discrimination that would make repaying the loan difficult. To earn a steady income as an owner-operator, a trucker needed to receive loads from brokers, shippers, or larger trucking firms willing to contract out hauls. Even when the dispatchers for such firms were willing to offer paying loads, receiving firms were likely to refuse loads delivered by black drivers. Local chapters of the Teamsters union commonly participated in such discriminatory arrangements. An owner-operator trucker did not necessarily need to belong to the Teamsters to make deliveries, but when delivering to a warehouse organized by the union he needed the cooperation of the workers there to unload his truck. Teamster locals in the urban North, in particular, were dominated by tightly knit groups of ethnic whites who treated membership in their union as a prerogative of whiteness. The national leaders of the union in the 1940s and early 1950s—Daniel Tobin and Dave Beck—did little to counteract the racial exclusion built into many local Teamsters chapters. Even when James R. Hoffa took over the IBT in 1957 after having gained a reputation as a champion of African American access to decent jobs, the union's headquarters did little to rein in the formal and informal rules used by local chapters to prevent blacks from rising in the trucking ranks. Both white and black truck drivers faced challenges in escaping their "sharecropper" status to become full-fledged owners, but the challenges faced by African Americans seeking the "independence" of truck ownership were extraordinary.[8]

For both white and black truckers seeking to become small business owners, membership in the Teamsters often presented an obstacle rather than an opportunity. Conservative politicians seized on this fact in the late 1940s and into the 1950s to undermine the power of organized labor within the nation's economy. The Republican-led passage of the Taft-Hartley Act in 1947 over President Truman's veto had placed significant checks on organized labor's power, but union membership nonetheless continued to swell in the 1950s. By 1955, one-third of all nonfarm workers in the nation belonged to unions. Despite gains in membership, national union leaders such as Walter Reuther of the United Auto Workers made deep compromises in the labor movement's agenda. Labor leaders accepted annual cost-of-living adjustments and expanded fringe benefits, while retreating from demands for systemic political and economic changes that would benefit not only white, northern, industrial workers but also women, black, southern, and unorganized farm workers. Although such compromises were widely hailed at the time by journalists and corporate leaders as a new "social compact" based on a "labor-capital accord," many rank-and-filers in the labor movement continued to agitate for better economic opportunities and increased autonomy in the workplace and within their unions. Over the course of the supposedly quiescent 1950s, organized labor averaged 352 massive work stoppages per year; the largest strike in U.S. history occurred not in the 1930s but in 1959 when over half a million steelworkers walked off the job for 116 days. Although such massive strikes helped many workers make important gains, they also encouraged corporations and conservative groups such as the National Association of Manufacturers to redouble their efforts to quash labor militancy through anti-Communist propaganda, political lobbying, and welfare capitalist strategies. But the strike wave of the 1950s also highlighted the growing sense among not only conservatives and corporate leaders but also liberal politicians and the general public that organized labor had become overly greedy, self-interested, and undemocratic.[9]

The Teamsters in particular came under repeated fire in the 1950s as the epitome of "Big Labor," with widely publicized scandals involving bribery, organized crime, and embezzled pension funds bringing government and public censure. From 1957 to 1959, Senator John L. McClellan (D-AR) chaired a special investigatory committee that heard testimony from over 1,500 witnesses, the bulk of whom either charged the Teamsters Union with shocking and systemic corruption or refused to speak up on behalf of the positive contributions the union had made to the living standards of millions of working Americans. The conservative southerner McClellan was joined by a northern Democrat, Robert F. Kennedy, who served as the McClellan Committee's chief counsel and who considered himself a friend of labor but bitter enemy of James R. Hoffa. Together McClellan and Kennedy denounced Teamsters leaders for having abused their power at the expense of the U.S. public and of the rank-and-file members of the working class. The McClellan Committee convinced many Americans that the 1954 film *On the Waterfront* accurately represented organized labor's betrayal of the rank-and-file working class. The committee also signaled the willingness of key liberals within the Democratic Party—including Robert Kennedy—to defect from that party's tight alliance forged with organized labor during the Roosevelt-Truman era. Furthermore the Mc-Clellan hearings boosted corporate lobbyists' ongoing efforts to pass a severely restrictive piece of labor legislation: the Landrum-Griffin Act of 1959. Landrum-Griffin clamped down on secondary boycotts and empowered the Labor Department to closely regulate union financial affairs. Government oversight of union finances probably helped existing union members by limiting opportunities for embezzlement and pension fraud, but the crackdown on secondary boycotts spelled the doom of Teamster power. Although the Taft-Hartley Act had technically outlawed the secondary boycott twenty-two years earlier, the Teamsters had nonetheless continued to use their most effective organizing tool by exploiting a technical loophole. Landrum-Griffin closed that loophole, forcing the union to rely solely on less effective organizing methods, such as picketing and firm-by-firm balloting. Without the secondary boycott, the Teamsters faced an almost impossible battle in efforts to organize the small, rural firms that would spring up in the countryside in the 1960s and 1970s—particularly in the strongly antiunion Sunbelt South, where state "right-to-work" laws already constricted labor organizing and provided a probusiness "corporate climate."[10]

Neither conservative nor liberal attacks on the Teamsters explain, however, why so many long-haul truckers would choose to work either for themselves or for small nonunionized firms despite the economic risks involved. The blue-collar culture of trucking cultivated a deep sense of separation from bourgeois urban society. Understanding this oppositional culture helps to explain why rural owner-operator truckers could fully realize that they worked within a capitalist world of rigid class lines, yet would nonetheless maintain a deep hostility to labor unions. Working-class manhood, particularly in a rural context, has traditionally been defined less by whether one owns the means of production than by an ethos shaped by economic uncertainty and the pride of overcoming that uncertainty on one's own terms. As George Raft's character, Joe Fabrini, stated in *They Drive by Night,* working for a guaranteed salary was "the easy way." Yet the masculine ideal portrayed by George Raft in *They Drive by Night,* even if it was rooted in an oppositional ethos, nonetheless made respectability in the eyes of the bourgeois world a valid goal. Joe Fabrini was willing to use his fists in defense of his perceived rights, but he did right by women, refused to drink alcohol, and avoided unnecessary violence. Joe Fabrini was a man to be admired—as indicated by Raft's eagerness to take the part to shed his reputation as a "heavy" in gangster films such as *Scarface.* The image of the respectable trucker circulated outside the world of Hollywood in the 1950s, as truckers became known as "Knights of the Road" for helping stranded motorists and using their blinkers and headlights as courtesy signals. This image was further reinforced by the standard driver's uniform of the era: trim, neat pants and buttoned shirt and a chauffeur's cap. The masculine mythologies of trucking moved increasingly into a wider cultural world in the 1950s and 1960s, as the image of the truck driving man was reflected back to truckers by movies and music. However, the greater currency of this imagery should not be taken to imply that truckers necessarily "bought" those ideas wholesale—or that by buying those ideas they were duped into a sense of "false consciousness," preventing them from understanding the exploitative nature of their work. Truckers were continually aware that the economic and political machinery that their work contributed to quite literally rode on their backs—and yet, they had legitimate reasons to value their work culture as distinct from other jobs that might well have earned them higher incomes.[11]

Above all, long-haul trucking provided many white rural men the chance to maintain a sense of rural identity and rootedness in an urban-industrial world. Country music artists and marketers were among the first to recognize this in the 1950s, which helps explain why nearly all trucking songs are country songs. Country music as a commercial form of entertainment was distinguished from other popular music forms primarily by its reliance on the lived experiences of rural people, particularly southern whites, as the inspiration for its tales and sonic textures.[12] Working-class whites fled the rural South in waves in the 1940s and 1950s, seeking industrial employment in the booming wartime and postwar factories of the urban North, West, and Sunbelt. Country musicians, dance hall operators, and record producers sought out these recently urbanized audiences and their crisp new dollar bills, offering everything from fast-paced bluegrass to jazzy western swing to "hillbilly" honky-tonk to sell tickets and records on a national scale. All of these relatively new forms of country music explored the intersection of white rural culture and urban industrial life, though in distinct ways. The bluegrass of performers such as Bill Monroe, Flatt and Scruggs, and the Stanley Brothers melded jazz-like musical virtuosity with traditional acoustic instruments and nostalgic lyrics about the "old home place." Western swing bandleaders such as Bob Wills and Spade Cooley cribbed simultaneously from the big band standards and "cowboy" tunes popular in the 1930s and 1940s, while mixing jazz instruments such as vibraphones and saxophones with pedal steel guitars and fiddles—whatever it took to draw huge crowds of white factory workers to the dance halls dotting the southwestern and western landscapes of the emerging Sunbelt. In the honky-tonk subgenre of postwar country music, musicians used electric guitars and pedal steels to fill smaller venues with emotionally raw, hard-driving music for hard-working folks. Honky-tonkers such as Ernest Tubb, Faron Young, and Kitty Wells crafted lyrics and tunes that, much as electric bluesmen John Lee Hooker and Muddy Waters were doing at the same time for black audiences in Detroit and Chicago, dealt with the day-to-day concerns of working-class rural migrants into urban environments. Country music of the 1940s and 1950s was far whiter in terms of musicians and audiences than jazz, blues, or rock n' roll, but even influential black artists such as rocker Chuck Berry and soulman Ray Charles recognized the power of country music's working-class narratives and the raw emotive power of "hillbilly" music. Blues musician Jimmy Witherspoon, for instance, declared that "if Chuck Berry was white . . . he would be the top country star in the world." Ray Charles famously despised rock music, yet declared he "could do a good job with the right hillbilly song"—and proved his case when he released *Modern Sounds in Country and Western* in 1962, which quickly became his most popular record. Country music of the period was white music, but just as importantly it was working-class music with rural roots.[13]

Trucking songs would figure most prominently within the honky-tonk wing of country music in the 1940s and 1950s, as songwriters and record producers began to see truck drivers—whether southern or not—as a distinct working-class market segment with disposable incomes. The first original song about truck driving appeared in 1939 when Cliff Bruner and His Boys recorded Ted Daffan's "Truck Driver's Blues," a song explicitly marketed to roadside café owners who were installing jukeboxes in record numbers to serve truckers and other motorists. Bigger truck driving hits followed on the tails of Daffan's tune, particularly "I'm a Truck Driving Man" by Art Gibson (1947) and Terry Fell's "Truck Drivin' Man" (1954). Besides being a rollicking harmonica-driven tune, Fell's song used an ingenious marketing device, referring to itself being played on a truckstop jukebox in the chorus ("I'll put a nickel in the jukebox / And play the 'Truck Drivin' Man'"). Less upbeat was Joe "Cannonball" Lewis's

"Truck Driver's Night Run Blues" (1951), which narrates the tale of a southern cotton farmer, who, forced off the land and into a truck cab in a northern city, wishes that he "had stayed down South, this night run's killin' me."[14]

In their effort to merge rural cultural traditions with the realities of urban-industrial lifestyles, musicians who recorded early trucking songs adapted country music's long-lived theme of the "wanderer." By singing about stopping at a "roadhouse in Texas / A little place called Hamburger Dan's," Terry Fell helped promote the idea that a trucker's life consisted mainly of playing pinball while sipping coffee poured by a red-headed waitress. The truck driver, as a man in control of his time and possessing an untamed sexuality, was the antithesis of the "organization man" or the "man in the gray flannel suit" or the member of the "lonely crowd" that sociologists of the 1950s identified as the primary victim of an increasingly corporatized, bureaucratic urban society. Few truckers would have taken Terry Fell's song as an accurate representation of their work culture, yet few would dispute that the sense of mobility that trucking provided was an important attraction of the work. When a man's workplace was the road, a trucker took no orders from the factory foreman and faced no line speed-ups or stopwatch-toting scientific managers. Trucking firm owners did attempt to gain control over the work process of truckers in the postwar period, but with little success. The tachograph was a good example. Introduced to U.S. markets in 1940 by the Sangamo Electric Company, the tachograph supposedly provided an objective measure of a driver's productivity by measuring distance traveled, speed, and the frequency and duration of stops, recording these data on a wax chart. An advertisement for Wagner Electric's version proclaimed in 1956 that a tachograph would provide clear evidence of a trucker making "unscheduled stops," a point graphically presented as a trucker drinking coffee and chatting with a truck-stop waitress. Tachographs proved easy for truckers to outwit, however, as the manager of a trucking firm found in 1960 when he noted that "90% of the cutting knives in the doors of the tachograph clocks have been removed and destroyed by drivers." Besides breaking the machine, drivers could leave the clock open while driving, or set the clock back or ahead, falsifying the machine's records. The company manager was quite familiar with these tactics, stating that he knew "there are exactly 41 ways that tampering has appeared on these clocks and every one of them [is] known to management." But because the manager could not actually ride in the cab with each driver, there was no way to prevent such tampering. Although premised on the methods of scientific management, the tachograph could not bring factory-style discipline to the cab.[15]

Truckers could thus imagine themselves as relatively independent workers while on the road, even if they also knew that the image of the "knight of the road" was more façade than reality. For the thousands of rural men who worked as truckers in the 1950s and 1960s, even the possibility of being something more than a highway version of a sharecropper seemed better than casting one's lot as a farmer within the economic strictures of capital-intensive agribusiness. Farm boys who made the choice to become truckers in the 1950s and 1960s did so in a world not of their own making, yet had legitimate reasons to believe that trucking—especially unregulated, nonunionized trucking—would offer a sense of independence akin to that of the small business-owning farmer. But as truckers became responsible for hauling the majority of U.S. farm and food products by the early 1960s, "independent" truckers also became fully integrated into the modern marketing machinery of the agroindustrial complex. By hauling live cattle, dressed chickens, pasteurized milk, milled grain, and packaged processed foods from factory farms to suburban supermarkets, independent truckers contributed to a resurgence of economic conservatism in farm politics.

THE FARM PROBLEM AS INDUSTRIAL PROBLEM

Ezra Taft Benson never touched the steering wheel of a big rig, but as secretary of agriculture from 1953 to 1961, he understood that transportation technology provided a powerful tool for undermining political support for unions and state regulatory policies within the farm and food economy. Benson claimed to be "above politics" due to his deep Mormon faith and his training as an economist, but his actions as head of the USDA were explicitly aimed at dismantling the centralized planning of New Deal agricultural policy. Brought on board by Eisenhower to woo the farm vote away from Democrats after five consecutive presidential losses for the Republicans, Benson worked to develop cooperative relationships between the federal government and private industry to solve the farm problem in the ostensibly "free" market. Under Ezra Taft Benson, the Department of Agriculture's efforts to solve the farm problem would shift away from planned scarcity or antitrust actions toward full-fledged efforts to boost the marketing power of food processors and factory farmers. Trucks driven by nonunionized drivers were central to this new distribution- and marketing-driven approach to the political economy of farm production and food consumption. Agribusinesses and agribusiness-friendly bureaucrats quite literally worked to engineer the increasingly conservative consumerism that characterized the 1950s and 1960s, by making low-priced foods available to U.S. consumers in a lightly regulated, increasingly nonunionized food economy. The privatized, individualistic landscape of mass consumption in the postwar economy emerged from transformations in the rural United States as well as in suburbia, impacting farm producers, rural and urban workers, and supermarket shoppers alike.[16]

In direct contrast to his predecessor Charles F. Brannan, Ezra Taft Benson harbored a lifelong mistrust of New Deal farm policies. Born in Whitney, Idaho, in 1899 to descendants of pioneers who had followed Brigham Young westward in 1847, Benson was raised as a devout Mormon, keen Boy Scout, and avid Republican. While running his father's farm from 1923 to 1929, Benson studied agricultural economics at Brigham Young University and Iowa State College. In the early 1930s he worked as a county agricultural agent for the University of Idaho Extension Service. From 1933 to 1939 he served as secretary of the Idaho Cooperative Council, a group dedicated to boosting Idaho farm incomes through voluntary marketing associations—a form of political-economic organization closely aligned with the associationalist approach of the Hoover era. Benson took his associationalist faith to Washington in 1939, when he became executive secretary of the National Council of Farm Cooperatives—a lobby group representing powerful agricultural marketing associations such as the California Fruit Growers Exchange (producers of Sunkist brand products), the California Associated Raisin Company (Sun-Maid), and the giant Land O' Lakes dairy cooperative, along with a host of smaller concerns. As head of the National Council of Farm Cooperatives, Benson was a reliable source for journalists and congressional leaders seeking a quotable critique of New Deal farm and food policies. Benson often decried the "paternalistic government" of Franklin D. Roosevelt for quashing "free enterprise" in U.S. agriculture and rallied members of the National Council of Farm Cooperatives to fight the actions of the Office of Price Administration during the war. In later years, Benson would make much of the fact that during his time as a farmer, he "never took a subsidy" from the federal government (though, of course, his farming experience predated the New Deal). In 1944 Benson left Washington to assume a position with the Quorum of Twelve Apostles, the ruling body of the Church of Latter-Day Saints. He returned to his political calling in 1953 after Dwight Eisenhower, unable to convince his brother Milton Eisenhower to accept the helm of the Department of Agriculture, tapped Benson instead—partly to appease conservatives within the Republican Party who demanded an ardent anti–New Dealer for the post.[17]

Immediately after taking office in 1953, Benson set about the task of dismantling New Deal farm policy. At his first press conference he distributed copies of a 1,200-word "General Statement on Agricultural Policy," a free-market manifesto that declared, among other ideas, that "a completely planned and subsidized economy weakens initiative, discourages industry, destroys character, and demoralizes the people." Benson's primary goal was to scale back the

New Deal price-support system, which he believed drained government coffers and stifled free enterprise. Much as Charles F. Brannan had learned before him, however, Benson's efforts to dramatically revise farm policy ran up against a Congress dominated by an unbending farm bloc wedded to maintaining the New Deal economic safety net for farmers. Paying lip service to "free enterprise" was one thing; slashing payments to commercial farmers whose votes kept many southern, midwestern, and western legislators in office was entirely another. Although Benson succeeded in convincing Congress to revise agricultural price support formulas in 1954 to allow for "flexible" payments, Congress refused to significantly overhaul the crop subsidy system. In fact, Benson's ardent attempts to undermine the price support system made him a widely reviled figure among many farmers, even among Republicans who otherwise backed President Eisenhower's procorporate policies. Contemporary political commentators blamed Benson's heavy-handed approach to the price-support issue for preventing the Republicans from retaking control of Congress after Democrats won the majority in 1954. A 1957 *Wallace's Farmer* poll found that only 15 percent of Iowa farmers believed Eisenhower was doing a poor job as president, while 60 percent rated Benson's performance as poor. Despite repeated calls for his dismissal both from the Democratic and Republican sides of the congressional aisle, Benson continued in his Cabinet post through the entire Eisenhower presidency.[18]

Benson failed to eliminate the price-support system, but he successfully used government funds to usher in an era of corporate-dominated agribusiness. Just after proclaiming his "General Statement on Agricultural Policy" in 1953, Benson eliminated the Bureau of Agricultural Economics (BAE), claiming that too much of the BAE's economic research supported statist New Deal policies.[19] In the BAE's stead, Benson erected two agencies, the Agricultural Research Service and the Agricultural Marketing Service. Benson expected these agencies to redirect the work of agricultural engineers and economists toward what he considered more "objective" marketing research. Though Benson summed up his approach to agricultural policy as the "freedom to farm," the term "agribusiness" was a more accurate descriptor. "Agribusiness" was a neologism proposed in 1955 by Harvard Business School professor John H. Davis. Davis was in many ways Benson's protégé; Benson had selected Davis to take over his position as executive secretary of the National Council of Farm Cooperatives in 1944, and Davis served as Benson's assistant secretary of agriculture from 1953 to 1954. Davis defined the word "agribusiness" in inherently political terms, declaring that "the old idea of trying to solve the farm problem on the farm is outmoded." Rather than use New Deal-era price supports and production controls to keep farm prices high, Davis declared that government agencies and corporations should cooperate to boost the marketing of farm products. The "objective" marketing research undertaken by Ezra Taft Benson's reorganized Department of Agriculture during the era of agribusiness was thus fully intended to be most beneficial to nonfarm agricultural industries, especially food processors and supermarkets.[20]

The intent of Benson's "objective" approach was to convert the farm problem into an industrial problem. Much as the Research and Marketing Act of 1946 had promised to do, Benson expected the engineers and economists in the permanently funded Agricultural Marketing Service to place in the hands of private industry, rather than the federal government, the burden of assuring high prices for farmers while offering consumers abundance at acceptable prices. As Bushrod Allin, a sympathetic agricultural economist, explained to Benson's assistant secretary of agriculture, Earl Butz, in 1956, the department's new focus on marketing research was "safe, sane, conservative [and] socially desirable [because] everybody, including farmers, stands to gain from it." But the new approach to marketing research was not entirely without controversy. Wesley McCune, a journalist who served as an agricultural policy advisor to Charles F. Brannan in the Truman administration, attacked Benson's reorganization plan as a corporate plot to remake farm policy in the interests of big business: "Everyone expected a certain amount of change in personnel at the Department of Agriculture when the political majority changed, but a shift toward middlemen was hardly expected." Benson's overhaul of USDA research was also unpopular within the department itself, as Harry C. Trelogan, director of the USDA's Marketing Research Division, noted in responding to Bushrod Allin's letter. In particular, the applications of marketing research appeared to be most directly beneficial to food processors and supermarkets rather than to farmers or consumers. The term "agribusiness," though still not in wide circulation, could hold negative connotations for economists who did not fully agree with the corporate-welfare vision of Ezra Taft Benson. Trelogan's note exposed a tension within the USDA's ranks. While Secretary of Agriculture Benson touted "objective" marketing research as a means of using state power to influence practices in private food distribution, some agricultural economists who had been transferred from the Bureau of Agricultural Economics to the Agricultural Marketing Service preferred a "strong program of fundamental longer-run research" rather than "being too closely associated with 'action' programs." In the long run, though, Benson's approach won out within the USDA, as he pushed the Agricultural Marketing Service to work closely with private industry, particularly food processors and supermarkets, to develop lower-cost marketing and distribution methods as a demand-side approach to increasing the farmer's share of the consumer's dollar.[21]

Benson thus built upon the efforts of his liberal predecessor, Charles F. Brannan, by defining the farm problem as an issue to be confronted through abundant marketing rather than planned scarcity. During the Great Depression, agricultural experts had seen the farm problem as an issue of overproduction. But in a Cold War political culture focused on maintaining economic stability and growth without the use of "socialistic" methods of heavy-handed government economic intervention, the problem seemed to be "underconsumption"—a product of inefficient marketing. Agricultural economists came to see marketing—understood as "the link between production and consumption . . . assembly, transportation, packing, packaging, processing, preservation, storing, wholesaling, and retailing—all the steps between producer and consumer"—as the point of attack. Efficient marketing machinery could simultaneously bring abundance to consumers and high prices to commercial farmers—and, in marked contrast to the Brannan Plan, without government support of the incomes of small farmers or of the wage demands of organized laborers in the food distribution economy. In particular, if the cost of transportation could only be kept down, argued a 1956 USDA pamphlet entitled *Food Transportation and What It Costs Us,* farmers' incomes would automatically rise even as consumer prices dropped. According to the USDA's economic research, the cost of transportation since the end of World War II had outpaced all other inflationary factors in the farm and food economy, simultaneously making food more expensive for consumers while taking a larger piece of the farmer's share of the farm marketing dollar (see figure 4.1).[22]

Long-haul trucking provided the essential mechanism for driving down the cost of transporting food from factory farm to suburban supermarket. Whereas the farming communities and food processors of the nineteenth century relied upon railroads to market their products to urban consumers, by the 1970s empty train tracks ran parallel to jam-packed highways in the rural landscape. Trucks increasingly replaced trains as the transportation mode of choice for farmers and food processors and retailers—not because trucking was inherently "better" or less costly than shipping by rail, but because trucks provided the technological flexibility required for the new distribution methods that supported Ezra Taft Benson's vision of marketing-driven agribusiness. This flexibility took several forms. For one, trains were tied to steel rails, but trucks could travel anywhere a road led. A trucker could thus haul directly from point-to-point, from loading dock to unloading dock—allowing for speedier service and just-in-time deliveries. This geographical mobility was in great part a product of political action, as truckers relied upon government-subsidized construction of highways in the mid-twentieth century, particularly the 41,000 miles of high-speed interstate highways funded under the Federal-Aid High-

CHANGES IN LAST DECADE

TRANSPORTATION PORTION

Of The Retail Food Dollar

 5.5¢    6.9¢    8.0¢

Of The Marketing Dollar

 10.7¢   12.7¢    13.2¢

1945   1950   1955

Figure 4.1. Transportation Portion of the Food Dollar, 1945–55.
Department of Agriculture economists in 1956 declared that transportation costs had risen more rapidly for both food consumers and farm producers than any other component of the food dollar since World War II. In this image the price of transportation is depicted eating away at the purchasing power of retail consumers and the incomes of farmers who marketed agricultural commodities. From *Food Transportation and What It Costs Us* (*Source*: Washington: USDA, Agricultural Marketing Service, 1956).

way Act of 1956. As engineers expanded and modernized the nation's highway network, truck and trailer manufacturers sold larger machines capable of competing directly with railroads on long-haul (rather than just short-haul) trips. While trains remained far more fuel- and cost-efficient over long hauls, tractor-trailers offered the flexibility of traveling either long or short distances. Trains undergirded the expansion of the U.S. industrial manufacturing economy in the late nineteenth century, but highways formed the backbone of the post–World War II "postindustrial" economy of fast-paced, retailer-driven distribution.

The nation's railroads faced stiff competition from truckers in the 1950s and 1960s. Rails increasingly lost valuable freight to truckers so that railroads' share of gross freight revenues dropped from 80 percent in 1944 to 52 percent in 1958, while truck revenues increased from 15 to 39 percent of total revenues in that period. Railroads continued to haul nearly twice as much freight as trucks by

1960, as measured in ton-miles (one ton of freight carried one mile), but trucks increasingly captured the market for short- and medium-length hauls of higher-value freight. Lower labor costs were not the primary reason for trucking's successful capture of market share in the 1950s and 1960s. Trucking firms did, on average, pay lower wages per employee than did the nation's railroads in the period. Despite paying higher wages per employee, however, railroads consistently enjoyed lower labor costs in proportion to their operating revenues. Railroad workers were also far more productive, in terms of ton-miles hauled per employee, in the postwar period. As the data in table B.6 (see appendix B) illustrate, railroads in 1960 had operating revenues 1.64 times as great as wage costs, while the ratio for trucking firms was 1.56. Railroads paid their employees better than trucking firms did in that year, but were also nearly 2.2 times as productive in terms of ton-miles carried per employee. Railroads would continue to outpace trucking firms in terms of operating efficiency and employee productivity through the end of the century.[23]

The efficiency and labor productivity of railroads could not, however, trump the flexible, customized service provided by trucking firms in the postwar "just-in-time" economy. Trucks, unlike railroads, could provide customized hauling for particular loads of goods—particularly for highly perishable (and more valuable) items such as frozen foods, milk, and beef. Trains hauled an incredibly diverse range of products, but even with specialized railcars, each load was just one unit among many with widely varying needs and destinations. Each semi-trailer, on the other hand, hauled only one commodity, directly from the point of origin to its destination. When shipped by truck, the commodity itself rather than the transporter's cost structure determined the type of hauling equipment used. Furthermore truckers could provide the specialized service needed to make sure that each load arrived quickly at its destination with little damage—an issue that, as we shall see below, was particularly relevant for highly perishable goods such as frozen foods. Trucks did not replace trains in the 1950s and 1960s; they simply replaced trains as the primary general-purpose mode of freight transportation, while trains became specialized carriers—primarily for bulky, low-value freight traveling long distances (such as coal). But although trucks would dominate general freight hauling after 1960, they would never capture the overwhelming market share and extraordinary revenue production that railroads had enjoyed at the start of the century. Whereas railroads of the early twentieth century had carried passengers as well as all types of freight, by the late twentieth century the nation's transportation system was highly fragmented. Trucks provided general freight transport, but railroads, pipelines, barges, and airplanes carried specialized freight loads, while airplanes and automobiles became the preferred modes of passenger travel. In 1970, motor carriers' revenues accounted for 1.34 percent of the gross national product, compared to the railroads' contribution of just over one percent of the GNP (see table B.6). Both figures paled in comparison to the railroads' 6.7 percent share of GNP in 1900.[24]

Trucking firms made their most impressive gains in agricultural and food hauling in the post–World War II period. By 1958, nearly 90 percent of all agricultural commodities traveled from farm to first market by truck. This was especially the case for highly perishable commodities such as milk, fruits and vegetables, and livestock. Take the case of cattle: in 1945, a little more than half—58 percent—of cattle arrived at livestock terminals by truck; by 1958, 88 percent did so, and a decade later nearly all cattle traveled to market in trucks. At the same time, trucks became the primary transportation mode for foodstuffs; in 1964, half of all foods (by volume) moved by truck. Trucks were especially important in moving meat, milk, cheese, and frozen foods, though railroads continued to be the primary transporters of less perishable goods such as grain mill products and canned foods. But the shift from trains to trucks in agricultural and food hauling was not an automatic consequence of the availability of good roads and big trucks, as if the technology itself were driving history. Instead the flexibility that trucking provided was crucial to the construction of Ezra Taft Benson's vision of a countryside populated by large-scale industrial farmers and nonunionized transportation and food industry workers. The example of the frozen food industry, one of the fastest-growing agribusinesses during Benson's years in office, provides a window into the ways in which the flexibility of country trucking helped transform Benson's antiunion, procorporate farm and food politics into material reality.[25]

Frozen Food and the Political Economy of Convenience

In January 1955, *Life* magazine published a photo spread on Seabrook Farms of New Jersey, calling it the "Biggest Vegetable Factory on Earth." The article sought to show *Life*'s readers how frozen vegetables started life on an industrial farm and ended up in suburban home freezers. For readers of *Life,* many of whom were new inhabitants of the booming postwar U.S. suburbs, the photo essay promoted a vision of a miraculous new food economy. Food processors like Nabisco had pioneered the packaging of cereals decades before, replacing anonymous barrels with branded boxes. But the postwar food economy brought *vegetables* in a box, processed at a megascale industrial plant, and delivered at low prices with guarantees of uniformity and "freshness" via self-serve supermarket shelves. Vegetables had once traveled to consumers either unprocessed or processed to the point of tastelessness; now they flowed through Ford-style assembly lines, but still emerged with their flavor and color preserved by freezers and plastic wraps. The *Life* article was just one entry in a long line of extravagant promises for frozen food. During the early years of the frozen food industry in the 1930s, frozen food promoters touted the product as a way for private industry to rationalize food production and marketing along Fordist lines—to make the luxury of, say, orange juice in the wintertime available to Americans of even modest means. In reality, however, it was not until the postwar expansion of long-haul trucking and new refrigeration technologies became available that frozen food processors achieved mass distribution of their product. The success of mass marketing in the 1950s gave frozen food a powerful political valence. Economists and policymakers in the era of agribusiness, including Ezra Taft Benson, hailed frozen food as a symbol of the power of "free enterprise" to trump New Dealism in the farm and food economy.[26]

The General Foods Corporation introduced Birds Eye brand frozen food as the "Most Revolutionary Idea in the History of Food" on March 8, 1930. Within seven years, Birds Eye frozen food could be purchased in over 3,000 retail and wholesale outlets in forty-five states. Expecting to make even fresh unbranded produce and seafood into profitable, branded, nationally distributed packages, General Foods invested heavily in the enterprise for several decades. The company also teamed up with Charles F. Seabrook, owner of the aforementioned southern New Jersey farm who earned the sobriquet "the Henry Ford of Agriculture" for his efforts to mass produce spinach; by 1938, Seabrook produced two-thirds of the nation's frozen vegetables. But despite the fact that General Foods pumped millions of dollars into the Birds Eye brand, while farmers such as Seabrook produced vegetables and fruits in mass quantities, frozen food was anything but a revolutionary industry through the 1940s—in fact, it remained dismally unprofitable until the 1950s. *Fortune* magazine wryly pointed out in 1946 that the "vast to-do" regarding frozen food involved "a line of merchandise whose total national tonnage does not yet equal that of sauerkraut and pickles."[27]

Despite the promises of a revolution in food production and marketing, frozen food fulfilled only one half of the Fordist equation of mass production until the mid-1950s. The industry could produce standardized commodities and branded goods in mass volumes, but could not move those goods to the masses. Even though a package of frozen food might leave the factory as a "perfect piece of merchandise" (as Edwin W. Williams, editor of *Quick Frozen Foods,* put it in 1939), too often it would arrive in the consumer's hands as either a product of dubious quality or at such a high price as to discourage mass consumption. "Distribution," opined Williams, "there's the rub." Distributing frozen food required technological systems of unprecedented scale, scope, and complexity—systems that simply did not exist in the 1930s. The refrigeration equipment required to maintain frozen food at extremely low temperatures was rare or nonexistent in most warehousing, transportation, and retail facilities. Although an extensive nationwide network of refrigeration existed, that distribution network had been built primarily for the movement of Chicago dressed beef, California produce, and midwestern butter and cheese—all products that required cool temperatures, not freezing temperatures. But in the 1950s, frozen food packers relied on new warehousing and transportation technologies to convince U.S. consumers that frozen orange juice and TV dinners were truly "luxuries for the masses." In doing so, frozen food producers contributed to the post–World War II transformation of the U.S. economy, as manufacturing took a back seat to distribution and retailing in driving economic growth and consumer abundance.[28]

The first step to achieving economically viable nationwide distribution was to find a cost-effective method for storing frozen food on its way to the supermarket. In the decade following World War II, warehousing underwent a dramatic if largely invisible revolution.[29] The change came as a response to the high cost of storage, a problem that was especially apparent in the frozen food industry. In 1946, the *Wall Street Journal* estimated that the cost of storing frozen food amounted to $0.025 per pound per month. This seems like a miniscule amount, but when frozen food packers computed the expense of holding several million tons at 3 cents per pound per year, the impact on price structures became dramatically apparent. Perhaps most important, frozen food warehousers were confronted by Benjamin Franklin's famous maxim that "time is money." The longer food remained frozen in a warehouse, the more it cost. This was partly due to the cost of electricity needed to run refrigeration equipment, but even more a result of the fact that a package of frozen food in storage represented tied-up capital. Not only was the stored package not earning profits for food processors in the marketplace, but its production required capital investment that accrued interest charges as it lay—quite literally a frozen asset.[30]

The postwar revolution in warehousing centered on achieving a steady flow of goods to minimize time in storage. Two key technologies lay at the heart of the new system: forklift trucks and standardized pallets, both of which were first used together on a large scale by the U.S. military during World War II. Forklifts and pallets made it possible to move and stack enormous quantities of goods at stunning speed, especially when compared to the previously widespread practice of moving irregularly shaped cartons with hand-operated two-wheeled trucks or dollies. As the navy discovered in a 1947 study, palletized loading could allow one man to accomplish in two hours a job that would otherwise take fourteen men four hours. Commercial warehousers quickly recognized the potential of palletization to reduce labor costs; with fewer workers required to move much greater quantities of goods, managers could limit their single largest category of operating expense while simultaneously minimizing the power of unions to dictate work conditions. As one distribution executive noted in 1968, "[Mechanical] equipment is never absent or temperamental and draws no fringe benefits." Palletization greatly amplified the power of an individual warehouse worker at the expense of his laid-off compatriots, but its impact on a warehouse's rate of throughput was just one part of a larger effort of mechanization. Ultimately warehouse designers and managers hoped to reconceptualize the warehouse as a place of dynamic movement rather than "dead" space. Continuous-flow principles of assembly line manufacturing were imported to the warehouse, with overhead or in-floor towlines and conveyor belts installed in single-story structures to move goods horizontally rather than vertically (as in older multistory buildings). One of the best examples of the modern continuous-flow warehouse was the 7.5 million cubic foot Alford Refrigerated Warehouse constructed outside Dallas, Texas, in 1949. "Keep it moving, preferably by machinery," was the motto of Fred F. Alford, who could brag that his new structure was not only the largest of its kind in the world, but was also capable of moving packages of frozen food from the "in" to the "out" dock without ever being touched by a human hand.[31]

The search for efficiency in frozen food warehousing gained new urgency in 1951 when Birds Eye announced a paradigm shift in its distribution policy. For the previous two decades, the Birds Eye division of General Foods Corporation had relied on independent wholesalers to distribute its products to retailers, but as of June 1951, the firm decided to sell as much as possible directly to supermarkets to drive up sales volume. Known as "direct selling," the new approach to frozen food distribution threatened to bypass independent wholesalers both economically and literally. Economically independents were increasingly excluded from getting their fingers in the markup pie; whereas distributor markups prior to 1950 averaged around 30 percent, by 1954 the average wholesale markup had dropped to 16 percent. Most large chain store buyers could get a cheaper price by buying directly from a processor like Birds Eye. Wholesalers were also literally bypassed in the distribution chain, as both packers and supermarkets built their own warehouses (or leased space in existing warehouses) to gain control of distribution logistics. The new machinery of movement radically restructured time as a factor in the cost of distributing frozen food, as the traditional role of the warehouse as a place of storage was increasingly replaced by the warehouse as a place of movement. The warehouse "middleman" either had to adopt the new creed of speed or else get out of the supply chain. These techniques, first developed in the food distribution industry, would later play a key role in the business models of discount retailers such as Wal-Mart, helping to drive down consumer prices for everything from clothing to televisions.[32]

Long-haul refrigerated trucking tied the dynamic warehouses of the streamlined frozen food industry to the supermarkets of booming suburbia. With supermarkets and warehouses dedicated to high-volume, high-turnover throughput of frozen food by the mid-1950s, the speed of transportation among the nodes in the distribution network became more essential than ever before. Frozen food packers relied on trucking to fundamentally reshape the economic geography of production in the early 1950s. Before then, the majority of frozen food factories were located on either the East Coast or the West Coast, primarily in New York, New Jersey, Oregon, Washington, and California. Beginning in 1944, however, Birds Eye began a five-year program of building and buying plants throughout the country, following the expanding federally funded highway system into the rural Midwest and South. Birds Eye's managers sought to supply their factories with raw materials from "widely dispersed" sites in order to be "practically weatherproof." Selection of new factory sites was far from random; Birds Eye and other major packers sought to gain access to harvests in places where the environment—including not only weather and soil conditions, but also the cost of land and labor—suited the production of particular fruits and vegetables at the lowest possible cost. Furthermore the climate and soil conditions at those sites would ideally allow harvests to fall in different times of the year so that the firm's factories could maintain a steady flow of production, allowing popular items to be marketed throughout the year, while simultaneously minimizing the time any one particular lot of frozen food had to spend in storage.[33]

In order to realize the advantages of decentralized production, however, packers had to rely on flexible transportation to move their products from farm regions to suburban consumers. One of the great economic promises of freezing food was the theoretical ability to remove perishability as a factor in distribution, allowing agricultural production to take place where and when it could be done most cheaply, yet permit placement of those goods on the market where and when they would bring the best prices. With packers moving to decentralized production after the war, the distance between producers and consumers expanded quite dramatically, increasing the necessity for reliable long-haul transportation. Railroads might have seemed the logical choice for long-distance transportation, because the unit cost of moving goods over distances of several hundred miles or more has always been lower for rails than for trucks, primarily because of lower fuel costs. But at the same time as frozen food packers began decentralizing their production, they were also faced with an increasing decentralization of consumption as Americans and their supermarkets moved into suburbs following World War II. Furthermore the sprawling one-story warehouses supplying these suburban centers of consumption required large plots of land, which could only be had cheaply in suburban or rural areas. This often meant the new warehouses had only highways, not rails, connecting them to their customers. In the postwar geography of suburban consumption, shipping by truck became necessary to move frozen food from rural areas of production to the suburban areas where warehousers, supermarkets, and consumers were located. Geography did not dictate a shift to shipment by truck, but for frozen food packers seeking to distribute their products as widely as possible, trucks became an increasingly attractive mode of transportation despite the higher cost compared to railroads. As a North Dakota food processor noted in a 1963 survey, "Trucking can go anywhere. Rail can't."[34]

Trucks also provided a form of technological flexibility—mechanical refrigeration—that proved essential for the frozen food industry to cultivate a mass market for its goods in the postwar period. Mechanical refrigeration became cheap, reliable, and widely available in truck trailers in the late 1940s. "Reefers," as the devices were known, were not new; an African American inventor named Frederick McKinley Jones had developed a mechanical refrigerator small and lightweight enough to be used in truck trailers in 1938. After establishing the Thermo King Corporation with a business partner, Jones sold thousands of his reefer units just before the war, especially to meat haulers anxious to reduce the spoilage common with the use of ice. The popularity of the first Thermo Kings came from their ability to provide truck drivers with an unprecedented degree of control over the temperature maintained in a trailer. Mechanical refrigerators work by forced convection of air past coils filled with compressed refrigerant; unlike ice or cold plate systems, a mechanical refrigerator does not merely absorb ambient heat but continually circulates cold air through a space. As a result, a mechanical system's degree of refrigeration is controllable and adaptable to multiple conditions (such as either cold or hot outside temperatures). Ice, on the other hand, refrigerates by absorbing heat at a more or less constant rate; temperatures can only be controlled by changing the quantity of ice used. Shippers had long recognized the theoretical advantages of mechanical refrigeration; the Pacific Fruit Growers Express company had been working on a mechanical unit to be used in railcars since the early 1930s. Until the arrival of the Thermo King, however, such efforts were impeded by the expense of constructing a unit that was simultaneously lightweight, compact, and yet able to operate reliably under the constant strain of vibration experienced in transit.[35]

With the release of the Thermo King Model R in 1949, frozen food shippers gained the power to maintain unprecedented control over their products in transit. Prior to the Model R, Thermo Kings had been designed and used primarily to keep meat and produce in the 35° to 45°F range, not to keep frozen food near 0°F. The Model R packed a more powerful 4-cylinder gasoline engine than previous Thermo Kings, allowing the compressor to produce extremely low temperatures. This engine was coupled to an automatic electric starter, allowing for constant operation of the unit's compressor even when the truck engine was not running. Controlled by a thermostat, the electric starter allowed a steady temperature to be maintained by starting, stopping, and restarting the compressor motor as needed. As a result, the Model R could not only produce very low temperatures, but it could do so by operating its engine only when needed to achieve the desired temperature. Furthermore the Model R incorporated Frederick McKinley Jones's latest innovation—a feedback device that kept the unit's engine running at peak efficiency at multiple settings. With these innovations, the Model R needed only a relatively small amount of fuel to keep an entire load of frozen food at or near 0°F. In a 1957 study, for instance, a group of agricultural engineers found that on a shipment of frozen food from Waseca, Minnesota, to Jersey City, New Jersey, a mechanical reefer used $20 of fuel and maintained a steady temperature of 0°F in transit, while an iced railcar used $214 of ice and salt with temperature spikes up to 14.6°F. As a consequence, frozen food packers quickly found mechanical reefers to be the cheapest and most reliable form of refrigerated transportation available.[36]

Mechanical refrigeration was cheaper and more reliable than ice, but even so the cost of shipping frozen food over very long distances by truck usually made rail shipment more economical. For instance, a survey of frozen food processors in 1955 found that the primary reason shippers chose rails over trucks was the simple fact that it was "cheaper"—in some cases, truck rates from West Coast factories to markets east of Chicago were as much as 62 percent higher than rail rates. But taking advantage of mechanical refrigeration necessitated the use of tractor-trailer transportation in the late 1940s and early 1950s, because railroads proved reluctant to adopt mechanical reefers. The Fruit Growers Express Company teamed up with Frigidaire to deploy the first large-scale fleet of 102 diesel-powered mechanical reefer railcars in 1951, but even four years later the nation's railroads had only 934 mechanical units in operation. As late as 1958, mechanical reefers represented less than 2 percent of the total number of refrigerated rail cars in use. Railroad managers were reluctant to invest $20,000 for each reefer car in the 1950s because, for three-quarters of a century, railroads had sunk significant capital into ice manufacturing and harvesting plants. Converting to mechanical reefers would make the rails' ice-producing infrastructure obsolete. Many trucking firms, on the other hand, had just entered the transportation business following the war's end, had no capital sunk in ice-making systems, and saw investment in specialized reefer equipment as a means to gain customers. In 1949, for instance, while railroads had no commercially available mechanical reefers, approximately 11,000 mechanical units were installed in the nation's trucks. If frozen food packers wanted to mass distribute frozen foods to suburban supermarkets without incurring significant losses in quality, truck transportation was essential.[37]

By the mid-1950s, the integration of long-haul reefer trucking and modern warehousing significantly reduced the cost of frozen food distribution, paving the way for mass consumption of the product for the first time in history. In 1953, truckers using mechanical refrigeration hauled the vast majority of frozen food—72 percent of all shipments by volume. Four years later, when that proportion had risen to 77.7 percent, an industry observer noted that "the only proper way [to distribute frozen foods] is in a refrigerated truck." Trucking tied together a distribution system characterized by decentralized mass production, low-margin direct selling to suburban supermarkets, and minimal time in transit and storage. The combination allowed frozen food packers to achieve reliable profits by selling high volumes on thin margins. Frozen food finally became price-competitive with canned food in the early 1950s. In 1953, for the first time in history, an average package of frozen peas could be purchased for less than a comparable can of peas. Improved distribution not only brought lower prices, but helped convince consumers that frozen food was a good value. Through the 1930s and 1940s, frozen food packers had faced considerable resistance from consumers who associated quick-freezing with spoilage, often with good reason. By shifting to a distribution system based on speedy movement and reliable refrigeration, packers were able to change many consumers' minds about the quality of the product. From 1949 to 1956, consumer purchases of frozen food expanded dramatically, accounting for $2 billion or 3.93 percent of total food store sales in the latter year. Frozen food outpaced the sales growth of all other food items in this period. This increased consumption came at the expense of fresh and canned fruits and vegetables. Although overall consumption of fruits and vegetables dropped in the period, consumption of frozen produce increased by a remarkable 170 percent. Especially popular were peas, green beans, lima beans, asparagus, and spinach, as well as orange juice concentrate. Advertisements of the period proclaimed frozen food to be "fresher than fresh," offering consumers a convenient and nutritious product at a low price. Improvements in distribution made such claims more than just empty rhetoric.[38]

Consumer acceptance of frozen food as a "convenience food" carried significant implications for the political economy of agribusiness in the era of Ezra Taft Benson. Marketers increasingly found consumers "more than willing to pay extra" for frozen food that provided consistent flavor and required only minimal preparation time. As one frozen food marketer put it in 1957: "Mama buys frozen foods not because they are cheaper but because of their superior taste, quality, and convenience." And the new frozen food items marketed in the 1950s were convenient, as packers unveiled a string of products to capitalize on consumer demand for simple foods that could be easily prepared. Frozen orange juice concentrate paved the way; after 1948, when Minute Maid began mass-marketing the product first developed by USDA researchers under an army contract during the war, frozen orange juice quickly became the nation's favorite breakfast drink. Birds Eye unveiled the "fish stick" in 1951 after seven years of research and development to assure consumer acceptance. The work paid off, as consumption of fish sticks rose from 7 million pounds in 1953 to 44 million pounds a year later. Pot pies, TV dinners, french fries, and pizzas all achieved similar instant success in the mass market over the next four years. Sales of potatoes for use in frozen french fries, for example, increased 1,800 percent between 1946 and 1956, driven largely by the rise of the McDonald's fast food chain—the most recognizable symbol of Americans' desire for convenience food in the period. It would seem easy to write off french fries and fish sticks as examples of consumers being duped by corporate marketers, but evidence suggests that consumers understood such foods to be truly convenient. Especially among working-class families in which women performed the "double duty" of working for pay outside the home and working without wages inside the home, consumers who bought frozen food such as pot pies or TV dinners generally did so because they appreciated the speed of preparation and believed that freezing provided the most nutrition and flavor for the money. For instance, a 1957 marketing survey of Birmingham, Alabama, steelworker families found that working-class purchases of frozen food were increasing at a much faster rate than purchases by higher-income groups.[39]

The most "convenient" aspect of frozen food, however, may have been its potential to restructure the political economy of food in the 1950s. Ever since the passage of the Agricultural Adjustment Act in 1933, farm policymakers had sought politically acceptable means for getting consumers to pay more money for their food products to help stabilize farm incomes. Through the Depression and World War II, organized consumers and economic liberals had fought to keep New Deal farm policies from driving up the retail price of food, with only mixed success. But when postwar consumers willingly paid higher prices for frozen food for its convenience, they helped push pricing decisions "downstream" in the agrofood economy. That is, food processors and supermarket managers gained increasing power to determine the prices paid to farmers and by consumers, rather than having such decisions made "upstream" by farmers or government planners. Consequently food processors and super-markets could boost their profits significantly even when consumers believed frozen food to be a good value. Consumers did, in fact, pay handsomely for the convenience of having some of the work of food preparation transferred out of the kitchen and into the factory. In 1939, the value added to the food economy by manufacturing amounted to $3.5 billion; by 1954, that amount had risen to $13.5 billion. Even after adjustment for inflation, consumers paid an additional $4 billion per year for convenience in the latter year, prompting two agricultural economists to observe that "it is obvious that [processed] food does cost more." But because consumers proved willing to pay for conven-ience, there was no sustained political protest from consumer groups about the fairness of price or the problem of monopoly in frozen food as had occurred in the milk and beef industries since the early twentieth century. The actual cost of convenience foods was further masked by the rapid decline of food costs as a percentage of family budgets in the postwar period; in 1947, U.S. families spent on average nearly 24 percent of their disposable income on food, but a decade later spent only 18 percent on food. Consumers spent more in ab-solute terms on food in 1957 than they did in 1947, but food costs remained low relative to increasing household expenditures on other consumer goods such as automobiles, televisions, and the many other conveniences of postwar suburban living. Furthermore the farmers who provided the raw materials that allowed frozen food packers and supermarkets to profit from the manufacture of convenience never took political action against the increasingly "down-stream" economy. Because frozen food packers bought agricultural products in large volumes and on contract, farmers valued the security of selling their pro-duce at a fixed, guaranteed price. Much like the price supports of New Deal farm policies, food processor contracts assured some measure of economic sta-bility—if only for the largest farmers, such as Seabrook Farms, willing to in-vest in the capital equipment necessary to produce farm commodities in mass quantities. Quick freezing would consequently appear to agricultural policy-makers in the 1950s to be an ideal solution to one version of the "farm prob-lem," simultaneously bringing high prices to produce farmers and high value to consumers without the need for significant state intervention in either pro-duction or marketing decisions within the economy.[40]

The upshot of this was that in the 1950s the Department of Agriculture cooperated closely with frozen food packers to consolidate their power in the food economy. Secretary of Agriculture Ezra Taft Benson was one of the most avid supporters of quick freezing as a solution to the surplus problem.

Speaking to a group of frozen food industry leaders in 1954, Benson congratulated them on their "spectacular achievements" in "revolutioniz[ing] the marketing of oranges." As Benson saw it, quick freezing replaced seasonal marketing of perishable commodities with "year-around markets for products in essentially fresh form." As the frozen orange juice example took hold among other fruits and vegetables, Benson predicted the achievement of "real stability of prices of so many highly perishable foods which traditionally sold for a song when the markets were glutted at harvest time." Such a statement may seem inconsequential in terms of agricultural policy goals, given its context as a laudatory speech at an industry banquet, but this was exactly the point. Benson's speech was not a statement of a new governmental approach to the surplus problem, but a pat on the frozen food industry's back for taking care of the problem themselves, without the need for government regulation of production or marketing. Benson literally showed his appreciation by presenting a certificate of achievement to Charles G. Mortimer, president of General Foods Corporation. But Benson offered more than just a plaque to the frozen food industry. As he continued his speech, Benson explained his faith in government research in science and technology, when undertaken "in close cooperation" with industry, to achieve the surplus-reducing goals of New Deal-era agricultural policies—without the policies. In particular, Benson offered to the frozen food industry the services of agricultural engineers and scientists working on improved methods for "processing, transportation, distribution, and storage of frozen foods." As Benson saw it, state-funded research on specific technological problems of the frozen food industry could create not only higher farm incomes, but also industrial stability.[41]

Perhaps most significantly, bureaucrats in Ezra Taft Benson's USDA pursued an ambitious deregulatory agenda in the realm of food transportation politics. Because the cost of transportation played such a crucial role in the profit structure and mass distribution capabilities of frozen food processors, any change in transportation regulatory structures could have a transformative effect on the industry. In particular, agribusiness-friendly economists in the USDA understood that unregulated, nonunionized trucking could put significant downward pressure on food prices through cut-rate competition with regulated, unionized freight truckers and railroads. The crowning triumph of this effort to inject more "flexibility" into the highway transportation system came in 1956 in a bizarre legal-ontological debate over whether a frozen chicken was in fact a chicken.

The chicken quandary arose after a series of battles between the Department of Agriculture and the Interstate Commerce Commission in the mid-1950s over the agricultural exemption clause of the 1935 Motor Carrier Act. As explained in the previous chapter, the USDA's efforts to broaden the exemption clause of the act took shape during the tenure of Charles F. Brannan, when Department of Agriculture bureaucrats sought to help small, decentralized trucking firms haul agricultural commodities to and from anywhere, at rates of their own choosing, without first receiving authority from the ICC. In the case of frozen food, the USDA's legal team came to believe in the mid-1950s that if truckers hauling frozen goods were exempt from ICC regulation, they would be able to provide geographically flexible service that would benefit both farmers and processors. As Mark L. Keith of the Farm Bureau Cooperative Association stated the farmers' interest in exemption in 1957, farmers selling perishable products to frozen food packers required "complete flexibility of truck service . . . so that trucks [can] move from producing areas to any market dictated by the 'unpredictable' forces of supply and demand." In other words, farmers wanted trucks to be available on short notice to haul produce to whichever processor was offering the best price at any particular moment. For regulated truckers who were not exempt from ICC regulations, this was often not possible, considering that they might not have the ICC-sanctioned operating authority to haul loads to or from certain states. And in any case, the regulated trucking firms also generally paid union-scale wages to their organized drivers. The "flexibility" of long-haul trucking was thus as much a product of political maneuvering as it was of the technological ability of a truck to travel anywhere at high speed.[42]

Some processors, meanwhile, had also sought help from the USDA to make the transportation of frozen food exempt from ICC regulation. Like farmers, some frozen food packers saw the geographical flexibility of exempt trucking as a way to minimize the risks of selling semiperishable goods in an unpredictable market. For instance, in the early 1950s a group of Florida orange juice processors called on the USDA to help them solve a growing transportation crisis. Few Florida processors had access to sufficient cold storage warehouse space at the time, meaning that packers often had to search far and wide for a warehouse capable of storing cans of orange juice during busy processing seasons. Even when the juice processors were able to ship their products directly up the coast to the major consuming centers of the Northeast, they generally found that truckers did not have operating authorities that would allow them to bring back a cost-reducing backhaul of, say, meat or dairy products. Both of these situations could be easily fixed, the processors told the USDA's legal team in 1953, if the truck transportation of frozen orange juice were exempted from ICC regulation. Exempt truckers could haul juice to any available warehouse space without going through the expensive and time-consuming process of receiving additional geographic operating authority from the ICC. In this particular case, the USDA's legal team successfully petitioned the ICC to grant temporary authority to eight Florida trucking firms to haul frozen orange juice. At the same time, the USDA hoped to find a more permanent expansion of trucking services available to frozen food processors.[43]

The opportunity arose in 1955, when Frozen Food Express, a regulated trucking company based in Texas, sued the ICC in federal district court. Frozen Food Express argued that the ICC was usurping its regulatory authority to deprive the firm of the right to haul frozen poultry to and from all points within the United States. The Department of Agriculture's solicitor general signed on to the case as an intervening plaintiff, seeing an opportunity to broaden the agricultural exemption to include frozen food. The Federal District Court for the Southern District of Texas decided against the plaintiffs in 1955, but Frozen Food Express and the USDA appealed the decision, bringing it before the Supreme Court in the spring of 1956. In the hearings before the Supreme Court, USDA lawyers argued that a frozen chicken maintained a "continuing substantial identity" with an unfrozen chicken. In simpler words, if a frozen chicken still looked like a chicken, it was still a chicken. Because the chicken had not taken on a new name or identity through the process of freezing in the way that, say, crude oil became polyurethane, the chicken was not "manufactured" and thus should be exempt from ICC regulation. Perhaps surprisingly, the Supreme Court agreed with the USDA, stating that "A chicken that has been killed and dressed is still a chicken. . . . We cannot conclude that this processing which merely makes the chicken marketable turns it into a 'manufactured' commodity." This decision was soon made applicable to nearly all frozen foods in November 1956, when the Supreme Court affirmed a lower court decision that had granted the Home Transfer and Storage trucking firm the right to haul frozen fruits and vegetables without first receiving ICC authority.[44]

As a consequence of these two cases, the ICC declared all frozen food to be exempt from economic regulation in late 1956, providing a template for later efforts to deregulate the entire trucking industry. One year after the Supreme Court's decisions in the *Frozen Food Express* and *Home Transfer and Storage* cases, over half of all frozen food shippers began relying on exempt truckers to haul their products. The cost of shipping frozen food dropped rapidly in response to the exemption decision. Two USDA economists, James Snitzler and Robert Byrne, found that in the two years following exemption, motor carrier rates on frozen food shipment dropped by 19 percent overall, and up to 36 percent on certain frozen items, even as railroad rates rose from 6 to 14 percent. This finding, as we shall see in chapter 7, would be cited in the 1970s by both neopopulist truckers and neoliberal economists as clear evidence that deregulation benefited both producers and consumers. In fighting to broaden the applicability of the agricultural exemption in the 1950s, Ezra Taft Benson's USDA created a template and a justification for the deregulation of highway transportation several decades before Jimmy Carter and Edward M. Kennedy pushed the Motor Carrier Act of 1980 through Congress.[45]

The time was not yet ripe, however, for full deregulation of the trucking industry. Outside the world of agribusiness transportation in the mid-1950s, relatively little support existed for efforts to limit the ICC's authority. In 1955, for instance, Secretary of Commerce Sinclair Weeks called for limited deregulation of railroad and trucking freight rates, intending to help railroads compete more effectively with truckers. The well-organized American Trucking Associations, however, waged a massive publicity campaign in the nation's newspapers, attacking the railroads as "monopolies" bent on gouging U.S. consumers during a period of inflation. Supported by the ICC—which saw the Weeks proposal as an attack on its institutional authority—and by the Teamsters—who denounced rate deregulation as a threat to their hard-won wage gains since 1935—the ATA wielded its lobbying power in Congress to crush the Weeks proposal.[46]

Even within agribusiness hauling, not all shippers agreed that the "free-market" approach to trucking was as beneficial as USDA economists declared it to be. Some frozen food shippers determined in 1957 that exempt hauling, rather than providing needed flexibility, posed serious threats to their industry. Ray V. Harron, traffic manager at Birds Eye, decided that even if exempt haulers provided more flexible service, regulated carriers provided better equipment. As a general rule, regulated truckers were larger firms with greater financial stability, able to invest in the latest refrigeration equipment. Good refrigeration was no small matter in an industry that for decades had found it difficult to deliver a high-quality product to consumers. By 1958 several large packers had decided that exemption had gone too far. Led by Birds Eye, Welch's Grape Juice, and Stokely-Van Camp, frozen food packers joined up with the ICC and regulated common carriers to petition Congress to amend the Motor Carrier Act to exclude frozen food from the agricultural exemption clause. Ironically one of the common carriers joining in the effort was Frozen Food Express— the firm that had initiated the court case that led to the Supreme Court's definition of a frozen chicken as a nonmanufactured chicken. Apparently the firm's chairman of the board, Cyrus B. Weller, had found that a year's worth of exemption had brought too much competition into the field of frozen food hauling. Whereas Frozen Food Express had previously argued that a frozen chicken was not manufactured, in testifying before Congress Weller argued that "Frozen fruits and vegetables are not farm commodities. They are the products of a substantially centralized, highly competitive industry characterized by large commercial firms." As Weller and the ICC saw it, frozen foods were manufactured goods, and so should be forced to travel to supermarket consumers via ICC-regulated carriers.[47]

Other groups who maintained a stake in a sound regulatory structure also contested the USDA's efforts to expand the agricultural exemption to all frozen foods. The American Trucking Associations, the Teamsters, and the nation's railroads were particularly concerned. Howard G. Freas of the ICC testified before the House Interstate Commerce Committee that the USDA's efforts to broaden the agricultural exemption threatened to destabilize the entire transportation industry. The exemption that Congress had originally intended to allow farmers to truck their products to market with minimal oversight was becoming, according to Freas, a free pass for agribusinesses to ship processed foods via "gypsy" truckers who would drive regulated carriers out of business. The American Trucking Associations agreed, informing William Crow at the USDA that the department's transportation work, which had previously served only farmers, was now "serving processors and manufacturers." The USDA admitted that food processors benefited most from the exemption, but insisted that farmers also gained from the flexibility of just-in-time transportation services. As George Dice, a USDA transportation economist, informed Congress: "There can be no question but that efficiencies and economies which are injected into the marketing process at any point affect producers [i.e., farmers]." The Farm Bureau agreed, stating the antiunion implications of exemption quite clearly by arguing that exempt hauling prevented the Teamsters from instituting "the same featherbedding and make-work practices that add costs to rail and truck common carrier operations," practices the Farm Bureau saw driving up the price of food for consumers while depressing farm prices. Nonetheless, with the two largest frozen food packers (Birds Eye and Stokely-Van Camp) calling for an end to the exemption, the passage of an amendment to the Motor Carrier Act was inevitable. The amendment came as part of the Transportation Act of 1958, which proclaimed frozen food to be ineligible under the agricultural exemption clause of the Motor Carrier Act of 1935.[48]

This was the first and last setback the USDA would ever be dealt in its efforts to use deregulatory politics to boost agribusiness firms' marketing power and limit the power of the Teamsters Union in the food economy. The episode demonstrated that "flexibility" was itself a flexible concept. For the economists and bureaucrats who served in Ezra Taft Benson's Department of Agriculture, "flexibility" represented a high degree of competition, even chaos, in the transportation industries, characterized by thousands of small trucking firms unfettered by ICC restrictions or by union organizers. Frozen food packers found significant drawbacks to the system, however, after experiencing this kind of flexibility for a year and a half. They appreciated the lower rates, faster service, and unrestricted point-to-point delivery of deregulated trucking. But some found that "flexibility" entailed reliance on carriers who often used ineffective refrigeration equipment and were likely to go out of business at any moment— the kind of truckers that *Nation* writer Alfred Maund had labeled "sharecroppers" in 1953 and that Teamster president Daniel Tobin had called "trash" in the early 1930s. Although frozen food packers agreed with Ezra Taft Benson that transportation costs had to be driven down—and also that the Teamsters should have less power in the food transportation industry—frozen food businessmen did not agree with agricultural economists who believed the "free market" was the most effective means of achieving more efficient transportation. Just as Progressive-era and New Deal-era big businessmen had come to accept certain government regulations as essential tools for achieving business and labor stability, the post–World War II frozen food packers who participated in the Eisenhower-era "corporate commonwealth" expected and even desired some degree of state intervention in the economy.[49]

By the end of Ezra Taft Benson's time in office, a great irony of the agricultural exemption clause of the 1935 Motor Carrier Act had been exposed. Farm-state congressmen had intended the exemption clause to help family farmers haul their own products to market, but by the end of the 1950s, the loophole had become a powerful tool for agribusiness corporations to drive down the labor costs of marketing processed foods. As of 1961, the Interstate Commerce Commission estimated that at least 37,000 exempt motor carriers operated more than 199,000 vehicles in the nation. Because these unregulated carriers did not need to report their activities to federal agencies, the ICC could not determine either the exact number or their geographical location or even what these truckers were hauling. Reports from ICC field officers, though, confirmed that much of the "gray area" of unregulated truck transportation was undertaken by drivers who illegally abused the agricultural exemption clause of the 1935 Motor Carrier Act to avoid regulatory oversight. The American Trucking Associations estimated that as of 1960 unregulated motor carriers hauled two-thirds of the nation's highway tonnage (see table B.5 in appendix B). In January 1961, a special congressional study group on national transportation policy condemned the USDA's efforts over the previous decade to expand unregulated trucking at the expense of the stable, unionized, regulated general freight trucking force. "Much is made of the benefits of motor carrier exemptions to the small farmer or fisherman whose personal labor directly produces our perishable foods," noted the study group. "Less is said about the benefits of bargain [trucking] rates to the corporations that assemble, process, and distribute these foodstuffs." Acknowledging that exempt long-haul trucking provided needed flexibility in terms of geographical reach and on-demand service for U.S. agriculture, the study group nonetheless questioned whether "these [exempt] carriers represent a more economic means of transportation or . . . a cutrate, sweatshop operation" that served large agribusiness corporations more effectively than either family farmers or independent truck drivers.[50]

While the case of frozen foods demonstrated that at least some agribusinesses realized that the "flexibility" of a hypercompetitive trucking market based on sweated labor might not redound to their economic benefit, two other agribusinesses of the 1950s and 1960s would accept the free-market ideology of the USDA's transportation economists. In the beef and milk industries—the subjects of chapters 5 and 6—corporate agribusinesses would come to see exempt trucks piloted by antiunion "asphalt cowboys" as effective tools for dealing a fatal blow to economic liberalism.

CHAPTER FIVE

Beef Trusts and Asphalt Cowboys

In October 1953, Bob Douthitt of Huntington Park, California, penned an angry diatribe to Secretary of Agriculture Ezra Taft Benson. The retail price of beef was skyrocketing even as cattle farmers saw their profits plummeting, and Douthitt was certain Benson could do something about it: "Men who work for a living can't pay such prices. . . . What can you do between the cattle men and the Butchers? Get busy or get out [of office]." Benson ordered economists in the Agricultural Marketing Service to investigate the beef price spread. As the study progressed, both farmers and consumer advocates encouraged the USDA to consider the problem of monopoly power. A Georgia cattle producer informed Benson, "There is too much spread between the price paid for live cattle and the price of steak and roast in grocery stores. Somebody is getting a heck of a profit! Didn't Swift show a 12 million dollar gain in NET profits this year over last?" The Brooklyn Tenant Welfare and Consumer Councils saw the high cost of meat as a case of "obvious price fixing" and demanded a "thorough investigation" of meatpackers.[1]

Even in the probusiness political climate of the Eisenhower years, the political problem of monopoly in beefpacking continued. The consumers and livestock raisers who had supported massive state intervention in the meat economy during World War II called upon Benson to pursue the antitrust powers granted to his office by Congress back in 1921. But Benson, under the advice of his like-minded undersecretary, Earl Butz, refused to blame the high price of meat on packers' profits. Instead Benson declared that strong labor unions and high wages were driving up the price of beef. In particular, he believed the 1955 successes of unionized meatpacking workers in gaining a $50 million wage boost had pushed up the cost of processing meat while forcing cattlemen to "tak[e] lower prices for meat animals." If meatpackers had the tools to drive down labor costs, consumer prices would drop without driving down farm prices. Benson would promote market forces, not state intervention, as the solution to the problem of monopoly in the beef economy.[2]

In fact agribusiness did gain the tools to introduce a radically transformed "free market" to beef production and marketing in the 1950s and 1960s, but it was not the Big Four packers who benefited. Much as Sam Walton's Arkansas-based discount retail store would launch an all-out war on old-line retailers Sears and Montgomery Ward in the 1960s, a group of upstart beefpackers located deep in the rural countryside relied upon trucking technology in the 1950s and 1960s to overthrow the Big Four by offering remarkably low-priced beef to U.S. consumers. Reliable mechanically refrigerated truck trailers made it possible for these new meatpackers, especially the viciously antiunion firm IBP, to bypass the railroad-based distribution system that had allowed the big packers to maintain their monopoly power since the beginning of the dressed beef trade in the 1880s. As beef prices dropped for U.S. consumers, while cattlemen raked in record profits by feeding cattle on outdoor industrial feedlots, the age-old problem of monopoly lost its political thrust. The postwar beefpackers satisfied two of the key goals of New Deal-era economic liberalism—low consumer prices and high farm prices—without the need for significant state intervention, particularly antitrust action, in the beef economy. In constructing a new "Jungle" in the feedlot country of the southern plains, however, firms such as IBP crippled the strong unions that had achieved high wages and decent working conditions for workers in the Big Four's urban factories after the organizing drives of the late 1930s. The new beef empire became a standard bearer for all that was considered "American" about industrial agriculture by the 1970s—free enterprise, high farm prices, low worker wages, and low consumer prices. The truck drivers who helped make this system work were ideal representatives of this contradictory economic culture that paid homage to a sense of independence reminiscent of the open range of the Old West while practicing a winner-take-all approach to the spoils of industrial capitalism.

Reefers and Cinderblocks

Mechanically refrigerated trailers, or reefers, allowed independent packers to bypass the Big Four's rail-based distribution system in the 1950s, setting in motion a decades-long restructuring of the nation's beef economy. Once reliable reefer units came into widespread use in the postwar period, small meatpackers could ship fresh beef carcasses directly to wholesalers. The distribution of beef increasingly relied on independent firms called "breakers," "boners," and "peddlers," rather than packer-owned branch houses. These firms delivered partially broken-down carcasses to institutional buyers—restaurants, schools, hospitals, and supermarkets—who wanted specific cuts of beef in quantity, rather than the entire carcasses delivered by the Big Four to their own branch houses. The monopoly power of big packers crumbled as independent wholesalers more than doubled in number from the 1930s through the early 1950s, even as the Big Four shut down the branch houses anchoring the rail-based distribution system. Small meatpackers who did not own branch houses could now effectively compete with the Big Four in interstate trade without having to invest in expensive capital equipment. Trucking firms cooperated in this antimonopoly crusade, providing reefers to move the carcasses from plants to wholesalers. Unlike the railroads of the late nineteenth century that refused to provide refrigerated railcars for dressed beef packers, truckers in the postwar period readily purchased the necessary equipment for the new wholesaling industry. Reefer fleets rapidly expanded over the next two decades; by 1963, trucks hauled 60 percent of the nation's refrigerated meat. As a consequence, beefpacking would undergo an economic and geographical transformation in the 1960s that witnessed the demise of the Big Four packers, the decimation of their unionized workforces, and the decline of midwestern cities such as Chicago and Omaha as central players in the beef economy.[3]

Direct shipping via reefer trailers made it possible in the 1950s for small independent packers to move away from the old meatpacking metropolises and locate plants nearer to rural cattle-producing regions. These packers built single-story plants, derided by the big Chicago packers as "cinderblocks" (a reference to the cheapness of their construction) in smaller cities and towns of the rural Midwest, West, and South (see figure 5.1). Thousands of firms adopted this relocation strategy in the late 1940s and 1950s, with one of the most successful companies being Hygrade Food Products, which built or acquired slaughtering plants in the 1940s and 1950s in places like Vernon, Texas; Storm Lake, Iowa; Mishawaka, Indiana; Orangeburg, South Carolina; and Hialeah, Florida. Many of the facilities that companies like Hygrade purchased were former plants of the independent slaughterers who had used illicit practices to gain market share during the price control efforts of World War II and the Korean War. The cinderblock operators found rural workers willing to work for much lower wages than the employees of the big urban packers, most of whom had been successfully organized by labor unions such as the CIO Packinghouse Workers Organizing Committee in the 1930s and 1940s. A 1966 government study found that average hourly wages at rural single-plant firms were seventy-five cents lower than those of workers at multiplant urban firms. The lowly reefer truck allowed between two and three thousand small, rural meatpackers to undermine the Big Four's monopoly power more effectively than any antitrust legislation had ever done.[4]

Faced with their first real competition since the late nineteenth century, the Big Four meatpackers saw their profits and market share greatly decline in the 1950s. In 1956, the Big Four slaughtered only 30 percent of the nation's cattle, down from 50 percent in 1920. This decline in slaughter occurred even

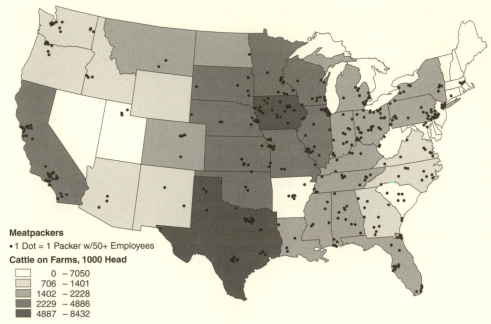

Figure 5.1. Meatpacker Locations and Beef Cattle on Farms in 1959.
Beefpacking decentralized both economically and geographically in the 1950s, as small "cinder-block" factories moved into rural cattle-feeding areas, particularly in the Midwest and Southeast (*Sources*: U.S. Bureau of the Census, *County Business Patterns* 1959; USDA, National Agricultural Statistics Database).

as the nation's demand for beef increased, meaning that the Big Four became increasingly unable to maintain even their original sales volume. In 1955 *Business Week* reported on the dour state of the big packers, pointing out that none of them had earned a net return of more than 1 percent on sales after taxes in the previous three years; most U.S. companies at the time counted on 5 or 6 percent to remain in business. Desperate to regain market share, Swift petitioned a federal district court in 1956 to be allowed to violate the Consent Decree of 1920 by selling meat at the retail level. This effort failed when Judge Julius Hoffman declared that although the Big Four had lost significant market share, they were still large enough to warrant continued compliance with the decree. But if Judge Hoffman believed that a monopoly still existed in meat marketing, the Big Four could not have disagreed more. The growth of trucking over the previous three decades had made it possible for smaller competitors to steadily erode the power of the big packers to control either the price of cattle in stockyards or the retail cost of beef. The Beef Trust had effectively dissolved as a material fact and as a matter of concern for cattlemen, consumers, or the USDA.[5]

Over the next several decades, however, trucking would ironically play a central role in developments that eventually led to a reemergent monopoly in the beef industry. New forms of economic concentration appeared in the 1960s. First came an industrialized and highly concentrated system of raising beef cattle—the modern feedlot—enabled by long-haul trucking. Second, rural meatpackers such as Iowa Beef Packers (IBP) transformed themselves from cinderblock operators into fearsome corporations. By establishing dominance in the distribution of beef via refrigerated truck trailer, IBP and a handful of similar firms drove competitors both small and large out of the beef business. Agricultural policymakers made little effort to prevent the rise of this new "Beef Trust." IBP and other new-era meatpackers so thoroughly revolutionized the beef industry that agricultural economists and policymakers in the Packers and Stockyards Administration saw efficiency where they might otherwise have seen monopoly. Although political figures publicly acknowledged the existence of a new beef monopoly in the 1970s, they did not consider the issue to be a significant problem. Instead congressional leaders in both rural and urban districts declared the new beef monopoly to be the product of the "logic" of industrial capitalism, providing high prices to farmers without driving up consumer supermarket tabs.

THE INDUSTRIAL STEER

The first stage in the reemergent beef monopoly was the transformation of the beef steer into an efficient meat producer in factory-style feedlots on the southern plains in the mid-1950s. These modern beef factories, holding tens of thousands of cattle in confined pens, were nothing like the Corn Belt feedlots that had dominated beef cattle feeding since the late nineteenth century. Corn Belt feedlots rarely held more than 1,000 head at a time and were operated by farmers who used cattle feeding primarily to supplement income from crop sales. The methods for beef feeding in the early twentieth century also relied on a complex relationship between ecological conditions and commodity markets that determined where and how a beef cow would spend its days before slaughter. For instance, the bluestem pastures of the Flint Hills of eastern Kansas provided succulent grazing for cattle who could either enjoy several unhurried years of grass feeding before slaughter, or be shipped off to spend their final months on the rich-soiled corn farms of Iowa or Nebraska to be "finished" at a higher weight with more impressive fat marbling in preparation for sale to hotels and discriminating restaurateurs. These ecological and economical niches allowed cattle raisers to decide which fate would bring the most profit from a steer in any given year, depending on the relative price of grain feeds versus the price that could be had for a grass-fed steer. Cattle feeding up to the early 1960s was a highly unsystematic business, with relatively small and widely dispersed individual operators comprising the vast majority of feeders. This situation would rapidly change. By 1965 nearly 60 percent of Kansas's cattle were fed in large commercial lots; in 1975 the number was nearly 90 percent. *Successful Farming* informed readers in 1969 that "the Corn Belt is giving way to a new area—the Feedlot Belt," and recommended that midwestern cattle feeders "get big (at least 500 head a year) and adopt a business approach" to compete with the large-scale commercial feeders of the plains. Cattle feeding was becoming big business, and although that big business would never exercise the same economic power as meatpackers, the industrial feedlot formed the backbone of the new beef economy of the 1960s.[6]

The industrial approach to cattle feeding appeared in the 1950s and became widespread by the mid-1960s, providing an anchor for the hypercapitalist meatpackers that would soon take the place of both the Big Four and the cinderblock rural packers. Whereas Corn Belt feeders had treated beef cattle as supplemental income (and manure) producers, the modern commercial lots focused solely on getting cattle up to slaughter weight as quickly and efficiently as possible. Their only source of income came through "custom feeding," that is, charging cattle owners a daily fee for yardage plus the cost of the feed required to "finish" the animals. Perhaps most important, the concept of industrial feeding was premised on abstract ideas of transportation economics rather than lived experiences of ecological niches in relation to seasonal grain markets. Modern feedlot operators reconceived cattle feeding by moving the steer to the feed, rather than the feed to the steer, much as Henry Ford's assembly line had moved the product to the worker rather than vice versa. Ideally, feedlot builders realized, the steer—which even in the industrial model still had to spend the first two years of its life eating grass on the open range—would not have to move very far to get to the feed. As a consequence, the modern feedlot system arose in the southern plains of Kansas, Texas, Oklahoma, Nebraska, and Colorado, in the middle of both the nation's great grain-producing region—the Breadbasket—and yet not far from the range lands of the northern plains and Texas where most beef cattle continued to be born and weaned (see figure 5.2).

Many agribusinessmen helped develop this industrial feeding approach, but one of the most important was Earl C. Brookover. As the man who brought the modern feedlot to southwestern Kansas—the nation's leading region of commercial cattle feeding by the turn of the century—Brookover possessed the farming experience, business acumen, and engineering skills requisite in

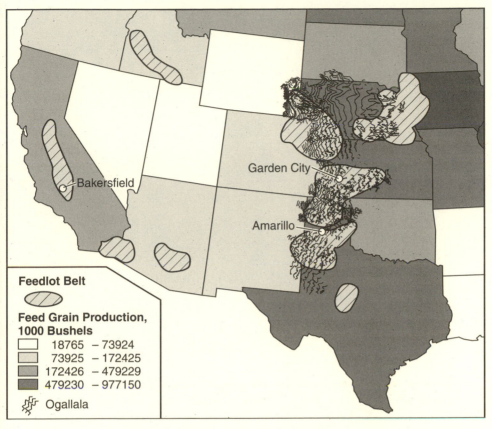

Figure 5.2. The Feedlot Belt and Feed Grain Production in 1965.
The giant cattle feedlots of the 1960s moved into the heart of feed grain production in the southern plains atop the Ogallala aquifer, reducing transport costs (*Source*: Krause, *Cattle Feeding*, 9, 11).

the new industrial beef regime. Born in 1906 in Scott County, Kansas, he worked in his youth for a neighbor who was one of the first to practice irrigated agriculture in that region of the state. After traveling to Peru to drill wells and install water pumps on sugar cane plantations, Brookover returned to Kansas to gain a degree in civil engineering—which he later recalled "was about as close as you could come to irrigation engineering at the time"—from Kansas State University in 1934. Upon graduation, Brookover bought a potato farm in southwestern Kansas and began installing irrigation systems on his and his neighbors' farms. It was sometime in the 1940s that he happened to travel with a friend out to California, where he witnessed the operation of pioneer commercial cattle feedlots near Bakersfield. Although impressed by the scale of the Bakersfield operations, Brookover was less impressed by their location. Bakersfield was a long distance from feed grain supplies and from the major cattle-producing ranges of the plains, making transportation costs a serious drain on profits. Brookover realized that with the help of irrigation his home state of Kansas was poised to become one of the nation's largest producers of feed grains; if he were to establish a giant feedlot back in Kansas, he would have a convenient "home market" of cattle-customers who could turn all that grain into handsome profits. In other words, Brookover saw industrial cattle feeding as a way to make more money out of grain farming—in contrast both to Corn Belt farmers who fed cattle primarily as a backup to grain production and to California feeders who finished cattle mainly for meat sales. In 1951, Brookover convinced an old friend with deep pockets and faith in Earl's vision to fund the construction of the first commercial feedlot in Kansas, just outside Garden City. Brookover opened this first feedlot with just a few hundred "four-legged customers" driven by hoof from nearby farms, but within a decade the scale of operations had increased in steady increments of 10,000 head every few years. By the turn of the century, Brookover had three feedlots with over 100,000 head capacity each.[7]

Brookover understood that irrigation was essential for industrial cattle feeding on the southern plains. The area of western Kansas that Brookover helped develop into a major producer of feed grain was also a place so arid that "old-timers once believed nothing would grow but wheat and sagebrush"—and of course old-time wheat farmers had confronted the extremes of aridity during the Dust Bowl of the 1930s. But Brookover realized that the bone-dry soils of southwestern Kansas lay atop one of the largest aquifers in the United States. The mighty Ogallala, a subterranean formation of thick calcareous sands, gravels, and sandy clays, trapped waters that had run off from the formation of the Rocky Mountains in the Tertiary Period. More than 800 miles long and 400 miles broad at its widest point, the Ogallala aquifer lay beneath parts of Texas, Oklahoma, New Mexico, Colorado, and Nebraska, as well as Kansas (see figure 5.2). Large-scale tapping of the water resources began in the early 1950s, when center-pivot irrigation systems powered by cheap natural gas made it possible to draw enormous quantities of water to the surface. In just five years between 1962 and 1967, western Kansas farmers filed more than 3,200 applications to install irrigation systems on their lands, certain that they could "grow virtually anything" if they had the water. Western Kansas was transformed in the 1950s and 1960s from a land of dry-farmed wheat fields to a patchwork of circular plots of green grain sorghums and roughage (such as hay) for cattle feed. As Brookover understood, it would be much less expensive to feed cattle in the heart of feed grain country, and he was proven correct in the mid-1960s when feedlot managers located above the Ogallala were able to buy feed grain for $12 to $15 more cheaply per ton than could California feedlots.[8]

Beyond recognizing the importance of new methods of irrigation, Earl C. Brookover envisioned cattle feeding in engineering terms. The essential problem, as he understood it, was how to efficiently transform a set of inputs (feed grains) into a high-value product (beef), all the while keeping in mind environmental constraints and opportunities as well as the economics of transporting supplies and finished products. As his son recalls, Brookover believed "engineering was the basis for everything." Having grown to adulthood in the era of Henry Ford's greatest successes in mass production, Brookover sought to develop a complex of technology, science, and traditional farming skills that would allow the mass production of beef cattle. Indeed modern feedlots like the one Brookover built outside Garden City, Kansas, increasingly came to resemble outdoor factories in the 1960s. At the heart of this factory floor was an automatic feed mill, erected to transform raw grains into efficient meat-producing proteins. First the raw grain, whether milo (grain sorghum) or corn, would be steam pressure-cooked to improve its digestibility, allowing cattle to gain more weight from less eating. Next the grain would travel from giant storage elevators via gravity chutes to the automated mixing mill. There, on-site nutritionists pulled levers and punched buttons to arrive at an appropriate ration for each group of cattle in the lot. This was important, because young cattle fresh off the grasslands of Montana or Colorado needed to be broken into their new life of eating as much as they could in the shortest amount of time—and so would be fed higher ratios of roughage (such as hay) for a time before they were ready for "hot rations." Besides steam-flaked grains and hay, these "hot rations" would generally contain urea or soy or cottonseed meal for added protein, along with a dash of molasses for palatability. Growth hormones such as diethylstilbestrol, antibiotics like Aureomycin, and manufactured protein supplements, especially the amino acid lysine, could further boost the weight gains. This scientific feeding allowed feedlot managers to reduce the amount of feed required to produce a pound of beef from nine pounds in the mid-1950s to around seven pounds in 1968; since then, even greater efficiency has been achieved.[9]

Steers that had previously spent time doing something other than eating now had little choice but to pack on the pounds. Once the rations left the mixing elevator, they moved via constant-flow gravity feeds into the beds of parked feed trucks. These trucks, equipped with self-unloading augers, would then be driven around acres of cattle pens, delivering the meals directly to concrete feed bunks. The cattle, with nothing else to do, need only move a few feet to dine. Meat production was maximized. Amidst all of this faceless feeding technology, a human element still remained crucial, in the form of "cowboys" who "rode pens" on horseback, checking the cattle for any signs of illness to keep disease from spreading among the tightly confined population. At Brookover's feedyard, this job was done by men who maintained the "reddened face, rugged costume and cattle-savvy of the traditional cowboy," their very names—Sanky Ruth and "Pappy" Palen—evoking a more rustic world of open ranges. But their cowboy duds contrasted starkly with the spotless white uniform of the feed mill technician, standing amidst a rectilinear grid of steel fences surrounding meat-producing biomachines. High-speed throughput was as essential on these outdoor factory floors as in any automobile factory. As one feedlot manager remarked in 1958, "Anyone buying steers wants them to finish fast. The quicker you can turn them in the feedlot, the more money you'll make." To help speed up the process, state agricultural experiment stations and land grant university researchers developed new cattle breeds, mixing Herefords, Brahmans, Shorthorns, and Angus into leaner, taller, meatier animals such as the Beefmaster, designed "for efficiency, not show ring standards." As with the Beefmaster, the modern feedlot was a place where function took precedence over form—and the sole function of both was to produce as much meat in as short a time as possible.[10]

Irrigation and feed grains made the southern plains an attractive place to locate the modern feedlots, but it was highways and long-haul trucks that made the system possible. Whereas in the early twentieth century urban stockyards in cities such as Chicago and Kansas City had served as "hotels" for cattle traveling from all over the country to central slaughtering plants, in the 1960s rural feedyards took over this role, providing housing for cattle on their way to the decentralized cinderblock slaughtering plants that arose in the 1950s. Feeder cattle, though riding in ventilated semi-trailers rather than air-conditioned Airstream RVs, came like tourists from grasslands all over the West, South, and Midwest, gathering for some hedonic dining at the feedlot trough for 90 to 120 days. So many four-legged tourists began arriving at the enormous Monfort feedlot constructed near Greeley, Colorado, in 1970 that the left lane on Interstate 80 became known as "the Monfort Lane." But once the cattle had arrived at a feedlot, they did not have much farther to go. Packer buyers began coming directly to the feedlot "hotels" to shuttle the animals to rural slaughtering plants; on the appointed day, truckers came directly to the cattle, rather than farmers or truckers taking the cattle to a market to be sold. One consequence of this more direct movement of cattle was that the animals lost significantly less weight since they rarely had to walk under their own power. Another result was that the local auction markets that had begun replacing central stockyards in the 1930s began to close as an era of large-scale direct marketing began. By the 1970s, both the stockyards of Chicago and the auction markets of small crossroads towns would close as the industrial feedlot became the locus of cattle selling and buying.[11]

Direct marketing relied upon the "bull hauler," immortalized as the "Asphalt Cowboy" in a country song performed by the appropriately named musician Sleepy LaBeef in 1970. The independence and strong work ethic of the "asphalt cowboy" helped make cattle trucking into an extraordinarily flexible form of transportation that served the purposes of the industrial feedlot quite well. From the beginning of large-scale beef production in the United States in the mid-nineteenth century, meatpackers faced the extraordinary challenge of gathering cattle from widely distributed ranches and farms and moving them to consumers without losing profits due to shrinkage, bruising, or early death. Transporting the animals safely required skilled laborers, whether actual cowboys, railroad stock handlers, or eventually truckers. But finding workers willing to put up with the stench and the demanding work required to convince stubborn cattle to take long rides in a confined space was not always easy. As a consequence, the average bull hauler in the twentieth century was usually a beginning trucker, someone who took the job as an entry-level position on the way up the trucking ladder to hauling cleaner, more respectable loads. As one experienced cattle trucker put it, "other truckers . . . think that we are the most stupid, stinking, sons-a-bitches on the road" and preferred not to have to park next to cattle trailers at truck stops. Still for a bull hauler willing to work hard and long hours providing quality service to livestock shippers, there was decent money to be made; in the early 1970s, a Nebraska trucker earned up to $1 per mile for cattle hauls. Money alone, however, did not define the experience of the bull hauler. Instead a sense of rugged independence permeated the culture of cattle truckers, often explicitly understood as a modern-day invocation of the idealized cowboy life of the Old West. It was this independence that livestock shippers and a new breed of hypercapitalist meatpackers encouraged and exploited in the 1960s and 1970s to gain market power in the beef industry.[12]

Part of the reason for this deeply felt sense of independence among cattle haulers was the widespread recognition that the job demanded impressive skills. Driving the truck was the easy part; the owner of one livestock hauling firm believed that he "could teach any idiot how to drive a truck," but finding drivers who also knew how to properly load and care for animals was a great deal more difficult. The bull hauler who believed that other drivers thought of his ilk as "stinking sons-a-bitches" defended his chosen line of work as more skilled than that of general freight haulers, noting that "hauling the big brutes is actually a delicate task [because] the animals bruise easily." Bruising made for unsaleable meat and was not kindly accepted by either farmers or packers who stood to lose money when truckers drove too fast, stopped too quickly, turned too sharply, or packed the cattle too tightly into a trailer. The "twentieth century trail boss" needed to keep as close an eye on his doggies as the cowboy of yore.[13]

Although Sleepy LaBeef sang with tongue firmly planted in cheek about the "asphalt cowboy" riding in his "air-conditioned seat," many cattle haulers believed themselves to be direct reincarnations of the Old West drovers. Floyd P. Mounkes of Emporia, Kansas, wore cowboy boots and a fine hat while "stand[ing] tall in the saddle" of a "modern highway truck which efficiently and economically transports a rancher's cattle to the market of his choice." But while the modern bull hauler moved cattle more quickly than the drovers of the Chisholm Trail, notions of efficiency and economy took a backseat to masculine ideals. This was most evident in the cattle hauler's preference for powerful trucks. C. R. Ballstadt, for instance, began hauling cattle in Iowa in 1933 with a Model T pulling a four-wheeled trailer, but by 1970 had assembled a small fleet of giant rigs, including a Kenworth, two Peterbilts, and three International Harvesters. Although high-horsepower engines were not particularly necessary for the job—particularly on the flat prairies and plains of the Midwest—Ballstadt had 335hp Cummins diesels installed in the Peterbilts and the Kenworth, earning him a highly coveted photo spread in *Overdrive* magazine. Cattle truckers who traveled any distance over a few hundred miles used the length of their trips to justify the purchase of big diesel rigs rather than gasoline straight trucks. Turbo-charged diesel engines could provide up to 40 percent better fuel economy per unit of engine weight than a gasoline engine, but the greater weight of a diesel engine required a trucker to invest in a bigger tractor and a longer trailer to realize any economic efficiencies gained by switching to diesel. The size and power of a diesel was not economically necessary, but an impressively powerful engine made the job worth doing. The culture of cattle hauling was permeated by a sense of independent manhood, defiantly upheld in an era of big business, big government, big labor unions, and, of course, big meatpackers.[14]

Truckers who considered themselves independent were, however, deeply embedded in a web of regulatory structures and capitalist machinery. Both livestock producers and meatpackers came to depend on truckers to operate a flexible transportation system that would allow them to increase their control over beef marketing in the late twentieth century. The technology of trucking provided a certain inherent flexibility, insofar as a big rig could travel down a ranch's dirt path almost as easily as it could cruise an interstate highway. But neither this physical freedom of motion nor the bull haulers' culture of manly independence was enough to guarantee that trucking would provide feedlot operators or meatpackers with new forms of economic power. Instead feedlots and packers encouraged the flexibility of trucking through subtle manipulations of state power. First, livestock hauling was exempt from ICC rate and market entry regulation; as explained in chapter 2, any agricultural commodity, not including "manufactured products thereof" (which included live cattle), did not fall under the ICC's regulatory ambit. The politics of livestock hauling in the state of Kansas offer useful insights into the importance of the federal agricultural exemption, because Kansas was one of the few states to regulate the industry. This was done through the Kansas Corporation Commission (KCC), a bipartisan regulatory body originally founded in 1911 in response to Populist anger at railroad rates. Although the KCC maintained a close watch over trucking rates beginning in the 1930s, it did allow farmers who hauled their own or their neighbors' cattle directly to market to do so without registering for a permit or filing their freight rates with the state. This exemption caused tensions between cattle raisers and regulated freight truckers, because Kansas farmers would have greatly preferred to have cattle hauling in their state be unregulated as it was in most other states. Kansas cattlemen did not merely complain about the KCC; they also regularly gave their business to truckers who did not have KCC hauling authority. In 1950, truckers who had received proper authority from the KCC began a two-decades-long effort, spearheaded by the proregulatory Kansas Motor Carriers Association, to combat the increasing prevalence of these "bandit truckers" who were "running scott-free" and creating "complete chaos" by not paying state fees and taxes. Where the KCC and Kansas Motor Carrier Association saw "chaos," cattle producers saw opportunities for cheaper, faster shipping of their cattle to market, and so found ways to avoid the very regulations that their Populist forebears had demanded for railroads. Kansas cattlemen might have envied their competitors in the state of Georgia, where farmers could rely on an unregulated livestock trucking industry in which competition was so fierce that truckers had to scramble to make enough money to pay for their equipment and fuel.[15]

Most of the nation's cattle producers relied on the flexibility of unregulated trucking services, and so lobbied Congress and the USDA to keep the federal exemption in effect from the 1930s through the 1970s. But while the USDA's agricultural economists officially approved of the agricultural exemption, some realized that the flexibility it entailed might add unnecessary costs to the marketing of beef cattle. Truckers in a highly competitive marketplace gained business not so much by lowering their rates, but by offering improved service to shippers. This meant, for instance, that a trucker would travel directly to a farm or a feedlot immediately when a cattleman called, even if this meant the trucker had to go significantly out of his way to get there. Furthermore, although trucks arriving directly on farms allowed cattle to move shorter distances on the hoof to get from a pasture to a feedlot to a packinghouse, each of these separate movements along the highway could quickly add up. As one cattle hauler noted in 1965, "it isn't unusual for us to haul the same cattle four or five times." The cattle producer's demand for a flexible transportation system was not the product of an abstract ideal of economic efficiency, but of a desire to use transportation networks to increase his ability to attain a desirable price for his cattle by selling them where and when he wished. Much as Wal-Mart, in later years, would rely upon information technologies, high-tech warehouses, and fleets of trucks to ship goods to stores "just in time" and on demand, the feedlots of the 1960s relied upon bull haulers to drive a load of cattle wherever and whenever the cattle owner wanted them shipped.[16]

With the flexibility of long-haul trucking propping up the industrial feedlots of the southern plains by the mid-1960s, a new form of monopoly power arose in cattle country. The modern feedlot created monopsonistic conditions in cattle marketing, as the number of buyers of cattle narrowed while the number of cattle sellers, spread throughout the ranges of the West and the Corn-Belt of the Midwest, continued to be large. As feedlots grew larger and more concentrated, fewer sales outlets existed for the cow-calf raisers of the nation's grasslands who produced feeder cattle. In the local auction markets of the 1930s and 1940s, cow-calf raisers from the grasslands of the West had always had the opportunity to sell their young cattle either directly to packers or to any one of thousands of Corn Belt feeders; even at the height of the Big Four's monopsony power, there were always plenty of other potential buyers for any individual steer. By 1968, however, cattle feeding had become remarkably concentrated. Although large-scale commercial lots accounted for only 1 percent of the nation's feedyards in that year, that handful of feedlots marketed half of all fed cattle. But unlike the packer-owned terminal stockyards of the early twentieth century, the new monopsony in cattle marketing drew almost no criticisms from cattle producers. One of the primary complaints livestock raisers had lodged against the urban terminal stockyards in Chicago and Kansas City was that cattle prices fluctuated from day to day, and yardage charges often seemed arbitrary. At a modern yard practicing custom feeding, however, cattlemen simply paid a flat yardage charge (five cents per day was common in 1960) plus the cost of whatever feed the steer ate while in residence. Cattlemen could count on relatively stable costs in the industrial feedlot system. Furthermore a modern feedlot such as Earl Brookover's kept highly trained sales specialists on staff, who kept in daily contact with packer buyers and made every effort to negotiate the best selling price possible for their customers. As Lucky Lilleqvist, the manager of a southwestern Kansas feedlot, noted in 1978, farmers who hauled their cattle into a terminal market like Kansas City might find upon arrival that buyers were offering $1.50 per hundredweight less than the price broadcast on the morning radio program. At that point a farmer would, according to Lilleqvist, have to say: "What am I gonna do? I've already unloaded my cattle. If I take them out of the stockyard and put them back in my truck, it's costing me money." But out at the feedlot, the cattle would not be loaded until the price was right; "farmers [got] a better deal selling directly to the packer." Feedlots became giant cattle factories not just because they could achieve economies of scale and greater throughput in cattle production, but because their very size provided cattle farmers with more formidable power in the market.[17]

Agricultural policymakers in the USDA viewed the growing marketing power of industrial feedlots as a permanent solution to the old problem of a large number of unorganized producers selling cattle in a noncompetitive marketplace. As the new forms of direct marketing took hold in the late 1950s, urban stockyard managers—still tied to the aging rail-based cattle marketing system—made efforts to have the Packers and Stockyards Division implement rules that would slow the geographical movement of cattle marketing into the countryside. Bureaucrats in the USDA, however, refused to put any limits or regulations on direct buying at feedlots. In 1961 representatives of the central stockyards convinced the House Agriculture Committee to hold hearings on the problem of direct buying by packers. Direct marketing had led to precipitous declines in sales of slaughter cattle at terminal markets since the 1920s; it appeared by 1961 that the central stockyards in cities such as Chicago and Kansas City were nearing extinction. In 1960, the members of the American Stockyards Association received only 59 percent of the nation's cattle for slaughter; as late as 1952, the percentage had been as high as 89 percent. This was a problem, argued A. Z. Baker, president of the American Stockyards Association, because it made possible the "concentration of buying power in fewer hands," with transactions occurring almost secretly in the countryside. R. E. Cunningham, representing the seven largest terminal stockyards at the hearings, pointed out that in ancient Constantinople, lamb slaughterers who bought animals outside the city were "beaten, shorn, and banished" for direct buying; Cunningham implied that he would like to see Congress pass a similar law to prevent the decline of the central stockyard. The USDA offered no support to the rail-based central stockyards, however. As Assistant Secretary of Agriculture John Duncan informed the House committee: "The Department believes that packers and other buyers should be free to purchase, and that producers and other sellers should be free to sell, livestock for slaughter at any point." In making this pronouncement of free-market ideology, the USDA agreed with meatpackers and the American National Cattlemen's Association, who argued that direct buying *increased* competition in the livestock marketplace, because "the livestock producer today has the widest possible choice of markets in which he may elect to sell."[18]

Only the National Farmers Organization (NFO) supported the central stockyards in their belief that the decline of terminal marketing would limit the choices that cattlemen had within the "free" market. The Iowa farmers who formed the NFO in 1955, in fact, believed the "free" market in agriculture was a sham and that individual farmers needed to organize to counteract the growing power of agribusiness corporations in the farm economy. The NFO recruited tens of thousands of members in grain-growing and livestock-raising midwestern states in the late 1950s by promoting the concept of collective bargaining among farmers. Unlike the heads of older farm organizations such as the Farm Bureau and the National Farmers Union, NFO leaders such as Oren Staley believed that political alliances with either the Republican or Democratic parties would not effect the immediate change needed in U.S. farm policy, and that more direct action within the farm economy was necessary. Reviving the ideas of Milo Reno's Depression-era Farmers Holiday Association and Walter Singler's Wisconsin Cooperative Milk Pool, the leaders of the NFO advocated the use of grain, livestock, and milk withholding actions by farmers facing declining prices. Withholding was a weapon for the weak, but a weapon of last resort, insofar as keeping farm products off the market was a gamble that could easily backfire if even a small percentage of desperate farmers broke ranks and shipped goods to market. Even if farmers banded together and stuck together through a concerted withholding action, the NFO understood that the tactic would never work without centralized marketing facilities like the urban cattle stockyards. As Robert Casper, vice president of the National Farmers Organization, informed the House Agriculture Committee in 1961, the central terminal markets for cattle were "the only price-basing mechanism the livestock industry now has." If government-regulated central markets were replaced by commercial feedlots and direct-buying schemes, farmers seeking to sell their live cattle would be forever forced to bargain as individuals in a lightly regulated marketplace. Individual farmers would be "free" to choose where and when they sold their cattle, but the power to set prices would remain primarily in the hands of far more tightly organized cattle buyers.[19]

As it soon turned out, the National Farmers Organization was right, even though the group struggled mightily to prevent the revival of unrestrained monopoly capitalism in cattle marketing. On Labor Day 1962, the NFO orchestrated a massive withholding action of livestock, demanding that meatpackers pay $32.45 per hundredweight of Choice grade cattle. To maintain unity and prevent farmers from surreptitiously shipping livestock to market, NFO members attacked bull haulers with bottles thrown at windshields and nails spread on highways. A week later, Chicago's Union Stock Yard reported cattle receipts 14 percent below those recorded in the same week of 1961. The Farm Bureau, fearing a mass defection of midwestern farmers to the direct-action NFO, circulated press releases predicting—apparently without irony—that the NFO would soon face antitrust charges from the Department of Justice. Meatpackers developed an even more effective strategy, offering irresistibly high prices to individual cattle sellers. By the third week of the withholding action, NFO members as well as nonaligned cattle farmers began rushing cattle to market to cash in while they could. On October 2, with defections rampant, the NFO called off the protest. By mid-October cattle prices had fallen back to their earlier levels. Within a few years the terminal marketing system would collapse almost entirely, making even a strongly coordinated withholding action even less likely to succeed than the NFO's abortive but hard-fought 1962 attempt. Chicago's Union Stock Yard closed in 1970 for lack of business, while the terminal markets that remained in cities such as Omaha and Kansas City began to focus solely on sales of feeder cattle, rather than slaughter cattle bound for packing plants. Local auction yards and independent sale barns also closed down, useless in an age of direct feedlot buying. Cattlemen could still choose to sell their animals to any buyer in the "free" marketplace, but cattle buyers now purchased stock almost entirely via direct sales at commercial feedlots.[20]

Following the expanding interstate highways of the 1950s and 1960, the antistatist marketing machinery of the new beef industry penetrated deep into the countryside. Encouraged by lax government intervention, cattle raisers throughout the country relied on the modern feedlot, decentralized rural meatpackers, and asphalt cowboys to boost their marketing power in the 1960s. Whereas cattle farmers had looked to the federal government to administer cattle prices to prevent the Big Four packers from abusing their monopoly power since the Depression of the 1930s, now they looked to the industrial feedlots spread throughout the southern plains to gain higher prices. Soon, however, a new monopoly power emerged to ratchet up the stakes in this "free" market, defying government regulators while decimating meatpacking unions in the name of low consumer prices. Few cattlemen, however, would object to the "logic" of this rural hypercapitalism.

The "Logic" of Boxed Beef

Before many U.S. consumers decided that cholesterol-laden red meat was unhealthy in the 1970s, they could barely spend their dollars fast enough on beef. In the 1960s—a decade of rising real wages—backyard suburban barbecues groaned under the increasing weight of Choice and Prime steaks, as annual per capita consumption of beef rose from 57 pounds in 1955 to 70 pounds in 1965, reaching a peak of nearly 80 pounds of beef per American in 1970. By that time, demand began outpacing the supply of beef, causing inflation that *Time* magazine blamed on the "increasing affluence" of consumers and their "long-standing love of beef." Beef steaks reached record high prices in the summer of 1969, and although "housewives seem[ed] hardly daunted" by the costs that year, the rising price of meat would within a few years cause a significant consumer backlash. In a last-gasp renewal of consumer-driven economic liberalism within the food economy, activist housewives demanded that President Richard Nixon institute price controls similar to those he had learned to despise as a young lawyer working for the Office of Price Administration during World War II. Nixon did so, although federally administered price controls would not satisfy consumer demands for cheaper beef. Instead new meatpacking firms emerged in the 1970s, using long-haul trucking to revolutionize the production and distribution of beef so thoroughly—and driving the price of beef so low—that consumers had little reason to protest the emergence of a new monopoly in beef production that dwarfed the power of the old rail-based Big Four.[21]

The price of meat skyrocketed in the early 1970s, driving a renewed sense of purchasing-power liberalism among U.S. consumers. In early 1973, when the price of meat rose by as much as 75 percent in a matter of weeks, consumers across the country decided that Nixon's secretary of agriculture, Earl Butz—the protégé of Ezra Taft Benson—was to blame. The previous August, Butz and Secretary of State Henry Kissinger had engineered a massive sale of U.S. grain to Soviet buyers. The sale was meant to further Kissinger's *détente* policies, while Butz expected a windfall for U.S. grain farmers—but the Soviets surprised everyone by snapping up $750 million worth of U.S. government-subsidized grain in a single purchase rather than over three years as planned. With less grain to feed domestic livestock, U.S. farmers kept cattle off the market, pushing up meat prices. The press dubbed the incident the "Great Grain Robbery," criticizing Butz, the Soviets, and grain-trading agribusinesses such as Cargill for driving up domestic food costs at taxpayer expense. Housewives around the country demanded action. President Nixon scolded the women, informing them that government intervention could not repeal the laws of supply and demand. Under continued pressure, though, Nixon announced a freeze on the wholesale and retail prices of meat on March 29, 1973—a remarkable action considering his undisguised hatred for price controls. Unsurprisingly, however, Nixon refused to strongly enforce the price controls or crack down on meatpackers' schemes for evading the regulations. Beef prices continued to climb. On April 1 a spontaneous grassroots meat boycott erupted across the nation, orchestrated by middle-class consumer groups such as Fight Inflation Together (Atlanta), Women's War on Prices (Wilmette, Illinois), Citizens Action Program (Chicago), and the Consumer Federation of California. Retail sales of meat dropped by 50 to 80 percent during the weeklong boycott, but supermarkets generally refused to lower their prices; the manager of Big Bear Stores defended the decision, saying "We can't price by emotion." But emotions ran high among consumers who, accustomed to low-priced beef, sought easy solutions to complex economic problems. With neither an obvious Beef Trust to attack nor a government willing to enforce strong OPA-style price controls, *Fortune* magazine predicted that only a "profound change in the techniques of . . . beef production" could bring prices down. As the magazine's editors knew, just such a free-market transformation was already underway in the beefpacking industry.[22]

Corporate powerhouses, rather than government action, fulfilled consumer expectations for low-priced beef in the 1970s. Firms such as Iowa Beef Packers (IBP), Spencer Foods, National Beef, and Excel and Missouri Beef (later merged as MBPXL) began as relatively small firms in the early 1960s. By 1980, a few of these firms—especially IBP—would establish a near-complete monopoly on beef processing and distribution, but in the beginning they could barely be distinguished from other cinderblock packers in the rural Midwest. Like the earlier generation of rural meatpackers that relied on reefers to challenge the branch-house rail-based system of the Big Four, the new packers deployed a strategy of building single-story slaughterhouses in rural areas of plentiful cattle and cheap labor. But the most profitable upstart packers ratcheted this relocation strategy up several notches, aiming for a degree of rural industrialization that would give them unprecedented control over livestock prices, worker wages, and retail distribution of meat.[23]

A renewed westward movement of meatpacking factories was the first stage of the rural industrialization strategy, as new meatpackers headed for the heart of the feedlot belt (see figure 5.3). As industrial feedlots sprang up on the southern plains in the 1960s, many meatpackers realized they were wasting money by transporting live cattle all the way from western Kansas or Colorado to slaughterhouses in Iowa or Illinois. No meatpacking firm was more focused on moving its factories to the new center of cattle supply than IBP. Under the

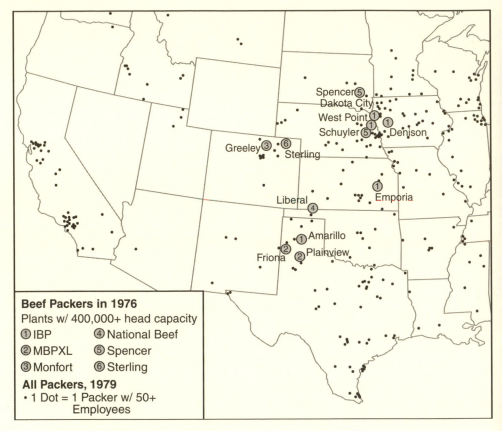

Figure 5.3. Rural Meatpacking in the 1970s.

Beefpackers such as IBP undertook a "rural industrialization" strategy in the 1970s, beginning in western Iowa and ultimately locating their largest factories in the heart of the western feedlot belt by the late 1970s (*Sources*: U.S. Bureau of the Census, *County Business Patterns* 1979; Williams, *Changing Patterns,* 17).

leadership of two previous unknowns in the industry, Currier J. Holman and Andrew D. Anderson, IBP built its first plant in Denison, Iowa, in 1961 with—ironically—the help of a Small Business Administration loan. From its small-business midwestern roots, IBP built successively larger plants over the next two decades, each one deeper in the heart of the feedlot belt—in Dakota City, Nebraska (1967); Emporia, Kansas (1968); Amarillo, Texas (1974). In 1979, IBP began construction of what remains the largest beefpacking plant in the world, just outside Garden City, Kansas—seven miles west of Earl Brookover's original feedlot. Though IBP was the largest, other firms such as National Beef, Missouri Beef, Excel, and Spencer followed its lead, establishing giant plants in the southern plains in the 1960s and 1970s. Whereas the mixed farming operations of the prairie Midwest had fed the nation's growing appetite for cattle from the late nineteenth to the mid-twentieth century, by 1977, nine western states accounted for 70 percent of the nation's beef slaughter. The wheat country of Kansas, just recently converted to industrial cattle feeding, was quickly becoming the nation's center of beef slaughter.[24]

Did the "logic" of industrial capitalism compel these meatpackers to move into the heart of cattle country? *Forbes* magazine declared so in 1968, calling IBP's strategy a "triumph of logic," allowing the packer to reduce transportation costs to a minimum by placing plants within an hour's trucking distance from feedlots. For contemporary admirers of IBP's methods, a circle seemed to have been completed. The nation's beef industry had begun with cattle drives to Old West towns such as Dodge City, Kansas, where cattle embarked on long railroad trips to the halfway point of Chicago's giant meatpacking factories, in order to continue the journey to the populous East as swinging carcasses. By the late twentieth century, Dodge City, Kansas, was once again a booming cowtown, but this time the cattle did not begin their long journeys eastward until they had been slaughtered in rural factories. Packers no longer had to swallow the expense of shipping inedible hides, hooves, and entrails halfway across the country. This "logic," however, did not become possible until modern highways and refrigerated trailers allowed speedy long-distance transportation of slaughtered meat. Furthermore the "logic" of IBP's strategy of rural industrialization—predicated upon a ferocious opposition to organized labor—did not become politically acceptable until after U.S. consumers had grown so accustomed to inexpensive beef that they were willing to accept a new monopoly in order to get it.[25]

And a monopoly they did receive. The new meatpackers reinstated an impressive control over the prices and terms on which they purchased live cattle, much as the Big Four had done by controlling railroad-based stockyards in the early twentieth century. In the mid-1960s packers such as IBP perfected the system of direct buying. IBP's buyers traveled by car each day from feedlot to feedlot, using two-way microwave radios to keep in constant contact with each other as well as a central dispatcher in Dakota City, Nebraska. This instantaneous feedback on market conditions prevented them from ever having to buy at a price that did not meet with approval from headquarters, just as the telegraph had allowed nineteenth-century Chicago packers to administer prices at stockyards around the country.[26]

Gaining control of cattle supplies was merely a precursor to selling meat to consumers at rock-bottom prices while reaping steady profits. IBP's managers did not necessarily entertain proconsumer sentiments; instead low retail prices merely offered a means of achieving market domination by underselling all competitors. The path to driving down prices began with capturing control of cattle supplies, but continued with the exploitation of unorganized rural workers. IBP was widely admired by other meatpackers in the 1960s for its steadfast refusal to peacefully negotiate wage contracts with meatpacking unions. The company made every effort to avoid the master contract achieved by employees at all of the old-line packing firms such as Armour, Swift, and smaller independents like Oscar Mayer in the early 1950s. Proving that rural Americans were not inherently hostile to labor militancy even in the 1960s, strikes were commonplace in IBP plants. A remarkably violent episode occurred at the Dakota City, Iowa, plant in 1969, as meatpacking unions fought to bring the renegade firm's wages in line with the rest of the industry. IBP's first president, Currier J. Holman, was so resolved to keep wages low that he told his management team to prepare to have one of every three plants out on strike at any given time. A union representative recalled in 1977 that Holman "once said you run a business the way you run a war, and he certainly applied that to labor." Even a former IBP executive found the firm's antilabor culture to be downright militant: "Iowa Beef makes the Marine Corps look like pantywaists." In addition to substandard wages, IBP demanded incredible productivity from workers. A worker on the kill floor of IBP's Garden City plant found the pace of work so intense that he did not "have time to sweep sweat from [his] face." Managers realized that few people could maintain such a pace for very long, and so considered an annual employee turnover rate of up to 96 percent to be "low."[27]

Driving down worker wages coincided with efforts to transform the process of cattle slaughter in the age of high technology. IBP introduced minute divisions of labor throughout the slaughtering process, requiring less skill from each employee, allowing the company to hire raw recruits and train them in a matter of hours—an essential tactic when turnover rates neared 100 percent. Plants were carefully designed to allow rapid, horizontal flow of the carcass through intensely refrigerated spaces, dramatically reducing shrinkage of the meat. In 1964, IBP took a live animal from the load-in dock to the load-out cooler in only thirty-two minutes; a decade later the company had the process down to twenty minutes. The combination of low wages, deskilling, division of labor, and rapid throughput allowed a modern IBP-style plant to slaughter a cow for less than $15 in the late 1970s, while old-line packers experienced costs of $18 to $20 per head. Packers sought further cost advantages by finding profitable uses for the byproducts of slaughter. Armour had pioneered the profitable sale of byproducts—such as hooves and horns for buttons and bones for fertilizer—in the early twentieth century, but the arrival of plastics and chemical fertilizers had wiped out the market for most of those items by the late 1950s. IBP began selling liver, tongue, sweetbreads, and cheek meat to French chefs as "variety meats," while blood became animal feed, hearts and meat scraps became hamburger, and hides became shoes. By shaving costs and boosting production, IBP could undersell nearly all of its competitors while making remarkable profits. The tiny company that began in 1960 with a $300,000 Small Business Administration loan became a ranking member of the *Fortune* 500 by 1969, with $534 million in annual sales.[28]

Despite its impressive growth in the 1960s, IBP would not achieve low prices and monopoly power to rival the strength of the old Beef Trust until it gained control over the distribution of fresh meat. This came with the firm's introduction of boxed beef in 1969, a technology that quickly proved as transformative as Gustavus Swift's refrigerated railcar had been in the 1880s. The concept of boxed beef was simple. Rather than ship entire carcasses to wholesale or retail butchers to be deboned and cut into consumer-sized portions, IBP cut ("broke") carcasses down into consumer cuts at its own rural plants, starting in Dakota City in 1969. These retail-ready cuts were wrapped in vacuum-sealed plastic bags, placed in cardboard boxes, and trucked via refrigerated trailer directly to the loading docks of supermarkets. Shipping boxed beef led to enormous savings in transportation costs—as much as 30 percent less than swinging beef—since only the meat that would end up in the retail meat case made the trip to the city. Boxed packaging also allowed for much more efficient use of trailer space; unlike the awkward shape of a swinging carcass, a box could be tightly stacked from wall-to-wall and floor-to-ceiling. Truckers could thus haul 4,000 more pounds of boxed beef than carcass meat. On top of all of this, the vacuum-sealed Cryovac bags extended the shelf life of fresh meat by nearly a month, making the distance between Dakota City and New York a relatively trivial matter. Despite the obvious theoretical advantages of the new technology, though, IBP did not achieve immediate success with boxed beef.[29]

Urban wholesale and retail butchers were especially unwilling to allow the "logic" of boxed beef to unfold. Members of the powerful Amalgamated Meat Cutters union correctly understood that boxed beef would allow companies like IBP to transform butchering into a job for low-wage rural workers. Over the entire history of beef distribution, skilled butchers had played a central role in delivering meat to consumers. Even the introduction of self service meat departments in supermarkets in the late 1940s had not eliminated the need for a skilled butcher to make meat cuts attractive to customers. Boxed beef, on the other hand, required only one or two cuts from retail butchers, making jobs in meatcutting departments little different from the least-skilled and lowest-paid jobs in the supermarket, such as stocking shelves. Realizing this, the

Amalgamated Meat Cutters refused to accept shipments of boxed beef at super-market receiving docks in cities such as New York, Chicago, Milwaukee, and St. Louis. The Amalgamated received significant cooperation from meat-hauling members of the Teamsters Union, who hoped to continue hauling beef carcasses for the old-line meatpackers such as Swift and Armour, whose shipping depart-ments maintained nationally bargained contracts with the truckers' union.[30]

IBP was committed to achieving control of beef distribution, however, and made every effort to break the resistance of organized labor. IBP president Currier J. Holman broke into the lucrative New York market by paying bribes to union officials and providing secret rebates to supermarket meat buyers, a strategy that would land him in federal court on conspiracy charges. But even more importantly, IBP cut the price of boxed beef so low that it simply became irresistible to supermarket managers, who realized they could eliminate the jobs of skilled butchers who made $2 to $3 more per hour than the workers needed to package and stock boxed beef cuts. By 1972, IBP had so many cus-tomers for boxed beef that it was making a profit of $5 million a year on sales of over $1 billion, despite the razor-thin profit margins required to keep the wholesale price attractive to retailers. In the mid-1970s, boxed beef quickly be-came the standard method of distributing fresh meat; MBPXL built a boxed beef plant in Wichita in 1975, Monfort built one in Oakley, Kansas, in 1978, and by 1979 nearly 44 percent of beef was sold in boxed form.[31]

Shipping beef in boxes required the services of truckers willing to drive al-most anywhere. In the era of rail-based branch house distribution, packers had moved fresh beef to small towns and cities by relying on a combination of rail-cars, cold-storage warehouses, and small delivery trucks. In an era of giant supermarkets widely distributed in suburban shopping centers, however, tractor-trailers were the only machines capable of delivering in volume to geographi-cally diffuse customers. Boxed beef distribution required IBP to ship directly to supermarket loading docks rather than to centralized receiving depots. Truckers hauling boxed beef might have to make multiple daily stops at super-markets across a broad territory to dispose of a full trailer load of meat. Even if one particular retail store called in a large meat order, the meatpackers needed truckers to be flexible. This was because no beef carcass was ever ex-actly like another, even in the age of scientific breeding and feeding, so if a super-market demanded an entire load of beef matching its precise specifications, the packer might have to assemble the order by bringing in carcasses from multiple plants. This assembly had to occur within a matter of hours to satisfy the large-volume supermarket customer, and so truckers might be called upon to drive from Kansas to Nebraska to Iowa with little advance warning. Modern beef-packing was a fast-paced industry, demanding instant delivery of both raw materials and finished products; only truckers traveling on good roads at high speeds and at any hour of the day could fulfill such expectations.[32]

Meatpackers relied on the independent streak of highway haulers to achieve market domination. This became especially apparent during a violent strike at IBP's Dakota City plant in 1969, when the Amalgamated Meatcutters Union convinced the Teamsters Union to refuse to accept loads of boxed beef bound for New York City. IBP responded by convincing the Interstate Commerce Commission to grant "emergency temporary authorities" to nonunionized independent truckers to get the meat through. Following this episode, IBP sought a more permanent solution by helping independent truckers gain ICC authority to compete with the unionized haulers. The firms' distribution manager described this effort in a transportation trade journal as "a quest for new blood," perhaps unintentionally evoking Karl Marx's image of capitalists as vampires sucking the very life out of workers. Not every new-breed meatpacker tasted blood at the sight of an independent trucker; some firms treated truckers as the aristocrats of their labor force. Monfort, for instance, bought its own fleet of fifty brand-new Kenworths with sleeper cabs in 1970 with the explicit intention of attracting good drivers who appreciated fine equipment. Monfort understood that some truck drivers might be willing to work without union representation if they had access to a manly rig like a Kenworth conventional (i.e., a truck with an extended nose, as opposed to the flat-fronted cab-over design). With their garish orange, white, and yellow color scheme, the Monfort trucks attracted attention. Edward Miller, a former steel hauler from McVeytown, Pennsylvania, remembers "riding along, kinda tired and in need of coffee" when he saw a Monfort rig on the highway, "sat up straight in [his] seat," and decided to become a Monfort driver. The sex appeal of the machine was not the only attraction of the job; Monfort had a reputation for treating its drivers well, even though traffic managers expected the truckers to drive "hard and fast." The modern meat hauler may have been an asphalt cowboy with an "air-conditioned seat" (and an air-conditioned trailer) but the sweated nature of his work was absolutely essential to the operation of the union-busting plans of the new rural meatpackers.[33]

Boxed beef hauled in tractor-trailers provided the basis of a new form of monopoly power for companies such as IBP. Boxed beef, like dressed beef before it, required enormous capital investments to make the system work. Unlike the dressed beef packers, however, the new breed of meatpackers did not have to invest in an expensive distribution infrastructure of branch houses and railcars; boxed beef distribution required only a fleet of refrigerated trucks to deliver meat directly to supermarket coolers. However, the low prices demanded by cost-conscious consumers and supermarket managers forced boxed beef producers to price the product so cheaply that only economies of enormous scale could produce profitability. Boxed beef producers built new plants of unprecedented size, dwarfing the output of the Chicago factories of the original "Beef Trust." The IBP plant opened near Garden City, Kansas in 1982 was officially publicized as having a daily slaughter capacity of 4,000 head, but in reality the number was closer to 5,500. This capacity was so large that anyone familiar with the beefpacking industry at the time would have thought, according to Earl Brookover, Jr., that the directors of IBP "had lost their minds." IBP's main competitors—MBPXL, Spencer, Monfort, and National Beef—were among the only companies able to secure enough capital to build the huge-capacity plants required to successfully market boxed beef. For both smaller beefpacking firms and the old-line packers such as Swift and Armour, the investments required to enter the boxed beef trade were prohibitively expensive. Because boxed beef distribution erected insurmountable barriers to entry, the number of meatpacking firms declined by 25 percent from 1970 to 1979, with small firms suffering the most. Those smaller rural firms that survived, such as Dubuque and Hyplains, did so by selling carcasses to IBP to be boxed, becoming "captive firms" in the process. In 1978, IBP alone slaughtered at least 16 percent of the nation's cattle—a remarkable share considering that even Swift at the height of its power had probably never slaughtered more than 18 percent.[34]

This new beef monopoly, however, never drew the sustained outrage of livestock producers or consumers as the Big Four had done in previous decades. IBP brazenly announced its plans to dominate the beef industry, as when Director of Public Affairs Charles Harness announced in 1982 that IBP simply wanted "to make a buck. We think we have to grow to make a profit." The low retail prices that accompanied boxed beef distribution made for good politics in an age of declining real wages. Robert Peterson—who replaced Currier Holman as president of IBP following Holman's indictment for bribing New York union officials—announced in 1981 that "the principal beneficiary of [boxed beef] is the consumer. The price of beef is still within the reach of the average consumer largely due to economy of scale." Congressional small business committees investigated the growing monopoly power of IBP during the late 1970s and early 1980s, but as Republican Representative Toby Roth of Wisconsin argued, "Looking at it through the housewife's view, I could care less about Iowa Beef." Although the congressional investigations resulted in charges of "predatory pricing practices" by IBP in dumping boxed beef below cost on retail markets, the main concern that arose from the hearings was not with monopoly of beef marketing, but with the potential of the big packers to gain control of the nation's cattle supply.[35]

Livestock raisers, though, generally had few complaints about the monopsony power of IBP. When the firm opened its record-capacity plant near Garden City in 1982, Kansas cattlemen announced that they were "gleeful" to have such a large buyer in their backyard. IBP's insatiable demand for cattle allowed raisers and feeders near a plant to increase their production without fear of losing their market. The Big Four packers, located hundreds or thousands of miles away, had never offered such convenience. IBP not only bought live cattle in steady volumes, but also tried to offer livestock producers higher prices than its competitors in order to maintain control of supplies. In 1981, the firm offered as much as $20 more per head than other packer buyers. Democratic Representative Frederick Richmond of New York could thus agree with his Republican colleagues in summing up the lack of government concern about IBP's power: "If indeed the IBP can pay more for the cattle, which is good for the farmers, if they can deliver a more efficient box of boxed beef to the East, [then] the basic concept is good, isn't it?" The "free market," though heavily concentrated in a few corporate hands, seemed to be delivering exactly what liberal New Dealers had been seeking to achieve with the farm policies and antitrust actions of the 1930s—farm prices remained steady even as consumers enjoyed reasonable prices. Of course, not all cattle producers were exactly "gleeful" to have IBP dominate cattle buying. In 1976, Iowa livestock feeders filed a federal price-fixing suit against the firm, and others have done so since, although collusion was difficult to prove in a direct-buying market shrouded in secrecy. In any case, IBP and other producers of boxed beef had so fundamentally restructured the economic geography of beef production and marketing that federal trustbusters would have been hard-pressed to break the new monopoly through administrative or judicial methods.[36]

With consumers satisfied by cheap T-bones and most cattle raisers content to sell at high prices to IBP, the issue of monopoly in beef production was no longer a significant political concern by the 1980s. Even before the Reagan administration dismantled the antitrust powers of the federal government in the 1980s to conform to the theories of the Chicago School of economists, the revitalized beef industry had demonstrated to policymakers and the public that low prices for meat trumped any vestigial concern about concentration of economic power in beef production and marketing.[37] The issues in the new beef industry that grabbed headlines and spurred government intervention were not primarily questions of political economy, but of environmental and food safety. Suburban residents in the vicinities of feedlots complained of groundwater and odor pollution, manure-laden dust, and piles of dead flies on their doorsteps, but state governments in the feedlot belt generally refused to limit the growth of industrial cattle feeding. Feedlot operators easily convinced state officials, eager to create economic growth, that the odors emanating from the yards were not the smell of manure, but "the smell of money." Monopoly had once again become a fact in the beef industry, but it was no longer a pressing political problem. Thirty-two years after IBP introduced boxed beef, the firm merged with Tyson Foods, making Tyson the source of one of every four pounds of beef, chicken, and pork in the United States. The top four meat firms controlled 85 percent of beef marketing in the country at the onset of the twenty-first century. *Business Week* identified Tyson as the "Wal-Mart of Meat" in 2004, but even Wal-Mart—usually capable of cowing its suppliers into submission—found the new meat mega-monopoly's economic power daunting. Both Tyson Foods and Wal-Mart relied on the political support of "New Democrats" such as Arkansas governor William Jefferson Clinton—who, after his successful, Wal-Mart-backed bid for the presidency in 1992, would oversee a booming consumer-driven, deregulatory, free-trade, antiwelfare economy beset by rising inequality of income. "Free enterprise" ruled in the new beef economy, as rural packers hidden from the view of suburban consumers captured markets, decimated organized labor, and undermined consumer and Democratic support for strong government intervention in the food economy.[38]

The problem of monopoly lost its political heft in the agribusiness-era beef economy. As the next chapter shows, new trucking technologies and the rising economic power of suburban supermarkets likewise spurred a fundamental restructuring of the production and marketing of fluid milk. As in the beef economy, this "postindustrial" restructuring pushed small farmers to industrialize operations while milk processors relied on highway transportation to slash wages and prices in the urban food economy. Nonunionized truck drivers contributed to these efforts. Like the asphalt cowboys who hauled feedlot cattle and boxed beef, rural milk haulers valued their economic independence even as they recognized that they worked within an "economic jungle" of cut-throat capitalist competition. Unlike bull haulers, however, the modern milk haulers of rural Wisconsin would directly challenge the monopoly power of milk processors in the 1960s, drawing on a Progressive-era critique of abusive corporate power that had underwritten New Deal liberalism within the farm and food economy since the 1930s. In failing to unite with organized labor to achieve better pay or working conditions, however, Wisconsin's rural milk haulers foreshadowed the antiunion hostility that would characterize independent trucking throughout the nation in the 1970s.

CHAPTER SIX

The Milkman and the Milk Hauler

In September 1960, forty Indianapolis milkmen invaded a local supermarket, commandeered all of its shopping carts, and jammed the aisles to protest the store's policy of underselling home-delivered milk by 28 cents per gallon. As the Indianapolis milkmen realized, chain supermarkets relied upon cheap milk to lure waves of suburbanites into their stores at least once per week; by using milk as a "loss leader," however, the stores priced the organized milkmen out of the Indianapolis dairy market. The livelihoods of these Teamster drivers were on the line as they confronted the customers who, like millions of other Americans in the 1950s and 1960s, began buying their milk in paper cartons at stores rather than having glass bottles delivered to their doorsteps. For an organization that had achieved its strength in the dairy industry through hardheaded organizational drives earlier in the century, the Indianapolis milkmen's protest starkly demonstrated the Teamsters' growing inability to gain sympathy from consumers in the supermarket age. The milkmen who wore white chauffeur's caps and clean overalls while collecting union-scale wages were being swept into the nostalgic dustbin of history as milk traveled from factory farm to supermarket in trucks driven by nonunionized milk haulers.[1]

The political economy of milk underwent fundamental transformations from the 1950s through the 1970s, as powerful agribusinesses triumphantly used new trucking technology to drive down wages and prices in the farm and food economy. The coalition of inner-ring dairy farmers, urban milk dealers, and organized milk deliverymen that had monopolized the fluid milk industry since the 1930s lost their dominance as outer-ring farmers, rural milk processors, and nonunion milk haulers launched an assault on the tightly regulated, inflationary milk marketing system erected during the New Deal. Consumers purchased low-priced milk at the supermarket while Teamster power waned in the milk economy, eliminating protests from the two strongest groups that had animated economic liberals' attempts to restructure milk marketing since the 1930s. This assault on economic liberalism, however, did not overturn the New Deal-era farm policies that encouraged monopoly power within the dairy economy. The federal milk marketing order system first erected in the Chicago region in 1933 continued in full strength through the end of the century, as USDA administrators and economists guaranteed that farmers would receive relatively high prices for their milk if only they boosted farm production on an industrial scale and joined the "super-coops" that came to rule the dairy market by the 1970s. The industrialization of the milk economy, to an even greater extent than in the beef industry, forced waves of small farmers off the land as they struggled to keep pace with the demands of modern agribusiness. Some of those squeezed out of dairying chose to become truck drivers, hauling milk in the giant bulk tanks that were essential to the milk marketing machinery of the era. Within this highly competitive industrial dairy economy, some Wisconsin milk haulers organized in the 1960s seeking to boost their incomes and improve working conditions. As "independent" truckers who refused to join the Teamsters, modern milk haulers contributed to the rural working class's increasing acceptance of the "free enterprise" vision promulgated by Ezra Taft Benson and like-minded policymakers bent upon undermining organized labor's power within the farm and food economy. These fiercely independent rural truckers did not turn their backs on economic liberalism because they were inherently conservative, however; instead they had legitimate reasons to believe that neither labor unions nor government regulators had the power to protect their economic interests.

THE END OF HOME DELIVERY

The assault on economic liberalism in the dairy economy began at the point of consumption. Since the late nineteenth century, urban Americans had received milk in glass bottles delivered to their doorsteps, but by the end of the 1960s, most Americans purchased milk at the supermarket. The introduction of the paper milk carton in the 1950s, hailed by its producers as an extraordinarily convenient package for consumers, proved instead most convenient to supermarkets and a new crop of small-town milk processors who succeeded in driving the organized milk deliveryman out of the dairy economy. Despite efforts by the Teamsters to salvage what they could in a hostile economic environment, the adoption of the paper carton meant that milk dealers could ship their product directly to supermarket loading docks via tractor-trailers, limiting the power of the union to shape milk dealers' business practices. Even during a decade when the Teamsters Union as a whole gained its most impressive expansions in membership and bargaining power, the union lost influence over the politics of a "fair price" for milk by the end of the 1960s.

In the 1950s paper milk carton producers touted their product as if it were a revolutionary force that would bring better living to consumers through the miracles of modern science and technology. Consumers, however, had remained nonplussed for several decades after the Ex-Cell-O paper carton first arrived on the scene in 1936. Consumers distrusted the carton because they could not see the "cream line" that indicated the fat content of the milk, as they could with a transparent glass bottle. In an era when high fat content was seen as an indicator of quality (rather than of artery-clogging cholesterol), the paper carton was by no means an obvious form of technological progress. An opaque carton might very well be hiding an inferior product, and since the Progressive era milk consumers had learned to mistrust milk dealers who might adulterate "nature's perfect food" with water, chalk, formaldehyde, or even ground sheep brains. Furthermore many cities and states outlawed paper containers for sanitary reasons through most of the 1940s. Because consumers and public health officials viewed the paper carton as inferior to glass, only 5 percent of milk was packaged in paper as of 1940. By 1952, however, over 40 percent was sold in paper packages. By 1956, the makers of Pure-Pak confidently advertised their product on national television as the most convenient package in history. Advertisers declared that paper cartons were light and easy for children to handle, disposable (with no need for washing, deposits, or returns like glass bottles), and took up little space in the refrigerator. Consumer surveys tended to verify these claims; a 1956 study found that "among those families who prefer paper containers," all agreed that "the superiority of this milk container stems principally from its greater all-round convenience and time-saving features."[2]

Milk distributors found paper packages even more convenient. First, even though paper packaging was more expensive than glass, it required no system of returns. Consumers were notorious for holding on to glass bottles to use for watering plants, holding flowers, and so on. Consumers saw the bottle as free while milk dealers saw it as a significant business expense. Furthermore milk dealers did not have to wash paper cartons and paper cartons, unlike glass containers, did not break. When flattened, paper took up one-tenth as much valuable floor space as glass bottles in the milk plant. For milk dealers, the paper carton was an obvious improvement over glass. But even more important than any of this was the fact that paper packaging helped large milk dealers expand their marketing range. Selling milk in paper cartons would justify an intense consolidation of the milk distribution industry and allow milk dealers to undermine the power of organized labor within the milk economy.[3]

The use of paper cartons, in contrast to glass bottles, allowed milk dealers to shift their plant locations away from urban centers. Prior to the mid-1950s, milk dealers tended to be located in the heart of a city, with most of their customers residing nearby. Because glass bottles broke in transit, dealers had to maintain distribution centers close to their customer base. Dealers were willing to accept a certain amount of breakage as the cost of doing business, but a rule of thumb in the early 1950s stated that any trip longer than forty miles caused too much breakage. The cost of replacing the bottles wiped out any potential profits to be made on the unbroken containers. Paper cartons, on the other hand, could be transported much farther than forty miles, allowing milk dealers to move their plants away from crowded urban centers.[4]

Paper milk cartons were shatterproof, but expensive to assemble, so dealers who made the switch from glass expanded the scale of their operations to drive smaller competitors out of business. The capital investment required to purchase paper packaging machinery meant that the companies converting to paper were also the largest. In Wisconsin in 1952, for instance, 41 out of 459 of the state's milk dealers had paper packaging facilities. Plants using only glass bottled 851 quarts of milk per day on average, compared to 21,350 quarts per day for those with paper packaging equipment. Producing such high volumes of milk encouraged companies to seek sales outlets far outside their own city limits in order to justify the expense of the new machinery. In 1952, Wisconsin paper milk dealers shipped their packaged milk as far as 278 miles from the plant, with most dealers extending their sales routes fifty miles outside city limits. Small-town milk dealerships either had to install their own paper packaging machinery to compete, or else drop out of the market. Those milk dealers who were most successful in making the shift to paper packaging were those who had established their businesses in city centers during the 1920s and 1930s, but relocated their plants from the high-rent downtown districts in the 1950s to small towns or rural areas where taxes, wages, and land costs were all much lower.[5]

The trend to paper accelerated in the late 1950s, encouraged by economists in the USDA's Agricultural Marketing Service who realized its potential for dismantling the milk problem. John C. Winter of the Agricultural Marketing Service recognized the importance of distribution costs. "In recent years," Winter wrote his supervisor in 1957, "the marketing margin has exceeded the farm value of milk. A large share of the marketing margin consists of packaging and related costs." As an employee of the USDA, Winter's primary duty was to devise and implement methods for raising farmers' incomes. However, as Winter recognized, if the cost of distribution continued upward, this goal could not be achieved without raising the cost of milk to consumers. In keeping with Secretary of Agriculture Ezra Taft Benson's demands that USDA researchers devise "objective research" plans that would boost farm incomes without raising consumer food costs, Winter proposed a research project in the winter of 1956 to develop "cheaper containers." The new paper cartons, Winter declared, would require less skilled handling by unionized employees, could be manufactured more cheaply, and would entail less transportation expense. Importantly the members of the committee reviewing Winter's proposal included representatives from national milk distributors, inner-ring dairy farmer cooperatives, and economists trained in the land-grant university complex. No consumers, Teamsters, or outer-ring dairy farmers were present. This committee, which had congressional authority under the Research and Marketing Act of 1946 to approve, disapprove, or prioritize the milk marketing projects of the USDA, pushed Winter's "cheaper containers" project to top priority in 1957. In other words, the most powerful actors in the milk economy agreed that paper cartons, unlike price supports, provided a politically acceptable method for redistributing milk money to farmers. This was an example of the "objective" marketing research touted by Ezra Taft Benson—after all, who could doubt the benefits of less expensive paper cartons?—as private agribusiness firms sought government help in streamlining the food economy.[6]

Milk dealers, in particular, understood that the paper carton could "rationalize" milk marketing by reducing the strength of the Teamsters in the dairy industry. Ever since the Teamsters Union had emerged in 1899 as a federation of craft unions of urban wagon deliverymen—many of whom delivered milk to doorsteps—the organization had gained ever more influence in the dairy economy. After the successful organizing drives of the late 1930s and 1940s, the Teamsters essentially controlled the delivery of bottled milk in every major city in the Midwest and Northeast. Teamster power within the dairy industry was predicated upon the vast numbers of milkmen who delivered milk door-to-door. By 1952, according to the Bureau of Labor Statistics, one-third of the dairy employees in the country were organized delivery drivers. Strength lay in numbers, as the union used its core strength in milk delivery to organize "inside" dairy plant workers who might otherwise have turned to a rival AFL or CIO union. Some milk dealers, seeking to weaken the Teamsters' ability to dictate business practices in the early 1950s, began employing drivers only during weekdays. Such a change in business practice, however, required tense negotiations at the bargaining table, and the Teamsters were nothing if not hardnosed business unionists who would accept such a change only if it came with higher wages and other concessions from management. No bargaining table was necessary, however, for management to introduce paper packages—and paper cartons offered dealers a chance to eliminate Teamster control over the terms of milk delivery. Insofar as the vast majority of paper deliveries were to suburban supermarkets and convenience stores, dealers could contract with independent over-the-road truckers to deliver their milk, or allow the supermarkets to take care of the delivery themselves with their own drivers.[7]

Figure 6.1. Borden Milk Company Deliverymen.
Milkmen, such as these drivers photographed in Milwaukee in 1948, were salesmen as well
as teamsters; clean white uniforms were part of the job of being the public face of the milk
industry as well as a driver of a delivery vehicle (*Source*: Wisconsin Historical Society, WHi
31172).

The Teamsters correctly interpreted this shift to "dock deliveries" or "drop
shipments" as a direct attack by supermarkets and large milk dealers on the
union's core membership. Milkmen in trim white uniforms, the familiar public faces of the milk industry since the late nineteenth century (see figure 6.1),
were being slowly replaced by nonorganized truckers hauling trailer loads of
milk cartons to the rear docks of supermarkets for straight hourly wages. The
Teamsters Mid States-East Coast Dairy Conference, recognizing the implications of the trend in 1959, called upon Teamster president James R. Hoffa to
put the combined strength of the region's organized dairy, warehouse, and
chain store workers to the task of ending the "drop-load delivery system."
There was little hope for effective union resistance, however. All too often, the
best the union could do was bargain for a slowdown in the rate of expansion
of the dock delivery system. Milk dealers in the 1950s saw their profits being
steadily squeezed by supermarket demands for large volumes of milk at low
prices, making home delivery routes increasingly expensive to maintain. To rid

themselves of the trouble, large milk dealers began offering their home delivery drivers unbeatable deals on used trucks and exclusive rights to delivery routes, thereby turning milkmen into independent salesmen-contractors rather than organized employees. Hoffa decried this maneuver as an effort to create a "phony façade of small business enterprise" among milk deliverymen, but milkmen often saw the chance to establish their own milk route as irresistible. The only other option—to go on strike—risked alienating home delivery customers. New York City Teamsters discovered this during a two-week strike in late 1961. Although the drivers won their wage concessions, 10 percent of home delivery routes in the city were permanently cancelled by angry customers whose milk had not appeared on their doorsteps during the strike. Consumers who had come to expect cheap milk from their supermarkets were not particularly interested in paying more for "nature's perfect food" just to satisfy the demands of Jimmy Hoffa's union—especially after the 1957–58 Senate anti-racketeering hearings spearheaded by legal counsel Robert Kennedy heaped damning charges of corruption upon the union.[8]

Paper cartons hastened the decline of home delivery not only by circumventing the Teamsters but also by solidifying the role of supermarkets in selling milk, spurring the wave of consolidations and mergers that characterized the milk industry in the 1950s. In Wisconsin in 1952, only a few dealers sold milk primarily to supermarkets or stores; well over half of the volume of milk deliveries was still directly to homes. However, as the cost of installing paper packaging equipment forced milk dealers to increase their sales volume and expand their marketing range, supermarkets became increasingly attractive customers. Signing a contract with just one supermarket was far easier than signing up hundreds of individual consumers, and guaranteed that a milk distributor would have a high-volume customer for years to come. Losing home delivery customers did not necessarily hurt business, because most would simply begin buying their milk at the store rather than from their milkman. By 1954, the *Milwaukee Journal*'s annual consumer survey reported that for the first time, more than half of Milwaukee consumers bought their milk at grocery stores. Milwaukee consumers, like consumers around the country, knew that they could buy their milk more cheaply at the supermarket than they could at their doorstep.[9]

Store-bought milk was cheaper than home delivered milk primarily because supermarket managers relied on milk to increase store traffic. Finding that customers made regular trips to the supermarket to stock up on low-cost staples like milk and bread, store managers used cheap milk to lure customers into buying higher-margin items such as meat and packaged foods while in the store. Milk dealers whose business remained centered on providing the convenience of home delivery to consumers decried the fact that supermarkets used milk as a "loss leader." Dealers were particularly unhappy about having to give supermarkets secret rebates in order to assure shelf space and prominent display of their products. Nonetheless there was little that the milk dealers could do to stop this trend, particularly once they had invested in paper packaging machinery. As supermarkets strengthened their position in food marketing in the 1950s, milk dealers could be kept in line simply by threatening to take over milk distribution entirely, as the Kroger, A & P, and Safeway grocery chains all did at various times. If dealers did not cooperate with the supers, they would be forced out of business entirely. Furthermore supermarkets benefited from state legislatures' repeals of price-fixing laws within milk economies in the 1950s, allowing the chain stores to drive retail milk prices far below the prices charged by milk dealers.[10]

Milk dealers who wanted to stay in business in the 1950s were forced to accept the lower profit margins of store delivery. Surviving required further increases in sales volume, and as a consequence, only the largest dairies were able to adjust to the new milk distribution system. Bowman Dairy Company, one of the largest milk dealers serving the Chicago area, decided in 1956 to increase its rebates to large chain stores such as A & P to 16 percent, keeping its discount for independent grocers at 11.5 percent. In 1960 Bowman outlined a plan for a long-term commitment to provide chain stores with an increased volume of milk, with dock delivery costs to be split between the dealer and the chains. Small milk distributors had little power to resist this collusion between supermarkets and large dealers. Between 1950 and 1962, the number of milk dealers serving city markets declined by half in the United States and by over 60 percent in the North Central region. Most dealers going out of business were small firms. By the early 1960s, then, a new form of "orderly marketing" emerged in the milk industry. With the low retail prices offered by supermarkets, consumer resistance to the price of milk essentially disappeared; no longer would consumers call upon congressional leaders to investigate the "milk trust" or consider price controls to keep milk affordable. Supermarkets did the job quite well, even if they incurred losses on milk sales to get consumers into the store every week.[11]

THE BULK TANK SYSTEM

As the Teamsters lost power within the milk economy and consumers gained high-quality milk at low prices, the only major fault line left in the decades-old "milk problem" was that between outer-ring and inner-ring dairy farmers. Although New Deal-era federal marketing orders had eased tensions between inner-ring fluid milk producers and outer-ring cheese dairymen, upstate farmers continued to seek access to the more lucrative urban milk markets. The widespread adoption of the bulk tank, encouraged by agricultural extension agents and economists serving under Ezra Taft Benson in the USDA-land-grant complex, would help to eliminate this remaining point of contention in the milk economy. As rural farmers adopted the bulk tank system in the 1950s and 1960s, they also adopted the industrial premises of Benson's agribusiness vision of a vigorously anti–New Deal form of "free enterprise" in farm country.

The bulk tank system, which replaced milk cans, provided the basic infrastructure for the transformation of dairy farming into dairy agribusiness. Well into the 1950s, most farmers stored their raw milk in ten-gallon cans. Since the late nineteenth century, cans had effectively and inexpensively kept milk free from dirt and other foreign matter. However, full milk cans weighed about 115 pounds, requiring time-consuming, back-breaking labor to be transferred to a truck for hauling to the dairy plant. As a consequence, milk truck drivers were limited in the number of farms they could visit on any given day. Furthermore because the glass-lined milk cans provided only minimal thermal insulation, they required daily pick-ups, making can hauling an expensive proposition. The cost of transporting can milk to the plant encouraged dairy plants to discriminate against outer-ring farmers, just as the Prussian gentleman farmer Johan von Thünen had theorized in 1826 and as agricultural economist John D. Black had explicated in 1935. Bulk tanks offered a means of breaking down this geographic barrier, boosting the economic power of outer-ring farmers in ways that the violent milk strikes of the 1930s had failed to do.[12]

Bulk tanks were not a particularly complex technology, but their adoption involved complex political negotiations. Milking machine pumps attached to a cow's udders sent raw milk into the tank, where refrigeration cooled the fluid to a bacteria-discouraging temperature of 40°F. The term "bulk" was apt, because the stainless steel tanks could hold anywhere from several hundred to several thousand gallons—generally the equivalent of two or more days' worth of milkings. The great advantage of the system was its simplification of the farm-to-plant transportation process. A milk hauler—a trucker who traveled from farm to farm collecting dairy farmers' milk for delivery to the processing plant—need only attach a suction hose between the truck tank and the farm tank, making for quick and easy milk transfers. Bulk tanks allowed bigger trucks operated by fewer drivers to visit more farms spread out over longer distances (see figure 6.2). Companies that manufactured bulk tanks, including Mojonnier Brothers of Chicago and the Heil Company of Milwaukee, promoted the system as the greatest advancement in milk technology since pasteurization. As a 1953 advertisement for Heil bulk tanks proclaimed, "Farmer—hauler—

Figure 6.2. Bulk Milk Truck.
Bulk milk trucks such as this one parked in a farm yard near Madison, Wisconsin, in the late 1950s, convinced agricultural experts that a "direct pipeline" from cow to consumer would fundamentally alter the politics and geography of dairying (*Source*: Wisconsin Historical Society, MJS-31170).

dairy—consumer—all benefit when a modern Heil farm pick-up tank and refrigerated farm storage tanks replace the back-breaking labor, expense, and investment of 10-gallon can operations." Dairy plant managers and agricultural economists likewise touted the system as a way to reduce transport costs and thereby transform the political economy of milk. Secretary of Agriculture Ezra Taft Benson hailed the system in 1953 as a "direct pipe line" from the cow to the dairy that would markedly "reduce the cost of marketing dairy products." Economists, dairy plant managers, and farm journalists envisioned the system increasing the volume of milk produced, thereby increasing farm incomes without a corresponding rise in consumer price. For milk plants needing large volumes of cheap but sanitary milk to satisfy their supermarket contracts, the bulk tank system eventually became a necessity. Major milk processors, such as Consolidated Badger in Wisconsin (bottlers of "Morning Glory" milk products), began to require farmers to install bulk tanks on their farms in the mid-1950s.[13]

Many farmers in the 1950s, however, like the consumers who had refused to see the paper carton as a marker of technological progress, were not convinced that installing a bulk tank would automatically improve their lives. Bulk tanks were expensive. In 1956, a 200-gallon tank that would hold only one day's worth of milkings during the flush spring season cost from $1,800 to $2,500. Especially in the outer rings of milksheds, farmers had never needed to invest in such expensive cooling equipment. Outer-ring farmers were precluded from entering city fluid milk markets by federal regulations that upheld the monopoly power of inner-ring farmers and urban milk dealers. City markets offered higher prices, but also required elaborate and expensive sanitation equipment to meet public health standards. Outer-ring farmers who produced milk only for less demanding cheese and butter factories were able to rely on less costly methods—such as submerging milk cans in cold spring water—to keep their milk cool. Farmers who produced milk mainly for cheese and butter also tended to have barns that lacked the separate milkhouse needed to accommodate the giant electric cooling tanks; adopting the bulk tank would entail the further expense of erecting a new structure and stringing electric lines to it. Furthermore in order to justify the cost of a bulk tank system farmers had to invest in a cattle herd that could produce enough milk to fill the tank regularly. Dairy cattle of the 1950s had recently become an expensive commodity, after scientific breeding programs transformed the animals into industrial organisms; between 1940 and 1980 selective breeding doubled the milk production of the average cow, but also made the average cow a costly investment. Because of the expense of installing the bulk tank system, only 45 percent of Milwaukee-area milk producers had converted to bulk tanks by 1956, and only 40 percent of Chicago producers had done so. Those who did make the switch were prosperous farmers who, when they approached a bank for the requisite loan, would be immediately identified as "progressive" and therefore creditworthy. Less successful dairy farmers need not apply.[14]

Ezra Taft Benson's dream of a "direct pipeline" would only come true, however, if every farmer, no matter how "progressive," installed the system. If some farmers refused to adopt the bulk tank, dairies would have to send out both bulk and can hauling trucks, making a partial conversion even more expensive than maintaining the old can system alone. Because dairy farmers tended to be organized into farmer-owned cooperatives, decisions about conversion lay largely in the hands of the farmers themselves, who used their power as shareholders in the enterprise to direct the cooperatives' business decisions. Milk processors who hoped to convince cooperative farmer-members to transform their farming practices thus required the intervention of outside experts who had no investment in the status quo. Extension agents, as members of the Federal

Extension Service established in 1914 by the Smith-Lever Act, were charged with disseminating the scientific and technological findings of land-grant university researchers to every farmer in every county in the country. Extension agents provided just the right kind of expertise to win over obstinate farmers who felt that learned economists waxing about the wondrous possibilities of this "direct pipeline" had little real-world understanding of the expense involved in setting up a bulk tank. Dairy cooperatives such as Consolidated Badger turned to extension agents based at the University of Wisconsin to help them convince farmers of the need to increase milk volumes. The most effective method, extension agents argued, was for the cooperative directors to offer low- or no-interest loans and a premium payment to farmers who made the conversion. Dairy farmers who wanted to continue shipping their milk to a dairy were offered an irresistibly higher price for their product, if only they would put themselves in debt to dramatically boost their herd size and install expensive marketing machinery on their farms. By 1958, over 11,000 Wisconsin farmers had installed tanks, up from only 30 farmers in 1952 and up from 3,500 in 1956. Extension agents worked closely with dairy cooperatives to spread the industrial ideal that had taken hold of grain farming in the 1920s to the recalcitrant dairy farmers of the 1950s.[15]

The bulk tank system forced farmers to ramp up the volume and expense of milk production, and in doing so, transformed the economic geography of midwestern dairy farming. In the first half of the twentieth century, thousands of outer-ring dairy cooperatives populated the Wisconsin countryside, with small plants processing farmer-members' raw milk and cream into cheese, butter, and evaporated milk. Unlike the large inner-ring fluid milk cooperatives such as the Milwaukee Cooperative Milk Producers and the Chicago-area Pure Milk Association, outer-ring cooperatives were rural, local institutions, often having no more than a few dozen members. Mottoes such as "Co-Operatives are the Small Man's Means of Doing Big Things" indicated the rooting of these enterprises in the agrarian cooperative movement of the early twentieth century, and by extension the Rochdale cooperative movement of nineteenth-century rural British weavers. For example, the Hillpoint Cooperative Creamery Association was established in 1904 in the village of Hillpoint, Wisconsin, approximately 150 miles west-northwest of Milwaukee. Begun by seven farmers looking for a market for their milk, the Hillpoint Cooperative served only twenty-five farmers in its first decade of operation, processing their cream into butter and skim milk into powder. The members made only conservative capital investments in the plant, with the democratic setup of the cooperative's decision-making structure encouraging each member to keep his share of the profits for himself rather than plowing proceeds back into the enterprise. As the cooperative gained more members through the 1940s, it expanded its operations slightly, buying an evaporated milk plant from the Nestlé Company in the larger town of Reedsburg in 1946. Even with this expansion, the cooperative shared in only a minute fraction of the market for manufactured dairy products, as it competed with thousands of similar cooperatives in the state. As a form of economic democracy in action, small cooperatives like Hillpoint provided reliable markets for outer-ring farmers, but by no means guaranteed wealth or market power.[16]

With the arrival of the bulk tank system in the 1950s, agribusiness-minded extension agents began to view small cooperatives like Hillpoint as outmoded throwbacks to an era of small-scale agriculture. Extension agents such as Truman F. Graf, a marketing economist at the University of Wisconsin, advocated a wholesale "dairy reorganization" to help outer-ring farmers "[do] a better job of marketing their milk and aid them in obtaining a higher price for their products." This "dairy reorganization" plan aimed to consolidate small outer-ring cooperatives into much larger cooperatives. All farmers would have to upgrade their cattle herds and barns to meet public health standards in order to produce milk for both manufacturing and fluid use. Small farmers who had been producing only Grade B milk for butter and cheese now had to join with inner-ring farmers in producing Grade A fluid milk, or else give up farming entirely. To implement this consolidation, Graf and his extension colleagues provided legal services and marketing studies to the three most powerful outer-ring cooperatives in the state—Lake to Lake, Badger Consolidated, and Wisconsin Dairies.[17]

These large cooperatives began aggressively absorbing their smaller competitors in the 1950s and 1960s. Cooperatives like Wisconsin Dairies would most often lure away a smaller organization's most productive farmers by offering a higher price than that offered by their local cooperative. Directors of small cooperatives like Hillpoint, seeing their most productive members flocking to the larger organizations, faced a choice between losing the majority of their milk supply or merging with the larger coop. Hillpoint held onto its independence slightly longer than many small coops, lasting into the mid-1960s by shutting down its low-volume plants and expanding its sales of fluid milk in Chicago, Milwaukee, and Madison. By the mid-1960s, however, Wisconsin Dairies had swallowed twenty-one smaller cooperatives, giving it almost complete control over central Wisconsin milk supplies. Hillpoint's directors threw in the towel in April of 1967 and convinced their farmer-member stockholders to vote for merger with Wisconsin Dairies.[18] Some small cooperatives proved more uncooperative in the consolidation scheme, particularly when farmer-members realized that a merger would lead to the closing of the "little farmer factory in [their] neighborhood." In these situations, cooperatives such as Lake to Lake and Badger Consolidated pursued the more aggressive strategy of hostile takeover through stock purchase. By 1967, this merger wave led to a decrease in the number of outer-ring dairy cooperatives in the Midwest by more than one-third since the end of World War II, even as their sales more than doubled. Farmers who could not make the capital investments in bulk tanks and selectively bred dairy herds were left out of the consolidation wave.[19]

Economists such as Truman Graf phrased this consolidation process in terms of "efficiencies," a word that masked the new power relationships at hand. The old class division between outer ring farmers and inner ring farmers that had ignited the violent strikes of the early 1930s began to dissolve in the 1960s as all Wisconsin farmers—at least those able to stay in the business—began producing Grade A milk. The giant cooperatives could sell this Grade A milk on either fluid or manufactured milk markets, whichever gained the highest price; no longer did the inner-ring cooperatives maintain monopoly control over urban milk supplies. Furthermore because bulk milk tanks and tank trucks made it possible to cheaply collect and ship milk long distances, outer-ring cooperatives could successfully send their milk to high-priced city markets like Chicago, or even further if the price warranted. In 1965, Wisconsin dairies shipped 119 million pounds of fluid milk out of state; just one year before, out-of-state shipments totaled only 70 million pounds. Much of this milk headed to Chicago, but some truckers hauled bulk loads as far as Indianapolis, Oklahoma, and even Texas when shortages developed in those areas.[20]

The USDA's federal milk marketing orders, predicated on the distribution of milk within 100- to 150-mile zones, were consequently becoming obsolete in the late 1960s. Wisconsin's outer-ring cooperatives banded together with other states' cooperatives in organizations such as Chicagoland Dairy Sales and Associated Dairymen to create "superpools" of milk for sale in Chicago and other distant cities. Associated Dairymen, Inc., created in 1964 as a marketing organization for farmers previously excluded from federal milk orders, included members in a swath from Texas west to Colorado and north to Wisconsin and Minnesota. Its leaders hailed the megamerger as an opportunity to garner higher prices for outer-ring farmers without driving up the consumer price of milk. The cost of fluid milk production was generally lower on outer-ring farms, where dairymen whose land remained less costly than inner-ring farmers could afford to grow their own hay for cattle feed. The merger trend went one step further in 1969 with the creation of Associated Milk Producers, Inc. (AMPI) out of twenty-one cooperatives. With the encouragement and help of Wisconsin extension agents, particularly economist Hugh L. Cook, AMPI developed a "unified marketing program" by coordinating the milk sales of 45,000 farmers—one-tenth of the nation's dairy farmers. Known as a "super-coop," AMPI effectively wrested control over the sale of fluid milk away from inner-ring milk distributors by the early 1970s. Whereas organized inner-ring farmers had called upon the federal government to boost their monopoly power in the 1930s, the organized outer-ring dairy farmers of the 1960s relied upon new technologies to make those New Deal-era regulatory structures obsolete, even as the structures themselves continued to guarantee government-supported prices for dairy farmers.[21]

Ironically this upheaval in the economic geography of milk marketing achieved the goals of the 1933 Wisconsin Cooperative Milk Pool strike. As explained in the first chapter, the Milk Pool strikers had unsuccessfully called upon government policymakers to use state power to break up the milk monopoly of inner-ring dairy farmers so that outer-ring farmers could ship cheaper milk to urban consumers. The milk marketing orders drawn up during the 1930s had, however, used state power to preclude just such a situation. The reorganization of dairy marketing set in motion by the bulk tank system, however, made it possible for outer-ring farmers to sell their lower-priced milk to city consumers in the 1960s, without the need for government agents to rewrite the milk marketing orders. The bulk tank system, then, offered a "free market" solution to the farm strife at the heart of the "milk problem." Percy S. Hardiman, the son of the founder of a successful Milwaukee fluid milk dealer, appreciated the irony of this situation in a 1976 oral history. By merging the interests of agricultural economists, large dairy cooperatives, and outer-ring farmers willing to convert their farms into factories, AMPI had achieved, without violence or significant public outcry, "pretty much what the Milk Pool was thinking about." John D. Black would also likely have approved the outcome, because the primary objective of AMPI as stated during its formation embraced Black's favorite phrase: "To provide for better prices to dairy farmers through more orderly marketing." But where John D. Black had looked to urban milk dealers and "progressive" inner-ring farmers as the source of that "orderly marketing" in the 1930s, by the early 1970s rural super-coops had achieved higher prices for their members without driving up consumer milk costs.[22]

THE MODERN MILK HAULER

The new milk marketing system of the 1950s and 1960s drove thousands of small farmers out of dairying. Some migrated to cities while others continued farming but sought off-farm employment to make ends meet. Because the new marketing machinery relied on trucks for its operation, some farmers decided to get behind the wheel of a milk truck to eke out a living without leaving their rural homesteads. In making that choice, however, milk haulers confronted the political and economic realities of the new agribusiness order in the midwestern countryside. These truckers were not the long-haul or over-the-road drivers that inspired popular culture romanticization of "kings of the open road." Nor was their situation similar to that of the Teamsters whose control of city milk delivery waned in the 1960s. The modern milk hauler was rural, not urban, and "independent," not organized. Although some Wisconsin milk haulers would decide in the 1960s that they were being exploited by the agribusiness order, they refused to join the Teamsters to boost their economic power. Like the "independent" truckers who would rally behind Mike Parkhurst to protest their condition in the 1970s, the rural milk haulers of the 1960s remained unconvinced that either the Teamsters or government regulators could provide them with the job stability and remuneration they believed they deserved.

In one of its early issues, the trade journal *Modern Milk Hauler* (first published in October 1960) reported the results of a survey intended to describe its target audience. The "average bulk milk hauler," the journal found, was 34.5 years of age, married, with 2.5 children. He had entered the business because "he likes to be independent" and preferred working outdoors; his wife, meanwhile, fulfilled the gender norms of the period by staying indoors keeping the company's books or dispatching drivers. The average bulk hauler owned a truck and a half, each machine fitted with an 1,800-gallon tank. The average haul had by this time expanded to 90 miles a day, although with fewer, larger farms to visit, the number of stops averaged just over 12. A flesh-and-blood version of these statistics was Archie Lawrence of the tiny town of Brooklyn, Wisconsin. Although owning a slightly larger tank than average (2,200 gallons) and running a longer daily route (125 miles), Lawrence and his bookkeeping wife considered their business to be relatively small. Neighborliness lay at the core of the enterprise, as the Lawrences offered to paint their farmer-customers' bulk-tank milkhouses for nominal fees. Some haulers ran larger operations with hired drivers. Even so, haulers like Spencer Findlay of Whitewater, who owned six trucks, represented the upper end of the size spectrum. Most milk hauling businesses were small, family enterprises, and like many of the farms they served, relied on unpaid women's work in order to stay afloat.[23]

The individual hauler may not have run a large operation, but his work was essential for creating the enormous volumes of milk needed by super-coops of the 1960s. As an editorialist in the haulers' trade journal put it in 1973: "Milk transportation or hauling, if you please, has given a big boost to milk marketing. Selling of milk by co-ops isn't on a provincial basis anymore. Milk is now transported and sold where it is needed." Bulk haulers not only made high-volume, long-distance marketing possible, but they served as indispensable intermediaries between producers and processors. Haulers were responsible for maintaining milk quality in the new all-Grade A system. Besides being expected to "have clean and tidy personal habits and . . . wear clean clothing," the hauler had to be able "by sight or smell . . . to distinguish non-conforming [i.e., off-flavor or dirt-contaminated] milk, since with him rests the decision to reject or accept the milk." Furthermore butterfat samples taken by the hauler at each farm would help determine the amount of the farmer's paycheck for a particular load, while bacteria samples guaranteed a processor's adherence to health standards. Bulk haulers were thus recognized by both farmers and milk processors as highly skilled and essential workers.[24]

Despite this acknowledged importance and skill, many bulk haulers in Wisconsin felt unfairly treated by dairies in the 1960s. In the bulk system's "scramble to gain volume," cooperatives set their haulers' rates as low as possible in order to offer farmers a higher price for their milk. In order to pay the expenses of a bulk tank truck, gasoline, insurance, and taxes, haulers were forced to increase the length of their routes. According to one haulers' advocate, this "creates a substantial problem for the milk hauler. Such a hauler, affected by high daily mileage and resulting high variable costs . . . is presently *subsidizing the processor* in his desire to obtain far-out product." The cooperatives' aggressive quest for volume reinforced itself and increased tensions in the industry, as bulk haulers sought to fill their ever-larger tanks by urging farmers on their routes to boost their yields and install bigger bulk cooling tanks. Haulers who did not sufficiently expand the volume of milk they delivered to a processor faced cancellation of their contracts. Wisconsin Dairies, for instance, helped finance haulers' truck tanks, but craftily maintained half ownership of the equipment in order to easily buy out, if necessary, low-yielding haulers. The "sharecropper" syndrome that Alfred Maund had discovered in Alabama in 1953 also characterized the milk hauler of rural Wisconsin.[25]

Haulers concerned with these problems formed an organization in 1957 to negotiate with dairies for higher pay and standardized work conditions. Despite the nature of its demands, the Wisconsin Milk Haulers Association (WMHA) did not consider itself a labor union, but rather a trade association representing the interests of small businessmen. The essence of the problem, argued leaders recruiting members for the WMHA, was that the bulk hauling business was *too* small within the "economic jungle" of the dairy industry. Truckers spread out over great distances had little opportunity to learn what other haulers charged for their services, and so had to fend for themselves in setting rates that would justify their investments in trucks and tanks. Haulers, as independent businessmen, theoretically "negotiated" with processors on pay scales, but "since the hauler is dealt with individually he has little or nothing to say about the hauling rates." The WMHA likened this situation to the feudal manors of medieval Europe, with haulers as the vassals "of their overlords, the operating dairies." Dairies encouraged haulers to act as "independent" owner-operators, but controlled their incomes through arbitrary rate manipulation. If an individual trucker asked for higher rates, as one Mr. Heding did at a meeting of the board of directors of Wisconsin Cooperative Creameries in 1955, the cooperative simply threatened to do its own hauling.[26]

Joining the International Brotherhood of Teamsters might have seemed an appropriate solution to these "feudal" conditions. In fact, the Teamsters made an effort to organize bulk hauling in the 1950s, gaining some success with larger private companies such as Borden, where the union already had strong representation among "inside" plant workers. The Wisconsin Teamsters gained a significant achievement in 1953 when they signed a number of dairy processors and larger trucking firms to a Statewide Milk Tank Agreement, establishing a minimum milk hauler's wage of $1.65 per hour with overtime and seniority provisions. The firms that accepted the contract sought to stabilize wages across the industry, preventing individual firms from gaining a competitive foothold by slashing labor costs. The "statewide" agreement, however, covered relatively few firms or employees; Teamsters Local 695 of Madison signed up only six companies, with forty-nine drivers, in the 1950s. Less than one-quarter of the haulers in Wisconsin gained union contracts by the end of the decade.[27]

The contract also proved hard to enforce in the hypercompetitive atmosphere of postwar milk marketing. Individual firms had significant incentives to disregard the contract to undercut their competitors on labor costs. Teamster locals repeatedly complained to state union officials that dairies broke the agreement by using out-of-state drivers and nonunion "wildcat" haulers. The Teamsters' difficulty was compounded in 1958 when the National Labor Relations Board instructed the union to cease and desist from using its power to coerce dairies into refusing milk from nonunion trucking firms. The three largest private dairies in Wisconsin took the ruling as a cue to ignore the Milk Tank Agreement for the next three years.[28]

An even more fundamental problem was the aversion of the rural milk hauler to labor unions. The Teamsters, in particular, conjured up images of boss unionism and coercive tactics. A 1974 editorial in the bulk haulers' trade journal explained this attitude as a consequence of the average hauler's "farm heritage" that encouraged an "independent spirit" like that of "farmers, who have been traditionally opposed to unionism." Midwestern farmers had not always been opposed to labor unions, of course; during the Progressive era, farmer-labor alliances such as the Minnesota-based Farmer-Labor Party (founded in 1918) and the North Dakota Nonpartisan League (1915–1922) achieved impressive state-level political successes in uniting the interests of urban workers and rural farm owners against those of monopoly capitalists. Even after New Deal agricultural policies had driven a wedge between farm interests and urban laborers, some dairy farmers continued to believe that alliances with organized labor could be fruitful. In December 1941, the United Dairy Farmers of Flint, Michigan, voted to join John L. Lewis's United Mine Workers. Lewis then announced a plan to organize all the nation's 3,000,000 dairy farmers into his industrial union, and in 1942 successfully enrolled 22,000 members of the Dairy Farmers Union in upstate New York, Pennsylvania, and Vermont. Most dairy farmers, however, already had strong collective bargaining groups of their own—in the form of milk producers' associations, backed by New Deal-era milk marketing orders—and viewed themselves as hard-working businessmen, not working-class laborers. Farm groups across the political spectrum, including the Farm Bureau, the Grange, and the Farmers Union, united in opposing Lewis's efforts to craft a new farmer-labor alliance in dairy country, painting Lewis as a greedy racketeer who drove a 12-cylinder Cadillac. Lewis's 1942 effort to organize dairy farmers as union members soon collapsed, but its brief successes demonstrated that rural hostility to organized labor was not an inherent product of a "farm heritage," but instead of the growing divergence between farm politics and labor politics in a post–New Deal political climate. By the late 1950s midwestern dairy farmers had come to view the labor movement's demands for higher wages—and in particular, the Teamsters' power within milk processing and delivery—as direct challenges to farm prosperity. In this context, the fact that milk haulers of the 1960s thought of themselves as businessmen—or rather, "skilled, qualified, licensed professional[s]"—made them inclined to side with farmers rather than organized labor. In an industry where haulers' customers were both farmers and neighbors, furthermore, joining a union would likely lose them business and lead to social ostracization. This attitude was not confined to Wisconsin. William I. Miller, who ran a three-truck milk hauling operation in Fisherville, Kentucky, felt that he did not receive fair pay for his skilled work, but he was "definitely opposed to unions" nonetheless. The New York State Teamsters Council complained in the early 1960s that bulk haulers who refused to unionize were mere "farmers who have quit farming" and thus not "legitimate truckers." Milk haulers retorted that they were "individual owners and not subject to union jurisdiction." Compounding the antiunion sentiments of milk haulers, the Teamsters faced the challenge of a 1960 National Labor Relations Board ruling that "bulk milk drivers are independent contractors and not employees within the mean-ing of the Taft-Hartley Act." Even if the haulers risked alienating their farmer customers by joining the Teamsters, then, they had no state-backed guarantee that their economic lot would improve.[29]

Within this rural "economic jungle" in which unionization offered little hope, milk haulers in Wisconsin pursued the Progressive-era tradition of seek-ing state regulation to boost their economic power. In February of 1961 the Wisconsin Milk Haulers Association filed a petition with the Wisconsin Pub-lic Service Commission—a body created in the early twentieth century when the reformer, legislator, governor, U.S. senator, and Progressive Party Wiscon-sinite Robert "Fighting Bob" LaFollette, Sr., called for state and federal gov-ernments to uphold the "public interest" by improving working conditions and wages in the industrial economy. The progressive spirit of "Fighting Bob" LaFollette remained intact in 1961 when the WMHA requested that the Pub-lic Service Commission investigate conditions in the bulk milk hauling indus-try. The Public Service Commission was the state equivalent of the Interstate Commerce Commission, in that it required new trucking firms to obtain a certificate of public convenience and necessity in order to conduct business in the state. In other words, if an individual wanted to start a new trucking busi-ness to haul milk within the state of Wisconsin, that individual had to prove to the commission that the new firm would not create unnecessary competi-tion for existing firms. The commission also administered Wisconsin's bulk hauling licensing exam, written by the state's Department of Agriculture and the Board of Health to assure milk quality in the bulk handling system. These regulatory structures were meant to assure that trucking firms received reason-able rates for their services, and that milk haulers would maintain the public health by developing the skills necessary to handle milk properly. Despite these layers of regulations, however, the commission treated milk truckers as farm-to-market haulers. Since 1931, the commission had exempted truckers hauling farm products to market from rate control and some forms of taxation. Just as the federal Motor Carrier Act of 1935 exempted farm truckers from Interstate Commerce Commission regulations, the state-level agricultural exemption in-troduced an element of chaotic competition to Wisconsin milk hauling. When the WMHA requested an investigation into hauling rates in 1961, they were attempting to counterorganize by using the power of the state to inter-vene on behalf of weakly organized milk haulers.[30]

The WMHA argued before the Public Service Commission that the regu-latory exemption for milk haulers created unfair conditions for the independ-ent businessman. Without regulation requiring dairy cooperatives to pay uni-form and fair rates, bulk milk haulers faced bankruptcy; as a consequence, the stability of the entire bulk handling system, and thus the public's interest in a safe milk supply, was threatened. The Public Service Commission agreed in February 1961 that this was legitimate grounds for consideration of the WMHA's request, but requested data from the trade association to back up the assertion that haulers did not receive fair rates. After a year of consultation with lawyers, the WMHA came up with the desired numbers. With the goal of guaranteeing the average hauler $450 in monthly earnings, the trade association asserted that the cost of equipment, taxes, and insurance required a rate of 16.8 cents per hundredweight of milk—two cents higher than the generally prevailing rate. Remarkably the dairies publicly agreed that the haulers' request was fair in nonbinding negotiations, but it soon became apparent to the WMHA that the dairies did not intend to put the higher rates into effect. Declaring that "the time for pussy footing is over," the haulers returned to the Public Service Commission in 1964, demanding state intervention to assure a "fair return" on truckers' investments. The dairies, however, were supported in the hearings by the Wisconsin Department of Agriculture, the state Farm Bureau, and agricultural extension agents—a far more strongly organized set of interest groups than the small, recently established haulers association. The Public Service Commission denied the WMHA's request in February 1964, asserting that evidence was insufficient to prove that haulers as a group were "not realizing satisfactory profits." The state's milk haulers would continue to be exempt from rate regulation, and therefore forced to continue to negotiate rates with dairies as individual contractors. Even in the state of Wisconsin, where Progressivism had flowered since the early twentieth century, milk haulers could not count upon state regulatory agencies to confront the entrenched power of agribusiness. If anything was "the matter" with Wisconsin milk truckers (to riff on Thomas Frank's criticism of rural working-class Kansans), it was not their inbred conservatism or hostility to liberal elites, but was instead the product of the inability of either labor unions or state regulators to satisfy the economic demands of rural milk haulers.[31]

Wisconsin's independent milk haulers, unable to rely upon either the Teamsters Union or the regulatory power of the state, had failed to counterorganize against the powerful interests running the postwar milk marketing machine. This episode illustrates more than just the problems faced by a relatively small group of rural workers. Like the Milk Pool strikers of 1933 who demanded government intervention to improve their lot in the hard times of the Depression, or the Teamsters milk deliverymen who used their strength in numbers to achieve job stability and decent wages in the 1930s and 1940s, or the consumers who looked to the Office of Price Administration for lower milk prices during World War II, the modern milk haulers in 1960s Wisconsin felt that the price of milk was unfair. Unlike those earlier episodes, however, the milk haulers' protests against low hauling rates gained little public attention or policy response. The consumers, workers, and small farmers who had driven the economic liberalism of the New Deal era either no longer had a reason, or no longer had the power, to contest the "fair price" of milk. When a group of economists investigated the price of milk in 1970, they determined that the interests of consumers were satisfactorily met by the monopoly power of supermarkets in the industry becuase milk had become a low-cost "staple grocery item." Outer-ring dairy farmers were also less likely to take political action against milk monopolies, having successfully taken control of the marketing of most of the nation's fluid milk supply. But if consumers benefited from inexpensive milk while outer-ring dairy farmers gained new opportunities, the agribusiness approach to milk marketing left many in the lurch. Small rural dairies devoted to cooperative marketing were consumed by super-coops uninterested in stakeholder democracy. Organized milk deliverymen faced permanent unemployment. Small farmers bankrupted by the bulk tank system left dairying in droves; in Wisconsin, an average of a dozen farmers per day decided to quit dairying between 1964 and 1966. Rural milk haulers revived the Progressive specter of Fighting Bob LaFollette to demand decent pay, but the radically transformed milk economy muted their protests. The price of milk had become a matter for contestation in the marketplace—not on the bargaining table, not on the front pages of newspapers, not in antitrust hearings before Congress, and not in violent milk-dumping actions by farmers.[32]

The one great exception to the rule was the milk withholding actions of the National Farmers Organization in March 1967. Dairy farmers in twenty-five states refused to send their milk to market that month, demanding a 2-cent per quart increase in milk payments. The most dedicated members of the NFO resided in the outer-ring regions of Wisconsin and Minnesota, although strong supporters of the withholding action were found as far west as Idaho and as far east as New Jersey. At a time when the hourly earnings of the best-equipped dairy farmers peaked at $1.50 (compared to $2.71 per hour for industrial workers), farmers felt they had little to lose by dumping milk on the ground. NFO president Oren Lee Staley recycled the rhetoric of milk strikers of the 1930s, declaring that the organization was "only trying to get a fair price for dairy farmers." The *New York Times,* however, confirmed the political divide between farm interests and consumers that had developed since the failure of the Brannan Plan in 1949, noting that "any increase in the farm price of milk often brings a larger increase in the price to consumers." Violent tactics made consumers unlikely to sympathize with the strikers, as NFO members sought to prevent nonaligned dairymen from shipping milk to market by shooting at bulk tanks, milk haulers, and processing plants in Wisconsin, Missouri, New Jersey, and elsewhere. Their anger touched a nerve in the nation's capital, where Democrats feared that a farmer uprising, coupled with mounting opposition to the Vietnam War, would nix President Lyndon B. Johnson's chances for reelection in 1968. Johnson's secretary of agriculture Orville B. Freeman suffered repeated attacks from farmers who declared that his Department of Agriculture, just like that of his Republican predecessor Ezra Taft Benson, aimed "to keep farm prices low." The NFO adopted a political slogan: "Sell your milk and dump L.B.J.!" Freeman nonetheless attempted to reach out to the protestors, declaring in a news conference that dairy farmers had "every right to organize and hold their products from the market place," although he admitted that milk-dumping would lead to higher consumer prices. The Department of Justice, though, determined that the NFO did not have a right to prevent nonmembers from shipping milk to market, and filed an antitrust suit against the NFO on March 30. Faced with the cruel irony of being prosecuted for violating the Sherman Antitrust Act in their efforts to challenge the monopoly power of agribusiness milk processors, on April 7 the farm group announced an end to the milk strike. Oren Staley announced that "Phase 2" of the NFO's plan to boost farm prices had begun. Rather than withhold milk from the market, members of the NFO would now ship their milk solely to cheese and butter processing plants that contracted directly with the organization. In making this shift, the NFO gave up on 1930s-style efforts to confront monopoly power in the milk economy—a là Milo Reno's Farmers Holiday Association or the Wisconsin Cooperative Milk Pool strikes of 1933. Despite acknowledging the desperate straits that would lead dairy farmers to shoot at their neighbors' milk trucks and tanks, the NFO's leaders felt compelled to submit to the new agribusiness order. In fact, the NFO became complicit in that order by creating its own version of a super-coop to compete with AMPI on essentially the same terms—that is, milk checks cut to NFO members would be determined by what the consumer-driven market would bear, not by a "fair price" set within a fundamentally altered milk marketing order.[33]

The failed protests of milk truck drivers in the WMHA and dairy farmers in the NFO foreshadowed the events of the 1970s, when nonunionized truckers across the nation resorted to violent civil disobedience to demand an improvement in their economic lot. The thousands of rural truckers who rallied behind *Overdrive* editor Mike Parkhurst in the 1970s in calling for an overthrow of the Teamsters Union and the Interstate Commerce Commission's regulatory policies, however, did not look to the legacy of Progressive-era reformers such as Robert LaFollette or Depression-era farm activists such as Milo Reno for their inspiration. Instead they invoked the agrarian language of the Populist movement of the late nineteenth century as they called upon Democratic politicians such as Edward Kennedy and Jimmy Carter to dismantle the regulatory policies of the New Deal. Unlike Wisconsin's milk haulers, Mike Parkhurst's followers would get what they asked for.

CHAPTER SEVEN

Agrarian Trucking Culture and
Deregulatory Capitalism, 1960–80

Born in 1933, Mike Parkhurst grew up hoping to be a journalist. He instead found himself behind the wheel of a milk truck after graduating from high school. Soon he was hauling watermelons, potatoes, fertilizer, and paper on irregular routes from Ohio to Florida to cities on the East Coast, and by 1953 Parkhurst had saved up enough money to buy a used F-7 Ford tractor and a thirty-three-foot trailer. He soon discovered constraints to the "independence" of the owner-operator trucker; one morning he awoke to a pounding on his cab door at 6 AM in Mansfield, Ohio, where a Teamster organizer informed him that he would have to pay union dues to unload his produce. The Teamsters, along with the "stifling bureaucracy" of the Interstate Commerce Commission, Parkhurst came to believe, had "strangled the healthy growth of the free enterprise system." So in 1961 Parkhurst sold his tractor-trailer and used the proceeds to establish *Overdrive* magazine—the "Voice of the American Trucker"—published out of a spare room in his Los Angeles apartment. At first, *Overdrive* sought to unite like-minded truckers across the nation by railing against filthy truckstops and picturing scantily clad women splayed across the hoods of Kenworths. But in February 1962 Parkhurst took an explicitly political direction, declared himself a "radical conservative," and issued a manifesto for the independent truckers of the world: "Today, the small businessman is being swallowed up by the big businessman. . . . Yet, there remains a combination small businessman and adventurer [who] is commonly referred to as a trucker. While this may seem to be a romantic description of a tired ex-farmer from Iowa, that is just what many thousands of truckers are." Parkhurst vowed to fight for this independent trucker, whom he believed represented the only hope for a society overrun by union, corporate, and government control. As he later told a reporter for *Time,* he wanted "to wake the truckers up to the fact that they're slaves to a monopoly." Waking them up, Parkhurst believed, required deregulation of the trucking industry: "I want competition, open and fair competition. I want unregulated trucking." In 1979, Parkhurst helped to orchestrate a nationwide protest by tens of thousands of "tired ex-farmers," who stormed the nation's highways demanding the elimination of federal economic regulations that had stabilized labor and business relations in the freight trucking industry since the New Deal.[1]

Though the independent trucker strikes of the 1970s were sparked by concerns over the price of diesel fuel, the shutdowns drew on a deeper set of populist grievances that had simmered in the rural landscape of independent trucking since the 1930s. As previous chapters have shown, would-be farmers took to the highways and interstates in the mid-twentieth century to seek the economic independence that farming no longer provided in an age of industrial agribusiness. The antiauthoritarian, antistatist, and antiunion rural trucking culture that resulted spawned country music hits about spending "Six Days on the Road" avoiding the ICC, while "outlaw" country singer Kris Kristofferson would play an industrial bandit in the 1978 Hollywood neowestern *Convoy.* This rural, hypermasculine, neopopulist culture would reverberate throughout the entire nation's political economy in the 1970s. In that decade, rural truckers who had tasted the sense of freedom provided by the unregulated "open road" of exempt agricultural hauling decided that neither the Teamsters Union nor federal regulators could effectively provide wage stability or job security to surmount the era's "stagflationary" economic woes. The neopopulist politics of independent truckers, cultivated in rural soil since the 1930s, erupted in a series of violent protests that contributed to a broader repudiation of economic liberalism in U.S. political culture.

THE RURAL ROOTS OF NEOPOPULISM

Mike Parkhurst's description of the typical independent trucker as a "tired ex-farmer" pointed to the deep rural roots of the deregulatory politics of truckers in the 1960s and 1970s. By the time of Parkhurst's statement, the life of most rural Americans was defined less by productive relations to the land than by the demands of agribusiness corporations, the federal government, and distant consumers. "Rural" no longer correlated closely with "agriculture." One consequence of this shift was the erosion of the political and cultural sway of the agrarian myth, a widespread conviction held since the colonial era that men (and they were always men) who worked the soil were the backbone of American republican democracy and the anointed repositories of moral virtue. By the 1960s, however, the cultural power of the myth faded dramatically, as the industrialization of agriculture made even family farming so highly capitalized and commodity-oriented that the agrarian myth's ever-tenuous connection to rural reality became farcical. Furthermore as farms consolidated and rural people rapidly migrated to cities in the twentieth century, the population base of the rural United States collapsed, bringing down with it the power of the agrarian myth to dominate the nation's political arrangements. This became most apparent in the "one-man, one-vote" decisions of the Supreme Court in 1964, which tied congressional representation and electoral votes to population rather than geography, breaking centuries' worth of rural dominance in the nation's legislative domain.[2]

The postwar culture of long-haul trucking emerged within this context to present a reinvigorated form of the agrarian myth that corresponded more closely to the new social and economic realities of America's rural industrial landscape. At the heart of the old agrarian myth was a faith, not necessarily based in reality, that working the land could provide a man with the ability to control his own destiny. Self-directed work, as opposed to industrial wage labor, defined the core of rural manliness. As the economic basis of this ideal eroded in the twentieth century, rural men were forced to look elsewhere for a chance to cultivate their masculinity, and long-haul trucking proved fortuitous in this search—at least for white men. Truck driving provided white rural men with meaningful work opportunities, allowing them to imagine themselves as bearers of traditional values of manhood in an industrial context. Encouraged by country music and film representations of trucking culture, these men came to believe that trucking provided a sense of economic independence akin to that previously imagined for farming. Popular paeans to the truck driver as the "last American cowboy" in the 1970s, however, defined rural manhood as a matter of fierce independence rather than social belonging, contributing to the increasingly divisive political culture of the post–World War II United States.[3]

Like the old agrarian myth, the dream of economic independence in 1960s trucking was based only tenuously in reality. An "independent" trucker often relied on a larger trucking firm that had received operating authority from the Interstate Commerce Commission to provide him with legal loads. Large firms such as Yellow Freight and Consolidated Freightways cornered the market on government operating authorities, prompting William J. Hill, an owner-operator who agitated for deregulation during the independent trucker strikes in the 1970s, to state: "As things stand now, we're nothing but sharecroppers." The pages of *Overdrive* magazine regularly displayed a similar frustration with the unrealized promise of economic independence. Hank Miller, for instance, wrote a lengthy letter to the editor expressing a common sentiment: "Didn't most of us as children dream of going into the trucking business when we grew up? And if we worked hard, maybe own a fleet of trucks. . . . Like all the Horatio Alger stories all you had to do was work hard and have a little luck to achieve success. What a grand illusion!" Or as Otto Riemer, an owner-operator from Wisconsin who spent several decades hauling produce and dairy products, summed up his life's work: "selling out your body to haul someone else's dirty freight, is why some drivers look like old men early in life." Truckers were fully aware of the chimerical nature of "independence," but they clung nonetheless to the masculine goal of self-directed work, for the myth held special resonance in a rural context.[4]

As industrialized agriculture created larger but fewer farms in the postwar period, trucking became one of the few available occupations for rural men who might otherwise have been farmers. This helps explain why the Interstate Commerce Commission found in 1978 that the "typical owner-operator . . . is a male residing in Iowa." For example, writer Frederic Will asked a man named Chuck how he had become a trucker in the 1960s: "I'd been brought up on a farm, back-country, real quiet. I'd handled farm vehicles but I got out onto the highway pretty much by accident, helping a farmer haul potatoes. . . . I signed on with a refrigerated foods company out of Louisville . . . and that was that. It was the best work I could find." Such drivers recognized the limited range of their choices in an economic world not entirely of their own making, yet in choosing to become truck drivers they also carved out a space in that world where economic independence at least seemed possible.[5]

It was in this context that country musicians of the 1960s and 1970s lauded the independent trucker, the "King of the Open Road," as a working-class hero directly descended from the range-riding cowboy of the Old West. As discussed in chapter 4, trucking songs first emerged in the 1940s and 1950s as jukebox ditties aimed at truckers. But in the 1960s trucking songs transcended the roadside café jukebox and contributed significantly to country and western's efforts to become the nation's working-class music. Often referred to as "countrypolitan" or "the Nashville Sound," much of the country music recorded in the 1960s sought to reach out to broader audiences by discarding what *Newsweek* derided as the "raw, nasal 'hillbilly' sound, alien to urban ears." Under the guiding hands of record producers Owen Bradley and Chet Atkins, country artists such as Roger Miller, Patsy Cline, and Eddy Arnold scored hits by minimizing twang and deploying smooth vocal choruses, clean electric guitars, tight drums, and lush orchestral arrangements. As a consequence, country music, which had started its career denigrated by city folks as "hillbilly music," accounted for four out of ten record sales in 1966. The growth in sales was due not only to savvy record producers and polished artists, but to the rapid spread of all-country music radio stations in the 1960s and 1970s. Country music had long been a staple of radio programming, particularly on Atlanta's WSB, Chicago's WLS (known for the *National Barn Dance* show), and Nashville's WSM (of *Grand Ole Opry* fame). But each of these stations merely interspersed country music within a much broader spectrum of music, from light classical to rock 'n' roll. The first radio station to feature an all-country format was KDAV in Lubbock, Texas, starting in 1953. A decade later, the Country Music Association sponsored a nationwide survey of country music radio listeners, finding them to have significant loyalty to the genre as well as impressive disposable incomes that would appeal to advertisers. As urban rock 'n' roll radio stations found their own markets increasingly competitive, many turned to the all-country format and saw their ratings and revenues jump dramatically. By the early 1970s, country music could be heard, at any hour on any day, in northern and urban regions just as readily as in southern and rural areas.[6]

As country music gained national respect and radio play, trucking songs formed a sizeable subgenre in their own right, particularly after the 1963 release of Dave Dudley's recording of "Six Days on the Road." Despite being sung by a previously obscure artist from Spencer, Wisconsin, "Six Days on the Road" hit number two on the country charts and number thirty-two on the pop charts. The fact that Dudley professed to be a "Yankee," and that his song first became popular on Milwaukee radio stations, was a significant indicator of the changing market orientation of 1960s country music. The new listeners wanted modern-sounding music with a rural sensibility, not "hillbilly" music. The song was written and performed to be a hit—to appeal not only to truck drivers with spare nickels, but to a much broader audience who would see in the truck driver, rather than the railroad man, a "new folk hero," as a *New York Times* reviewer put it in 1966. Key to this strategy was the song's shearing off of the nostalgic overtones that characterized so much of the train song oeuvre; the song was hard-driving, modern, even industrial in its sound and story, as it sought to make the lived experiences of rural people relevant in a postwar context. Especially important was the song's signature sound—a combination of a mildly distorted "fuzz box" electric guitar riff, a "tick-tack" bass line, and the deep baritone vocals of Dudley. As Dudley later put it, "that shotgun guitar came through real good," giving the song an electric energy that has brought sales to date of over one and a half million records and inspired dozens of covers by artists as diverse as Junior Brown, Taj Mahal, and Country Joe McDonald.[7]

Along with the "shotgun guitar" sound, "Six Days on the Road" brought something new to trucking music: it was based in the experiences of actual truckers. The trucking songs of the 1940s and 1950s were primarily written by artists whose first-hand experience of trucker culture was confined to roadside cafés. By contrast, the writers of "Six Days on the Road"—Earl Greene and Carl "Peanut" Montgomery—had spent years hauling flooring products from Tuscumbia, Alabama, up and down the eastern seaboard. The reference to having "Georgia overdrive" came from their familiarity with throwing a truck's transmission into neutral on steep mountain downgrades in the South. Greene and Montgomery may also have chosen to call this action "Georgia overdrive" to avoid the equally common, though more offensive, terms "Mexican overdrive" and "Jewish overdrive." Other phrases in the song conveyed a similar familiarity with real trucker lingo and concerns—"Jimmy" (GMC truck), the "ICC" (Interstate Commerce Commission), and "little white pills" (amphetamines). The lingo was fascinating to nontruckers, but "Six Days" was also appreciated by truckers as a song that had more to do with driving on roads than with stopping at cafés.[8]

The remarkable success of "Six Days on the Road" encouraged other artists and producers to record a raft of trucking tunes in the 1960s and 1970s. One key figure was Don Pierce, the owner of Starday Records in Nashville. Pierce's Starday sold country music exclusively, unlike larger labels such as Mercury, Columbia, and Decca, where country contributed only a minority of records to catalogs dedicated mostly to pop, jazz, classical, and rock. Pierce was a marketer extraordinaire; among other strategies, he used direct-mail catalog campaigns to reach rural customers and jukebox operators. For Pierce, the whole point of recording country music was to sell country music: "Music that doesn't sell [is] obviously music that isn't communicating," he once stated. "You have got to be commercial! A song can involve itself with basic things such as women, drinking, gambling, death, and traveling BUT it's got to have something fresh." After the release of "Six Days on the Road," Pierce jumped on the chance to sell "something fresh" in the form of trucking music; as Starday producer Tommy Hill later recalled, Pierce "wanted to record every truck song that came through the door." Among the Starday artists who recorded hit trucking songs in the 1960s were the Willis Brothers ("Give Me 40 Acres") and Red Sovine ("King of the Open Road" and "Teddy Bear").[9]

Meanwhile, labels on the West Coast also contributed to the growing catalog of trucking songs. Many of these were part of the "Bakersfield Sound," distinguished from the Nashville Sound by its unapologetic use of hard-driving guitars, pedal steels, and honky-tonk harmonies. Ken Nelson was a West Coast country music producer who became particularly intrigued by the marketing potential of trucking songs in the 1960s. Nelson had already produced a string of country music hits for Capitol Records—the chart-topping, rebel-rousing, explicitly working-class country music of artists like Buck Owens, Rose Maddox, and Merle Haggard—when he asked Joe Cecil "Red" Simpson to write an album of trucking songs in 1965. Red Simpson learned to play guitar and fiddle during the Depression, living in a migrant settlement outside of Bakersfield, California, with his "Okie" farm-worker family. By 1965 he was a highly respected songwriter in the Bakersfield scene, having penned over thirty hit tunes for the Farmer Boys and Buck Owens. Ken Nelson had tapped Simpson's songwriting skills before, but his request of 1965 was slightly different. The astounding 1963 chart success of "Six Days on the Road" inspired Nelson. The time seemed ripe to establish trucking songs as a full-fledged subgenre of country music, thereby carving out a new market segment for Capitol Records's expanding and increasingly popular country catalog. The great market potential Nelson saw for trucking music drove him to first ask his biggest talent, Merle Haggard, to write some hit highway songs. Although Haggard would later record one of the most poetic songs of the genre—"White Line Fever"— he turned Nelson down in 1965, thinking that songs about truck-stop waitresses and pinball machines might tarnish his reputation as a serious writer of songs for the working man.[10]

Red Simpson proved Haggard's reservations unwarranted with his first hit record as a singer. Simpson's mid-tempo "Roll, Truck, Roll" was released in 1966. With lyrics about a trucker losing touch with his family, sung and spoken in Simpson' deep baritone and complimented by a melancholy, shimmering pedal steel guitar, the song became an instant classic on truck-stop jukeboxes and late-night AM radio. Although the only truck Red Simpson ever drove was a Good Humor ice cream delivery van, he was suddenly a "homespun, country-boy folk hero to the thousands of drivers who pilot the big transport rigs across the nation's highways." It was a "funny thing," according to Simpson: "It used to be that no one thought much about trucks or the people that keep them running. Now everyone—men, women, and kids all across the nation, are truck song fans.'" Simpson devoted two full-length albums to truckers, joining artists of the 1960s and 1970s such as Red Sovine, Dave Dudley, Kay Adams, Del Reeves, the Willis Brothers, and Dick Curless who transformed trucking songs into what country music historian Bill C. Malone has called the "single largest category of modern work songs."[11]

Behind the marketing efforts of country music producers lay the recognition that truck drivers, as a distinct demographic, *liked* country music. Truck drivers, reasoned Ken Nelson, spent hours "driving long and lonely miles with only their radios for company," making them an ideal audience for "a type and style of music and lyric with which they could personally identify." C. O. Bruce, Jr., a trucker from Blum, Texas, wrote to *Overdrive* in 1966 to complain about radio stations that played light classical music in the early morning hours: "I am sure that there are a lot of truckers who like [classical music], but I believe that 50% more truckers would rather hear country music on the road as it is the only kind you can understand what they are saying. . . . What we want is country music from 12 AM to 12 AM." The key phrase here was "you can understand what they are saying," indicating truckers' belief that only country musicians wrote songs that spoke to drivers' real-life concerns. Leo Hayes, whose route regularly took him from Amarillo, Texas, to New York City, claimed that "he [had] always been a country boy and the country will never leave him," which led him to grumble that "one of the greatest misfortunes bestowed on mankind is that New York [City] doesn't have a country station." Vern Husband, an owner-operator from Hooker, Oklahoma, tried to avoid such misfortunes by keeping a list of the nation's all-country radio stations in his cab "so I know where to tune in wherever I am."[12]

Although country music should not be taken as a direct reflection of the historical experiences of rural people, there is significance in the fact that nearly all trucking songs are country songs. As music reporter Virginia Alderman wrote in 1975, "The combination of truck drivers and Country music is a 'natural' as most everyone knows," noting that truck drivers were "some of the best fans country music has." But this "natural" connection was deeply tied to the social transformation of the U.S. countryside in the mid-twentieth century. A song like Red Simpson's "Roll, Truck, Roll" was not a paean to the open road. Instead the song describes a man yearning to return to his home and family. Likewise "Six Days on the Road" was as much about "mak[ing] it home tonight" as it was about evading Smokeys on the interstate. This implicit tension, between escaping society's bonds and remaining faithful to one's roots, is a defining theme in nearly all country music—particularly railroad and hobo songs—helping explain the appeal of trucking culture for country musicians seeking to sell records to rural audiences. Country trucking songs evoked a middle ground between the romance of the range-riding cowboys of the Old West and the socially sanctioned life of the farmer whose hard work fed the nation and upheld its moral values.[13]

In that middle ground between individual freedom and social responsibility, between defying social norms and upholding them, the mythology of the American trucker reflected a paradox that defined rural life in the late twentieth century. As small, family-owned farms faded from the landscape, rural Americans struggled to maintain a sense of rootedness in the land and in their small communities, even as their lives became enmeshed in an increasingly individualistic and technologically complex urban society. This tension would define the neopopulist cultural politics of independent truck drivers in the 1970s, feeding into the antistatist, antiunion sensibilities of the thousands of truckers who followed Mike Parkhurst in his quest to deregulate the trucking industry in the summer of 1979.

Country trucking songs sold a contradictory vision of rural masculinity in the 1960s and 1970s, simultaneously imagining the truck driving man as a renegade wanderer and as a faithful family man. The idea of the "rambling man" has been a consistent theme in commercial country music, from Jimmie Rodgers's statement that "when a man gets blue, he grabs a train and rides," to Hank Williams's declaration that the Lord had made him a rambling man. Just as prominent in country music has been the importance of settling down to a stable home and family life, from songs waxing nostalgic for the "old homeplace" to moralistic warnings against marital infidelity and the lure of the honky-tonk. These contradictory themes worked their way readily into trucking songs. From Johnny Dollar's "there ain't no place that I ain't been" to Red Simpson's plaintive worry about his son "not doing too good in school," the truck driving man's torn allegiance to roaming and returning home served as the narrative fuel for many a country song. But this tension did more than just help sell records. It also helped truck drivers negotiate a meaningful sense of manhood, an explicitly rural masculinity rooted in a deep resistance to becoming a "desk-pilot" or a "factory hand" simply for the sake of a stable home life. This cultural conflict between personally satisfying work and the economic rewards of truck driving would play a significant role in the neopopulist politics of independent trucking of the 1970s.[14]

Trucking culture was infused with the romance of the "open road," a space of mobility where a man could imagine himself being his *own* man. This was the central theme of countless trucking songs, from Asleep at the Wheel's "I've Been Everywhere" (in which the narrator rattles off a seemingly endless list of places across the nation that he's visited) to Dave Dudley's "Rollin' Rig" (which tells of a trucker's addictive need to roam, something his wife and children simply cannot understand). The metaphor of the alluring "long white line" that truckers must follow at all costs figured prominently in songs performed by Moore and Napier and Merle Haggard, among others. The draw of the open road, however, was much more than a country music phenomenon; it was often the most important value that a truck driving man attached to his work. As an anonymous trucker told writer/photograph Robert Krueger in 1975, "[The highway] is sort of the last frontier, where a guy can roam, be his own boss." Work on the road was still work, but that work was not performed under the constraints of walls, foremen, managers, or union organizers. As one woman described her husband's love of driving in a 1965 letter to *Overdrive,* "He has been offered office jobs and each time we talk it over again together and decide against it. We both know that he could never be happy behind a desk." For a truck driving man, the long white line traced a path of flight from the watchful eyes of authority figures. A trucker named Chuck, who was born in a small Texas town, told writer Axel Madsen in the early 1980s: "What I like about truckin' is that even if you drive for someone else, there ain't anybody

TABLE 7.1

Women in the Labor Force and in Trucking, 1960–80

	1960		1970		1980	
	Labor Force	*Trucking*	*Labor Force*	*Trucking*	*Labor Force*	*Trucking*
Number of Women	22,466,500	11,600	30,974,300	30,700	44,592,100	65,100
Percent Female	32%	1%	37%	2%	42%	3%

Source: IPUMS 1960–80.

standing over you when you're out there on the highway." When a man's workplace was the road, there were no orders from the foreman or middle management and no line speed-ups or stopwatch-toting scientific managers.[15]

The appeal of mobile, task-oriented work was not solely confined to men. Women who wished to defy the constrictions of indoor work in the home, office, or factory joined the trucking field in increasing numbers, particularly in the 1970s. By 1980, approximately 65,000 women were truck drivers, a 112 percent increase since 1970 (see table 7.1). Such statistical measures do not, of course, take into account the unpaid workforce of women who kept the books and paid the bills for their owner-operator trucker husbands—just as rural women whose work in barnyards and in farm home offices rarely qualified them as "farmers" in the eyes of census agents.[16] Unpaid bookkeepers remained invisible to census enumerators, but even women who were subject to the statistician's gaze remained a rare sight in trucking until the 1970s. In a 1933 survey of 4,000 drivers, not a single woman was employed as a driver, though around 400 worked for trucking firms as cashiers, bookkeepers, and clerks. In 1955, the trade journal *Power Wagon* noted that Martha Thomas was one of only three female drivers in the entire state of Florida. As late as 1979, a survey of over 9,000 long-haul truckers found only 57 women employed as drivers. The exclusion of women from the trucking workforce can partly be explained by policies of the International Brotherhood of Teamsters, which barred women from membership until government pressure forced a change during World War II. Even afterward, many Teamster locals instituted separate pay scales and seniority rules for men and women, often designating "men's jobs" (driving) and "women's jobs" (inside work). "Women's jobs" paid significantly less than "men's jobs," although the 1963 passage of the Equal Pay Act opened opportunities for women to challenge such dual wage structures. The act did not call for equality in pay for women and men who worked jobs of similar character, but instead called for equal pay for equal work, leaving the dual wage structure of the U.S. economy intact. The Equal Pay Act nonetheless opened a window for women's groups to contest the discriminatory practice of codifying certain jobs as male and others as female in order to keep working women's pay low. Most effective was the National Organization for Women's successful lobbying of President Lyndon Johnson to include "sex" along with "race, creed, color, or national origin" in his Executive Order 11246 of 1967. By empowering the Equal Employment Opportunity Commission to enforce the sex nondiscrimination clause of Title VII of the Civil Rights Act of 1964, Johnson's order paved the way for women to gain access to jobs that had formerly been explicitly codified as "men's jobs," including long-haul trucking.[17]

It was precisely this gendered distinction however—whether codified or implied—that drew thousands of defiant women into trucking in the 1960s and 1970s. Within a year of the publication of Betty Friedan's *Feminine Mystique* and the passage of the Equal Pay Act of 1963, a flood of letters arrived at the desk of the editor of *Overdrive* from women who saw trucking as a means of liberation from the confines of the home. In 1964, Linda Buis, who team-drove with her husband, explained that the time had come for women to be treated as equals on the highway: "'Company policy' tells me that I should be content in our little cottage, to keep a lamp in the window and stick to my knitting. . . . [But] we are both truck drivers and proud of it." Though most of a truck driver's working hours were spent in a cab much more confining than even the smallest cottage, the lure of the "open road" was at least as appealing to women as it was to men, especially insofar as "women's work" had for so long been defined by enclosure—whether in a suburban home or in a factory. As Monti Tak explained her decision to become a trucker in the early 1970s: "If you know what trucking is, I don't have to explain it to you. . . . I enjoy traveling and seeing new sights and faces. Like most truckers, I feel closed in if I work indoors." Judy Kuncher, "a small platinum-blonde woman of 27 years and 124 pounds," took a driving job for "the freedom; that's what I like. My time is my own." While appreciating the degree of control over her time, she had originally been drawn to trucking by the stories her husband told of seeing the West Coast—"I wanted to get out there, too." Such defiance of gender stereotypes inspired the 1966 country hit "Little Pink Mack," in which Kay Adams sneered that she was a "gear-swapping mama" who didn't "know the meaning of fear."[18]

But wandering was at its core reserved for men. In the eyes of male truckers, women who worked not only outside the home but *outside* were crossing a dangerous line. Men's interpretations of female truckers ranged from the patronizing—such as an article in the *Modern Milk Hauler* that applauded truck driver Shirley Genrich for her ability to remain "at heart . . . a homemaker [who] likes to cook and bake"—to downright chauvinistic, as when trucker Charlie Johnson shook his head in disbelief upon sight of Judy Kuncher, exclaiming: "A woman driving a damn big rig like this!" Truck driving men often remarked on the slight frames of women drivers, implying (incorrectly) that the height and weight of the driver was a marker of the ability to control a big rig—even one with hydraulic power steering (readily available by the late 1950s). A writer for the *Kansas Transporter* profiled Marie Jones, of Jones Heavy Hauling in Topeka, in 1954, noting that she pitted "a little over 100 pounds against an 80,000-pound cargo," which seemed "pretty rough odds." Though the difference between a 200-pound man and a 100-pound woman would seem inconsequential when measured against a 15- to 30-ton tractor-trailer combination, the incongruity was enough for the writer to label Jones, in an otherwise laudatory article, a "diminutive 'trucker.'" Surrounding her job title with patronizing quotation marks was symptomatic of a wider perception that anyone could become a *driver,* but becoming a *trucker* required more testosterone.[19]

Furthermore many male truckers believed that women who became truckers would lose their femininity, possibly threatening the gender hierarchy not only of trucking but of the entire nation. In dozens of letters to the editor that appeared in *Overdrive* magazine in the 1960s discussing the topic of women drivers, the subject of greatest concern for male writers was that women truckers might become gender-confused when they donned overalls and dirtied their hands with grease and coffee. One writer for *Overdrive* described with obvious dismay that Corinne M. White, despite having spent almost twenty years behind the steering wheels of buses, taxi cabs, and trucks, appeared to "feel more comfortable in men's clothes than in more feminine attire." Mike Parkhurst echoed a common theme when he told an interviewer, "Nothing turns a [male] driver off quite as quickly as being seated next to a 176-pound, muscle-bound mama whose clothes appear to be cast-offs from the Ringling Brothers tent department." Perhaps just as discomforting to male truckers, however, were women drivers such as Pam Pantelis who took pride in their feminine appearance. In a 1967 letter to *Overdrive* Pantelis explained that she kept a full-length mirror in her truck's sleeper cab, because she could not "stand NOT to look like a girl; and no one has mistaken me yet [for a man]!" Women drivers who were comfortable in their sexuality and in their work clothes— whether baggy overalls or tight blue jeans—transgressed the boundaries of "normal" gender behavior in the hypermasculine world of long-haul trucking, in which it was assumed that attractive women at truck stops could only be prostitutes, not drivers. Resistance to women drivers may have been further influenced by the popular notion that trucking culture was infused with sexual deviance in ways that threatened the very sanctity of American woman-hood—that, in fact, truck stops were nothing more than modern-day broth-els. Songwriters told of truckers with "girlfriends everywhere," of a "Truck Driving Son of a Gun" who liked his women "everywhere I go," of a "Truck Drivin' Cat with Nine Wives." Cal Martin's "Diesel Smoke, Dangerous Curves" warned of the perils faced by a manly trucker—and the "curves" in question were not those of twisting roads. Truck driving men were imagined to have a remarkable gift, even a compulsive need, for sexual conquest as they traveled from one truck stop to another.[20]

Many male truckers undoubtedly felt threatened by women in the highway workforce because they strongly believed a "man's job" was to support "his" home and family. After Judy Kuncher began driving a truck, her husband left her, declaring that she had become "too independent." For such men, women's liberation challenged their patriarchal authority as breadwinners. A truck driv-ing man, contrary to the popular imagery of sexual promiscuity, was generally a committed family man who took pride in providing for his family. When so-ciologist John Runcie asked a group of truckers in the late 1960s who the most important people were in their lives, the truckers uniformly responded "fam-ily." The data on marriage and divorce rates presented in table B.2 (see appen-dix B) show that truck drivers were consistently more likely to be married and less likely to be divorced than the average member of the labor force for the entire period from 1930 to 1980. The reality of the truck driving man as a fam-ily man may not have inspired as many country songs as did the truck-stop waitress, but the theme was surely prevalent. Singer Red Sovine became par-ticularly famous for his songs about the family values of truck drivers, espe-cially "Woman behind the Man behind the Wheel" and "Giddy-Up Go." Dave Dudley, for his part, believed that the theme of a trucker desperate to get home, as explored in "Six Days on the Road," explained the song's appeal to truck drivers who "were really a family guy [*sic*]. And they wanted to get home to the wife and kids. And Labor Day, play in the back yard. . . . That was the idea." After all, the narrator of "Six Days on the Road" claimed that he "could have a lot of women," but he wasn't "like some other guys" who would cheat on their wives. Kay Adams, who recorded the "answer" to "Six Days on the Road" with "Six Days Awaiting," amplified this theme, declaring that her truck driving man "*better* make it home tonight." For every song about "Movin' On" (Merle Haggard), there was another about "Comin' Home" (Johnny Horton). As in country music more generally, trucking songs imagined working-class manhood as a constant negotiation between the poles of promiscuity and fidelity.[21]

The work experience and cultural mythology surrounding truck driving provided men with opportunities to cultivate a meaningful sense of manhood—a sense of empowerment that many would see as threatened by government regulators and union organizers in the 1970s. Men whose culture taught them to admire both the wanderer and the stable breadwinner could use trucking to navigate their way between these contradictory ideals. Particularly in a rural context, this negotiation mattered. But manhood was not only about the degree to which one wandered; it was also about *power*—or at least a feeling of such. A modern tractor-trailer was a very large machine. Though by definition its operation required the existence of an extensive technological system of highways, warehouses, manufacturers, shippers, fuel providers, and so on, the truck itself was under the complete control of one person. Guiding a machine weighing up to thirty tons down the highway could provide a driver with a feeling of immense power. Especially for someone with little education and limited economic opportunities, the sense of control that came with piloting a big rig could make a man feel that he, as an individual, mattered. This feeling helped shape a belief that truckers were the "backbone of America"— a phrase notable not only because it appears on so many belt buckles sold in modern truckstops, but because it is a direct extension of the agrarian myth's contention that farmers were the nation's backbone. As the agrarian myth had once declared that men who worked the soil held a privileged and separate place within the moral and political universe, so truckers by the late 1970s came to define themselves as a group apart from, yet central to, U.S. society at large. As Merle Haggard declared in 1975, it took "a special breed to be a truck driving man."[22]

The experience of being behind the wheel of an enormous machine empowered truckers as a social group riding high above mere "civilians" in their "four-wheelers." Particularly after the Citizens' Band radio craze of the mid-1970s, truckers spoke their own lingo, referring to an unmarked police car as a "Smokey in a plain wrapper" or a low overpass as a "barbershop," and often bragged of being able to find the shortest route between two cities or the best restaurant in any small town. Taking on a CB "handle" (nickname) or mastering the intricacies of double-clutching was not enough, however, to make a driver into a fully empowered truck driving man. In the words of Otto Riemer, "a truck does not a trucker make," by which he meant that a true trucker was one who could harness the power of his machine to drive safely and courteously, maneuver easily in tight positions, and maintain a consistent speed in all types of terrain. Truckers understood possession of such skills to be the essential distinction between themselves and "civilians" whose small, maneuverable four-wheeled automobiles did not require the ability to "anticipate situations a block ahead of you . . . because you can't stop like a car's gonna stop." Only a professional driver could control the raw power contained under the hood of a big diesel rig. Furthermore a professional driver could come to feel so intimately connected to his equipment that, as one trucker put it, "a ground gear is a feeling of pain as real as a cut or scratch would be to the operator." Becoming one with the machine in this context made a man feel larger than himself, rather than a mere cog swallowed up and unmanned by the scale of industrial machinery, as depicted most famously by Charlie Chaplin in the 1936 film *Modern Times.*[23]

Truckers' sense of separateness was further encouraged by the rise of the truckstop as a space of male working-class culture. The modern truckstop appeared in tandem with the nation's interstate highways in the late 1950s and 1960s. Small mom-and-pop roadside cafés lost business to full-service multiplexes, operated as chains by a few large petroleum companies with the resources to buy up real estate at interstate exchanges. Built to lure truckers who spent hundreds of dollars for fuel at each stop, the new truckstops offered some combination of food, coffee, truck washing and repair, truck scales, restrooms and showers, lodging, and a place to meet other truckers. To help truckers avoid interaction with despised "civilians," most truckstops created separate dining rooms and rest areas for "professional drivers only." As Kirk Slack, the owner of a stop outside Tampa, Florida, advertised in 1965: "We cater strictly to Truckers and not to tourists." Truckstops pointedly defied middle-class notions of dress, behavior, and taste. Men wore overalls and work boots or cowboy hats and big belt buckles, while eating meals where quantity took precedence over quality. Despite a widespread belief that tourists could find the best road food "where the truckers eat," the truckers' use of the phrase "choke and puke" for the average roadside diner had a ring of truth. The issue was not that truckers did not prefer "good" food, but that their definition of "good" was dictated by the speed of service, the size of portions, the amount of meat, and the overall ability of a meal to provide a sensation of fullness for a reasonable price. As Emily Viparina, co-owner of Little Mike and Little Em's Truck Stop in upstate New York, recalled in 1975, "We tried to cook so it was a man's food and not fancy, fancy stuff, but it was food that they enjoyed." The truckstop was a place for truckers to bond, however briefly, as working-class men; all others were unwelcome.[24]

There were limits to the working-class solidarity of trucking culture. Particularly for African American truckers, the hope that one's identity as a truck driving man could take precedence over one's racial identity too often proved unobtainable. A black trucker named John J. Harris, for instance, wrote a letter to *Overdrive* in 1963 to complain of separate but unequal facilities at truck stops in certain southern states: "When I start on duty at my job I automatically lose

my [racial] identity and become a 'trucker' and I sincerely feel and will demand the same treatment and respect as any other 'trucker.'" But, as Harris
noted, that respect was clearly lacking in segregated washrooms that did not
provide "the same decent and modern facilities as [those available to] the white
driver." Harris further recognized that the "professional drivers only" section
of the restaurant often implied "white drivers only," as "if they don't want us
there." As in the case of women, black truckers often found it difficult to be
accepted as a "true" trucker in an occupation dominated by white men.[25]

Discrimination against black truckers was not confined to truck stops in
the Jim Crow South, however. White truckers in both the North and the
South assumed that the color of their skin entitled them to higher incomes
than blacks and feared that race-based competition for good-paying jobs
would drive down wages for all drivers. As a consequence, African American
truckers suffered from informal and formal arrangements in Teamster locals
that defined long-haul driving as a white man's job, reserving for black men
lower-paying jobs in warehouses, local delivery driving, and "spotting" (guiding trucks to delivery docks). These jobs not only paid less on an hourly basis
than over-the-road driving jobs, but also tended to be part-time rather than
full-time; as of 1960, only 54 percent of African Americans employed in the
trucking industry held full-time jobs. African Americans who worked for
wages in the trucking industry consequently earned significantly less than their
white counterparts. The wages of whiteness are quantifiable; as the data in
table 7.2 illustrate, in 1960 black truckers earned barely more than half as
much as white truck drivers. This situation began to change in the 1960s, however, after the civil rights movement achieved passage of the 1964 Civil Rights
Act. Title VII of that act authorized the Equal Employment Opportunity
Commission (EEOC) to hear cases involving individual workers who faced
discrimination from either employers or labor unions. In an early discrimination case filed against the Federal Paper Board Company of Bogota, New Jersey, the EEOC brokered settlements in 1966 with both the firm and with the
United Papermakers and Paperworkers union to force changes in seniority
rules that would open up more driving jobs for black employees. Other cases,
particularly those involving chapters of the Teamsters Union, proved more
difficult to resolve. More often than not, the EEOC would fail to negotiate a
settlement that both management and union leaders agreed upon. African
Americans who wished only to be considered for promotion to over-the-road
driving jobs thus had to take their cases to court, where they could expect to
spend several years fighting against firms and unions better equipped to hire
lawyers capable of stalling litigation.[26]

Even so, some African American truckers did make important strides in at-

TABLE 7.2
Truck Driver Income by Race, 1960–80

	1960		1970		1980	
	White	*Black*	*White*	*Black*	*White*	*Black*
Median Income†	$11,820	$6,814	$14,953	$10,449	$14,005	$10,005

Source: IPUMS 1960–80.

† 1980 dollars, using Consumer Price Index.

taining higher-paying jobs. By 1970 the disparity between white and black truckers' incomes had narrowed somewhat (see table 7.2). As important as those higher incomes must have been for black trucking industry workers, however, many continued to resent the widespread discrimination that prevented most African Americans from attaining the best jobs as over-the-road drivers. For instance, one of the largest trucking firms of the time, T.I.M.E.-D.C., employed 1,820 white long-haul drivers in 1971 but only 8 black over-the-road drivers, spurring a lawsuit that was not resolved until it reached the Supreme Court in 1977. T.I.M.E.-D.C. and the Teamsters contested district court and appeals court decisions that favored black plaintiffs, arguing that more minorities had been hired by the firm since 1971 and would soon have enough seniority built up to advance to over-the-road jobs. In 1977, however, the Supreme Court ordered the firm and the union to make long-haul driving jobs immediately available to black workers who had already earned seniority rights to promotion through years of working as local drivers, warehousemen, or spotters.[27]

Faced with frustratingly few achievements under Title VII of the Civil Rights Act or in the courts, black leaders created an organization in 1975 to help African American truckers become "kings of the open road." The Minority Trucking-Transportation Development Corporation (MTTDC), "dedicated to the economic interest of all minority truckers," enrolled "several hundred members" by mid-1976. Taking to heart President Richard Nixon's 1969 call for an expansion of "Black Capitalism," Timothy Person of the MTTDC petitioned Nixon to consider appointing two black citizens as ICC commissioners to address historic discrimination in long-haul trucking. Person's petition did not succeed; Nixon's call for Black Capitalism was made with the intent not of promoting black business ownership but of forestalling political demands for affirmative action. The MTTDC nonetheless remained active at the local, state, and federal levels until 1980, running educational, research, and lobbying campaigns and providing legal counseling to black drivers seeking to break down the color barrier in long-haul trucking. For instance, the group rallied behind the efforts of Allstates Transcontinental Van Lines to gain ICC operating authority, which, if granted, would have made the company the first black-owned interstate hauler of household goods. The committee saw a black-owned furniture mover with interstate operating rights as an important business not only for providing incomes to black drivers who would be hired by the firm, but also as a way to provide a needed transportation service to African American residents of the nation's inner cities—areas where, the MTTDC noted, most white-owned furniture haulers refused to proffer their services. This effort also failed, as the ICC declared that the areas to be serviced by Allstates were already served by existing van lines. The ICC refused to grant the black-owned firm operating authority despite overwhelming evidence that existing white-owned van lines did not, in fact, serve urban areas with majority black populations. Testifying before the Senate Commerce Committee in the summer of 1979, M. Harrison Boyd of the MTTDC summed up the extraordinary sense of frustration the Allstates case engendered in the black trucking community: "How is it that more than $100,000 in legal and professional fees, support from the [Carter] administration, the Congress, three Government agencies and various institutions in the private and public sectors cannot get a minority the first national van line authority in the history of our Nation?" Despite the MTTDC's efforts, structural barriers—in addition to outright racial bigotry—prevented African Americans from joining the ranks of long-haul truckers.[28]

Racial conflicts over access to good-paying jobs were sharpest and most bitterly fought within the regulated, unionized sector of the trucking industry. These firms tended to be organized by the Teamsters Union—the locals of which often fiercely guarded the "possessive investment in whiteness" that secured higher wages and more stable employment for white truckers. But in the unregulated sector of the trucking industry, small firms and owner-operator truckers dominated the field—and this sector of trucking was so overwhelmingly white as to make racial conflict a non-issue for most rural, unregulated, and owner-operator truckers. While many white truckers who worked for wages felt compelled to fight to keep black truckers from rising through the ranks, white truckers who worked for themselves or for a small firm could ignore the possibility that blacks might also wish to gain the sense of empowerment and economic opportunity provided by driving a big rig across the country. While the color line in regulated trucking was bitterly contested, the color line in unregulated trucking was nearly invisible because blacks were so thoroughly excluded. As the census data presented in table 7.3 show, the overwhelming majority of owner-operator truck drivers from 1960 to 1980 were white. These numbers include urban delivery drivers as well as long-haul drivers,

TABLE 7.3

Truck Ownership by Race, 1960–80

	1960		
	Total	*White*	*Black*
Number of Owner-Operators	135,571	126,507	8,865
Percent of Owner-Operators	100%	93%	7%
	1970		
	Total	*White*	*Black*
Number of Owner-Operators	121,300	110,100	10,600
Percent of Owner-Operators	100%	91%	9%
	1980		
	Total	*White*	*Black*
Number of Owner-Operators	188,900	173,400	13,200
Percent of Owner-Operators	100%	92%	7%

Source: IPUMS 1960–80.

however, and there is reason to believe that the long-haul industry was far whiter. For instance, business management researcher Richard Leone estimated in 1970 that only 2.4 percent of long-haul truck drivers were black. Leone's estimates were based solely on data provided by large, regulated freight carriers, since comprehensive data on unregulated over-the-road trucking firms' labor forces do not exist (see appendix A). It seems likely that unregulated long-haul trucking firms would have had a much lower proportion of black drivers. As small firms with few employees, they would not have appealed to EEOC or Department of Justice lawyers as worthwhile targets of antidiscrimination actions. Furthermore because truckers in the rural, unregulated sector tended to be recruited by family members or friends, the whiteness of this sector of the trucking industry would have been self-perpetuating. The U.S. Civil Rights Commission found in a 1974 analysis of the trucking industry that only a "miniscule number" of trucking firms were owned by blacks or other racial minorities. Without black ownership of small trucking firms, the opportunities for social recruitment of new black drivers into the over-the-road industry were inherently limited.[29]

With such structural challenges to integration of the long-haul industry in place, most white long-haul truckers in the 1960s and 1970s would have had little compulsion to militantly defend the color line. The "independent" white trucker of the 1960s and 1970s, as we shall see below, would have felt far more threatened by the Teamsters Union and the regulatory power of the ICC than by the possibility that black men might join their ranks as owner-operator truckers. Thus, although racial inequality and segregation pervaded long-haul trucking, making the prerogatives of whiteness "invisible" and seemingly "natural" to white drivers, both white and black truckers shared a common sense of antagonism toward unions and government officials. Much like the black truckers who formed the Minority Trucking-Transportation Development Corporation, white long-haul owner-operator truckers decided in the 1960s and 1970s that labor unions and the federal government were undermining the economic interests and opportunities of the common working man.

The act of driving a truck could be an empowering experience, providing a sense of controlling an enormous piece of machinery that marked a man as part of a distinctive social group. Because the pride associated with this sense of power was so important to white male truckers, they created carefully guarded boundaries to their group identity, excluding "civilians" and female and black truckers from full membership. Like the old agrarian myth that defined a farmer as a white man whose hard labor made the lifestyles of less industrious men possible, trucking culture imagined a truck driving man as both central to U.S. society yet essentially separate. In the 1970s, this sense of separateness would take on a new intensity as the truck driving man came to understand himself as the "last American cowboy," a cultural construction that helps to explain the intense neopopulist politics of the violent trucker shutdowns of 1973–1974 and of the summer of 1979.

The Neopopulist Moment

Antiestablishment sentiments ran strong in U.S. trucking culture from the earliest days of long-haul trucking, but emerged in the 1970s as a full-fledged repudiation of all large-scale institutions. In particular, many truckers came to deeply resent the very existence of the International Brotherhood of Teamsters and layers of government regulations. Truckers came to imagine themselves as outlaw figures resisting all efforts of liberal society to bring stability and social cohesion to American life—a process encouraged by a slew of popular culture representations of truckers as cowboys, bandits, and renegades both before and after the independent trucker shutdowns of the 1970s. This uprising, in both its political and mythological forms, drew from a wellspring of antiestablishment resentment long present in the rural social landscape, a resentment that had risen, abated, and yet lived on after the Populist agrarian movement of the 1880s and 1890s. In tune with a wider cultural moment in the 1970s when neopopulism became a means of protesting liberal social change rather than encouraging it, the "bandit" trucker who defied authority figures became a national (anti-)hero. The Populist movement marked a rural repudiation of industrial capitalists' laissez-faire ideology and ushered in the Progressive era of strong government intervention in social and economic affairs—including, notably, the regulation of interstate transportation. By contrast, the neopopulist protests of independent truckers in the 1970s marked a rural repudiation of economic liberalism, in ways that would benefit suburban U.S. consumers while simultaneously undermining the power of organized labor and calling into question the federal government's intervention in the economy.[30]

Independent truckers mounted a strong challenge to the Teamsters Union in the mid-1960s. For three and a half decades the Teamsters had honed a strategy that combined the use of brute force and pragmatic "business unionism" to organize large and medium-sized trucking firms, primarily regulated firms. The secondary boycott proved particularly effective, as Teamster locals would use their established power in certain industries to compel recalcitrant companies to sign labor contracts by cutting off a firm's supplies of fuel, tires, and truck parts delivered by organized drivers. After the 1959 Landrum-Griffin Act clamped down on the secondary boycott, the Teamsters lost their most potent organizing weapon, but under the leadership of James R. Hoffa the union continued to fight for higher wages for its members. In 1964, Hoffa attained one of the most impressive achievements in Teamster history, the National Master Freight Agreement, binding nearly every large unionized trucking firm in the country to a standard labor contract that covered approximately 450,000 truck drivers. Organized freight trucking provided job stability, seniority rights, strong wages, guaranteed pensions, and paid vacations. Teamsters benefited handsomely from union membership, especially in comparison to general trends in industrial wage gains. Hoffa's achievement of unprecedented national bargaining power for his union, however, came at the expense of an exceptionally undemocratic internal bureaucracy. Even when Hoffa brought shame to the union through shady deals with mobsters and earned a prison sentence for bribing a grand juror in 1964, however, many rank-and-filers remained deeply loyal to the union. Although Teamster leaders had utterly silenced individual members' voices in labor negotiations, Hoffa had brought the rank-and-file undeniable economic benefits.[31]

The signing of the National Master Freight Agreement in 1964, however, marked a turning point in the rise of Teamster power. Four years after the signing of the first master agreement, approximately 500,000 truck drivers belonged to the Teamsters (out of 1.6 million total members). By 1976, the number of unionized long-haul truckers had decreased to 280,000—a 44 percent decline in union membership in one decade. These decreases came at a time when overall employment in the trucking industry *increased*, indicating that individual truck drivers were rapidly fleeing not the industry but the Teamsters, even though the union continued to achieve gains in wages, benefits, and working conditions. A 1977 article in the conservative magazine *U.S. News & World Report* declared that the Teamsters Union was itself to blame for the trend, having been so successful at gaining wage increases over the years that "its members are being priced out of their jobs." This was not the case, however. Unprecedented economic opportunities were available to self-employed, nonunionized truckers in the 1960s; as the data in table B.3 (see appendix B) illustrate, this was the first decade in which self-employed truck drivers earned higher median incomes than truckers working for wages. Although these data do not take into account pension or health benefits or other noncash income, they show that by 1970, owner-operator truckers on average earned almost 8 percent more than their "company driver" counterparts. In 1960, by contrast, the median income of employed truckers was 14 percent higher than that of self-employed truckers. For Verla Bullard, who wrote to *Overdrive* magazine in February 1971 after having reread Vance Packard's 1959 book *The Status Seekers,* the rising incomes of independent truckers during the 1960s indicated that they belonged in the ranks of the "upper middle class," despite sociologists' continued definition of trucking as blue-collar work. Bullard—apparently anxious about her family's socioeconomic status—overstated her case, but captured the sensibility of truckers of the period who believed upward class mobility could best be achieved through self-employment rather than Teamsters membership.[32]

Even as the ink was drying on the National Master Freight Agreement, nonunion trucking firms began sprouting in rural regions of the country. Crippled by the Landrum-Griffin ban on secondary boycotts, the Teamsters of the 1960s and 1970s could do little to counteract the rise of new firms that relied on "independent" owner-operator drivers. Many of these firms started out small, such as the trucking company established by cattle farmer Lamar Beauchamp in Winter Haven, Florida, in the early 1960s to haul carcasses from midwestern beefpacking plants to supermarkets in the Southeast. What began as a fleet of five reefer trucks expanded dramatically in 1965, when Beauchamp decided to buy the Refrigerated Transport Company. Although Refrigerated Transport was one of the nation's largest unionized trucking firms at the time, it was on the verge of bankruptcy, and sold out to Lamar Beauchamp and his son Richard for only $600,000. By contracting solely with nonunion, owner-operator drivers, the Beauchamps were able to undercut the freight rates of unionized firms hauling perishables. By 1980 Refrigerated Transport had become the nation's largest refrigerated trucking firm. Such firms often practiced a form of welfare capitalism reminiscent of the 1920s, keeping drivers loyal to the "family atmosphere" of a company. This was the case at Merrill Transport of Maine, which maintained its status as the largest nonunion trucking firm in that state in the 1970s by offering profit-sharing plans, promotion to managerial status from within the ranks of drivers, and a "generous Christmas [pay bonus] program." The single largest nonunion trucking firm, Overnite Transportation of Richmond, Virginia, similarly relied on a welfare capitalist strategy in the 1970s to fend off the Teamsters. The company supplemented welfare capitalism with less benign tactics. Founded as a one-truck affair in the 1930s by Harwood Cochrane (a former dairy farmer), Overnite expanded rapidly in the 1960s and 1970s by buying up struggling unionized companies, laying off all the drivers, and filling the jobs with "extremely loyal people." Under Cochrane's direction, Overnite earned a reputation as a virulently antiunion company. In 1961 the company successfully sued the Teamsters for $863,193 in losses incurred during a secondary boycott that violated the provisions of the Landrum-Griffin Act. Companies such as Overnite were intent upon using the Landrum-Griffin Act not only as a weapon to fend off the Teamsters but as a means of gaining a competitive edge on established unionized trucking firms such as Roadway and Consolidated Freight.[33]

Along with Refrigerated, Merrill, and Overnite, thousands of smaller concerns emerged in the 1970s to challenge the regulated, unionized trucking sector's dominance of the motor carrier industry. As the data in table 7.4 illustrate, nearly 19,300 new unregulated trucking firms emerged between 1967 and 1972 (an increase of 44 percent), during which time the number of regulated trucking firms increased by only 10 percent. Most unregulated firms were tiny in comparison to their regulated counterparts, with average operating revenues per firm of approximately one-eightieth that of larger firms in 1972. Furthermore unregulated firms paid significantly lower wages to their employees; workers at regulated trucking firms earned on average 56 percent more per year than the almost 328,000 workers at unregulated trucking firms. By 1977, employees at regulated trucking firms earned 80 percent more than their unregulated counterparts. (Insofar as these data unfortunately represent only the wages of employees and not owner-operators contracted to the firms, there is no way to compare incomes of regulated and unregulated owner-operator drivers.) Further analysis of the Census Bureau's 1972 data on long-haul unregulated trucking firms (presented in table B.4 in appendix B) shows the rural concentration of enterprises that hauled freight across state lines yet remained outside the regulatory reach of the ICC—and generally beyond the organizational scope of the Teamsters Union. When states are ranked by the highest concentrations of unregulated long-haul trucking firm employees in relation to the statewide labor force in 1972, the top ten states include Arkansas, Montana, South Dakota, Minnesota, Nebraska, Idaho, Kansas, Iowa, California, and Wyoming—all states with large rural populations and economies heavily dependent on agriculture. Urban industrial states such as Connecticut, New York, and Massachusetts fall at the bottom of the list.

As nonunionized and unregulated trucking firms flourished in the 1970s, the "independent" owner-operator became a common figure in the trucking industry. In 1979, industry analyst Daryl Wyckoff estimated that approximately 100,000 of the nation's 500,000 long-haul truckers were owner-operators. The U.S. General Accounting Office reported that between 1972 and 1980, self-employment in the long-haul trucking industry increased by 43 percent while overall employment in the industry increased by only 15 percent. Furthermore as figure 2.1 illustrates, southern states such as Alabama, Arkansas, Oklahoma, Kentucky, and Tennessee witnessed rising concentrations of owner-operator truckers within their labor forces, although midwestern farm states such as Iowa and Minnesota continued to have the highest concentrations of self-employed

TABLE 7.4
Number, Revenues, Employees, and Compensation of Regulated and Nonregulated Motor Carriers, 1963, 1967, 1972, and 1977

| | 1963 | | 1967 | | 1972 | | 1977 | |
	Regulated	Nonregulated	Regulated	Nonregulated	Regulated	Nonregulated	Regulated	Nonregulated
Number of Carriers	1,175	42,986	1,389	43,628	1,525	62,924	835	58,335
Operating Revenues per Carrier	$5,978,723	$53,483	$5,586,200	$85,604	$9,832,131	$123,856	$26,970,060	$216,319
Total Number of Employees	351,104	167,500	508,930	192,688	580,000	327,770	473,073	333,612
Average Employee Compensation	$7,251	$5,081	$7,928	$6,663	$12,778	$8,195	$19,785	$10,916

Sources: ICC, Transport Statistics, 1963, 1967, 1972, 1977; 1963 Census of Transportation: Vol. IV; 1967 Census of Business, Selected Services, Subject Reports, no. 8; 1972 Census of Transportation, Selected Service Industries, S-7; 1977 Census of Transportation: Nonregulated Motor Carriers and Public Warehousing.
Note: Regulated refers to intercity Class I Common Carriers of Property only (1963–72: firms with over $1 million annual revenues; 1977: firms with over $3 million annual revenues). Nonregulated includes all trucking firms exempt from ICC regulation employing workers for wages, but does not included non-regulated self-employed truckers.

drivers. Just how many long-haul truckers were actually owner-operators was (and is) open to dispute, becuase many, if not most, worked in the unregulated trucking sector—generally hauling fruit, vegetables, milk, livestock, grain, and other "exempt" agricultural commodities—and thus evaded the ICC's statistical reporting requirements. Furthermore because owner-operators were not considered employees by the Census Bureau, they were not counted in the Bureau's 1963, 1967, 1972, and 1977 special reports on the unregulated trucking industry. For instance, the 1972 special census report on unregulated trucking firms found 10,812 establishments primarily engaged in transporting agricultural products, but that number included only those companies with at least one paid employee, thus excluding many self-employed owner-operators. With little reliable information available, contemporary estimates of the number of owner-operators in the country varied widely. A group called the National Independent Truckers Unity Committee claimed to have 150,000 members in 1976, while the National Association of Long-Distance Owner-Operators claimed 90,000 members. What was not up for debate was the fact that the vast majority of these owner-operator truckers did not belong to the Teamsters. At least 80 percent of owner-operator truckers were nonunionized.[34]

The decline of Teamster power was not solely due to Landrum-Griffin or to the rise of rural antiunion firms, for many truckers came to see the Teamsters as having lost touch with the common working man. As an owner-operator steel hauler (and former Teamster), told Studs Terkel in 1974, "Outside of the dues money [the Teamsters] take out of your check, they [do] absolutely nothing. They [do] less than nothing. . . . They're establishment." This statement from a steel hauler represented a broader sentiment among owner-operators in that industry, as became clear during a set of violent wildcat strikes in 1967 and 1970. A group of owner-operators organized a dissident faction called the Fraternal Association of Steel Haulers (FASH), determined to gain recognition within the Teamsters Union for their unique economic interests "as the semi-independent owner-operators of their own expensive equipment." The reason for holding wildcat strikes, one member of FASH declared, was that "The [T]eamsters say they represent you, but they don't. We're just dues payers." The formation of FASH was indicative of a much broader frustration with the Teamsters among many truckers in the 1970s. Rank-and-file Teamster members around the country demanded that their leaders revive the militancy that had made their union so strong in the late 1930s and immediate postwar years. In the spring of 1970 in Chicago, 40,000 Teamsters led by Louis Peick of Local 705 organized a massive strike to protest unsatisfactory wage increases agreed to by national leaders. The strike forced the national union to renego-

tiate better pay hikes for all its members in 1970, but under the leadership of
Frank Fitzsimmons from 1971 to 1981 the IBT suppressed the uprising by offering high-paying executive posts to Chicago rebels Peick and Ray Schoessling.
Even so, in 1976 over 440,000 Teamsters struck again, demanding wage increases that would keep up with runaway inflation. Although the 1976 strikers
achieved significant wage concessions, rumbles of discontent with Fitzsimmons's lackluster leadership led to the creation of the Teamsters for a Democratic Union (TDU). TDU members picketed the national convention in
1976 stating that "officials hold these conventions to steal our money." Fitzsimmons responded by telling the dissidents to "go to hell." For truckers who refused to join the increasingly passive and undemocratic union in the 1970s, the
pages of *Overdrive* magazine confirmed their anti-Teamsters sentiments. Mike
Parkhurst held a life-long grudge against the union, which he believed had
"forced" him to join and pay dues despite the fact that he owned his own truck
in the 1950s. In a 1974 call for independent truckers to unite in opposition to
the Teamsters, Parkhurst declared that "forced unionism or forced anything
has always been what most truckers call 'slavery.'" Truckers often wrote in to
Overdrive to express similar statements, such as Homer Hanna's 1966 declaration of independence: "I have lived for ten years without the Union and I can
say I've been really happy. . . . I was hired for my willingness and dependabil-
ity as a man. I don't have to sell myself to anybody to make a living." The measure of a truck driving man in this formulation was not merely the thickness
of his pay envelope, but his ability to fend for himself in a difficult economic
environment.[35]

Independent truckers came to despise, along with labor unions, the deep
involvement of government in regulating that economic environment in the
1970s. Even for the rural truckers who were exempt from the economic regulations of the ICC, the presence of agents of government—whether local,
state, or federal—was a persistent feature of the daily work experience. Just as
vexing as the "Smokeys" (state troopers) or "county mounties" (county police)
who issued speeding tickets were the bewildering array of state-level regulations and taxes. Each state set its own restrictions on maximum weight, height,
and length of trucks and trailers, and each state devised its own methods for
measurement. Interstate travel required a driver to have an intimate knowledge of all of these rules and hundreds more, a task that was still further com-
plicated by the fact that the rules were constantly changing and often arbitrarily enforced. As ex-trucker Jack Cady summed up in 1973, "Bureaucrats steal
more than money. They take a man's time, eat at his perception and life with
hot little worms of red tape." Truckers may have imagined themselves "kings
of the open road," but that myth was belied by their need to navigate through

a dense web of weigh stations, ports of entry, reams of paperwork, layers of taxation, and contradictory regulations.[36]

For Otto Riemer, who dedicated an entire chapter to "Government" in a 1985 memoir of his life in trucking, it was clear that big government and big business had aligned to subject the independent trucker to the arbitrary exercise of power. "Out on the road we are little more than checkers," wrote Riemer, "being moved on the boards of power by the agents of government. . . . Big Brother is no longer merely looking over our shoulders, he is slowly but surely taking complete control over our lives." Riemer's statements captured an antistatist sentiment that by the mid-1970s was a central component of trucker culture, as one can see by opening any issue of *Overdrive* magazine from the period. A 1966 article in *Overdrive* denounced the ICC as "octopustic" for maintaining a "perpetual banquet of privilege and power" that served only corporate trucking firms and the Teamsters Union while shutting independent truckers out of lucrative freight markets. In 1970 this interpretation of ICC malfeasance gained wider circulation when a group of Harvard Law students aligned with consumer advocate Ralph Nader published *The Interstate Commerce Omission*. Naderites attacked ICC commissioners for allowing giant railroad and trucking firms to maintain cartel-like power while driving up the cost of goods for the consuming public. In 1973 *Overdrive* interviewed libertarian economist Milton Friedman of the University of Chicago, lauding the free-market theoretician for his "daring and outspoken" belief "that governmental agencies are far worse than the problem they were created to solve" and that "there is no justification for the ICC whatsoever." In 1975, the magazine included a piece unironically praising New Left historian Gabriel Kolko's critique of the Interstate Commerce Commission as a corporate-liberal tool that provided large transportation firms with a government-sanctioned monopoly that they could not achieve in the marketplace.[37]

Otto Riemer, however, presumably never read Milton Friedman's manifestoes or Gabriel Kolko's revisionist histories of transportation policy. His self-published statement about Big Brother deserves further attention, though, because it was delivered as part of a complex political orientation that assuredly was not inspired by New Left politics, Naderite consumerism, or by academic libertarians in the Chicago School of economics. In a book ostensibly about his experiences as a truck driver, Riemer offered eloquent commentaries on a broad range of political topics. He was opposed to abortion and drugs and welfare and taxation and corporate capitalism. Riemer supported, however, animal rights, racial equality, New Deal-style public employment and poverty-reduction programs, and organized labor (but not the Teamsters). Though such a mix of views may seem contradictory, for Riemer the entire package was coherent in its concern for the people he saw as the primary victims of institutionalization, bureaucratization, and corporatization. Although Riemer might have agreed with the New Left's 1962 declaration in the "Port Huron Statement" that U.S. democracy suffered from an alienating "politics without publics," it seems unlikely that Riemer would have taken to the streets to demand an end to racial injustice, persistent poverty, and Cold War militarism. Nor would he have been likely to pound the pavement canvassing for libertarian Barry Goldwater in the 1964 presidential election, as many New Right college students and Sunbelt suburbanites did in their quest to scale back government intervention in the economy while strengthening government policing of moral affairs.[38] A neopopulist truck driver like Riemer would likely have had little taste for such divisive politics and little time for engaging in participatory democracy. Riemer's version of neopopulist politics was by no means his alone. As one driver told Studs Terkel: "It's a strange thing about truckers, they're very conservative. They come from a rural background or think of themselves as businessmen. But underneath the veneer they're really very democratic and softhearted and liberal. . . . You tell 'em they're liberal and you're liable to get your head knocked off. But when you start talking about things, the war, kids, when you really get down to it, they're for everything that's liberal." The rural backgrounds, daily work experiences, and absorbed mythologies of many truckers made them deeply resistant to intrusions of big labor and big government—but this did not make them inherently conservative or even necessarily libertarian in a dogmatic sense. Mike Parkhurst, who considered himself a "radical conservative," saw most truckers as "liberal-conservatives"— that is, they believed firmly in "as much freedom as possible on the highway," but had mixed views on every other political topic.[39] A trucker like Otto Riemer thus might have been drawn to the economic populism espoused by Independent American Party candidate George Wallace in the 1968 election, but would have been more likely to actually vote for Republican Richard Nixon as the "law and order" candidate who promised, however insincerely, a more moderate response to the racial tensions of the period. If Nixon became allied too closely with corporations or the Teamsters at a time of economic stagnation, however, that support was likely to vanish. Pocketbook politics— not socially conservative concerns about affirmative action, integrated schools, student radicalism, or women's liberation—were the key factors shaping independent truckers' rising tide of anger over what they saw as the interlocking of big government, big labor, and big business in the 1960s and 1970s.[40]

When truckers came to feel betrayed by arbitrary government regulations and the undemocratic Teamsters Union, radically libertarian politics came to the fore. "Stagflation," the combination of stagnant workers' earnings and rising prices that characterized the economy of the 1970s, helped fuel this neopopulist anger. In contrast to the 1960s, when owner-operator truckers had made impressive gains in income relative to their "company driver" counterparts, real income for owner-operators stagnated in the 1970s so that the median incomes of self-employed truckers were well below those of employed drivers by the end of the decade (see table B.3 in appendix B). Even as earnings fizzled, independent truckers found themselves opening their wallets wider to pay for rising costs of doing business. As trucks grew larger and trailers grew longer under liberalized state laws allowing bigger rigs on the nation's highways, independent truckers found themselves purchasing new equipment and paying higher insurance rates. As J. Gonzalez wrote to *Overdrive* in February 1973, "[Prices] in America are not going down. My fuel, tires, and oil went up. My take-home pay has gone down. I'd like to see the day when every owner-operator becomes organized, like the Teamsters (but NOT the Teamsters)." M. P. Funkhouser echoed Gonzalez's assessment, proposing in a September 1973 letter that independent truckers organize a nationwide strike. Funkhouser suggested darkly "if every steering-wheel holder stayed home for just the same three days, maybe then someone would sit up and take notice." Without a Teamsters strike fund to back up the action, Funkhouser realized his proposal might sound preposterous: "Don't get me wrong. I'm not making so much money that I can afford to sit home, but if I can realize some cash from it in the future, I'll eat beans for a week to get what I deserve for the time I spend at my job all day." Many independent truckers agreed that the time had come for a change—but as soon became clear, few were willing to settle for just a plate of beans.[41]

A series of violent independent trucker strikes erupted in the winter of 1973–74 and then again in the summer of 1979. Though the shutdowns were triggered by a sudden rise of fuel prices following the 1973–74 OPEC oil embargo and the 1979 energy crisis, the anarchic neopopulist protests drew on a long-standing set of grievances. Like the agrarian revolts of the late nineteenth century, the independent truckers who struck in the 1970s expressed an angry dissatisfaction with the broad contours of industrial capitalism, the distant powers-that-be that applauded the self-made man while simultaneously constraining his opportunities to be that man. Also like the agrarian protests, the shutdowns were characterized by the difficulties of organizing a political movement composed of fiercely independent individuals, making the truckers as unsuccessful as the Populists at achieving their direct demands for reform.

In the wake of the OPEC oil embargo, the price of diesel fuel rose from an average of 31 cents per gallon in May 1973 to 50 cents in September. Fuel became as scarce as it was expensive, prompting the Nixon administration to impose a nationwide fifty-five mile-per-hour speed limit in November to conserve fuel. Owner-operator truckers found themselves in a squeeze, forced to pay more for diesel while carrying fewer loads at lower speeds. A spontaneous protest erupted in December 1973 when three truckers with the CB "handles" Dopey Diesel, Big Sissy, and Doggy Daddy stopped their tractor-trailers in the middle of Interstate 84 on the New York-Connecticut state line. Owner-operator truckers soon began blocking roads and encircling fuel pumps around the country, prompting Mike Parkhurst to call on all owner-operators to unite in a simultaneous nationwide shutdown on December 13 and 14 to dramatize their plight. Thousands of drivers heeded the call, whether by parking their rigs in the middle of a highway or by simply staying home. Some owner-operators became more militant, seeking to prevent other truckers from moving on the highways by toting shotguns, puncturing tires, and throwing bricks and bottles at windshields. Angry truckers planted a bomb in an empty tractor cab in Arkansas. At least thirty-five episodes of gunfire were reported by December 15. On that date, the first shutdown officially ended, having achieved nothing but unsympathetic publicity and a determination among several leaders to coordinate a second and larger protest.[42]

That second protest came in January–February 1974, emerging out of a hastily organized conference at the Mayflower Hotel in Washington. Approximately nineteen different groups had arrived to represent the distressed owner-operator, bearing names such as American Truckers for the Country and the Council of Independent Truckers, along with already established groups such as the Fraternal Association of Steel Haulers (FASH) and the Mid-West Truckers Association. Seeking to make the second shutdown more than just a publicity stunt, the leaders of these groups hammered out a list of demands, which would be presented to the Congress and President Nixon by a five-man Truckers Unity Council, headed by William Hill, the president of FASH. Among the demands were a request to roll back the price of diesel fuel to May 1973 levels, a guarantee of fuel supplies for commercial use, and a public audit of petroleum firms. Like the 1892 Omaha Platform of the Populist Party, these demands called upon the federal government to exercise its power to protect the economic interests of common working men from the assumed predations of large corporations. Unlike the Populists, however, the Truckers Unity Council was not willing to wait for the next presidential election, nor were they interested in government ownership of the nation's transportation facilities. The council issued a statement calling for a nationwide shutdown on January 31, but the leader of the Ohio-based Council of Independent Truckers demanded the shutdown begin the day after the meeting, January 24. In response, the second shutdown began in Akron, Ohio, on the 24th, quickly spreading to Pennsylvania and then to most of the nation, from New Jersey to Oklahoma, in early February.[43]

Once again the protests were violent, as truckers demanded that the Nixon administration do something to alleviate their economic crisis. Gunshots and bricks thrown through windshields killed two drivers and injured dozens more. The governors of Florida, Pennsylvania, and Ohio called out the National Guard to ride shotgun with drivers who refused to be intimidated by the protestors. Even so the flow of commodities was drastically reduced, particularly impacting steel mills, meatpackers, farmers, and supermarkets. Beefpackers and steel plants in the Midwest, cut off from their supplies, laid off thousands of workers; Secretary of Agriculture Earl Butz predicted that farmers would lose millions of dollars as perishables rotted in storage; grocers warned of "serious shortages" as panicky consumers raided meat and produce cases; and McDonald's resorted to airlifts to bring hamburger patties to its midwestern restaurants. On February 6, 7, and 8, the Truckers Unity Council met with William J. Usery, Jr., head of the Federal Mediation and Conciliation Service and labor advisor to President Nixon, to present their list of demands. After tense negotiations, the government offered to freeze the retail price of diesel fuel until March 1 and grant a 6 percent surcharge on the rates of ICC-regulated trucking firms to absorb some of the cost of fuel. The offer was essentially meaningless, in that Nixon had already frozen the price of fuel, and the rate increase would provide no relief for the thousands of owner-operators who did not contract with ICC-regulated carriers (such as "exempt" produce and livestock haulers). Independent truckers thus refused to acknowledge the "so-called settlement," calling it "inadequate." By February 12, however, most truckers had given up on achieving more, and returned to the roads "trying to get a few bucks in their pocket." Mike Parkhurst, who had not participated in the negotiations, called the deal a "sellout" and used the pages of *Overdrive* to call for "The Real Shutdown" in May. The planned protest never materialized, though, because many truckers believed "they could not afford to shut down again." Nonetheless Parkhurst would spend the next several years attempting to convince the readers of his magazine that they could no longer expect the federal government to come to their aid. Only an overthrow of New Deal-era regulatory structures, Parkhurst believed, would level the playing field for the independent trucker.[44]

Fuel costs may have sparked the conflagration, but something much deeper was at stake. A truck driving man was supposed to be the king of the open road, the backbone of America, not a mere cog in the wheels of global energy politics. Harry Davis, an owner-operator hauling produce out of Florida, painted mottoes of the shutdown's mission on the side of his trailer: a "Fight for Freedom" and "The American Way." By refusing to haul the loads that made the U.S. consumer's lifestyle possible, truckers hoped to call widespread attention to their economic bind. Above all the federal government seemed directly to blame for the independent trucker's plight. "We can't afford to keep truckin' under these circumstances," declared Dee Jackson. "The government doesn't give a damn about the little man, never has, never will." Independent truckers who had come to feel betrayed by the Teamsters were now coming to feel just as betrayed by Richard Nixon. For truckers like Jackson, Nixon seemed completely out of touch with the experiences of the ordinary working man. Nixon's imposition of a fifty-five mile-per-hour speed limit drew the most heated criticism. Drivers insisted that they achieved better fuel economy at seventy miles per hour, because their engines were geared for greatest efficiency at high speeds. Richard Dewey informed sympathetic *Overdrive* readers that the speed limit forced him to use ten more gallons of fuel per day; in protest he pasted a sign on the back of his truck that read, "If I am slow—Cuss 'Tricky Dick'—Not Me." It did not matter that engineers at General Motors found that speeds above fifty-five increased air resistance and sharply reduced fuel economy. The very idea of a Washington politician—especially an advocate of a scaled-down "New Federalism" government—telling a professional driver how to do his job produced a deep sense of loathing. "Big John" Trimble, host of an all-night radio show dedicated to truckers, refused for years to say "55" on air, considering the term an "obscenity." Nixon further infuriated truckers who might have been expected to be members of his "silent majority" when he declared in a February 9 radio address that he refused to negotiate with "a handful of desperadoes." In response, a produce hauler declared in the pages of *Overdrive* that "when the next shutdown comes around . . . I'm gonna take my goddamn truck and burn it on the goddamn White House lawn." In July 1974, over one hundred truckers stood on the steps of the U.S. Capitol carrying signs reading "Impeach Nixon"—and they did not primarily have the Watergate scandal on their minds.[45]

Beyond an exasperation with Nixon, however, the truckers despised the very existence of the powers-that-were. Undemocratic labor unions and corporate-minded government regulators seemed to be sucking the economic lifeblood from the men who made the United States run. "We can't take no more," explained Joseph Lehoe, an owner-operator who participated in the shutdowns. "We're caught in the middle," he continued, meaning that maintaining his livelihood depended on the difference between the revenues gained from shippers—who pushed for the lowest possible freight rates—and the costs of trucking—which were pushed as high as possible by fuel companies and state and federal taxation and regulation. This feeling of economic helplessness explains why truckers like Lehoe—who, as an archetype of Nixon's "silent majority," professed to have been "enraged" by the student antiwar protests of the 1960s—would engage in violent mass protest even though most did not consider themselves radical. In fact, for many truckers the greatest achievement of the shutdowns was a renewed sense of independent manhood. As Mike Kortasz of Algonquin, Illinois—the ironically nicknamed "Big Sissy," one of the instigators of the first blockade on I-84 in Connecticut—put it: "Maybe we're all getting back our self-respect. Feels good to walk tall and look a man in the eye again, doesn't it?" The shutdowns failed to achieve any of the truckers' stated aims, but they provided a public forum for truckers to assert their importance to the U.S. economy and demand respect.[46]

That respect came in the mid-1970s, though perhaps not in the exact form desired, when a sudden outpouring of popular culture media celebrated the trucker as the "last American cowboy." Author Jane Stern used the phrase as the subtitle of her 1975 book *Trucker,* in which she admitted that "the reality can never match the legend," but nonetheless dedicated 163 pages of text and photographs to comparing truckers to the riders of the Old West. The term carried a certain irony, insofar as truckers used "cowboy" as a derogatory epithet for reckless drivers or ridiculous dressers—"Those who are just plain unable, mechanically speaking, to own and operate a rig. The ones with the 'double clutching boots' and the 'chain drive billfolds,'" as one driver put it. The idea of the trucker as a renegade figure who refused to bow to authority, however, gained purchase in the social climate of the 1970s. The "Southernization" of the United States brought an explosion of cultural forms celebrating individual freedom, family values, and hell-raising in the name of defying mainstream urban modernity. Merle Haggard's tongue-in-cheek 1969 hit song "Okie from Muskogee" celebrated moonshine and patriotism over marijuana and free love, defining a new subgenre of music known as "outlaw country." "Outlaw" artists such as Haggard, Johnny Paycheck, David Allan Coe, and Waylon Jennings used their prison records as marketing tools. Willie Nelson traded his turtleneck for a bandana while Johnny Cash dressed all in black and recorded live albums in prisons. By the end of the decade, Jennings sang the theme song to the television show *The Dukes of Hazzard,* in which "good ol' boys" Bo and Luke Duke used their souped-up Dodge Charger—painted with Confederate symbols and named the "General Lee"—to humiliate the witless police and greedy capitalists of "Hazzard County," Georgia.[47]

Sandwiched between the two cultural endpoints of "Okie" and the *Dukes of Hazzard* came a flood of trucking movies. The two most popular movies, *Smokey and the Bandit* (1977) and *Convoy* (1978), presented very different versions of the rebel trucker, though the narrative tension in both films centered on truckers flouting the long but incompetent arm of the law. Burt Reynolds, as "The Bandit," guided an 18-wheeler filled with contraband Coors beer and driven by "The Snowman" (Jerry Reed) from Oklahoma to Georgia, evading and taunting Buford T. Justice (played by Jackie Gleason) and a host of other "Smokeys" along the way. *Smokey and the Bandit* was the first widely viewed trucking movie since *They Drive by Night,* and the contrasts between it and the earlier film are striking. Where the 1940 film centers on the struggles of a common working man to become economically independent, *Smokey* imagines trucking as a hedonistic joyride, entirely divorced from economic reality. Burt Reynolds's character displays his manhood by seducing women, cavorting through the countryside, and otherwise defying establishment standards of propriety. Rather than challenging the economic injustice of the Depression-era United States as *They Drive by Night*'s Joe Fabrini had done, the Bandit's primary goal is to bed Carrie "Frog" (played by Sally Fields) while humiliating Buford T. Justice. Like the television show *The Dukes of Hazzard* that it helped to inspire, *Smokey and the Bandit* was an escapist fantasy, depicting the unbridled enthusiasm of rural southern outlaws resisting authority figures while cultivating an untamable sexual prowess (see figure 7.1).[48]

Unlike *Smokey and the Bandit,* the 1978 movie *Convoy,* directed by Sam Peckinpah, was intended to make a broader statement about the political culture represented by the trucking cowboy. Famed for his ultra-violent 1969 film *The Wild Bunch,* Peckinpah wanted *Convoy* to be a new kind of western. Mack trucks would replace quarter horses, Smokeys would replace federal marshals, and truckstops would replace saloons as the loci of spontaneous brawls. "Outlaw" country singer Kris Kristofferson plays the part of "Rubber Ducky," an independent trucker with an icy-blue stare whose control over his big rig is so complete that he needs not even a shirt to drive. Nor does he need the Teamsters, which he informs the audience "ain't my damn union." "I'm independent," declares the Duck, emphasizing that "there ain't many of us left." The Duck is a wanderer, his freedom constrained only by the exercise of state authority, represented by Sheriff "Dirty Lyle" Wallace. Lyle extorts a kickback out of the Duck and a group of fellow truckers caught for speeding, provoking the Duck into a retaliatory punch. Forced to flee as Lyle, handcuffed to a barstool, calls in backup, the Duck inadvertently becomes the leader of a "mighty convoy." With the help of CB radios, the convoy attracts hundreds of truckers who hail the Duck as a "people's hero" for his defiance of the fifty-five mile-per-hour speed limit. Federal Agent Hamilton arrives in a "bear in the air" (a police helicopter), using a "computerized system" to lock onto the truckers' CB frequency and inform the Duck that he is in violation of federal law. The convoy nonetheless continues to barrel down the highway, as the Duck sneers

Figure 7.1. The Bandit.
In contrast to the neatly uniformed driver of the 1940s, this renegade trucker wore his shirt half-unbuttoned when photographed by Marc F. Wise at a truck stop in Ontario, California, in 1988. The horse's-head belt buckle and the Confederate Battle Flag design on his long-nose Peterbilt publicly declared him as a "Bandit" (*Source*: Marc F. Wise, *Truck Stop* [Jackson: University of Mississippi Press, 1995]).

"piss on your law!" to Lyle, ultimately confronting the machinery of the state directly in an explosive Hollywood-style climax.[49]

Although the movie never makes clear what exactly the Duck was protesting, the broad appeal of the movie was explained by "C. W. McCall," a.k.a. William Fries, whose 1975 hit song "Convoy" was the inspiration for the movie. "'Convoy' appeals to the rebel instinct in Americans," said Fries, making it possible for he and Kris Kristofferson "to make a few statements—about how regulated our lives have become and how many of our freedoms we have lost." Like Peter Fonda's character "Captain America" in the 1969 film *Easy Rider*, the Duck was a renegade for whom the open road was a source of, and solace for, antiestablishment yearnings. Unlike Captain America, however, the Duck found that solace not in smoking marijuana and harboring an elitist grudge against small-town conservatives, but by embracing his traditional manhood in his lonely search for the soul of America. *Convoy* was panned by critics for its tackiness; the *New York Times* called the movie a "big, costly, phony exercise in myth-making," while a reviewer for *Time* wrote that watching the film was "roughly as much fun as a ride on the New Jersey turnpike with the windows open." The movie nonetheless struck a chord among truckers who, even though they deplored the movie's gross misrepresentation of the actual nature of their work, saw in the movie a dramatization of the fact, as one driver put it, that "Truckers ain't organization people!"[50]

One year after the release of *Convoy*, an actual independent trucker protest emerged, with angry drivers calling for the complete dismantling of federal economic regulations in the trucking industry. Like the protests of 1973–74, the shutdowns of the summer of 1979 were provoked by a rapid rise in fuel costs, as part of the energy crisis instigated by the overthrow of the Iranian Shah. After several years of gaining publicity as cowboys, however, truckers in the 1979 shutdown sought to demonstrate that their independent way of living was central to the U.S. economy. The shutdown began on June 5, 1979, when a convoy of truckers arrived in Washington and circled the Capitol. Mike Parkhurst, as president of a new group called the Independent Truckers Association (representing 30,000 drivers), seized the moment and called for a nationwide shutdown. By the end of June, approximately 75,000 truckers had stopped driving. Once again the protests were violent, as roving bands of truckers set fire to empty trucks and shot at the windshields of drivers who refused to stop. Nine states called out the National Guard to protect company drivers. By the time the shutdown ended in early July, one driver had been shot and killed, while dozens more were injured. As in the 1973–74 shutdowns, independent trucker groups formed a Unity Council, headed by William Hill. The coalition demanded the Carter administration reduce the price of diesel, raise the speed limit, ease size restrictions on highways, and provide a freight surcharge to compensate for rising fuel costs.[51]

In contrast to the shutdowns of 1973–74, however, independent truckers made a more organized effort to gain the ear of the president by garnering sympathy from consumers. Most of the independent truckers had entered the exempt hauling industry under the deregulatory umbrella established by farm interests in the 1935 Motor Carrier Act, meaning that they worked mainly as haulers of fresh produce, grain, live cattle, and milk. Thousands of truckers collaborated to block the movement of food from farms to supermarkets. As Oscar Williams, an official with Parkhurst's Independent Truckers Association, declared: "I can predict that when housewives in the major cities go to market and cannot find peaches, cherries, or fresh meat, or find they have to pay double for these goods, there will be one hellacious uproar in Washington." Trucking's importance in the agribusiness economy became apparent as meatpacking plants and grain elevators shut down. In Montana, where half of the state's truckers were owner-operators, deliveries of livestock to packing plants and of boxed beef to supermarkets halted almost completely. Produce began rotting across the country, from Washington State cherries, cucumbers, squash, and potatoes to North Carolina green beans and potatoes, to California strawberries and lettuce—all foods carried primarily by independent truckers. Peach growers in Georgia stopped harvesting; farmers in Pennsylvania dumped milk; and a Minnesota pork plant shut down. Truckers blockaded a Stop & Shop supermarket distribution center in Connecticut, making a direct appeal to consumers in New York City, New Jersey, Connecticut, and Massachusetts. The intent, as Independent Truckers Association spokesman Don Swanson argued, was to show consumers that the cost of diesel fuel translated directly into increased food costs. "We could go ahead and pay $2 for a gallon of diesel," stated Swanson, "but people are going to have to pay $6 for a pound of hamburger. We don't want to see that. We have to buy hamburger, too." Despite panic buying in supermarkets, however, the truckers' shutdowns and blockades proved too sporadic and disorganized to achieve a lasting impact on food supplies. Without an effective means of central organization, the 1979 shutdowns ended much like the first, with the Carter administration offering only limited concessions to the truckers. There was one important difference, however, between the results of the 1973–74 shutdowns and those of 1979. Although the 1979 strikes did not produce a "hellacious uproar" in Washington, they did lend support to President Carter's and Massachusetts senator Edward Kennedy's efforts to push deregulation of the trucking industry through Congress.[52]

Deregulatory Capitalism

With the passage of the Motor Carrier Act of 1980, Parkhurst saw his desire for a free-market revolution in long-haul trucking come true as Congress formally deregulated the U.S. trucking industry. This legislation could be seen as the culmination of a decade-long effort by economic advisors within the Nixon, Ford, and Carter administrations to implement a free-market ideology in response to pressure from consumers and business interests. Ralph Nader, for instance, attacked the ICC for gouging consumers by sanctioning freight monopolies, while shippers from grocery stores to auto manufacturers decried trucking regulation for driving up freight rates. These views resonated with economic advisors to Presidents Nixon and Ford—particularly James Miller III and Alan Greenspan—taken with economist Milton Friedman's neoliberal free-market theories. Jimmy Carter, determined to reform trucking policy as part of his broader efforts to pare back federal power, appointed a proderegulation commissioner to the ICC. In 1978, the newly antimonopolistic ICC defied Congress, the Teamsters, and the American Trucking Associations and began dismantling regulatory structures. That same year, Carter signed a law deregulating the domestic airline industry, capping five years of efforts by Senator Edward M. Kennedy (D-MA) to undermine the Civil Aeronautics Board's regulatory power. In the spring of 1979 Kennedy surprised Carter by proposing a sweeping deregulation bill, challenging Carter to deliver on his earlier promise to fully deregulate trucking. Kennedy enrolled a wide-ranging crew of supporters whose politics would, in prior decades, have aligned them with the Republican rather than the Democratic Party—including the National Association of Manufacturers on behalf of free-enterprisers, Mike Parkhurst representing independent truckers, and the American Farm Bureau Federation speaking on behalf of agribusiness. In June 1979, President Carter joined with Kennedy, and the two Democrats successfully pushed trucking deregulation through Congress within the year, despite heavy resistance by the American Trucking Associations and the Teamsters Union. The political climate of the 1970s, with its "mood for free enterprise," stagflationary economic woes, and repudiation of New Deal economic liberalism, made full deregulation of the trucking industry possible. But the roots of trucking deregulation lay in the social and political context of rural America that had bred the fiercely independent "tired ex-farmer" trucker who supported Mike Parkhurst's call to arms during the 1979 shutdowns.[53]

Violent strikes would not bring down the ICC, Mike Parkhurst realized. The legacy of the agricultural exemption clause of the 1935 Motor Carrier Act, however, could provide an effective lobbying tool before Congress. By the early 1970s, the agricultural exemption discussed in previous chapters had created an entire sector of the long-haul trucking industry that was free from regulatory oversight by the ICC. For promoters of antistatist approaches to national transportation policy, the agricultural exemption offered a model of free markets operating in the public interest. Mike Parkhurst was not the only one to argue along these lines; economists both within and without the USDA had been arguing along much the same lines for decades. For instance, Richard N. Farmer, a professor of business administration at the University of California-Los Angeles, argued in 1964 that the exemption reduced shipping costs, benefiting both producers and consumers of agricultural products. As Farmer put it, "To regulate for the sake of regulation, or to tidy up what seems to be a confusing, chaotic free market seems unsound." But it was Mike Parkhurst who fully realized the political power of the agrarian resonance of independent trucking in the 1970s. If agribusiness-friendly congressmen could be convinced that deregulated trucking would lower the price of food without lowering farm prices, independent truckers could attack the ICC as an outmoded relic and the Teamsters as selfish brutes who contributed to the inflation of the 1970s. The seeds of deregulation that had been planted by a farm-friendly Congress in 1935 and nurtured by the USDA through the 1960s were ready to bear fruit. Mike Parkhurst was prepared for the harvest.[54]

After gaining national attention in the 1973–74 shutdowns, Parkhurst regularly appeared as a witness before Senate and House committees considering trucking deregulation. Parkhurst repeatedly pointed to the exempt rural trucker as the backbone of the nation's food economy. In 1977 Parkhurst informed the sympathetic Senate Committee on Agriculture that "a lot of farmers around this country would like to be able to put their goods which are now being shipped by regulated carriers right on the backs of independent truckers." Speaking "from the standpoint of consumers" before the Senate Committee on Commerce, Science, and Transportation in March 1979, Parkhurst declared that with deregulation, "food costs could be brought down inasmuch as over 90 percent of all fresh fruits and vegetables are hauled by the small operator." As evidence for his claim, Parkhurst pointed to what he called an "invisible regulatory agency in the basement of the Department of Agriculture" that had driven down food prices by expanding the agricultural exemption for farm truckers since 1935. While the Teamsters and regulated trucking firms represented by the American Trucking Associations testified that deregulation would bring only chaos to the trucking industry, Parkhurst noted that farm trucking had long been deregulated, making it possible for independent truckers to provide consumers with fresh produce at low prices at any time of year. Calling upon independent truckers to "launch [a] much-needed letter-writing campaign" to Congress, Parkhurst urged truckers to "appeal to the consumer interests" in trucking deregulation as well as think about how deregulation would "put more dollars in your wallet [and] more steaks on your table." By easing ICC restrictions on market entry, deregulation would make it possible for thousands of small trucking firms, especially independent owner-operator truckers, to begin freely competing for general freight much as they had always been able to compete for farm and food hauls. A free market for truck transportation, Parkhurst declared, would benefit farmers, consumers, and independent truckers alike.[55]

Senator Edward M. Kennedy, unlike Mike Parkhurst, was no libertarian. Kennedy nonetheless understood the political resonance of the agricultural exemption as a model for trucking deregulation. As an early front-runner in the race to replace Jimmy Carter as the Democrat's presidential candidate in the 1980 elections, Kennedy saw trucking deregulation as an ideal issue that would allow him to reach out to the hard-working independent rural truck driver while still satisfying his urban and suburban working- and middle-class constituency. Carter had come into office proposing to deregulate trucking but had not fully delivered on his promise, so Kennedy pounced on the issue. In a craftily staged press conference in January 1979, Kennedy put trucking deregulation on the congressional agenda flanked by consumer crusader Ralph Nader, Carter's "chief inflation fighter" and point man on airline deregulation Alfred E. Kahn, along with representatives of the National Association of Manufacturers, the National Federation of Independent Businesses, and the Consumer Federation of America. All agreed that with inflation threatening the nation's consumer-driven economy, Congress could no longer bow to the special-interest demands of the Teamsters and the American Trucking Associations, who continued to fight any efforts to deregulate the industry. Introducing free enterprise to the trucking system, Kennedy believed, would simultaneously boost independent truckers' incomes while lowering consumer prices. Trucking deregulation thus appealed to libertarian and liberal interests simultaneously in an age of stagnating wages and inflationary prices. Kennedy's framing of the politics of trucking deregulation in this manner was part of a broader effort among Democrats in the period to distance themselves from the perception that liberal politics necessarily implied big bureaucracy, cozy relations with labor unions, and interventionist economic regulations. Just as his brother Robert Kennedy had done in formulating the McClellan Committee's anti-Teamsters attacks in the late 1950s, and as his other brother John F. Kennedy had done when proposing a dramatic tax cut in 1963, Edward Kennedy's proderegulation stance marked the culmination of a long-term shift within the postwar Democratic Party. By the 1970s, party leaders had defected from New Deal-style, class-based, equity-oriented economic liberalism enforced through regulatory governance. Both Kennedy and Carter represented the Democrats' new focus on rights-based social liberalism combined with growth-oriented economic policies that primarily benefited business interests and relatively affluent consumers. Carter soon offered his full support to Kennedy's efforts, and in June 1979, just as Parkhurst and his followers were gearing up for a violent blockade of the nation's farm and food transportation network, the two Democratic leaders proposed sweeping trucking deregulation legislation.[56]

Although Kennedy's support for deregulation reflected his efforts to pitch the Democratic Party as the party of economic growth, most of the hard work of making deregulatory ideology into material reality had already been done by agribusiness over the previous four decades. Kennedy's specific proposals for deregulation drew on the fact that rural trucking had remained unregulated since 1935. Appearing before the Senate Committee on Commerce, Science, and Transportation in late June, Kennedy explicitly drew legislators' attention to the agricultural exemption as a template for deregulation. "The best proof that trucking deregulation works," Kennedy intoned, "is the fact that more than half of the trucking industry has never been regulated." The success of the agricultural exemption in keeping rural trucking free from the heavy hand of government regulation, Kennedy announced, had been proven in 1956, when "fresh and frozen dressed poultry and frozen fruits and vegetables were declared exempt from I.C.C. regulation." Citing the USDA's study of the rapid drop in freight rates that came with the Supreme Court's 1956 decisions to allow transportation of frozen poultry and frozen produce without ICC regulation, Kennedy asserted that he could not "think of a single action that could deal more effectively with the problem of inflation than deregulation of the trucking industry." The "absurdities" of ICC regulation of trucking, according to Kennedy, "have an impact . . . from a consumer's point of view in terms of prices at the supermarket." Kennedy, like Mike Parkhurst, tied the pocketbook politics of rural anarchopopulist independent truckers to the inflationary fears of middle-class suburban consumers, proposing trucking deregulation as a simple solution to the era's complex economic difficulties.[57]

Farm lobbyists joined Parkhurst and Kennedy in this fight for deregulation. C. H. Fields, testifying before the Senate on behalf of the Farm Bureau, declared that the benefits of trucking deregulation had been proven since 1935 by the "tremendous success story" of the agricultural exemption clause of the original Motor Carrier Act. According to Fields, "55 percent of the motor carrier business is already free from ICC regulation," allowing independent truckers to haul farm products at lower prices and with greater flexibility than either regulated trucking firms or the railroads. B. H. Jones, representing the National Cattlemen's Association, agreed. "When nonregulated truckers can haul live cattle, hogs, and sheep to slaughter more expeditiously and at lower rates than the regulated trucks and rails can haul away the approximately 60 percent of that cargo which is meat, the need for a serious and thorough review of the intervention of government in the system is obviously overdue." Jones, echoing the sentiments of Mike Parkhurst, declared that "the Nation can no longer afford the luxury of overregulation on the part of Government." Ray Mackey, representing the Kentucky Farm Bureau, told the Senate that "overwhelming evidence points to the fact that less Government regulation and red tape in the trucking business and more freedom and competition will produce better service to all Americans." As if he had taken part in the trucker insurrection of the summer of 1979 himself, Mackey stated that "we believe that 45 years of restrictive regulation is enough for our Nation's trucking industry." Farm Bureau and other agricultural representatives, unlike Mike Parkhurst, were not revolting against government intervention in the economy per se; the Farm Bureau continued to support New Deal-era farm subsidies that benefited large-scale farmers at taxpayers' expense. Trucking deregulation, however, promised to unite the interests of commercial farmers with those of urban consumers, simultaneously raising farmers' incomes while reducing the price of food at the supermarket—much as Charles Brannan had unsuccessfully attempted to do back in 1949. In contrast to Brannan's proposal for a U.S. version of a Swedish social-democratic consensus among farmers, workers, and consumers on farm policy, however, the deregulation of trucking would ensure that private enterprises rather than public political coalitions would hold the reins in the food economy.[58]

The agricultural politics of trucking deregulation helped secure the passage of the Motor Carrier Act of 1980, which formally deregulated the entire trucking industry. The House committee that reported the final trucking deregulation bill to President Carter announced it had received "thousands of letters from consumers—from beef processors to independent owner-operators." With an oddly placed dash the House declared that beefpackers and truckers were "consumers," implying that all agreed with Senator Kennedy and President Carter on the need to deregulate transportation to keep consumer prices low. The House Committee on Public Works and Transportation summed up the aims of the Motor Carrier Act of 1980: "reduced regulation of the industry will indeed reduce prices and inflation." Allowing independent owner-operator truckers to transport processed food products as well as farm commodities would "result in cost savings to the consumer through increased service and price competition." The "ultimate beneficiary" of deregulation would be "the American consumer." The House report repeatedly referenced the USDA's study on the impacts of the 1956 deregulation of frozen food trucking as proof positive of deregulation's anti-inflationary potential. Thus, while the Motor Carrier Act of 1980 was crafted in direct response to the economic stagflation and political conservatism of the 1970s, the deregulatory impulse in trucking also had much deeper historical roots. Long before the word "deregulation" came into widespread use, rural trucking had always been unregulated, providing a model for the version of "free enterprise" pushed by Carter and Kennedy in 1979.[59]

After deregulation became political reality in 1980, independent truckers gained the freedoms they had so long demanded, but at a significant cost. Deregulation transformed the trucking industry in the 1980s, bringing chaotic and cut-throat competition reminiscent of the 1920s. By mid-1982, the American Trucking Associations reported that 188 formerly regulated motor carriers had gone bankrupt, while 40 percent of large trucking firms saw net losses. The easing of market entry restrictions encouraged the proliferation of small trucking firms located in rural areas, following the pattern set over the previous decades by the unregulated agricultural trucking industry. Larger firms, particularly J. B. Hunt, also joined in the competition. But whether the new trucking companies were small or large, nearly all were nonunion. Three years after the 1980 Motor Carrier Act became law, the number of nonunion motor carriers tripled. The Teamsters hemorrhaged members, so that by 1985 only 160,000 long-haul truckers belonged to the union—a 43 percent decline since 1976. With competition driving down freight rates, wage-cutting became a business imperative for both union and nonunion firms. By 1996, the nation's freight bill reached an all-time low, but at the cost of transforming big rigs into "sweatshops on wheels," as firms slashed wages while Teamster power collapsed in long-haul trucking. Some individual truckers benefited from the deregulatory regime, of course, considering that the easing of barriers to market entry allowed individuals previously unable to work as self-employed truckers to join in the competitive fray. For African American truckers in particular, the decline of Teamster power and the removal of regulatory barriers to black self-employment opened up new opportunities; black truckers were three times more likely to be owner-operators by 1988 than they had been in 1978. But because white drivers entered the ranks of owner-operators even more rapidly than African Americans after deregulation, blacks represented only 6 percent of owner-operators by 1988. In any case, declining incomes for both employees and owner-operators meant that new opportunities did not necessarily translate into economic security. Deregulation proved to work exactly as it had been intended—to place on "independent" truckers the brunt of the burden of satisfying both producers and consumers by driving down the cost of the transportation that connected them. Truckers who had all along sought to be independent men—free of government bureaucracy, corporate control, and dues-demanding unions—seemed to have achieved exactly what they wanted.[60]

Why would independent truckers fight so hard for a policy change that would prove so contradictory to their economic interests? William Hill, the head of the Fraternal Association of Steel Haulers, lamented the "farm background" of most of the truckers who participated in the shutdowns of the 1970s, implying that rural truckers fell prey to a form of false consciousness when they demanded independence at any cost. "All these guys have that American dream, man, that they're gonna work hard and they're gonna be millionaires," scoffed Hill. "And they'll own their own trucking company some day. Bullshit."[61] But while that "farm background" certainly drove owner-operators to attach great importance to unregulated long-haul trucking as a path to manly independence, they were not unthinking dupes of free-market ideologues. With few options for satisfying work in an era of industrial agri-business, rural men who chose to enter the relatively unrestricted world of agricultural trucking at mid-century did so in an economic world not entirely of their own making. Under the deregulatory umbrella established by a farm-friendly Congress in 1935 and expanded by the Department of Agriculture through the 1960s, farm and food trucking remained chaotic and hypercom-petitive even as the Teamsters Union and larger trucking firms cornered the market for more lucrative freight. The ideal figure of rural manhood within this agribusiness context became the "bandit" trucker, who proved willing to embrace laissez-faire ideology even if that meant a return to the economic chaos that had characterized trucking in the 1920s. By the 1960s and 1970s, the fierce independence of owner-operator truckers—intensified by country music, Hollywood films, Mike Parkhurst's libertarian screeds, and a sense that the Teamsters and the federal government had betrayed the working man's eco-nomic interests—created the conditions for a violent protest. When fuel prices rose in the 1970s, independent truckers demanded an injection of free enter-prise into the entire transportation economy. In doing so, truckers and congres-sional deregulators paved the way for the low-wage, low-price capitalism that would define the final decades of the twentieth-century U.S. political economy. Independent truckers helped to shift the machinations of deregulatory capital-ism into high gear in the late twentieth century, not out of ignorance of their own economic interests, but because they had few other economic choices.

The neopopulist sentiments that ignited the trucker protests of the 1970s helped to sweep Ronald Reagan into the presidency in 1981. Fed up with the failed economic policies of the Nixon, Ford, and Carter administrations, independent truckers were among those who firmly believed that Reagan had an answer to stagflation. Robert Thompson of Whiteville, Tennessee, explained to *Overdrive* magazine that "the economy hasn't been too good the past year," and that he expected Reagan "to be better." Richard Mumford of Mononga-hela, Pennsylvania, agreed, noting that "the price of just about everything is killing us," and that Reagan also seemed likely to "put the speed limit back at 65 mph"—after all, the candidate had maintained that government was the problem, not the solution, ever since praising Barry Goldwater's presidential nomination at the 1964 Republican National Convention. Bob Vetters of St. Petersburg, Florida, worried that the hawkish Reagan might "get us into a war," but still believed that "he's going to make a much better President than Carter." J. R. Ellis of Belton, Missouri, had "found out from people in California" that Reagan "did a good job when Governor of that state"—although he qualified his statement by pointing out that he had "expected a lot from Carter, too." Bob Bunch of Knoxville, Tennessee, showed a similar mix of optimism and uncertainty about Reaganomics—"I support his tax cut [but] if taxes are cut too much, it could hurt the whole country." After a decade of stagnant economic growth and rising prices, independent truckers were ready for the changes promised by Ronald Reagan and the new ultraconservative Republican Party. Even so, however, they remained concerned about a sustained rollback of government power that might threaten their livelihoods. Independent truckers faced a new era of deregulatory capitalism with a mix of hope and trepidation. Despite their anarchic behavior over the previous decade, they were not dupes of neoliberal economists nor of Commie-taunting, Bible-thumping conservative politicians. Reagan's promise of a "free market" with higher speed limits and lower taxes, however, seemed better than any alternatives being offered by the Carter administration, the Democratic Party, or organized labor.[1]

Reagan delivered on his "free market" message, of course. After mounting a fierce attack on organized labor during the PATCO air traffic-controller's strike in August 1981, he signed into law a massive tax cut a few days later. During Reagan's eight years in office, social welfare programs saw funds dry up while defense spending on such dubious projects as the Strategic Defense Initiative ("Star Wars") rose rapidly. Combined with intentionally regressive tax cuts that, according to supply-side economists, were meant to spur investment by wealthy Americans, the Reagan-era increase in military spending drove the federal budget deep into the red. Despite overseeing the booming economy of the 1980s, the Reagan administration implemented economic policies that put the press on working-class Americans; real wages for the bottom rungs of the economic ladder stagnated through the rest of the century. Under the Bush and Clinton administrations of the 1990s, attacks on the structures of economic liberalism continued; industries from energy to telecommunications were deregulated, social welfare policies were either scaled back or eliminated entirely, and corporate executives raked in record earnings while ordinary working Americans struggled to stay afloat. Few New Deal-era economic policies survived in the conservative era. Middle-class welfare programs such as Social Security remained intact, but the sweeping welfare reforms of 1996 charted a new course of economic uncertainty for the working poor and revived Social Darwinism as a seemingly valid social theory. New Deal-era farm policies also survived, but continued to disproportionately subsidize corporate agribusinesses while small farmers fell deeper into debt trying to purchase the machines, pesticides, and patented genetically modified seeds required to stay in the business.[2]

Independent truck drivers faced unprecedented economic uncertainty in the new era of deregulatory capitalism. One driver penned a 1983 *New York Times* editorial claiming that deregulation "created more gypsies than the market can bear," echoing Jack Keeshin's statement that trucking had been a "dog-eat-dog business" in the 1920s, before regulation. Owner-operator truckers who had called for deregulation during the shutdowns of the 1970s organized a very different kind of shutdown in May 1982, when the Independent Truckers Unity Committee decided that "deregulation . . . has caused such a drop in revenues that most owner-operators are operating at below what it costs them [to drive]." Though this shutdown did not gain widespread support, Mike Parkhurst initiated another full-scale protest in January 1983, after President Reagan signed a bill that increased the federal fuel tax and other fees for truckers. As in prior years, independent truckers' pocketbook politics trumped any tendency toward cultural conservatism or patriotic Reagan-worship. Parkhurst hoped to reverse the tax legislation by orchestrating a nationwide shutdown of truckers who were pressed not only by fuel costs but by the extreme competition that came in the wake of deregulation. Reagan scolded Parkhurst for his tactics, informing the truckers that they could simply pass on the increased costs of fuel taxes to consumers. The truckers retorted that the cut-throat competition under deregulation prevented them from doing so. In any case, that same competitive environment also discouraged most truckers from joining the shutdown, for fear of being driven entirely out of business.[3]

Meanwhile the deregulatory free-market ideology enshrined in the 1980 Motor Carrier Act began spreading across the highways of North America. In 1981, the United States Trade Representative, prodded by the American Trucking Associations, declared a "trucking war" against Canada, which refused to fully deregulate its trucking industry until 1989. Once Canadian trucking deregulation went into effect, that country's trucking firms and owner-operators faced chaotic competition that spurred a brief recession and mass protests. Canadian asphalt cowboys concerned about job losses due to U.S. competition blockaded the bridges over the Niagara, Detroit, and St. Clair rivers in May 1990, April 1990, and yet again in May 1991. The Ontario government commissioned a report to respond to the protestors' concerns; among other recommendations, the commission advised Canadian trucking firms to consider either setting up nonunion operations in the United States to counteract the higher incomes of Canadian employees or else begin "reviewing arrangements with [Canadian] unionized drivers." As the United States's largest trading partner, Canada faced a difficult choice between maintaining a commitment to worker prosperity and adopting the union-slashing requirements of "free" transborder trade. Meanwhile the Mexican government removed economic regulations on that country's trucking industry in 1989, although no U.S. fomented "trucking war" was involved. The Salinas government, elected in 1988, pushed trucking deregulation as part of a broader neoliberal economic reform package of slashed government spending, privatization of national resources, weakening of labor unions, and liberalized export policies in compliance with the demands of the International Monetary Fund. "Pirate" truckers who had been shut out of formerly state-backed Mexican *transportista* cartels could legally haul freight after deregulation, particularly agricultural produce, textiles, and electronics bound for export to the United States. To be a *troquero* after deregulation allowed thousands of Mexicans, many migrating from the devastated countryside to *maquiladora* industrial zones of the north, to become entrepreneurs—but only in a hypercompetitive market where kinship and patronage networks rather than state policy and labor unions provided any semblance of income stability.[4]

Exports of U.S. deregulatory ideology would seem to have taken another upturn after the signing of the North American Free Trade Agreement in 1993, although the impacts of NAFTA on North American highway transportation were mixed. While transborder highway shipments between the United States and Canada mushroomed after NAFTA, the highways between the United

States and Mexico continued to be deeply regulated. Opponents of NAFTA, including the American Trucking Associations and the Teamsters Union, declared Mexican truckers to be unsafe, underinsured, prone to overloading their aged trucks, and likely to bring illegal drugs over the border—much as proponents of the 1935 Motor Carrier Act had declared rural U.S. truckers to be "gypsies" and "fly-by-nighters," though this time around the debate was waged in unapologetically xenophobic terms. Despite efforts by U.S. food processing firms and supermarkets to push the George W. Bush administration to open up the border to certain Mexican trucking firms—which generally paid wages one-third lower than U.S. trucking firms—opposition to unrestricted transborder operations remained strong. The Teamsters, protectionist congressional Republicans, the editorial board of the *Wall Street Journal,* and xenophobic conservatives such as Phyllis Schlafly all declared Mexican truckers an unwelcome "menace" on U.S. soil. Whether U.S., Canadian, and Mexican truckers' incomes would be driven still lower by rampant transcontinental competition remained uncertain in the early years of the twenty-first century.[5]

The economic uncertainties of late twentieth-century capitalism were not confined to North American truckers, as rural residents of the United States faced new challenges from globalizing patterns of trade, production, and migration. Global economic events in the late 1970s and early 1980s—including Carter's 1979 embargo on Soviet grain shipments, Reagan's maintenance of tight monetary policies, and expanded grain production by Argentina, Australia, and Canada—led to a steep decline in U.S. farm prices, threatening family farmers with inescapable debt. Stories of midwestern farmers committing suicide haunted the nation in the 1980s, while angry farmers in the American Agriculture Movement drove in tractorcades to Washington, D.C., demanding relief. Willie Nelson and other country musicians held a series of "Farm Aid" concerts to help farmers facing foreclosure. Less publicized, but equally traumatic, was the lack of security for late twentieth-century rural Americans who did not have family farms to lose. Migrant farm workers, meatpacking employees, and workers in discount retail stores receiving substandard wages also found that rural realities did not necessarily live up to American dreams. Those dreams were increasingly hatched not in the rural United States but in Central America and Southeast Asia—regions of the world increasingly exporting the low-wage rural labor force that made the U.S. low-priced supermarket economy hum. Xenophobic calls for the construction of border fences began to resonate not only in California and Texas and Florida, where migrant and immigrant farmworkers had long toiled in the fields and factories of wage-slashing agribusinesses, but also in the beef, pork, and poultry packing communities of Kansas, Iowa, Georgia, and North Carolina.[6]

Were rural Americans—whether truckers, farmers, farm workers, or Wal-Mart employees—lulled into a state of "false consciousness" by tax-slashing, union-busting, corporate-friendly, anti-immigrant conservative politicians, as Thomas Frank has implied by asking *What's the Matter with Kansas?* The history of long-haul trucking in the rural countryside calls this interpretation into question. Although rural truckers did make choices both in their own work lives and in the voting booth that contributed to the rise of modern economic conservatism, they did so in an economic world shaped primarily by agribusinesses and procorporate politicians in both the Republican and Democratic parties. Certainly the "truck driving man" maintained a fierce sense of independence that fed into the free-market ideology of the late twentieth century. But as we have seen, that sense of independence emerged in the 1930s through the 1960s as rural men turned to trucking to escape the grim prospects of farming in an age of industrial agriculture. The rural transportation economy remained unregulated, with the support of USDA bureaucrats and agricultural policymakers, throughout the twentieth century. Agribusinesses such as frozen food producers, meatpackers, and milk distributors were thus able to rely on independent truckers to radically transform the economic geography of their industries. The "free enterprise" that characterized the modern agribusiness economy overturned the consumer-labor pocketbook politics that had animated liberalism in the food economy since the New Deal. Organized labor lost traction in the hypercapitalist rural meatpacking industry and milk distribution economy, while consumers had little reason to protest the cut-rate food prices offered in supermarket aisles. From the 1930s to the 1970s, then, rural truckers contributed to the undermining of economic liberalism in the farm and food economy—either by simply choosing to do the work that they did or by demanding that politicians overturn regulatory structures that privileged organized labor. In making these choices, however, truckers did so not because they ignored their economic interests and focused on the politics of "law and order," race-baiting, superpatriotism, or antielitism that defined the modern Republican Party. If anything was "the matter" with Kansas by the end of the century, it was the fact that the entire state smelled like "money" (i.e., manure) while working Kansans—whether truckers, small farmers, meatpacking employees, or truckstop waitresses—had neither the backing of consumers, organized labor, or a powerful state to confront the contours of deregulatory capitalism.

APPENDIX A

Note on Quantitative Data Sources

Despite a wealth of historical statistics on the U.S. trucking industry, no comprehensive data exist that would allow for quantitative analysis of several important issues discussed in this book. It is impossible, for instance, to compare the size of the regulated trucking industry to the size of the unregulated trucking industry—in terms of number of firms, number of employees, wages paid, tonnage hauled, revenues, profits, and so forth. By their nature, unregulated trucking firms evaded the oversight of government agencies responsible for compiling these statistics. Despite publishing detailed annual reports on the regulated trucking industry, the Interstate Commerce Commission never tracked unregulated firms. The Census Bureau undertook a special series of studies of the unregulated trucking sector in 1963, 1967, 1972, and 1977—but found it impossible to include unregulated trucking firms with no paid employees (that is, owner-operator truckers). Because owner-operators composed an important segment of the unregulated industry, this omission prevents even a gross estimate of the number of unregulated but self-employed truck drivers.

It is also impossible to construct reliable data on the number of long-haul truck drivers, contrasted to local delivery drivers, who worked in the United States in the twentieth century. The Interstate Commerce Commission kept detailed records only on long-haul drivers employed by Class I common carrier firms and not on workers employed by smaller Class II and Class III regulated firms. The Census Bureau and the Bureau of Labor Statistics generally treated long-distance and local driving as the same occupation (under Standard Industrial Classification [SIC] 421), and did not distinguish between drivers working for regulated and unregulated firms. Economic censuses, including the *County Business Patterns* series, distinguished between long-haul (SIC 4213) and local drivers (SIC 4214) in a few reports in the 1950s and 1960s. The economic censuses, however, included only firms with one or more paid employees, thus omitting the significant number of owner-operator long-haul truckers upon which this study is largely focused. I am not the first researcher to have spent many frustrated hours searching for such data; in 1966, transportation scholars George Delehanty and D. K. Patton noted that even within the regulated trucking industry, data on manpower were so sketchy as to be "a great distance from the hard data which has proven so useful in other areas of transportation." Even the Interstate Commerce Commission regretted the lack of accurate statistics on the trucking workforce during the protests of the 1970s. When asked by Congress in 1976 to provide "an accurate profile" of the owner-operator trucking sector, ICC chair George Stafford replied that there were too few sources, "and even those available are often incomplete and . . . not as reliable as would be desired."[1]

The only source that provides a comprehensive statistical window into the social and economic lives of U.S. truckers over the course of the twentieth century is the Integrated Public Use Microsample (IPUMS), a machine-readable database compiled and distributed by researchers at the Minnesota Population Center at the University of Minnesota. By providing census data on specific individuals and households, the 1/100 IPUMS samples allow researchers to develop detailed and customized tabulations of a remarkable variety of information. Most of the tables in appendix B were constructed from this data, and the tabulations contained therein are extraordinarily illuminating in many respects—particularly in terms of income, ownership status, race, gender, and geographical location of truck drivers. There are, however, significant limitations to the IPUMS data. First, as noted above, enumerators for the Census Bureau did not distinguish between long-haul and local truck drivers when coding individuals' occupations. This means that all references to truck drivers in the following tables include everyone from dump-truck drivers to package delivery drivers to long-haul over-the-road drivers of tractor-trailers. This lumping together of local and long-haul drivers significantly distorts certain variables in terms of the qualitative findings presented in this book. For instance, noncensus sources indicate that the proportion of African Americans employed in long-haul trucking was significantly lower than that in local trucking. For another, disaggregating long-haul drivers from local drivers would probably boost the proportion of rural persons engaged in long-haul trucking. Another limitation to the IPUMS data is that the Census Bureau has repeatedly redefined its measure of rurality, making precise distinctions between rural and urban populations impossible over time. I have consequently chosen to use the census variable on the metropolitan status of households, which was more consistently defined. The metropolitan status variable, however, does not provide clear distinctions between small towns, exurbs, and truly rural areas, and so should not be treated as an entirely accurate representation of rurality. Finally, certain variables were not reported for all census years covered in this study, making it impossible, for instance, to compare the incomes of truck drivers in 1930 to those of 1940. Neither can 1940 and 1950 income data be compared, as the 1940 census recorded only wages and salaries and not business income. In 1960 and 1970, the metropolitan status of households located in lightly populated regions and states were not included in the IPUMS samples due to confidentiality concerns, making data on metropolitan and nonmetropolitan populations in those years incomparable with data from other years. Despite these limitations, however, the IPUMS samples provide a useful window into trends and consistent patterns within the U.S. trucking industry.

Table B.1
Truck Drivers in the Labor Force, 1930–80

	1930		1940		1950	
	All Workers	*Truckers*	*All Workers*	*Truckers*	*All Workers*	*Truckers*
Total Labor Force	100%	3%	100%	2%	100%	2%
Metropolitan	54%	62%	57%	54%	61%	57%
Nonmetropolitan	46%	38%	43%	46%	39%	43%
Self-Employed	22%	9%	21%	12%	16%	10%
Median Income*	n/a	n/a	$4,697[†]	$5,152[†]	$7,355	$8,382
Male	78%	100%	76%	99%	72%	100%
White	88%	90%	89%	91%	90%	88%
Black	11%	10%	10%	9%	10%	12%
Average Age	37	32	39	35	39	35
Single	34%	32%	33%	24%	22%	17%
Married	65%	67%	65%	75%	72%	78%
Divorced	1.7%	1.2%	2.0%	1.7%	5.6%	4.9%

(continued)

TABLE B.1 *(continued)*

	1960		1970		1980	
	All Workers	*Truckers*	*All Workers*	*Truckers*	*All Workers*	*Truckers*
Total Labor Force	100%	3%	100%	2%	100%	2%
Metropolitan	60%	51%	65%	56%	77%	67%
Nonmetropolitan	25%	31%	23%	28%	23%	33%
Self-Employed	12%	8%	9%	7%	9%	9%
Median Income*	$10,430	$11,264	$12,196	$14,105	$10,570	$13,005
Male	68%	99%	63%	98%	58%	97%
White	89%	85%	89%	87%	85%	84%
Black	10%	14%	10%	13%	10%	13%
Average Age	40	39	39	41	37	39
Single	20%	13%	21%	11%	25%	16%
Married	75%	83%	73%	83%	65%	74%
Divorced	5.3%	4.6%	6.3%	5.7%	10.1%	10.2%

Source: IPUMS.

* In 1980 dollars, using Consumer Price Index.

† Does not include nonwage or nonsalary income (profits, dividends, etc.).

TABLE B.2

Income, Ownership, and Metropolitan Status of Truckers by Race, 1930–80

	1930		*1940*		*1950*	
	White	*Black*	*White*	*Black*	*White*	*Black*
All Truckers	90%	10%	91%	9%	88%	12%
Median Income*	n/a	n/a	$5,402[†]	$3,359[†]	$8,724	$5,303
Owners	92%	6%	93%	7%	94%	5%
Metropolitan	89%	11%	89%	12%	87%	13%
Nonmetropolitan	91%	8%	93%	7%	89%	11%
	1960		*1970*		*1980*	
	White	*Black*	*White*	*Black*	*White*	*Black*
All Truckers	85%	14%	87%	13%	84%	13%
Median Income*	$11,820	$6,814	$14,953	$10,449	$14,005	$10,005
Owners	93%	7%	91%	9%	90%	7%
Metropolitan	83%	17%	84%	15%	81%	15%
Nonmetropolitan	87%	12%	88%	11%	89%	9%

Source: IPUMS.

* 1980 dollars, using Consumer Price Index.

[†] Does not include nonwage or nonsalary income (profits, dividends, etc.).

TABLE B.3

Income and Metropolitan Status of Self-Employed Truckers and Truckers Working for Wages, 1930–80

	1930		1940		1950	
	Self-Employed	*Employees*	*Self-Employed*	*Employees*	*Self-Employed*	*Employee*
Median Income[*]	n/a	n/a	n/a	n/a	$4,961	$7,355
Metropolitan[†]	46%	64%	41%	56%	34%	59%
Nonmetropolitan[†]	54%	36%	59%	44%	66%	41%
	1960		1970		1980	
	Self-Employed	*Employees*	*Self-Employed*	*Employees*	*Self-Employed*	*Employee*
Median Income[*]	$9,873	$11,264	$14,953	$13,893	$13,505	$14,167
Metropolitan[†]	n/a	n/a	n/a	n/a	56%	68%
Nonmetropolitan[†]	n/a	n/a	n/a	n/a	44%	32%

Source: IPUMS

[*] In 1980 dollars, using Consumer Price Index.

[†] The 1960 and 1970 census samples do not identify the metropolitan status of households located in ligh populated regions or states.

TABLE B.4

Employees of Unregulated Long-Haul Trucking Firms Relative to Total Labor Force by State Rank, 1972

State	Number of Unregulated Firms	Number of Employees	% Total State Labor Force	Rank
Arkansas	126	1189	0.17%	1
Montana	68	442	0.16%	2
South Dakota	65	313	0.12%	3
Minnesota	323	1857	0.12%	4
Nebraska	168	702	0.11%	5
Idaho	65	316	0.11%	6
Kansas	125	829	0.09%	7
Iowa	224	980	0.09%	8
California	980	6609	0.08%	9
Wyoming	5	102	0.08%	10
. . .	. . .	. . .	. . .	. . .
South Carolina	85	248	0.02%	40
Tennessee	105	346	0.02%	41
Rhode island	7	81	0.02%	42
Maine	34	72	0.02%	43
Connecticut	46	238	0.02%	44
New York	158	1186	0.02%	45
Massachusetts	81	338	0.01%	46
New Hampshire	6	36	0.01%	47
D.C.	0	0	0.00%	48
Hawaii	0	0	0.00%	49*

Source: 1972 *Census of Transportation, Selected Service Industries, S-7: Nonregulated Motor Carriers and Public Warehousing.*

* Data on Vermont and Alaska employment figures is excluded due to confidentiality concerns.

TABLE B.5
Estimated Tonnage Carried by Regulated and Nonregulated Intercity Motor Carriers, 1950–79

| | 1950 | | 1960 | | 1970 | | 1979 | |
	Regulated	Nonregulated	Regulated	Nonregulated	Regulated	Nonregulated	Regulated	Nonregulated
Millions of Tons	213	581	387	794	661	1,167	973	1,321
Percent of Total	27%	73%	33%	67%	36%	64%	42%	58%

Source: American Trucking Associations, *American Trucking Trends*, 1978–79.
Note: Nonregulated carriers include private firms not primarily engaged in transportation.

TABLE B.6

Revenues, Employees, Wages, and Ton-Mileage of Railroads and Motor Carriers, 1940–80

	1940		1950		1960		1970		1980	
	Rail	Motor	Rail	Motor	Rail	Motor	Rail	Motor	Rail	Motor
Operating Revenues (billions of 1980 dollars)	$21,645	$5,091	$27,142	$12,785	$22,672	$20,064	$23,594	$30,934	$27,404	$43,000
Revenues as % GNP	1.07%	0.25%	1.48%	0.70%	1.11%	0.98%	1.02%	1.34%	1.85%	2.90%
Employees (thousands)*	1,046	n/a	1,237	619	793	856	577	1,083	532	1,280
Wages and Salaries (billions of 1980 dollars)	$11,221	n/a	$15,891	$7,346	$13,787	$12,844	$11,975	$19,920	$13,490	$24,146
Compensation per Employee (1980 dollars)	$10,727	n/a	$12,846	$11,868	$17,385	$15,005	$20,754	$18,393	$25,358	$18,864
Ratio of Revenues to Wages	1.93	n/a	1.71	1.74	1.64	1.56	1.97	1.55	2.03	1.78
Ton-Mileage (billions)†	379	62	597	173	579	285	771	412	932	568
Ton-Miles per Employee	362,333	n/a	482,619	279,483	730,139	332,944	1,336,222	380,425	1,751,880	443,750

Sources: ATA, American Trucking Trends 1979–80; Transportation Association of America, Transportation Facts and Trends 1982, Transportation in America 1989; Census Bureau, Historical Statistics of the United States.

Note: Railroads: ICC Class I and II only; Motor Carriers: ICC Regulated Class I, II, and III only.

* Trucking employee figures based on Bureau of Labor Statistics records of firms in Standard Industrial Classification 42 with at least one paid employee.

† Includes for-hire (regulated and unregulated) and private carriers (unregulated).

Abbreviations Used in Notes

Archives and Libraries

ATHS	American Truck Historical Society, Kansas City, Missouri
CHS	Chicago Historical Society, Chicago, Illinois
CMHF	Country Music Hall of Fame Library and Museum, Nashville, Tennessee
FCHS	Finney County Historical Society, Garden City, Kansas
KSHS	Kansas State Historical Society, Topeka, Kansas
NAL	National Agricultural Library, Beltsville, Maryland
NARA-II	National Archives II, College Park, Maryland
SECC	Seabrook Educational and Cultural Center, Upper Deerfield Township, New Jersey
SI-NMAH	Smithsonian Institution, National Museum of American History, Archives Center, Washington, DC
UWMARC	University of Wisconsin-Milwaukee Area Research Center, Milwaukee, Wisconsin
WHS	Wisconsin Historical Society, Madison, Wisconsin

Manuscript Collections

AMPI	Associated Milk Producers Incorporated Records, WHS
AMSR	Agricultural Marketing Service Records, RG 136, NARA-II
BDC	Bowman Dairy Company Records, CHS
BPSF	Beef Packer Subject File, FCHS
CBC	Consolidated Badger Cooperative Records, WHS
CIC	Cattle Industry Clippings, KSHS
FES	Federal Extension Service Records, RG 33, entry 1001a, NARA-II
FSF	Feedlot Subject File, FCHS
GG	Golden Guernsey Dairy Cooperative Records, UWMARC
GM	Gavin McKerrow Records, WHS
IBT 695	International Brotherhood of Teamsters Local 695 Records, WHS
IBTR	International Brotherhood of Teamsters, Chauffeurs, Warehousemen and Helpers of America Records, WHS
IHR	International Harvester Company Records, WHS
JDB	John D. Black Papers, WHS
KCC	Kansas Chamber of Commerce Records, KSHS
MCIC	Motor Carrier Industry Clippings, KSHS

MIC   Meat Industry Clippings, KSHS
NWAA   N. W. Ayer Advertising Proofsheets, SI-NMAH
NWLB-TC National War Labor Board, Trucking Commission Records, RG 202,
       NARA-II
OPAR   Office of Price Administration Records, RG 188, NARA-II
SAR   Secretary of Agriculture Records, RG 16, entry 17, Correspondence,
       NARA-II
USDAHC   United States Department of Agriculture History Collection, Special
       Collections, NAL
UWA   University of Wisconsin Archives, University of Wisconsin-Madison,
       Madison, Wisconsin
WCBA   Warshaw Collection of Business Americana, SI-NMAH
WDC   Wisconsin Dairies Cooperative Records, WHS

Periodical Literature

AH   *Agricultural History*
AM   *Atlantic Monthly*
ATN   *Ag Trucking News*
BHR   *Business History Review*
BW   *Business Week*
CR   *Congressional Record*
FFF   *Frozen Food Factbook*
FJ   *Farm Journal*
JFE   *Journal of Farm Economics*
KT   *Kansas Transporter*
MCN   *Music City News*
MD   *Milk Dealer*
MHFT   *Milk Hauler and Food Transporter*
MJ   *Milwaukee Journal*
MLR   *Monthly Labor Review*
MMH   *Modern Milk Hauler*
NR   *New Republic*
NW   *Newsweek*
NYT   *New York Times*
OD   *Overdrive*
ORPD   *Open Road and the Professional Driver*
PW   *Power Wagon*
QFF   *Quick Frozen Foods*
SEP   *Saturday Evening Post*
SF   *Successful Farming*
T&C   *Technology and Culture*

USNWR	*U.S. News & World Report*
WOT	*Wheels of Time*
WP	*Washington Post*
WSJ	*Wall Street Journal*

INTRODUCTION

1. Peter Bonventre et al., "Truckers in Revolt," *NW,* Jun. 25, 1979, 45; "One Hellacious Uproar," *Time,* Jul. 2, 1979, 22–27; *NYT,* Jun. 22, 1979, B4.

2. House Small Business Committee, *Regulatory Problems of the Independent Owner-Operator in the Nation's Trucking Industry, Part 1, Hearings,* 94th Cong., 2nd sess., May 19, 20, 26, Jun. 5, 1976, 195; House Public Works and Transportation Committee, *Examining Current Conditions in the Trucking Industry and the Possible Necessity for Change in the Manner and Scope of Its Regulations, Part 1, Hearings,* 96th Cong., 1st sess., Aug. 20, 21, Sep. 22, Oct. 4, 5, 27, Nov. 20, Dec. 28, 1979, 1089; Senate Agriculture Committee, *Agricultural Transportation Problems, Part 2, Hearings,* 95th Cong., 1st sess. Sep. 27, 28, 1977, 2.

3. Thomas Frank, *What's the Matter with Kansas?: How Conservatives Won the Heart of America* (New York: Metropolitan, 2004), 17, 136. A classic example of the white working-class "backlash" thesis is Peter Schrag, "The Forgotten American," *Harper's,* Aug. 1969, 27–34. A more elaborate version appears in Thomas Byrne Edsall and Mary D. Edsall, *Chain Reaction: The Impact of Race, Rights, and Taxes on American Politics* (New York: W. W. Norton, 1991). Racialized urban housing conflicts figure prominently in Thomas J. Sugrue, *The Origins of the Urban Crisis: Race and Inequality in Postwar Detroit* (Princeton, NJ: Princeton University Press, 1996); Becky M. Nicolaides, *My Blue Heaven: Life and Politics in the Working Class Suburbs of Los Angeles, 1920–1965* (Chicago: University of Chicago Press, 2002); Robert O. Self, *American Babylon: Race and the Struggle for Postwar Oakland* (Princeton, NJ: Princeton Univiversity Press, 2003); Kevin Kruse, *White Flight: Atlanta and the Making of Modern Conservatism* (Princeton, NJ: Princeton University Press, 2005); Matthew D. Lassiter, *The Silent Majority: Suburban Politics in the Sunbelt South* (Princeton, NJ: Princeton University Press, 2005). Lisa McGirr argues strongly that the politics of the "New Right" were not a form of "backlash," but instead the product of a "positive" grassroots movement based in the middle class (*Suburban Warriors: The Origins of the New Right* [Princeton, NJ: Princeton University Press, 2001]). Joseph Crespino has subtly undermined the concept of a white working-class "backlash," demonstrating the role of white elites in accommodating civil rights agendas in post-1954 Mississippi (*In Search of Another Country: Mississippi and the Conservative Counterrevolution* [Princeton, NJ: Princeton University Press, 2007]). In contrast to all of these works, I decenter urban racial conflict, Southern religious fervor, and "race-neutral," middle-class entitlement politics by focusing on the class-inflected politics of the American heartland. Neither race nor religion explain why working-class, nonsuburban Americans would align with economic libertarians in an era of increasing structural inequality.

4. As political scientist Larry M. Bartels has recently shown, data on voting patterns provide no evidence that cultural concerns gained any traction over economic concerns for working-class voters in the last half of the twentieth century. Larry M. Bartels, "What's the Matter with *What's the Matter with Kansas?" Quarterly Journal of Political Science* 1 (Mar. 2006): 201–26. Bartels, however, maintains that southern white voters, lured by the race-baiting politics of George Wallace and Nixon's "southern strategy," may have abandoned the class-based politics of the Democratic Party in the 1960s. Even this familiar interpretation of the repudiation of economic liberalism among working-class whites has recently come into question, however, in Byron E. Shafer and Richard Johnston, *The End of Southern Exceptionalism: Class, Race, and Partisan Change in the Postwar South* (Cambridge, MA: Harvard University Press, 2006). On twentieth-century populism more broadly, see Michael Kazin, *The Populist Persuasion: An American History* (New York: Basic Books, 1995) and David A. Horowitz, *Beyond Left and Right: Insurgency and the Establishment* (Urbana: University of Illinois Press, 1997).

5. The term "postindustrial," first proposed by sociologist Daniel Bell (*The Coming of Post-Industrial Society* [New York: Basic Books, 1973]), has become a rather vague shorthand for everything from deindustrialization to the rise of "knowledge work" to new forms of globalization—though it is inherently misleading, since industrial production continues to anchor the world economy, if not Detroit's economy. "Post-Fordism," a more deeply theorized term, refers not only to deindustrialization but to the collapse of collective bargaining arrangements, the abandonment of Keynesian economic theory in favor of neoclassicism, the rise of multinational corporations as contestants to nation-states, and a repudiation of modernist culture. See David Harvey, *The Condition of Postmodernity: An Enquiry into the Origins of Cultural Change* (Oxford: Blackwell, 1990); Michael Hardt and Antonio Negri, *Empire* (Cambridge, MA: Harvard University Press, 2000).

6. Certainly the New Deal order—even in matters of political economy—was never a monolithic entity; regional tensions, conflicts over gender, race, the war in Vietnam, and a host of other disagreements consistently belied a liberal "consensus." Furthermore Cold War national security concerns and attacks on "creeping socialism" tempered many of the postwar era's progressive impulses. Even so, I argue in the following pages that a strong sense of economic liberalism animated U.S. labor, consumer, and farm politics both before and after the height of New Deal liberalism in the mid-to-late 1930s.

7. Nelson Lichtenstein, ed., *Wal-Mart: The Face of Twenty-First-Century Capitalism* (New York: New Press, 2006).

8. Tracy Deutsch, "Untangling Alliances: Social Tensions Surrounding Independent Grocery Stores and the Rise of Mass Retailing," in *Food Nations,* ed. Warren Belasco and Philip Scranton (New York: Routledge, 2002), 156–74; Lizabeth Cohen, *A Consumers' Republic: The Politics of Mass Consumption in Postwar America* (New York: Knopf, 2003).

9. John Mark Hansen, *Gaining Access: Congress and the Farm Lobby, 1919–1981* (Chicago: University of Chicago Press, 1991); David E. Hamilton, *From New Day to New Deal: American Farm Policy from Hoover to Roosevelt, 1928–1933* (Chapel Hill: University of North Carolina Press, 1991); Theda Skocpol and Kenneth Finegold, "State Capacity and Economic Intervention in the Early New Deal," *Political Science Quarterly* 97 (Summer 1982): 255–78;

Allen J. Matusow, *Farm Policies and Politics in the Truman Years* (Cambridge, MA: Harvard University Press, 1967), 38–78; Jon Lauck, *American Agriculture and the Problem of Monopoly: The Political Economy of Grain Belt Farming, 1953–1980* (Lincoln: University of Nebraska Press, 2000); Sally H. Clarke, *Regulation and the Revolution in United States Farm Productivity* (New York: Cambridge University Press, 1994); Lyle P. Schertz and Otto C. Doering III, *The Making of the 1996 Farm Act* (Ames: Iowa State University Press, 1999). For histories of agriculture that treat technological change as a vital component of political change, see Deborah K. Fitzgerald, *Every Farm a Factory: The Industrial Ideal in American Agriculture* (New Haven, CT: Yale University Press, 2003); Pete Daniel, *Breaking the Land: The Transformation of Cotton, Tobacco, and Rice Cultures since 1880* (Urbana: University of Illinois Press, 1985).

10. My approach to the political history of the farm problem thus provides an implicit critique of the institutionalist and pluralist models of policy implementation. Historians and political scientists dealing with farm policy are wont to trace, in impressive detail, the relationship among farm lobbyists in the American Farm Bureau Federation, legislators in the congressional "farm bloc," and the bureaucrats and administrators of the Department of Agriculture. While the institutionalist approach is extraordinarily useful for explaining the genesis and original intent of particular pieces of legislation, as political history it too often leaves undiscussed the issue of how that legislation actually played out in the material and social world beyond Capitol Hill. An excellent review of the institutionalist literature is: Julian E. Zelizer, "Stephen Skowronek's *Building a New American State* and the Origins of American Political Development," *Social Science History* 27 (Fall 2003): 425–41.

11. Politicians, business leaders, and social reformers from the earliest years of the republic understood that transportation technologies provided powerful tools for shaping and reshaping the nation's political economy. Although historians have explored the politics of canal, river, railroad, and automobile transportation in great detail, relatively little work exists on the long-haul trucking industry of the twentieth century. See Ronald E. Shaw, *Canals for a Nation: The Canal Era in the United States, 1790–1860* (Lexington: University of Kentucky Press, 1990); George Taylor, *The Transportation Revolution, 1815–1860* (New York: Rinehart, 1951); Louis C. Hunter, *Steamboats on the Western Rivers: An Economic and Technological History* (Cambridge, MA: Harvard University Press, 1949); Colleen A. Dunlavy, *Politics and Industrialization: Early Railroads in the United States and Prussia* (Princeton, NJ: Princeton University Press, 1994); Steven W. Usselman, *Regulating Railroad Innovation: Business, Technology, and Politics in America, 1840–1920* (Cambridge, MA: Cambridge University Press, 2002); Bruce E. Seely, *Building the American Highway System: Engineers as Policy Makers* (Philadelphia: Temple University Press, 1987); Mark H. Rose, *Interstate: Express Highway Politics, 1939–1989*, 2nd ed. (Knoxville: University of Tennessee Press, 1990); William R. Childs, *Trucking and the Public Interest: The Emergence of Federal Regulation, 1914–1940* (Knoxville: University of Tennessee Press, 1985); Mark H. Rose, Bruce E. Seely, and Paul F. Barrett, *The Best Transportation System in the World: Railroads, Trucks, Airlines, and American Public Policy in the Twentieth Century* (Columbus: Ohio State University Press, 2006).

CHAPTER ONE: FOOD AND POWER IN THE NEW DEAL, 1933–42

1. Jerome Frank, Opinion in *Queensboro Farm Products vs. Wickard,* 137 F. 2nd 969, (2nd Cir. 1943), 974; "SEC Appointments," *NW,* Dec. 20, 1937, 42; Reinhold Niebuhr, "Jerome Frank's Way Out," *Nation,* Jul. 9, 1938, 45.

2. Lawrence Goodwyn, *The Populist Moment: A Short History of the Agrarian Revolt in America* (Oxford: Oxford University Press, 1978); Elizabeth Sanders, *Roots of Reform: Farmers, Workers, and the American State, 1877–1917* (Chicago: University of Chicago Press, 1999); Daniel T. Rodgers, *Atlantic Crossings: Social Politics in a Progressive Age* (Cambridge, MA: Harvard University Press, 1998), 318–66; David A. Lake, "Export, Die, or Subsidize: The International Political Economy of American Agriculture, 1875–1940," *Comparative Studies in Society and History* 31 (Jan. 1989): 91–94.

3. James Shideler, *Farm Crisis, 1919–1923* (Berkeley: University of California Press, 1957); Hansen, *Gaining Access;* Hamilton, *From New Day to New Deal;* Gilbert C. Fite, *George N. Peek and the Fight for Farm Parity* (Norman: University of Oklahoma Press, 1954).

4. Daniel, *Breaking the Land;* Gilbert C. Fite, *Cotton Fields No More: Southern Agriculture, 1865–1980* (Lexington: University of Kentucky Press, 1984); Fitzgerald, *Every Farm a Factory.*

5. Jacobs, *Pocketbook Politics,* 114–17; Richard S. Kirkendall, *Social Scientists and Farm Politics in the Age of Roosevelt* (Columbia: University of Missouri Press, 1966).

6. Persia C. Campbell, *Consumer Representation in the New Deal* (New York: Columbia University Press, 1940), 203–4; Howe quoted in Jacobs, *Pocketbook Politics,* 119; Peek quoted in Arthur M. Schlesinger, Jr., *The Age of Roosevelt: The Coming of the New Deal* (Boston: Houghton Mifflin, 1958), 52.

7. Jess Gilbert, "Eastern Urban Intellectuals and Midwestern Agrarian Intellectuals: Two Group Portraits of Progressives in the New Deal Department of Agriculture," *AH* 74 (Sep. 2000): 162–80; John C. Culver and John Hyde, *American Dreamer: The Life and Times of Henry A. Wallace* (New York: W. W. Norton, 2000); Robert Jerome Glennon, *The Iconoclast as Reformer: Jerome Frank's Impact on American Law* (Ithaca, NY: Cornell University Press, 1985); Peter H. Irons, *The New Deal Lawyers* (Princeton, NJ: Princeton University Press, 1982), 121–2.

8. Michele Micheletti, *The Swedish Farmers' Movement and Government Agricultural Policy* (New York: Praeger, 1990), 44–52; Rodgers, *Atlantic Crossings,* 315, 319; George N. Peek with Samuel Crowther, *Why Quit Our Own* (New York: Van Nostrand, 1936), 20; Irons, *New Deal Lawyers,* 10; Fite, *George N. Peek,* 243–66.

9. Robin D. G. Kelley, *Hammer and Hoe: Alabama Communists during the Great Depression* (Chapel Hill: University of North Carolina Press, 1990); Larry Grubbs, *Cry from the Cotton: The Southern Tenant Farmers' Union and the New Deal* (Chapel Hill: University of North Carolina Press, 1971); Neil Foley, *The White Scourge: Mexicans, Blacks, and Poor Whites in Texas Cotton Culture* (Berkeley: University of California Press, 1997), 186–201; Jack Temple Kirby, *Rural Worlds Lost: The American South, 1920–1960* (Baton Rouge: Louisiana State University Press, 1987), 51–79; Daniel, *Breaking the Land,* 65–151.

10. Theodore Saloutos and John D. Hicks, *Twentieth-Century Populism: Agricultural*

Discontent in the Middle West, 1900–1939 (Lincoln: University of Nebraska Press, 1951), 491, 219–54; David B. Danbom, *The Resisted Revolution: Urban America and the Industrialization of Agriculture, 1900–1930* (Ames: Iowa State University Press, 1979); Shideler, *Farm Crisis,* 127; Hansen, *Gaining Access;* Theodore Saloutos, *The American Farmer and the New Deal* (Ames: Iowa State University Press, 1982), 124–50; Hal S. Barron, *Mixed Harvest: The Second Great Transformation in the Rural North, 1870–1930* (Chapel Hill: University of North Carolina Press, 1997), 107–52.

11. Steve Fraser, *Labor Will Rule: Sidney Hillman and the Rise of American Labor* (New York: Free Press, 1991); Lizabeth Cohen, *Making a New Deal: Industrial Workers in Chicago, 1919–1939* (Cambridge: Cambridge University Press, 1990); Nelson Lichtenstein, *State of the Union: A Century of American Labor* (Princeton, NJ: Princeton University Press, 2002), 20–97; Jacobs, *Pocketbook Politics.*

12. Alice Kessler-Harris, *In Pursuit of Equity: Women, Men, and the Quest for Economic Citizenship in 20th Century America* (New York: Oxford University Press, 2001), 19–116; Patricia Sullivan, *Days of Hope: Race and Democracy in the New Deal Era* (Chapel Hill: University of North Carolina Press, 1996); Lawrence B. Glickman, "The Strike in the Temple of Consumption: Consumer Activism and Twentieth-Century American Political Culture," *Journal of American History* 88 (Jun. 2001): 99–128.

13. Ellis W. Hawley, *The New Deal and the Problem of Monopoly: A Study in Economic Ambivalence* (Princeton, NJ: Princeton University Press, 1966); Colin Gordon, *New Deals: Business, Labor, and Politics in America, 1920–1935* (Cambridge: Cambridge University Press, 1994); Alan Brinkley, *Voices of Protest: Huey Long, Father Coughlin, and the Great Depression* (New York: Vintage Books, 1983); Franklin D. Roosevelt, Acceptance of the Renomination for the Presidency, Philadelphia, PA, Jun. 27, 1936, in *The Public Papers and Addresses of Franklin D. Roosevelt,* vol. 5, ed. Samuel I. Rosenman (New York: Random House, 1938), 232–33; Brinkley, *End of Reform,* 48–64, 106–36, Ickes quoted on 57; Anthony J. Badger, *The New Deal: The Depression Years, 1933–1940* (New York: Hill and Wang, 1989), 105–6.

14. Jonathan J. Bean, *Beyond the Broker State: Federal Policies toward Small Business, 1936–1961* (Chapel Hill: University of North Carolina Press, 1996), 17–36; Jacobs, *Pocketbook Politics,* 160–63; Richard S. Tedlow, *New and Improved: The Story of Mass Marketing in America* (New York: Basic Books, 1990), 182–239.

15. E. Melanie DuPuis, *Nature's Perfect Food: How Milk Became America's Drink* (New York: New York University Press, 2002); Daniel R. Block, "The Development of Regional Institutions in Agriculture: The Chicago Milk Marketing Order," (Ph.D. diss., University of California-Los Angeles, 1997), 1–199.

16. William Cronon, *Nature's Metropolis: Chicago and the Great West* (New York: W. W. Norton, 1991), 46–54.

17. Daniel Block and E. Melanie DuPuis, "Making the Country Work for the City: Von Thünen's Ideas in Geography, Agricultural Economics and the Sociology of Agriculture," *American Journal of Economics and Sociology* 60 (Jan. 2001): 79–98; Gordon R. Lewthwaite, "Wisconsin Cheese and Farm Type: A Locational Hypothesis," *Economic Geography* 40 (Apr. 1964): 95–112; George Max Beal and Henry H. Bakken, *Fluid Milk Marketing* (Madison, WI: Mimir Publishers, 1956), 35–62.

18. Barbara Orland, "Turbo-Cows: Producing a Competitive Animal in the Nineteenth and Early Twentieth Centuries," in *Industrializing Organisms,* ed. Susan R. Schrepfer and Philip Scranton (New York: Routledge, 2004), 167–90; Eric E. Lampard, *The Rise of the Dairy Industry in Wisconsin: A Study in Agricultural Change, 1820–1920* (Madison: State Historical Society of Wisconsin, 1963).

19. John D. Black, *The Dairy Industry and the AAA* (Washington: Brookings Institution, 1935), 60–82, 463.

20. *NYT,* Aug. 13, 1933, 2; E. Wilson, "Milk Strike," *NR,* Sep. 13, 1933, 122–25; *MJ,* Feb. 7, 1933, 6; *MJ,* Feb. 19, 1933, 3; A. William Hoglund, "Wisconsin Dairy Farmers on Strike," *AH* 35 (Jan. 1961): 24–34; *MJ,* Feb. 8, 1933, 1; *MJ,* Feb. 15, 1933, 1, 2; *MJ,* Feb. 17, 1933, 1, 3; *MJ,* Feb. 18, 1933, 1, 3; *MJ,* Feb. 20, 1933, 1, 2; *MJ,* Feb. 21, 1933, 1, 2; Dr. Pilgrim, "Health Department Activities during the Milk Strike," 1933, box 14, folder 3, entry 27, AMSR.

21. Mr. Blatz to Rodger Crabtree, "Report on Trip to South Milwaukee Farmers," Apr. 13, 1934, box 46, folder 6, entry 27, AMSR; Percy S. Hardiman, Interview by Dale Trelevan, Aug. 3, 1976, Percy Hardiman Oral History, WHS, tape 3, side 1.

22. Milk Council, Inc., Chicago Milk Dealers Association, and Pure Milk Association to Henry A. Wallace, May 26, 1933, box 41, folder 9, entry 25, AMSR; Pure Milk Association to Wallace and George N. Peek, Jul. 5, 1933, box 1811, folder 3, SAR.

23. Clyde L. King, *The Price of Milk* (Philadelphia: John C. Winston, 1920); Block, "Development of Regional Institutions," 208; Milwaukee Co-operative Milk Producers, "Why Should I Sign a Marketing Agreement?" Pamphlet, n.d. (1933?), box 1, folder 5, AMPI; "Informal Conference on the Chicago Milk Agreement," Jul. 5, 1933, box 41, folder 9, entry 25, AMSR. Chicago came under Federal Milk Marketing Order No. 41 in 1937, continuing to this day with only a brief interruption in 1966.

24. "Informal Conference on the Chicago Milk Agreement," Jul. 5, 1933, box 41, folder 9, entry 25, AMSR; Hearings on Proposed Marketing Agreement, Washington, DC, Jun. 5, 1933, box 42, folder 1, ibid.; Block, "Development of Regional Institutions," 227–28; Carroll Lawrence Christenson, "Employment and Earnings in Commercial Milk Distribution, 1929–34," *MLR* 43 (Jul. 1936): 139–49; Jerome Frank to Glenn McHugh, Jul. 10, 1933, box 42, folder 2, entry 25, AMSR; Hearings before the Secretary of Agriculture with Reference to Modification of Any Provisions of the Marketing Agreement for Milk—Chicago Milk Shed (Agreement No. 1), Docket No. 1-C, vol. 2, Chicago, Nov. 30–Dec. 1, 1933, box 41, folder 1, ibid.; Hendrik Shipstead to Henry A. Wallace, Jul. 16, 1933, box 1811, folder 3, SAR.

25. "Distribution of Consumers' Dairy Dollar," 1934, box 1, entry 27, AMSR; Jerome N. Frank to George Peek, Mr. Brand, Chester Davis, Aug. 28, 1933, box 1811, folder 3, SAR; Chicago City Council to Franklin D. Roosevelt, Nov. 2, 1933, box 1814, folder 2, ibid.; Hearings before the Secretary of Agriculture, Chicago Milk Shed, Docket No. 1-C, vol. 1, Chicago, Nov. 27–29, 1933, 29–30, 33, 45, box 40, folder 9, entry 25, AMSR.

26. House Agriculture Committee, *Regulation of Milk Production, Distribution, and Pricing,* Unpublished Hearings on H.R. 8988, 73rd Cong., 2nd sess., May 3, 1934, 126–27; "Let 'em Drink Grade A," *Fortune,* Nov. 1939, 82–84, 131–32.

27. John S. Picago to Thomas Hughes, Apr. 3, 1938, reel 16, IBTR; "Milk in Chicago," *Fortune,* Nov. 1939, 80–81, 124–28; "Milk War in Detroit," *BW,* May 1, 1937, 28; "Milk

Strike," *NW,* Aug. 28, 1939, 38; "History and Business of Bowman Dairy Company," n.d. (1955?), 8–9, box 1, folder 1, series I, subseries 1, BDC; Alan Barth, "Only the Cows Are Contented," *Nation,* Jan. 1, 1938, 744–45; James Ernest Boyle, "Battle of Milk," *SEP,* Nov. 13, 1937, 18–19; "FTC Raps Big Dairies," *BW,* Jan. 9, 1937, 34, 37; John T. Flynn, "The Milk Monopoly," *NR,* Apr. 5, 1939, 250.

28. Temporary National Economic Committee, *Investigation of Concentration of Economic Power, Part 7: Milk Industry, Poultry Industry, Hearings,* 76th Cong., 1st sess., Mar. 9–11, May 1–3, 1939, 2778.

29. Wesley McCune, "Why Milk Costs So Much," *Harper's,* May 1942, 608.

30. Cronon, *Nature's Metropolis,* 225–34; Mary Yeager, *Competition and Regulation: The Development of Oligopoly in the Meat Packing Industry* (Greenwich, CT.: Greenwood Press, 1981), 17, 49–59; John H. White, Jr., *The American Railroad Freight Car: From the Wood-Car Era to the Coming of Steel* (Baltimore: Johns Hopkins University Press, 1995), 270–83.

31. Cronon, *Nature's Metropolis,* 235; Oscar Edward Anderson, Jr., *Refrigeration in America: A History of a New Technology and Its Impact* (Princeton, NJ: Princeton University Press, 1953), 145–46, 148–49; Lewis Corey, *Meat and Man: A Study of Monopoly, Unionism, and Food Policy* (New York: Viking Press, 1950), 46–49; Yeager, *Competition and Regulation,* 61–77.

32. Originally only a "Big Four"—Swift, Armour, Hammond, and Morris—successfully mass marketed dressed beef. Sulzberger & Sulzberger joined the field in 1897 and was renamed Wilson in 1916. The Cudahy company joined in 1900, but Hammond was acquired by Armour in 1901, keeping the number at five. Morris merged with Armour in 1923, making the Big Five the Big Four.

33. Yeager, *Competition and Regulation,* 260–61; Richard J. Arnould, "Changing Patterns of Concentration in American Meat Packing, 1880–1963," *BHR* 45 (Spring 1971): 20; Cronon, *Nature's Metropolis,* 245; Corey, *Meat and Man,* 75, Federal Trade Commission, *Report of the Federal Trade Commission on the Meat-Packing Industry, Part III* (Washington: GPO, 1919), 116, 117.

34. Corey, *Meat and Man,* 431; Federal Trade Commission, *Report, Part III,* 11, 15, 85–116; Arnould, "Changing Patterns," 22; Charles L. Wood, *The Kansas Beef Industry* (Lawrence: University of Kansas Press, 1980), 164, 165, 178–79.

35. Charles Edward Russell, *The Greatest Trust in the World* (New York: Ridgway-Thayer, 1905), 5; Paula E. Hyman, "Immigrant Women and Consumer Protest: The New York City Kosher Meat Boycott of 1902," *American Jewish History* 70 (Sep. 1980): 94; Upton Sinclair, *Autobiography* (New York: Harcourt, Brace, 1962), 126.

36. Federal Trade Commission, *Report of the Federal Trade Commission on the Meat-Packing Industry, Part I* (Washington: GPO, 1919), 72, 26, 68–70; ibid., *Part V,* 12–13; Jimmy M. Skaggs, *Prime Cut: Livestock Raising and Meatpacking in the United States, 1607–1983* (College Station: Texas A & M University Press, 1986), 106–7, 152; Corey, *Meat and Man,* 89; Arnould, "Changing Patterns," 25; Wood, *Kansas Beef,* 266.

37. *Stafford v Wallace,* 258 U.S. 495 (1922), 514–16; *NYT,* May 15, 1922, 8.

38. *NYT,* Jul. 15, 1933, 15; *NYT,* Sep. 13, 1935, 40; USDA Economic Research Service, "Food Consumption (Per Capita) Data System," http://www.ers.usda.gov/data/foodconsumption/; John T. Schlebecker, *Cattle Raising on the Plains, 1900–1961* (Lincoln: Univer-

sity of Nebraska Press, 1963), 153; *NYT*, Nov. 6, 1937, 7; H. S. Fain to Wallace, Oct. 27, 1933, box 1771, folder 14, SAR.

39. Frederic C. Howe, "Working Arrangement with Meat Packing Companies," Jan. 24, 1934, box 1995, folder 6, SAR; Jerome Frank to Tugwell, Ezekiel, Howe et al., "In Re: Packers," Jun. 29, 1933, box 1826, folder 5, ibid. (emphasis in original).

40. Ezekiel to Chester Davis, Jun. 11, 1934, box 1995, folder 6, SAR; Robert E. Sher, "Plan Proposed by Mr. F. H. Prince for Organization of Union Purchasing and Distribution Company," Jan. 26, 1934, ibid.

41. Ezekiel to Tugwell, "Packers' Agreement," Aug. 8, 1933, box 1826, folder 5, SAR; Jerome Frank, "Marketing Agreement with Packers," Aug. 11, 1933, ibid.; Swift to Wallace, Jan. 11, 1934, box 1995, folder 6, ibid.; Ezekiel, "Status of Negotiations with Packers," Jan. 17, 1934, ibid.; Fred Krey to Rep. John J. Cochran, May 10, 1934, ibid.; Wallace to R. C. Ashby, Jun. 27, 1936, box 2380, folder 4, ibid.

42. Charles F. Hurley to Wallace, Oct. 7, 1937, box 2589, folder 2, SAR; Wallace to Hurley, Oct. 23, 1937, ibid.; *NYT*, Sep. 17, 1935, 4; *NYT*, Nov. 10, 1935, 35; *NYT*, Apr. 7, 1936, 19; *NYT*, Apr. 7, 1936, 19; *NYT*, Oct. 6, 1936, 37; *NYT*, Jul. 6, 1938, 5.

43. Arnould, "Changing Patterns," 26; Corey, *Meat and Man*, 90–91; Robert Aduddell and Louis Cain, "Public Policy toward 'The Greatest Trust in the World,'" *BHR* 55 (Summer 1981): 238.

Chapter Two: Chaos, Control, and Country Trucking, 1933–42

1. *They Drive by Night*, directed Raoul Walsh, 97 min., Warner Bros., 1940, digital video disc.

2. Barron, *Mixed Harvest*, 30; Michael L. Berger, *The Devil Wagon in God's Country: The Automobile and Social Change in Rural America, 1893–1929* (Hamden, CT: Archon Books, 1979); Ronald Kline and Trevor Pinch, "Users as Agents of Technological Change: The Social Construction of the Automobile in the Rural United States," *T&C* 37 (Oct. 1996): 763–95; Christopher W. Wells, "The Changing Nature of Country Roads: Farmers, Reformers, and the Shifting Uses of Rural Space, 1880–1905," *AH* 80 (Spring 2006): 143–66; Joseph Interrante, "You Can't Go to Town in a Bathtub: Automobile Movement and the Reorganization of Rural American Space, 1900–1930," *Radical History Review* 21 (Fall 1979): 151.

3. Seely, *Building the American Highway*, 35–99; Bureau of the Census, *Historical Statistics of the United States: Colonial Times to 1970* (Washington: GPO, 1976), 710.

4. Gijs P. A. Mom and David A. Kirsch, "Technologies in Transition: Horses, Electric Trucks, and the Motorization of American Cities, 1900–1925," *T&C* 42 (Jul. 2001): 489–518; Robert F. Karolevitz, *This Was Trucking: A Pictorial History of the First Quarter Century of Commercial Motor Vehicles* (Seattle: Superior Publishing, 1966), 80–81; Louis Rodriguez, "The Development of the Truck: A Constructivist History," (Ph. D. diss., Lehigh University, 1997), 78–80; Roy Fruehauf, *Over the Road to Progress! Fruehauf Truck Trailers* (New York: Newcomen Society, 1957) and *Engineered Transportation* (Detroit: Fruehauf Trailer

Co., 1930), Transportation Subject File, box 2, folder 21, WCBA; James Harold Thomas, *The Long Haul: Truckers, Truck Stops, and Trucking* (Memphis: Memphis State University Press, 1979), 73.

5. James R. Wiley, *Motor Transportation of Hogs to the Indianapolis Market,* (Lafayette, IN: Purdue University Agricultural Experiment Station, 1927), 2; G. N. Motts, *Motor Truck Marketing of Michigan Fruits and Vegetables* (East Lansing: Michigan Agricultural Experiment Station, 1932); Harold G. Moulton, *The American Transportation Problem* (Washington: Brookings Institution, 1933), 576–77, 610–11; Thomas H. MacDonald, "Substitution of Highway Transportation for Unprofitable Branch Line Operations," May 16, 1933, box 1913, folder 3, SAR.

6. Federal Coordinator of Transportation, *Hours, Wages, and Working Conditions in the Intercity Motor Transport Industries* (Washington: GPO, 1936), 57; Henry A. Wallace, "High Freight Rates as a Retarding Factor in Agricultural and Industrial Recovery," statement at Hearings before the Interstate Commerce Commission, Docket Ex Parte 115, Dec. 7, 1934, box 2001, folder 7, SAR; Chad Berry, *Southern Migrants, Northern Exiles* (Urbana: University of Illinois Press, 2000); James N. Gregory, *The Southern Diaspora: How the Great Migrations of Black and White Southerners Transformed America* (Chapel Hill: University of North Carolina Press, 2005), 81–112.

7. Steven Ruggles, Matthew Sobek, Trent Alexander, Catherine A. Fitch, Ronald Goeken, Patricia Kelly Hall, Miriam King, and Chad Ronnander, *Integrated Public Use Microdata Series: Version 3.0* (Minneapolis: Minnesota Population Center, 2004). See appendix A for a methodological note on these data and other statistics derived from the IPUMS census samples.

8. "Trucks Are Going over the Top," *BW,* Sep. 12, 1936, 13–14; Childs, *Trucking and the Public Interest,* 35.

9. Dick Boyd, "'Blick's' Ideal Truck Lines Has Come Long Way Since 'Dirty 30s,'" *Norton (Kansas) Daily Telegraph,* May 31, 1978, MCIC; Harry D. Woods, *Woods Highway Truck Library,* New York Times Oral History Program (Glen Rock, NJ: Microfilming Corp. of America, 1975–77), interviews with Edward J. Buhner (#2), Henry E. English (#4), John F. Ernsthausen (#5), Carl Ozee (#11), Samuel Raitzin (#12); Marvin Schwartz, *J. B. Hunt: The Long Haul to Success* (Fayetteville: University of Arkansas Press, 1992); Kenneth Rhodes, "Arno Dalby Is Living Proof That Any Goal Is Possible If You Work for It," *Lubbock Avalanche-Journal,* Feb. 28, 1961, Loyd M. Lanotte Papers, Texas Tech University, Southwest Collection, Lubbock, TX, Reel 1; Paul Merrill, *Forty-Six Years a Truckman: The Story of Merrill Transport Company* (New York: Newcomen Society, 1975), 8–9.

10. Samuel E. Hill, *Teamsters and Transportation: Employee-Employer Relationships in New England* (Washington: American Council on Public Affairs, 1942), xii.

11. Thorp McClusky, "Truck Drivers Are Human, Too," *Christian Science Monitor Magazine,* Aug. 9, 1947, 13; "A Man's on His Own on the Highway," *ORPD,* Jun. 1967, 5.

12. Roy B. Thompson, "The Trucking Industry, 1930–1950," Interview Recorded with Corinne L. Gilb, Jun.–Aug. 1958, Industrial Relations Interviews, Bancroft Library, Berkeley, CA, 52; Harry D. Woods, *Woods Highway Truck Library,* interviews with John J. Brady, Sr. (#1) and "Mr. X" (#9); Hawley, *New Deal and the Problem of Monopoly,* 231–34.

13. State-level regulations preceded federal legislation. See Donald V. Harper, *Economic Regulation of the Motor Trucking Industry by the States* (Urbana: University of Illinois Press, 1950), 26–27, 32–34.

14. John Lewis Keeshin, *No Fears, Hidden Tears: A Memoir of Four Score Years* (Chicago: Castle-Pierce Press, 1983), 19–20, 32–33; Hawley, *New Deal and the Problem of Monopoly,* 19–71.

15. Childs, *Trucking and the Public Interest,* 101–14; Thompson, "The Trucking Industry," 100–76; Hawley, *New Deal and the Problem of Monopoly,* 127–29, 232–33. The word "Associations" (plural) was used because it was a national collection of dozens of state- and regional-level trucking associations that had sprung up in the 1920s to negotiate with state regulatory bodies.

16. *Report of the Federal Coordinator of Transportation on Regulation of Transportation Agencies,* 73rd Cong., 2nd sess., Mar. 10, 1934, S. Doc. 152; Senate Interstate Commerce Committee, *To Amend the Interstate Commerce Act, Part I: Motor Carrier Act of 1935, Hearings,* 74th Cong., 1st sess., Feb. 25–28, Mar. 1, 2, 4–6, 1935, 51, 50, 61–62, 66; Thomas K. McCraw, *Prophets of Regulation: Charles Francis Adams, Louis D. Brandeis, James M. Landis, Alfred E. Kahn* (Cambridge: Harvard University Press, 1984), 80–142.

17. Thomas, *Long Haul,* 93–110; Samuel Woolley Taylor, *Line Haul: The Story of Pacific Intermountain Express* (San Francisco: Filmer, 1959); Philip L. Cantelon, *The Roadway Story* (Rockville, MD: Montrose Press, 1996); James F. Filgas, *Yellow in Motion: A History of Yellow Freight System, Incorporated* (Bloomington: Indiana University Press, 1971); Kenneth D. Durr and Philip L. Cantelon, *Never Stand Still: The History of Consolidated Freightways, Inc. and CNF Transportation, Inc.* (Rockville, MD: Montrose Press, 1999); J. R. Halladay, *Partner in Progress: The Story of the American Trucking Associations* (Alexandria, VA: American Trucking Associations, 1994), i.

18. Ralph C. James and Estelle Dinerstein James, *Hoffa and the Teamsters: A Study of Union Power* (Princeton, NJ: Van Nostrand, 1965), 91; Lawrence S. Rothenberg, *Regulation, Organizations, and Politics: Motor Freight Policy at the Interstate Commerce Commission* (Ann Arbor: University of Michigan Press, 1994), 76–78.

19. Robert T. Schultz, *Conflict and Change: Minneapolis Truck Drivers Make a Dent in the New Deal* (Prospect Heights, IL: Waveland Press, 2000); James and James, *Hoffa and the Teamsters,* 91, 92–101.

20. Thaddeus Russell, *Out of the Jungle: Jimmy Hoffa and the Remaking of the American Working Class* (New York: Knopf, 2001), 18, 25–72.

21. J. B. Gillingham, *The Teamsters Union on the West Coast* (Berkeley: Institute of Industrial Relations, University of California, 1956), 6, 54–64; David Witwer, *Corruption and Reform in the Teamsters Union* (Urbana: University of Illinois Press, 2003), 134–37; Harold M. Levinson et al., *Collective Bargaining and Technological Change in American Transportation* (Evanston, IL: Transportation Center at Northwestern University, 1971), 18–19.

22. Charles W. Holman, "The Proposed Code of Fair Competition for the Trucking Industry," Dec. 4, 1933, box 1913, folder 9, SAR; Wallace to Rep. John McDuffie, Nov. 1, 1933, ibid.; Paul H. Appleby to Donald R. Murphy, Nov. 1, 1933, ibid.; Wallace, "Proposed Code on Fair Competition for the Trucking Industry," Nov. 2, 1933, ibid.

23. Fred Brenckman to Wallace, "Federal Regulation of Motor Trucks," Mar. 28, 1934, box 2032, folder 19, SAR; Senate Interstate Commerce Committee, *Amend the Interstate Commerce Act,* 504, 508; House Interstate and Foreign Commerce Committee, *Regulation of Interstate Motor Carriers, Hearings,* 74th Cong., 1st sess., Feb. 19–22, 26–28, Mar. 1, 4, 5, 1935, 291.

24. Eastman to Wallace, "Effect of the Proposed Motor Carrier Act on Farm Trucking," Mar. 16, 1934, box 2032, folder 19, SAR; *CR,* 74th Cong., 1st sess., Jul. 31, 1935, vol. 79, pt. 11, pp. 12,217, 12,221; Warren H. Wagner, *A Legislative History of the Motor Carrier Act, 1935* (Denton, Md.: Rue Publishing, 1935), 26–29.

25. Melvyn Dubofsky, *The State and Labor in Modern America* (Chapel Hill: University of North Carolina Press, 1994); Linda Gordon, *Pitied but Not Entitled: Single Mothers and the History of Welfare, 1890–1935* (New York: Free Press, 1994); Landon R. Y. Storrs, *Civilizing Capitalism: The National Consumers' League, Women's Activism, and Labor Standards in the New Deal Era* (Chapel Hill: University of North Carolina Press, 2000); Cindy Hahamovitch, *The Fruits of Their Labor: Atlantic Coast Farmworkers and the Making of Migrant Poverty, 1870–1945* (Chapel Hill: University of North Carolina Press, 1997).

26. "Can You Beat This 41 Year Record?" *MMH* (Nov. 1960): 23; "37 Years of Milk Hauling," *MMH* (Oct. 1960): 18–19, 23; "Milk Hauling Has Come a Long Way," *MMH* (Feb. 1961): 6–7; "Wisconsin Hauler on the Job 49 Years," *MHFT* (Apr. 1973): 18; "Wisconsin Man in 'Haul of Fame,'" *MHFT* (May 1973): 16.

27. Biographical notes, box 32, folder 1, JDB; Hamilton, *From New Day to New Deal,* 182.

28. Black, *Dairy Industry and the AAA,* 222, 302–3.

29. Black to James E. Russell, Mar. 2, 1934, box 5, folder 3, JDB.

30. Skaggs, *Prime Cut,* 134–35; Corey, *Meat and Man,* 131.

31. Cronon, *Nature's Metropolis,* 222, 236; J. S. Cotton, Edmund Thompson, and Jay Whitson, "Cost of Fattening Cattle," in *Report of the Federal Trade Commission on the Meat-Packing Industry, Part VI* (Washington: GPO, 1920), 64, 55–132.

32. Mordecai Ezekiel, "The Cobweb Theorem," *Quarterly Journal of Economics* 52 (Feb. 1938): 255–80; Kenneth H. Mathews, Jr. et al., *U.S. Beef Industry: Cattle Cycles, Price Spreads, and Packer Concentration* (Washington: Economic Research Service, 1999); Lee Searle, "Cattle Marketing: Cycles Still Control the Booms and Busts," *SF* (Aug. 1975): 22–23.

33. R. C. Ashby, *Livestock Truckage Rates in Illinois with a Comparison of Marketing Expense by Truck and by Rail* (Urbana: Illinois Agricultural Experiment Station, 1930); E. C. Johnson and E. A. Johnson, *Trucking Livestock to South St. Paul* (St. Paul: Minnesota Agricultural Experiment Station, 1931); G. F. Henning, *The Truck and Its Relationship to Livestock Marketing in Ohio* (Wooster: Ohio Agricultural Experiment Station, 1929).

34. J. R. Mohler to Wallace, Sep. 17, 1935, box 2209, folder 6, SAR; M. L. Wilson to Hugh M. Tate, Oct. 8, 1935, ibid.; "Record in Cattle," *Kansas City Times,* Oct. 19, 1943, CIC; Schlebecker, *Cattle Raising,* 167; American Trucking Associations, *American Trucking Trends* (Washington: American Trucking Associations, 1954), 7; ibid. (1963), 22.

35. George L. Schein, "Index and Abstract of Transcript of Hearings on Proposed Code of Fair Competition Submitted by the American Stockyards Association to the Agricultural

Adjustment Administration and the National Recovery Administration for Approval," Mar. 2, 3, 5, 6, 1934, 7, 14, 74–75, 79, box 2076, folder 4, SAR; Agricultural Marketing Service, Livestock Division, *Livestock, Meat, Wool, Market News,* Jan. 31, 1940, 1,148; J. D. LeCron to J. E. Renner, Dec. 18, 1934, box 2076, folder 4, SAR.

36. A. G. Black to N. K. Carnes, Dec. 28, 1938, box 2821, folder 13, SAR; Wood, *Kansas Beef,* 270.

37. Schein, "Hearings on Proposed Code," 102; House Agriculture Committee, *Prohibit Feeding of Livestock by Certain Packers, Hearings,* 89th Cong., 2nd sess., Apr. 21, 22, Oct. 5, 6, 1966, 106; Aly A. Abdou, "Economic Aspects of Motor Transportation in Marketing Livestock," *JFE* 39 (Nov. 1957): 961; Wood, *Kansas Beef,* 179.

CHAPTER THREE: FOOD FIGHTS IN WAR AND PEACE, 1942–52

1. Virgil W. Dean, *An Opportunity Lost: The Truman Administration and the Farm Policy Debate* (Columbia: University of Missouri Press, 2006); Robert Griffith, "Forging America's Postwar Order: Domestic Politics and Political Economy in the Age of Truman," in *The Truman Presidency,* ed. Michael J. Lacey (Cambridge: Cambridge University Press, 1989), 75–78; Alonzo L. Hamby, *Beyond the New Deal: Harry S. Truman and American Liberalism* (New York: Columbia University Press, 1973), 303–10.

2. "Peg Beef Prices," *BW,* Dec. 19, 1942, 70; Marshall B. Clinard, *The Black Market: A Study of White Collar Crime* (New York: Rinehart, 1952), 116–17; Jacobs, *Pocketbook Politics,* 192–94, 202, 207, 215; Amy Bentley, *Eating for Victory: Food Rationing and the Politics of Domesticity* (Urbana: University of Illinois Press, 1998), 9–29, 85–102.

3. Schlebecker, *Cattle Raising,* 171; "Boom in Beef," *BW,* May 30, 1942, 22; John D. Black and Charles A. Gibbons, "The War and American Agriculture," *Review of Economic Statistics* 26 (Feb. 1944): 14–16; Bureau of the Census, *Historical Statistics of the United States* (1976), 485.

4. Clinard, *Black Market,* 134, 142–43; John J. Madigan to Jerry Thorne, May 12, 1943, box 1, folder 1, entry 111, AMSR.

5. Judith Russell and Renee Fantin, *Studies in Food Rationing* (Washington: GPO, 1947), 265; "Milk Rations Seen," *BW,* Jun. 12, 1943, 57; *WSJ,* Feb. 10, 1942, 1; *NYT,* Dec. 31, 1941, 32.

6. McCune, "Why Milk Costs So Much," 604, 608.

7. Russell and Fantin, *Studies in Food Rationing,* 267–68; *Report of the Secretary of Agriculture* (Washington: GPO, 1943), 149; Hugh Rockoff, *Drastic Measures: A History of Wage and Price Controls in the United States* (Cambridge: Cambridge University Press, 1984).

8. Office of Price Administration, Press Release OPA-1415, Jan. 1, 1942, box 1.2/22, folder B4, USDAHC; "Milk Pinch Grows," *BW,* Aug. 28, 1943, 29; John C. Weigel, "Statement of Considerations for Regional Order No. 26," Feb. 1, 1943, box 4107, entry 476, OPAR; Raymond S. McKeough, "Opinion Accompanying Amendment No. 1 to Order No. G-4," Nov. 12, 1943, ibid.

9. Russell and Fantin, *Studies in Food Rationing,* 282–83; USDA, "Action Begun on

Milk Marketing Economy Program," Jan. 4, 1943, box 1.2/22, folder B4, USDAHC; "Dairy Dilemma," *BW,* Sep. 18, 1943, 19.

10. Labor Research Division, Mid-States Dairy Conference, Proceedings, Feb. 26, 1943, 18, box 119, folder 8, series II, IBTR.

11. Rogers to International Association of Milk Dealers, Mar. 16, 1942, reel 84, IBTR; Tobin to Rogers, Mar. 18, 1942, 1–2, ibid.; H. G. Burger to Thomas Flynn, May 14, 1942, box 119, folder 8, series II, IBTR.

12. *NYT,* May 24, 1942, 1, 39; *NYT,* May 29, 1942, 1, 10; "Milk Route Peace?" *BW,* Nov. 21, 1942, 112–13; Victor Jack Sheifer, "Technological Change and Collective Bargaining: Experiences in the New York Milk-Distributing Industry, 1939–1972" (Ph.D. diss., New York University, 1974), 326–27, 329.

13. "Prices Assailed," *BW,* Jul. 15, 1944, 28, 31; "Beef in Trouble," *BW,* Dec. 23, 1944, 17–18; "Ceiling on Beef," *BW,* Feb. 3, 1945, 24–26; Clinard, *Black Market,* 145–47; Porter to Bowles, Mar. 12, 1946, box 1340, folder 1, SAR; Jacobs, *Pocketbook Politics,* 227–31.

14. "Farm Bloc on the March," *BW,* Mar. 2, 1946, 15–16; Edward A. O'Neal to Anderson, Jan. 30, 1946, box 1340, folder 1, SAR; Anderson to Rep. Paul J. Kilday, Mar. 13, 1946, ibid.; *CR,* 79th Cong., 2nd sess., Jul. 23, 1946, vol. 92, pt. 8, 9770–71, 9777; ibid., Jul. 24, 1946, 9875–76; ibid., Jul. 25, 1946, 10108. Rural congressional districts after E. Scott Adler, "Congressional District Data File, 79th Congress," http://socsci.colorado.edu/~esadler/districtdatawebsite/.

15. J. B. Hasselman to Porter, Aug. 24, 1946, box 1339, folder 2, SAR; Brannan to Rep. Mike Mansfield, Sep. 9, 1946, folder 3, ibid.; Nelson G. Kraschel to Clinton P. Anderson, Oct. 14, 1946, folder 5, ibid.

16. Jacobs, *Pocketbook Politics,* 228–31; Matusow, *Farm Policies and Politics,* 52–61.

17. Corey, *Meat and Man,* 91–92, 186; William O'Dwyer to Anderson, Jun. 13, 1947, box 1471, folder 12, SAR; Jacobs, *Pocketbook Politics,* 235–36.

18. "Dairy Prices," *NR,* Sep. 16, 1946, 309; Advertisement for National Dairy Products Corp., "How Would YOU Lick the High Cost of Living?" 1948, box 354, folder 1, series 2, NWAA; National War Labor Board Trucking Commission, Case No. 111–15769-D, Jun. 18, 1945, box 29, folder 4, series II, subseries 4, BDC; "Milk Every Day?" *BW,* Sep. 22, 1945, 86; "Milk Delivery, How Often?" *BW,* Nov. 3, 1945, 83; "Tripped on Wages," *BW,* Apr. 27, 1946, 98; "Milwaukee Drivers Demand Daily Delivery, Settle for Pay Increase," *MD* (Jun. 1946): 118; "Resolution Regarding Grade A Milk Marketing Changes," Wisconsin Cooperative Creamery Association, Mar. 9, 1955, box 5, folder 10, WDC; Truman Torgerson, *Building Markets and People Cooperatively: The Lake to Lake Story* (Manitowoc, WI.: Lake to Lake Division of Land O'Lakes Inc., 1990), 2–32.

19. House Agriculture Committee, *Long-Range Agricultural Policy, Part 1, Hearings,* 80th Cong., 1st sess., Apr. 21, 22, 23, 1947; Matusow, *Farm Policies and Politics,* 3, 12; Dean, *Opportunity Lost,* 27; National Planning Association, *Dare Farmers Risk Abundance?* (Washington: National Planning Association, 1947).

20. *Current Biography* (1948), 57–59; Eleonora W. Schoenebaum, ed., *Political Profiles: The Truman Years* (New York: Facts on File, 1977), 51–53; Dean, *Opportunity Lost,* 80–81.

21. Matusow, *Farm Politics and Policies,* 110–44; Dean, *Opportunity Lost,* 19–48.

22. Hamby, *Beyond the New Deal,* 224; Matusow, *Farm Policies and Politics,* 178–87; Dean, *Opportunity Lost,* 97–108; Jacobs, *Pocketbook Politics,* 240–22.

23. Dean, *Opportunity Lost,* 131–46; Reo Millard Christenson, *The Brannan Plan* (Ann Arbor: University of Michigan Press, 1959); Matusow, *Farm Policies and Politics,* 191–201; Jacobs, *Pocketbook Politics,* 238–39.

24. David E. Lindstrom, "Farm Price Policies in Sweden," *JFE* 34 (May 1952): 267–74; David J. Vail, Knut Per Hasund, and Lars Drake, *The Greening of Agricultural Policy in Industrial Societies: Swedish Reforms in Comparative Perspective* (Ithaca, NY: Cornell University Press, 1994), 91–238; Matusow, *Farm Policies and Politics,* 119, 121–23, 195.

25. Matusow, *Farm Policies and Politics,* 201, 205; Dean, *Opportunity Lost,* 148, 152–53; Marie Murtaugh to Brannan, Aug. 18, 1949, box 1712, folder 1, SAR.

26. Dean, *Opportunity Lost,* 156–200. On Whitten, see Mary Summers, "The New Deal Farm Programs: Looking for Reconstruction in American Agriculture," *AH* 74 (Spring 2000): 241–57; James C. Cobb, *The Most Southern Place on Earth: The Mississippi Delta and the Roots of Regional Identity* (New York: Oxford University Press, 1992), 259–61.

27. Persia Campbell to Brannan, Oct. 12, 1949, box 1712, folder 2, SAR; Brannan to Kline, Sep. 23, 1950, box 1711, folder 2, ibid.

28. *NYT,* Jan. 21, 1951, 41; *NYT,* Jan. 19, 1951, 42; "Beef May Be Cheaper, But How Much Will We Get?" *SEP,* Jun. 23, 1951, 10–12; *NYT,* Jun. 27, 1951, 23; House Agriculture Committee, *Beef Ceiling Price Regulations,* 80, 78; *NYT,* Jun. 8, 1951, 1; *NYT,* Jun. 9, 1951, 11; "The Beef Price Control Program," *Consumer Reports,* Jul. 1951, 321–24; *NYT,* Jul. 25, 1952, 1, 15; *NYT,* Aug. 14, 1952, 1, 24; *NYT,* Apr. 1, 1951, 151.

29. National Planning Association, *Must We Have Food Surpluses?* (Washington: National Planning Association, 1949), 18; F. L. Thomsen, "Postwar Readjustments in Marketing and Distribution," Address before Annual Agricultural Outlook Conference, Washington, D.C., Oct. 20, 1943, box 2, folder 11, JDB.

30. *CR,* 79th Cong., 2nd sess., Jul. 15, 1946, vol. 92, 9031; *Statutes at Large* 60, 1082 (1946); House Agriculture Committee, *Agricultural Research,* 79th Cong., 2nd sess., Jul. 8, 1946, H. Rept. 2458; Douglas E. Bowers, "The Research and Marketing Act of 1946 and Its Effects on Agricultural Marketing Research," *AH* 56 (Jan. 1982): 249–63; James L. Forsythe, "Clifford Hope of Kansas: Practical Congressman and Agrarian Idealist," *AH* 51 (Apr. 1977): 407–20.

31. Paul Boyer, *By the Bomb's Early Light: American Thought and Culture at the Dawn of the Atomic Age* (New York: Pantheon Books, 1985), 109, 110–30; Jeffrey L. Meikle, *American Plastic: A Cultural History* (New Brunswick, NJ: Rutgers University Press, 1995), 168; Kenneth T. Jackson, *Crabgrass Frontier: The Suburbanization of the United States* (New York: Oxford University Press, 1985), 234–38; Daniel Horowitz, *The Anxieties of Affluence: Critiques of American Consumer Culture, 1939–1979* (Amherst: University of Massachusetts Press, 2004); Levitt quoted in David Halberstam, *The Fifties* (New York: Villard Books, 1993), 141; Cohen, *Consumers' Republic,* 217–21.

32. James C. Scott, *Seeing Like a State: How Certain Schemes to Improve the Human Condition Have Failed* (New Haven, CT: Yale University Press, 1998); Thomas P. Hughes,

Human-Built World: How to Think about Technology and Culture (Chicago: University of Chicago Press, 2004), 153–73; Lisa Rosner, ed., *The Technological Fix: How People Use Technology to Create and Solve Problems* (New York: Routledge, 2004).

33. Agricultural Research Administration, *Report of Activities under the Research and Marketing Act* (Washington: GPO, 1951–53); *WSJ*, May 26, 1954, 1, 17; *Farm-Retail Spreads for Food Products: Costs, Prices* (Washington: Agricultural Marketing Service, 1957); Ralph L. Dewey and James C. Nelson, "The Transportation Problem of Agriculture," in USDA, *Yearbook of Agriculture* (Washington: GPO, 1940), 720–39.

34. American Trucking Associations, *American Trucking Trends* (1949), 1, 4; Ruggles et al., *Integrated Public Use Microdata Series,* 1950 1% sample; *Thieves' Highway,* dir. Jules Dassin, 94 min., Twentieth Century Fox, 1949, digital video disc.

35. *Statutes at Large* 52 (1938): 36–37; Henry A. Wallace to Sen. J. P. Pope, Aug. 23, 1938, box 2839, folder 1, SAR; USDA Newsletter, "Bowling Saves Millions," Nov. 26, 1945, 4, box 6, folder 8, entry 42, AMSR; Production and Marketing Administration, *Transportation Activities: Semi-Annual Report of the Transportation Rates and Services Division,* Jul. 1947, 5, 52. On early uses of the term "deregulation" by railroad executives, see Rose, Seely, and Barrett, *Best Transportation System,* 99.

36. Interstate Commerce Commission, Docket MC-107669, *Norman E. Harwood Contract Carrier Application,* 47 M.C.C. 597, Dec. 16, 1947; Donald C. Leavens, "The Investigation Concerning Exempted Agricultural Commodities," Aug. 17, 1948, and "Agenda for Exempted Agricultural Commodities Advisory Committee Meeting," Aug. 17, 1948, box 5, folder 20, entry 42, AMSR.

37. Charles B. Bowling to All Parties of Our Record, "Determination of Exempted Agricultural Commodities," Aug. 10, 1949, box 5, folder 20, entry 42, AMSR; Interstate Commerce Commission, Docket MC-C-968, *Determination of Exempted Agricultural Commodities,* 52 M.C.C. 511, Apr. 13, 1951; Celia Sperling, *The Agricultural Exemption in Interstate Trucking: A Legislative and Judicial History* (Washington: Agricultural Marketing Service, 1957), 27–29.

38. R. Thayne Robson, "The Trucking Industry," *MLR* 82 (May 1959): 548; "Trucking Commission History," n.d. (1945?), box 2428, folder 1, entry 305, NWLB-TC; National War Labor Board Trucking Commission, In the Matter of Southeastern Area Employers' Negotiating Committee and International Brotherhood of Teamsters, Nov. 26, 1943, box 2423, folder 1, ibid.; Thomas E. Flynn to N. P. Feinsinger, Dec. 17, 1943, box 2413, folder 6, entry 303, ibid.; American Trucking Associations, "Argument of the Trucking Industry to the War Labor Board against Change in the Present Wage Stabilization Program," Oct. 14, 1944, box 2428, folder 2, entry 305, ibid.; Nathan P. Feinsinger, *Collective Bargaining in the Trucking Industry* (Philadelphia: University of Pennsylvania Press, 1949), 31.

39. Mildred R. DeWolfe, *For-Hire Carriers Hauling Exempt Agricultural Commodities: Nature and Extent of Operations* (Washington: Agricultural Marketing Service, 1963); Walter Miklius, *Comparison of For-Hire Motor Carriers Operating under the Agricultural Exemption with Regulated Carriers* (Washington: Agricultural Marketing Service, 1966).

40. Interstate Commerce Commission, "Lease and Interchange of Vehicles: Motor Carriers: Ex parte No. MC-43," *Federal Register,* Jan. 27, 1948, 369–72; Interstate Commerce

Commission, Ex Parte MC-43, *Lease and Interchange of Vehicles,* 52 M.C.C. 675, May 8, 1951, 691–92, 703, 714–15; Frank Tobin to Daniel J. Tobin, Dec. 18, 1951, box 1, folder 14, series V, IBTR; Senate Interstate and Foreign Commerce Committee, *Amendment to Interstate Commerce Act (Trip Leasing), Part 2, Hearings,* 83rd Cong., 2nd sess., May 10–11, Jun. 7, 8, 25, 1954, 209, 212.

41. Guy Black, "Agricultural Interest in the Regulation of Truck Transportation," *JFE* 37 (Aug. 1955): 444; U.S. Supreme Court Reports, 97 Lawyers Ed., *American Trucking Associations, Eastern Motor Express and Secretary of Agriculture* vs. *ICC,* 344 U.S. 298 (1953), 338, 352; John H. Davis to Charles E. Jackson, Apr. 1, 1954, box 2, folder 3, entry 18, AMSR; True D. Morse to Lee J. Quasey, Apr. 6, 1954, box 3, folder 5, ibid.; Senate Interstate and Foreign Commerce Committee, *Amendment to Interstate Commerce Act (Trip Leasing), Part 1, Hearings,* 83rd. Cong., 1st sess., Jul. 8–9, 1953, 7–11, 52; Ibid., *Part 2,* 399, 452–75, 503–9; Senate Interstate and Foreign Commerce Committee, *Amending Interstate Commerce Act with Respect to Trip Leasing,* 84th Cong., 1st sess., 1955, S. Rept. 1271, 3–4; House Interstate and Foreign Commerce Committee, *Trip Leasing (Interstate Commerce Act), Hearings,* 84th Cong., 2nd sess., May 16, 17, 21, 1956; Sperling, *Agricultural Exemption,* 14.

42. Ralph L. Dewey, "Regulations and Policies," in USDA, *Yearbook of Agriculture* (Washington: GPO, 1954), 109; Rose, Seely, and Barrett, *Best Transportation System,* 97–104.

CHAPTER FOUR: TRUCKING CULTURE AND POLITICS IN THE AGRIBUSINESS ERA, 1953–61

1. Robert Vandivier, interview by the author, Nov. 22, 2003, Lebanon, IN; Lawrence Pilgrim, interview by the author, Jul. 7, 2006, Cleveland, GA. On the rise of Jesse Jewell's poultry empire: Monica Richmond Gisolfi, "From Crop Lien to Contract Farming: The Roots of Agribusiness in the American South, 1929–1939," *AH* 80 (Spring 2006): 167–89; William Boyd and Michael Watts, "Agro-Industrial Just-in-Time: The Chicken Industry and Postwar American Capitalism," in *Globalising Food: Agrarian Questions and Global Restructuring,* ed. David Goodman and Michael Watts (London: Routledge, 1997), 192–223.

2. Bureau of the Census, *Historical Statistics of the United States* (1976), 457, 467–68, 483.

3. Key works on the industrialization of U.S. agriculture and its social and environmental impacts include Geoff Cunfer, *On the Great Plains: Agriculture and Environment* (College Station: Texas A&M University Press, 2005); Danbom, *Resisted Revolution;* Daniel, *Breaking the Land;* Fite, *Cotton Fields No More;* Fitzgerald, *Every Farm a Factory;* Steven Stoll, *The Fruits of Natural Advantage: Making the Industrial Countryside in California* (Berkeley: University of California Press, 1998); Mary Neth, *Preserving the Family Farm: Women, Community, and the Foundations of Agribusiness in the Midwest, 1900–1940* (Baltimore: Johns Hopkins University Press, 1995); Donald Worster, *Dust Bowl: The Southern Plains in the 1930s* (New York: Oxford University Press, 1979). On Iowa's transformation from a mixed farmscape into a monocropped outdoor factory, see Deborah K. Fitzgerald, "Eating and Remembering," *AH* 79 (Fall 2005): 393–408.

4. "Kansas Motor Carriers Plan 15th Annual Convention," *Wichita Eagle,* Sep. 3, 1950, MCIC; "Trucking Represents Second Largest Industry in Kansas," *Wichita Eagle,* Sep. 28, 1952, ibid.; Donald E. Church and Margaret R. Purcell, "From Farms to First Market," in USDA, *Yearbook of Agriculture* (1954), 87–92; Edwin G. Flittie and Zane P. Nelson, "The Truck Driver: A Sociological Analysis of an Occupational Role," *Sociology and Social Research* 52, 3 (1968): 207; John F. Runcie, "Social Group Formation in an Occupation: A Case Study of the Truck Driver," (Ph.D. diss., University of Michigan, 1971), 146; Richard Gingerich, "Growing up around Trucks," *WOT,* May 2005, 24, 26.

5. Joe Miller, "Dave Beck Comes out of the West," *Reporter,* Dec. 8, 1953, 21; "Who Are the Teamsters?" *USNWR,* Mar. 8, 1957, 134; Bureau of Labor Statistics, "Over-the-Road Truckdrivers," *Occupational Outlook Handbook* 1255, 4th ed. (1959): 420; Bureau of the Census, *Historical Statistics of the United States* (1976), 169, 173.

6. "Trucking Industry Second in Kansas," *Wichita Eagle,* Jun. 10, 1962, MCIC; "Hanefeld Trucking (Brothers)," n.d. (May 1960), box 37, folder 1, IBT 695; "Hanefeld Election . . . Eligibility List as Submitted by the Company," Jun. 1960, ibid.; A. E. Mueller to All Hanefeld Trucking Employees, Jun. 29, 1960, ibid.; National Labor Relations Board, Certification of Results of Election, Case No. 13-RC-7223, Jul. 18, 1960, ibid. On the agrarian myth and its gendered and racialized aspects, see Joan Jensen, *With These Hands: Women Working on the Land* (Old Westbury, NY: Feminist Press, 1983); Deborah Fink, *Agrarian Women: Wives and Mothers in Rural Nebraska, 1880–1940* (Chapel Hill: University of North Carolina Press, 1992); Mark Schultz, *The Rural Face of White Supremacy: Beyond Jim Crow* (Urbana: University of Illinois Press, 2005).

7. Alfred Maund, "Peons on Wheels: The Long-Haul Trucker," *Nation,* Nov. 14, 1953, 393; Bureau of Labor Statistics, "Over-the-Road Truckdrivers," 419; J. Wayne Flynt, *Poor but Proud: Alabama's Poor Whites* (Tuscaloosa: University of Alabama Press, 1989); Steven Hahn, *The Roots of Southern Populism: Yeoman Farmers and the Transformation of the Georgia Upcountry, 1850–1890,* rev. ed. (New York: Oxford University Press, 2006); Roger L. Ransom and Richard Such, *One Kind of Freedom: The Economic Consequences of Emancipation,* 2nd ed. (Cambridge: Cambridge University Press, 2001).

8. Richard D. Leone, *The Negro in the Trucking Industry* (Philadelphia: Wharton School, University of Pennsylvania, 1970), 28–30; Russell, *Out of the Jungle,* 120–28, 191–92; James and James, *Hoffa and the Teamsters,* 276. On the challenges and prospects of race relations in the union movement of the 1940s and 1950s: Robert Rogers Korstad, *Civil Rights Unionism: Tobacco Workers and the Struggle for Democracy in the Mid-Twentieth Century South* (Chapel Hill: University of North Carolina Press, 2003); Michelle Brattain, *The Politics of Whiteness: Race, Workers, and Culture in the Modern South* (Princeton, NJ: Princeton University Press, 2001); Bruce Nelson, *Divided We Stand: American Workers and the Struggle for Black Equality* (Princeton, NJ: Princeton University Press, 2001).

9. Lichtenstein, *State of the Union,* 98–177; Mike Davis, *Prisoners of the American Dream: Politics and Economy in the History of the U.S. Working Class* (London: Verso, 1986), 102–53; Dubofsky, *State and Labor,* 197–231; Judith Stein, *Running Steel, Running America: Race, Economic Policy and the Decline of Liberalism* (Chapel Hill: University of North Car-

olina Press, 1998), 15–26; Elizabeth A. Fones-Wolf, *Selling Free Enterprise: The Business Assault on Labor and Liberalism, 1945–1960* (Urbana: University of Illinois Press, 1994); Jacobs, *Pocketbook Politics,* 246–61.

10. Witwer, *Corruption and Reform,* 157–211; Lichtenstein, *State of Labor,* 162–66; Russell, *Out of the Jungle,* 171–212; Bruce J. Schulman, *From Cotton Belt to Sunbelt: Federal Policy, Economic Development, and the Transformation of the South, 1938–1980* (New York: Oxford University Press, 1991), 162–65; James C. Cobb, *The Selling of the South: The Southern Crusade for Industrial Development, 1936–1990,* 2nd ed. (Urbana: University of Illinois Press, 1993), 96–121.

11. "Divided Highway: The Story of *They Drive by Night,*" companion film to digital video disc.

12. The word "inspiration" is key here, because we can by no means take country music to be a faithful "mirror" of the historical experiences of rural people. Recorded country music has always been, after all, an inherently commercial art form. But one profitable way to get rural people to buy country records was to tell stories that at least *seemed* authentic. Furthermore the endless battles among country listeners about what constitutes "real country" involve constant negotiations of white rural identity. See James C. Cobb, "Rednecks, White Socks, and Piña Coladas? Country Music Ain't What It Used to Be and It Really Never Was," *Southern Cultures* (Winter 1999): 41–50; Richard A. Peterson, *Creating Country Music: Fabricating Authenticity* (Chicago: University of Chicago Press, 1997); Bill C. Malone, *Don't Get above Your Raisin': Country Music and the Southern Working Class* (Urbana: University of Illinois Press, 2002); Aaron Fox, *Real Country: Music and Language in Working-Class Culture* (Durham, NC: Duke University Press, 2004).

13. Gregory, *Southern Diaspora,* 32–33, 72–74, 173–83; Neil V. Rosenberg, *Bluegrass: A History* (Urbana: University of Illinois Press, 1985); Gerald W. Haslam, *Workin' Man Blues: Country Music in California* (Berkeley: University of California Press, 1999); Malone, *Don't Get above Your Raisin';* Jeffrey J. Lange, *Smile When You Call Me Hillbilly: Country Music's Struggle for Respectability, 1939–1954* (Athens: University of Georgia Press, 2004); Peter Guralnick, *Lost Highway: Journeys and Arrivals of American Musicians* (Boston: D. R. Godine, 1979); Howard A. DeWitt, *Chuck Berry: Rock 'n' Roll Music,* 2nd ed. (Ann Arbor, MI: Pierian Press, 1985), 14; Michael Lydon, *Ray Charles: Man and Music* (New York: Riverhead Books, 1998), 157, 418.

14. Dorothy Horstman, *Sing Your Heart Out, Country Boy: Classic Country Songs and Their Inside Stories, by the Writers Who Wrote Them,* 3rd rev. ed. (Nashville: Country Music Foundation, 1986), 326; Joe Fodor, "Truck Song, 1928–1965: 'Wreck on the Old Mountain Road' to 'Giddyup Go'" (draft of an unpublished paper), Trucking Songs Subject File, CMHF; Lewis Nichols, "The Ubiquitous Juke Box," *NYT Magazine,* Oct. 5, 1941, 22; Art Gibson, "I'm a Truck Driving Man," Mercury 6065; Terry Fell, "Truck Drivin' Man," RCA Victor X 0010 (lyrics reprinted by permission of Alfred Publishing); John George Seiter, "Truck Driver's Night Run Blues," performed by Joe Lewis, MGM 11071.

15. "Graphic Clocker," *BW,* Dec. 21, 1940, 36; "Watchman in the Cab," *PW* (Apr. 1956): 18–19, 47; International Harvester Co., Motor Truck Division, Motor Truck Circular 161, "Tachograph," Dec. 15, 1961, box 8, Motor Truck Circulars, IHR; Advertisement for Wag-

ner Electric Corporation, "5 Ways that Tachographs Can Improve Your Fleet Operation," *PW* (Mar. 1956): 9; G. M. Nequette to All Drivers, Terminal Managers and Mechanics, "Tampering with Tachograph Clocks," Jun. 15, 1960, box 13, folder 14, IBT 695.

16. A rich literature exists on the politics of postwar suburban consumerism, though neither consumption scholars nor historians of agriculture have successfully integrated the simultaneous shifts in U.S. farm politics and the rise of a "consumer's republic" of self-interested, "entitled" suburban consumption. See Cohen, *Consumers' Republic;* Jacobs, *Pocketbook Politics;* Lassiter, *Silent Majority.* Key works on 1950s agricultural policy, meanwhile, have tended to ignore the ways in which the rise of agribusiness and of suburbia were deeply linked; see Jon Lauck, *American Agriculture and the Problem of Monopoly: The Political Economy of Grain Belt Farming, 1953–1980* (Lincoln: University of Nebraska Press, 2000); Willard Cochrane and Mary E. Ryan, *American Farm Policy, 1948–1973* (Minneapolis: University of Minnesota Press, 1976); Trudy H. Peterson, *Agricultural Exports, Farm Income, and the Eisenhower Administration* (Lincoln: University of Nebraska Press, 1979).

17. *Current Biography* (1953), 63–65; Eleonora W. Schoenebaum, ed., *Political Profiles: The Truman Years* (New York: Facts on File, 1977), 34–38; Wesley McCune, *Ezra Taft Benson: Man with a Mission* (Washington: Public Affairs Press, 1958), 6. On associationalism and the farm cooperative movement, see Hamilton, *New Day to New Deal;* Victoria Saker Woeste, *The Farmer's Benevolent Trust: Law and Agricultural Cooperation in Industrial America, 1865–1945* (Chapel Hill: University of North Carolina Press, 1998).

18. Edward L. Schapsmeier and Frederick H. Schapsmeier, "Eisenhower and Ezra Taft Benson: Farm Policy in the 1950s," *AH* 44 (Oct. 1970): 376; Hansen, *Gaining Access,* 127–63; McCune, *Ezra Taft Benson,* 79.

19. Since its inception in the 1920s, the BAE cultivated a tight relationship to commercial agricultural interest groups to support its vision of centralized agricultural policy and planning. During the New Deal era, the BAE served as the central planning and policy wing of the USDA, gaining enemies on both the left and the right of the political spectrum. Ellis R. Hawley, "Economic Inquiry and the State in New Era America: Anti-statist Corporatism and Positive Statism in Uneasy Coexistence," in *The State and Economic Knowledge: The American and British Experience,* ed. Mary O. Furner and Barry Supple, 287–324.

20. Ezra Taft Benson, *Freedom to Farm* (New York: Doubleday, 1960); John H. Davis, "Business Responsibility and the Market for Farm Products," Address before Boston Conference on Distribution, Oct. 17, 1955, box 1, folder 2, John H. Davis Papers, NAL; John H. Davis, "From Agriculture to Agribusiness," *Harvard Business Review* 34 (Jan. 1956), 115.

21. Wesley McCune, *Who's behind Our Farm Policy?* (New York: Praeger, 1956), 312; Allin to Butz, Aug. 2, 1956, box 9, Public Relations 7 folder, entry 48, SAR; Trelogan to Allin, Dec. 21, 1956, ibid.; O. V. Wells et al., "The Fragmentation of the BAE," *JFE* 36 (Feb. 1954): 4, 6; Earl L. Butz, "USDA's Role in Marketing," *Marketing Activities* (Nov. 1954): 3–5, box 1.3/16, folder VI B4, USDAHC; "Food Distribution: Research, Educational, and Service Work of the USDA," Mar. 1955, 3–4, box 1, folder 14, entry 42, AMSR.

22. Roy W. Lennartson, "Between the Farmer and Consumer," in USDA, *Yearbook of Agriculture* (Washington: GPO, 1951), 49; *Food Transportation and What It Costs Us* (Washington: Agricultural Marketing Service, 1956).

23. American Trucking Associations, *American Trucking Trends* (1960), 11; William J. Hudson and Don C. Leavens, "The Kinds and Uses of Carriers," in USDA, *Yearbook of Agriculture* (1954), 96–97.

24. Albro Martin, *Railroads Triumphant: The Growth, Rejection, and Rebirth of a Vital American Force* (New York: Oxford University Press, 1992), 339–98; Bureau of the Census, *Historical Statistics of the United States* (1976), 224, 730, 733.

25. American Trucking Associations, *American Trucking Trends* (1970–71), 15; David E. Moser and Wesley R. Kriebel, *Transportation in Agriculture and Business* (Columbia: University of Missouri Extension, 1964), 4.

26. "Biggest Vegetable Factory on Earth," *Life,* Jan. 1955, 40–43.

27. *WSJ,* Mar. 26, 1930, 23; *Rewriting the Menus of the World: The Story of the Most Revolutionary Idea in the History of Food* (Boston: Birds Eye Packing Company, 1931); *WSJ,* Jun. 24, 1931, 13; *WSJ,* Aug. 27, 1931, 3; *WSJ,* Jan. 31, 1938, 1; "Let Them Eat Cake," *Fortune,* Oct. 1934, 135, 137; Bruce Barton, "You Don't Altogether Like Your Job?" *American Magazine,* May 1921, 114; John Seabrook, "The Spinach King," *New Yorker,* Feb. 20, 1995, 225; "Deerfield Packing Corporation Supervisors' Conference," 1939, Artifacts File, Deane Eadie Folder, SECC; "Frozen Foods: Interim Report," *Fortune,* Aug. 1946, 105.

28. Edwin W. Williams, "Are Frosted Foods at the Crossroads?" *QFF* (Mar. 1939): 22.

29. The role of the warehouse in the twentieth-century economy is something of a "black box," hidden from view and therefore largely taken for granted. Landscape historian J. B. Jackson is to my knowledge the only scholar to write, if briefly, on the "steady flow" concept of modern warehousing in *A Sense of Place, a Sense of Time* (New Haven, CT: Yale University Press, 1994), 173–85.

30. *WSJ,* Dec. 3, 1946, 1. On the history of time as a commodity, see E. P. Thompson, "Time, Work-Discipline, and Industrial Capitalism," *Past and Present* 38 (Dec. 1967): 56–97.

31. S. O. Kaylin, *Understanding Today's Food Warehouse* (New York: Chain Store Age Books, 1968), 50, 57–58, 63; "Modern Handling of Frozen Foods in Storage," *QFF* (Feb. 1948): 47–48; "Palletizing Solves Distributor's Problems," *QFF* (Jul. 1948): 42; "Mechanized Handling of Frozen Foods," *QFF* (May 1947): 58; "Industry-Wide Trend to New One-Story Warehouses," *BW,* Dec. 13, 1947, 24–25; "Newest Texas Whopper, the Biggest Refrigerator in the World," *BW,* Oct. 8, 1949, 22–23; "'Keep It Moving' Means Efficiency," *QFF* (Jan. 1949): 62.

32. Charles G. Mortimer, Jr., "A Statement of Birds Eye's New Distribution Policy," *QFF* (Jun. 1951): 54, 173–75; "What's Ahead for the Frozen Food Distributor," *QFF* (Mar. 1954): 77; "FF Warehouse Included in New Safeway Depot," *QFF* (Mar. 1955): 438; "Warehouse Acts as Chains' Distribution Center to Keep Pace with Frozen Food Trends," *QFF* (Apr. 1956): 184; Kenneth F. Stepleton, "New Warehouse Role in a Changing Economy," *QFF* (Aug. 1959): 119, 126.

33. "Frozen Foods: Interim Report," 109; General Foods Corporation, *Annual Report,* 1945; ibid., 1948.

34. Keith O. Burr and Lawrence S. Martin, "Transportation Requirements," *QFF* (Dec. 1946): 68; "Trucks Are Taking over for Frozen Food Transportation," *QFF* (Oct. 1951): 55; E. R. Wagner, "Choice of Carrier Is Decided By Market Conditions, In-Transit Rights,

Time of Shipment," *QFF* (Nov. 1955): 92; Forney A. Rankin, "Inherent Advantage of Trucks & Rails Make Both Necessary for Frozen Food Movement," *QFF* (Apr. 1962): 226; James F. McCarthy, *Highways, Trucks and New Industry: A Study of Changing Patterns in Plant Location* (Washington: ATA Foundation, 1963), 63.

35. "Trucking Exec's Challenge Spurred 'Refrigerator on Wheels,'" *Transport Topics* (Jul. 5, 1997); American Society of Mechanical Engineers History and Heritage Center, "Thermo King Model C Transport Refrigeration Unit," Oct. 1, 1996; J. W. Kalmes, "Thermo-King Refrigerator Units on Trucks and Trailers," Dec. 3, 1946, box 12, folder 4, Motor Truck Engineering and Product Bulletins/Reports, IHR; "Transporting Frozen Foods by Truck," *QFF* (Aug. 1946): 71, 75; Douglas Albert, "Truck-Trailer Refrigeration," *Refrigerating Engineering* (Jan. 1948): 31–32; William McGinnis Holroyd, "Influences and Challenges of the Growing Frozen Food Industry on Refrigerated Transport Equipment" (Ph.D. diss., Indiana University, 1960), 24–26.

36. "Pre-Cooling of Perishables," *PW* (Sep. 1948): 20; Holroyd, "Influences and Challenges," 14; G. D. Albert, "Truck-Trailer Refrigeration for Frozen Foods," *QFF* (Mar. 1949): 174; Russell H. Hinds, Harold D. Johnson, and Robert C. Haldeman, *A Performance Test of Refrigerated Rail Cars Transporting Frozen Foods* (Washington: Agricultural Marketing Service, 1957); "PIE Cites Contributing Factors that Led to Refrigeration Change," *QFF* (Apr. 1954): 141.

37. James R. Snitzler and Robert J. Byrne, *Interstate Trucking of Frozen Fruits and Vegetables under Agricultural Exemption* (Washington: Agricultural Marketing Service, 1959), 30, 34; "It's about Time," *QFF* (Nov. 1955): 87; A. L. Reneau, "Frozen Food Transportation and Distribution," *Ice and Refrigeration* (Oct. 1949): 19; Harold E. Sweeney to William C. Crow, "The Market for Transport Refrigeration," Sep. 26, 1949, box 5, folder 20, entry 42, AMSR.

38. "Motor Carriers Haul 72% of Frozen Food Output," *QFF* (Nov. 1953): 63, 109–10; "Motor Carriers Haul 77.7% of Frozen Food Shipments," *QFF* (Dec. 1957): 128; Louis Woehl, "More Attention Should Be Paid to Trucking Equipment," *FFF* (1957), 23; "Frozen Food Share of Grocery Store Sales, 1949–1956," *FFF* (1958); "Frozen Fruits, Vegetables Usage Continues Post-War Uptrend," *QFF* (Sep. 1957): 107–8; "Per Capita Consumption Comparison," *FFF* (1957): 91; Advertisement for Seabrook Farms Baby Lima Beans, "You Couldn't Grow Them Fresher in Your Own Back Yard," 1954, box 431, folder 2, series 2, NWAA.

39. George Egger, "Quality Is the Key to Further Expansion of Frozen Food Sales," *FFF* (1957): 29; Shane Hamilton, "Cold Capitalism: The Political Ecology of Frozen Concentrated Orange Juice," *AH* 77 (Fall 2003): 557–58; "Fish Sticks Score with All-'Round Convenience," *QFF* (Sep. 1953): 81–82; "Birds Eye Story," 91; *WSJ*, Feb. 3, 1954, 1; "French Fries Sales Climb 1,800% in Ten Years," *QFF* (Oct. 1957): 97–100; Eric Schlosser, *Fast Food Nation: The Dark Side of the All-American Meal* (Boston: Houghton Mifflin, 2001), 111–31; Daniel B. Levine, *Consumers Appraise Canned and Frozen Foods, Their Packages and Labels in Atlanta, Kansas City, and San Francisco* (Washington: Agricultural Marketing Service, 1958); "Frozen Fruits, Vegetables Widen Sales Base among Lower Income Groups," *QFF* (Mar. 1957): 44.

40. Mildred Boggs and Clyde Rasmussen, "Modern Food Processing," in USDA, *Year-*

book of Agriculture (Washington: GPO, 1959), 428, 429; USDA, Economic Research Service, "Food Expenditures by Families and Individuals as a Share of Disposable Personal Income, 1929–2006," http://www.ers.usda.gov/Briefing/CPIFoodAndExpenditures/Data/table7.htm.

41. Ezra Taft Benson, "Research Results in Progress," Address at a dinner in honor of the 25th Anniversary Celebration of the Founding of the Frozen Food Industry, Washington, D.C., Apr. 13, 1954, box 1.3/15, folder B3, USDAHC; *NYT,* Apr. 14, 1954, 43.

42. "Exemption Debate Moves Forward as Farm Groups Plan Own Study," *QFF* (Aug. 1957): 131.

43. Margaret R. Purcell, *Transportation of Florida Frozen Orange Juice Concentrate: A Case Study of Carrier Competition Induced by Dynamic Industry Growth* (Washington: USDA, 1955), 8, 31, 33, 37–38; "Asks Truckers for 'Greater Efficiency,'" *QFF* (Apr. 1953): 160.

44. *American East Texas Motor Freight Lines,* Inc. v. *Frozen Food Express,* 351 U.S. 49 (1956), quote at HR2; *Home Transfer & Storage Co. v. United States,* 141 F. Supp. 599 (1956); Sperling, *Agricultural Exemption,* 36–37; Neil Olmsted, "ICC Indecision Seen Forcing Fight to Widen Exempt Product List," *QFF* (Nov. 1956): 78.

45. Snitzler and Byrne, *Interstate Trucking of Frozen Fruits and Vegetables under Agricultural Exemption,* 1, 50.

46. Rose, Seely, and Barrett, *Best Transportation System,* 97–119.

47. "Effects of Agricultural Exemption Debated by Packers and Carriers," *QFF* (Feb. 1957): 163; John W. Burks to J. C. Winter, Jan. 11, 1957, box 2, folder 15, entry 42, AMSR; House Interstate and Foreign Commerce Committee, *Interstate Commerce Act: Agricultural Exemptions, Hearings,* 85th Cong., 2nd sess., Apr. 23–25, 1958, 288.

48. House Interstate and Foreign Commerce Committee, *Interstate Commerce Act: Agricultural Exemptions,* 4, 14, 24, 154, 378–79; John V. Lawrence to William C. Crow, Jan. 29, 1957, box 2, folder 15, entry 42, AMSR.

49. Robert M. Collins, *The Business Response to Keynes, 1929–1964* (New York: Columbia University Press, 1981); Robert Griffith, "Dwight D. Eisenhower and the Corporate Commonwealth," *American Historical Review* 87 (Feb. 1982): 87–122.

50. Interstate Commerce Commission, *Annual Report* (Washington: GPO, 1961), 136; Interstate Commerce Commission, Bureau of Transport Economics and Statistics, *Gray Area of Transportation Operations* (Washington: Interstate Commerce Commission, 1960); Senate Interstate and Foreign Commerce Committee, Special Study Group on Transportation Policies in the United States, *National Transportation Policy,* Committee Print No. 445, 87th Cong., 1st sess., Jan. 3, 1961, 516, 518.

CHAPTER FIVE: BEEF TRUSTS AND ASPHALT COWBOYS

1. Bob Douthitt to Benson, Oct. 1953, box 28, entry 11, AMSR; A. L. Ellis to Benson, Dec. 27, 1953, ibid.; Laura Hall to Dwight Eisenhower, Nov. 18, 1953, ibid.

2. Earl Butz to Sen. Ed C. Johnson, Sep. 3, 1954, box 2, folder 4, AMSR, entry 18; D. B. DeLoach to A. L. Ellis, Jan. 4, 1954, box 28, entry 11, AMSR; "Who Gets What You Spend for Food? Farmer's Share Shrinks, Labor Takes a Bigger Slice," *USNWR,* Mar. 9, 1956, 72–73.

3. Willard F. Williams, "Structural Changes in the Meat Wholesaling Industry," *JFE* 40 (May 1958): 322–27; "Who Gets the Money for Beef," *USNWR,* Feb. 17, 1956, 36–40; Dale E. Butz and George L. Baker, Jr., *The Changing Structure of the Meat Economy* (Cambridge: Harvard Business School, 1960), 51–52; Arnould, "Changing Patterns," 18–34; Skaggs, *Prime Cut,* 153; Milton D. Ratner, "The Role of Truck Transportation in Marketing Pre-Packaged Meats," *Refrigerated Transporter* (Feb. 1969): 14–17.

4. Butz and Baker, *Changing Structure,* 67; Senate Judiciary Committee, *Unfair Trade Practices in the Meat Industry, Hearings,* 85th Cong., 1st sess., May 1–3, 7–10, 15, 22, 1957, 280–81; Roger Horowitz, *Negro and White, Unite and Fight!: A Social History of Industrial Unionism in Meatpacking, 1930–90* (Urbana: University of Illinois Press, 1997), 1–141, 250–53; National Commission on Food Marketing, *Organization and Competition in the Livestock and Meat Industry* (Washington: GPO, 1966), 17.

5. Senate Judiciary Committee, *Unfair Trade Practices in the Meat Industry, Hearings,* 85th Cong., 1st sess., May 1–3, 7–10, 15, 22, 1957, 278; Robert Aduddell and Louis Cain, "The Consent Decree in the Meatpacking Industry, 1920–1956," *BHR* 55 (Autumn 1981): 359–61, 369–72.

6. Skaggs, *Prime Cut,* 178; James Whitaker, *Feedlot Empire: Beef Cattle Feeding in Illinois and Iowa, 1840–1900* (Ames: Iowa State University Press, 1975); "Cattlemen Must Neglect Feed Lot," *Topeka (Kansas) Capital,* Aug. 28, 1943, CIC; John M. Collins, "The Cowman Holds the Top Cards in Year's Biggest 'Poker Game,'" *Kansas City Star,* Aug. 27, 1944, ibid.; "Flint Hills Feed Vast Lowing Herds," *Topeka (Kansas) Capital,* Jun. 13, 1944, ibid.; "More Beef to the Acre," *Kansas Farmer,* Feb. 1952, 6, 32, ibid.; John H. McCoy and Robert H. Wuhrman, *Some Economic Aspects of Commercial Cattle Feeding in Kansas* (Manhattan: Kansas Agricultural Experiment Station, 1960), 6; Wood, *Kansas Beef,* 286; Dave Malena, "Just Ahead-A Turning Point in the Beef Industry," *SF* (Apr. 1969): 32. Similar increases occurred in Colorado, Nebraska, Oklahoma, and Texas; see Kenneth R. Krause, *Cattle Feeding, 1962–89: Location and Feedlot Size* (Washington: Economic Research Service, 1991), 15.

7. Tom Carlin, "The Man with a Different Point of View," *K-Stater,* Jul. 1982, FSF; Earl Brookover, Jr. and Ty Brookover, interview by the author, Mar. 23, 2004, Garden City, KS; Kathi Loper, "Earl Brookover's Achievements Far Ranging," *Garden City Telegram,* Oct. 8, 1976, BSF; "Farm Leader in State Dies," *Topeka (Kansas) Capital-Journal,* Nov. 14, 1985, CIC; John Fraser Hart, *The Changing Scale of American Agriculture* (Charlottesville: University of Virginia Press, 2003), 48–55. The California feedlots that Brookover saw may have been those of the Kern County Land Company in Bakersfield, which were organized by Dwight Cochran, a former vice president of marketing for Safeway Stores seeking to produce lean, grain-finished cattle in quantity for supermarket buyers; Skaggs, *Prime Cut,* 179.

8. "State's Cattle Industry Is in 'Revolution,'" *Topeka (Kansas) State Journal,* Aug. 16, 1967, CIC; "Kansas Beef Boom in Feedlots," *Kansas City Star,* Aug. 20, 1967, CIC; "To Build Big Feed Lot Near Leoti," *Hutchinson (Kansas) News,* Aug. 11, 1966, ibid.; Charles Pratt, "Beefing up on a Kansas Runway," *Topeka (Kansas) Capital-Journal,* Feb. 18, 1968, ibid.; John Opie, *Ogallala: Water for a Dry Land,* 2nd ed. (Lincoln: University of Nebraska Press, 2000), 138–81.

9. Earl Brookover, Jr., interview; Lawrence A. Mayer, "Monfort Is a 'One-Company In-

dustry,'" *Fortune,* Jan. 1973, 93–94; Wood, *Kansas Beef,* 292; "Even Better Beef Hormones?" *FJ* (May 1957): 39–42; Dick Braun, "New Feed Additive May Cut Beef Costs," *FJ* (Jun. 1960): 47; Orville Schell, *Modern Meat* (New York: Random House, 1984).

10. Michael Bates, "Paved Feedlot Increases Gain," *Topeka (Kansas) Capital-Journal,* Jul. 1, 1982, CIC; Charles Hammer, "Automation on the Kansas Prairie," *Kansas City Star,* Feb. 5, 1961, ibid.; "Steers that Finish Fast," *FJ* (Mar. 1958): 68L–68M; Charles E. Ball, "The New Beef Breeds Are Rolling," *FJ* (Nov. 1956): 63.

11. J'Nell L. Pate, *America's Historic Stockyards: Livestock Hotels* (Fort Worth: Texas Christian University Press, 2005); Mayer, "Monfort," 93; Wood, *Kansas Beef,* 292;" Revolution Hits Cattle Industry," *Topeka (Kansas) Capital-Journal,* Sep. 11, 1960, CIC.

12. Clark Bentley and Lawton Williams, "Asphalt Cowboy" (BMI / Shelby Singleton / Western Hills), recorded by Sleepy LaBeef, Plantation Records 66; Stan Holtzman, "The 'Bull Hauler': 'Other Drivers Call Us Stupid,'" *OD* (Jul. 1965): 42; "The Livestock Hauler: 20th Century Trail Boss," *OD* (Feb. 1972): 123.

13. Robert Vandivier interview; Holtzman, "'Bull Hauler," 44; "'5 Major Things to Watch' in Every Livestock Haul," *KT* (Feb. 1948): 14, 21; "Handle Stock Properly to Reduce Bruising," *KT* (Jul. 1954): 23; "Livestock Hauler: 20th Century Trail Boss," 118.

14. Donna Hobbs, "Business Surrounded by Atmosphere of the 'Old West,'" *KT* (Jul. 1962): 6–8; "Small Fleet of the Month," *OD* (Apr. 1970): 84; Tim Heerdt, "Hauling Livestock, A Boy's Perspective," *WOT,* Mar. 2004, 25; Earnest R. Sternberg, *A History of Motor Truck Development* (Warrendale, PA: Society of Automotive Engineers, 1981), 46.

15. "KCC History Goes back to March 1883," *Wichita Eagle,* Nov. 8, 1976, MCIC; Ted Blankenship, "KCC Isn't Just Another State Board," *Wichita Eagle,* Nov. 7, 1976, ibid.; L. A. Hoffman, P. P. Boles, and T. Q. Hutchinson, *Livestock Trucking Services: Quality, Adequacy, and Shipment Patterns* (Washington: Economic Research Service, 1975), ii; "Farm-to-Market Carriers Wage War on Violators," *KT* (Aug. 1950): 20–21; John Harvey, "What Good Are Ports of Entry?" *Kansas Farmer,* Jan. 20, 1951, 10; "Adequate Rates Major Problem Facing Bull Haulers," *ATN,* Jun. 1973, 32.

16. J. C. Winter to Charles B. Bowling, "Livestock Transportation Charges," Feb. 28, 1955, box 2, folder 2, entry 42, AMSR; Abdou, "Economic Aspects," 964; "Hauling as Many as 2900 Cattle a Day," *KT* (Apr. 1965): 4.

17. Ronald A. Gustafson and Roy N. Van Arsdall, *Cattle Feeding in the United States* (Washington: Economic Research Service, 1970), 24, 47; McCoy and Wuhrman, *Economic Aspects of Commercial Cattle Feeding,* 15; Earl Brookover, Jr., interview; Paul Stevens, "Feedlots Give Ranchers More Market Leverage," *Wichita Eagle,* Aug. 18, 1978, CIC.

18. House Agriculture Committee, *Equalize Livestock Marketing Competition,* 87th Cong., 1st sess., 3, 16, 29, 30, 55, 89.

19. Ibid., 71.

20. John T. Schlebecker, "The Great Holding Action: The NFO in September, 1962," *AH* 39 (Oct. 1965): 207–11; Skaggs, *Prime Cut,* 190; Mike Perrault, "On the Block: Remnants of Once-Flourishing Livestock Business to Be Sold," *Garden City Telegram,* Aug. 3, 1988, CIC.

21. USDA, Economic Research Service, "Food Consumption (Per Capita) Data System"; "Housewives' Beef," *Time,* Jun. 13, 1969, 94; "Beef Sales Boom and So Do Prices," *USNWR,* Jun. 9, 1969, 68.

22. Roger B. Porter, *The U.S.-U.S.S.R. Grain Agreement* (Cambridge, MA: Harvard University Press, 1984); *WSJ,* Mar. 29, 1973, 1, 30; *WSJ,* Apr. 9, 1973, 4; *WSJ,* Apr. 3, 1973, 2; *NYT,* Apr. 8, 1973, 1; *NYT,* Apr. 3, 1973, 1; Mayer, "Monfort," 91.

23. Michael J. Broadway, "From City to Countryside: Recent Changes in the Structure and Location of the Meat- and Fish-Processing Industries," in *Any Way You Cut It,* ed. Donald D. Stull, Michael J. Broadway, and David Griffith (Lawrence: University of Kansas Press, 1995), 27; Kathleen Stanley, "Industrial and Labor Market Transformation in the U.S. Meatpacking Industry," in *The Global Restructuring of Agro-Food Systems,* ed. Philip McMichael (Ithaca, NY: Cornell University Press, 1994), 129–44.

24. Dale C. Tinstman and Robert L. Peterson, *Iowa Beef Processors, Inc.: An Entire Industry Revolutionized!* (New York: Newcomen Society, 1981), 9; "Meat Plant to Garden City," *Topeka (Kansas) State Journal,* Sep. 4, 1979, MIC; "IBP Looks toward Moving In," *Garden City Times,* Apr. 10, 1980, ibid.; Fred Kiewit, "Kansas Beef to the Nation," *Kansas City Star,* Aug. 15, 1971, MIC. The states were Iowa, Nebraska, Minnesota, Missouri, Colorado, Kansas, Texas, Oklahoma, and New Mexico: Willard F. Williams, *The Changing Structure of the Beef Packing Industry* (Lubbock, TX: TARA, 1979), 56.

25. "Triumph of Logic," *Forbes,* Dec. 15, 1968, 48; House Agriculture Committee, *Prohibit Feeding of Livestock,* 24.

26. Jerry Fetterolf, "Final Touches Are Due on Emporia Packing Plant," *Wichita Eagle,* Apr. 27, 1969, MIC; "Ahead of the Herd in Automation," *BW,* Jun. 27, 1964, 106.

27. House Small Business Committee, *Small Business Problems in the Marketing of Meat, Part 5,* 9; Tinstman and Peterson, *Iowa Beef Processors,* 12; Horowitz, *Negro and White,* 253–68; Deborah Fink, *Cutting into the Meatpacking Line: Workers and Change in the Rural Midwest* (Chapel Hill: University of North Carolina Press, 1998), 51; "Fighting over the Cost of Cutting Meat," *BW,* Nov. 22, 1969, 74–76; *WSJ,* Jul. 29, 1970, 2; *WSJ,* Jun. 29, 1970, 26; "Bad Old Days," *Time,* Aug. 9, 1982, 47–48; James Cook, "Those Simple Barefoot Boys from Iowa Beef," *Forbes,* Jun. 22, 1981, 35; "Iowa Beef Becomes a Test for Management," *BW,* Mar. 14, 1977, 28–29; "Oxy's Bid to Blend Energy with Food," *BW,* Jun. 15, 1981, 37; Donald D. Stull and Michael J. Broadway, "The Effects of Restructuring on Beefpacking in Kansas," *Kansas Business Review* 14 (Fall 1990): 13.

28. House Small Business Committee, *Small Business Problems in the Marketing of Meat, Part 5,* 8; Tinstman and Peterson, *Iowa Beef Processors,* 8;"Ahead of the Herd in Automation," 106; "Rough Riders," *Forbes,* Jun. 15, 1974, 65; House Small Business Committee, *Small Business Problems in the Marketing of Meat and Other Commodities, Part 4, Changing Structure of the Beef Packing Industry, Hearings,* 96th Cong., 1st sess., Jun. 25, 26, 1979, 10; Evelyn Steimel, "French Chefs May Be Using Garden City Products," *Hutchinson (Kansas) News,* Mar. 4, 1969, MIC; "300,000 Pounds Dressed Beef a Day Is Goal," *Garden City Telegram,* Oct. 28, 1965, 2, BSF; "The Youngest Giant," *Fortune,* May 15, 1969, 293.

29. Tinstman and Peterson, *Iowa Beef Processors,* 8; House Small Business Committee, *Small Business Problems in the Marketing of Meat, Part 5,* 34; Ratner, "Role of Truck Transportation," 14–17.

30. "Meat Prepackaging Soars," *BW,* Oct. 25, 1947, 62–66; "Visible Meat," *BW,* Dec. 28, 1957, 109; Corey, *Meat and Man,* 161–63; William Burns, "Changing Corporate Structure and Technology in the Retail Food Industry," in *Labor and Technology: Union Responses*

to Changing Environments, ed. Donald Kennedy, Charles Craypo, and Mary Lehman (University Park: Department of Labor Studies, Pennsylvania State University, 1982), 41; Cook, "Simple Barefoot Boys," 33, 35.

31. *WSJ,* Mar. 12, 1973, 4; *WSJ,* Mar. 14, 1973, 4; *NYT,* Mar. 14, 1973, 1, 89; Lawrence A. Duewer, "Cutting Beef-Handling Costs," *National Food Review* (Fall 1985): 2; House Small Business Committee, *Small Business Problems in the Marketing of Meat, Part 5,* 14; "Beef Firm to Open $10-Million Facility," *Wichita Eagle,* Mar. 17, 1975, MIC; "Firm Plans Beef Plant at Oakley," *Wichita Eagle,* Aug. 30, 1978, ibid.

32. Starr H. Lloyd, "Food Distribution: A Study in Beef," *Transportation and Distribution Management* 12 (Sep. 1972): 21–24; "Amarillo's IBP: Where Beef Is King," *ATN,* Mar. 1977, 18.

33. Lloyd, "Food Distribution," 21, 23; "Private Fleet Cuts Delivery Time, Cargo Losses for Monfort of Colorado," *ATN,* Sep. 1973, 6; Edward Miller, "Monfort Pride," *WOT,* May 2007, 40–41.

34. Earl Brookover, Jr., interview; Williams, *Changing Structure,* 7, 15, 52; House Small Business Committee, *Small Business Problems in the Marketing of Meat and Other Commodities: Part 3, Concentration Trends in the Meat Industry, Hearings,* 96th Cong., 1st sess., May 1, 2, 14, Jun. 4, 1979, 8, 35; ibid., *Part 4,* 33, 50; ibid., *Part 5,* 11.

35. Ray Hemman, "Kansas 'Beef Factory' on Display for Empire Days," *Hutchinson (Kansas) News,* Jun. 5, 1982, MIC; Tinstman and Peterson, *Iowa Beef Processors,* 12; House Small Business Committee, *Small Business Problems in the Marketing of Meat, Part 4,* 42, 41; Skaggs, *Prime Cut,* 194–95; Williams, *Changing Structure,* 86, 92, 149.

36. Lynn O'Shaughnessy, "Plants Welcomed by Kansas Cattlemen," *Kansas City Times,* May 12, 1982, MIC; Cook, "Simple Barefoot Boys," 36; House Small Business Committee, *Small Business Problems in the Marketing of Meat, Part 5,* 69; *NYT,* Aug. 13, 1976, 78; "Lawsuit Claims IBP Cornered Market," *Garden City Telegram,* Dec. 29, 2001, 1, 2, BSF; Skaggs, *Prime Cut,* 193.

37. Chicago School economic theorists such as Richard Posner rejected decades worth of antitrust policy against firms that gained structural market power, arguing that government intervention was required only when monopolistic firms gained the power to distort prices. Price, rather than competition, became the guiding measure of economic "efficiency." The Reagan administration put these theories into action by appointing Chicago School lawyers and economists to the Antitrust Division of the Justice Department and by reorganizing the Federal Trade Commission. However, as Marc Allen Eisner has shown, the Chicago School-based transformation of antitrust policies was well under way in the Nixon, Ford, and Carter administrations. Even under Presidents Kennedy and Johnson the enforcement of antitrust laws was pursued with little vigor. See Marc Allen Eisner, *Antitrust and the Triumph of Economics: Institutions, Expertise and Policy Change* (Chapel Hill: University of North Carolina Press, 1991); James R. Williamson, *Federal Antitrust Policy during the Kennedy-Johnson Years* (Westport, CT: Greenwood Press, 1995).

38. *Dill* v *Excel Packing Co.,* 183 Kan. 513 (1958); "Wichitans Join War on Feedlot," *Wichita Eagle,* Jan. 8, 1966, CIC; Jackie Hellstrom, "Potwin Residents Disturbed over Feedlot Location," *Wichita Beacon,* Apr. 25, 1969, ibid.; Robert Trosper to the Editor, "Neighbor

Opposes Brookover Expansion," *Garden City Telegram,* Dec. 4, 1999, FSF; Wendy Zellner, "The Wal-Mart of Meat: Tyson Foods," *BW,* Sep. 20, 2004; *WSJ,* Apr. 11, 2000, 1. On Tyson's rise to dominance in the chicken industry, see William Boyd, "Making Meat: Science, Technology, and American Poultry Production," *T&C* 42 (Oct. 2001): 631–64; Steve Striffler, *Chicken: The Dangerous Transformation of America's Favorite Food* (New Haven, CT: Yale University Press, 2005). On Clinton's connections to Tyson, Wal-Mart, and economic inequality, see Roy Reed, "Clinton Country," *NYT Magazine,* Sep. 6, 1992, 32–34, 40–44; Mark Hodgson, *More Equal than Others: America from Nixon to the New Century* (Princeton, NJ: Princeton University Press, 2004), 22–23, 87–111.

Chapter Six: The Milkman and the Milk Hauler

1. "Indianapolis Milkmen 'Mass-Shopped,'" *MD* (Oct. 1960): 10.

2. "Container Conflict," *BW,* Mar. 21, 1936, 16, 19; "Can Paper Come In?" *BW,* Mar. 18, 1939, 14; Advertisement for Thatcher Glass, "Glass Bottles are Best," *MD* (Jun. 1953): 32; Sheldon W. Williams et al., *Organization and Competition in the Midwest Dairy Industries* (Ames: Iowa State University Press, 1970), 40; "How Fast Is the Trend to Paper Containers?" *MD* (May 1953): 4–5; Advertisement for Pure-Pak Milk Cartons, "The New Story of Milk: A Fresh New Container with Every Quart," *MD* (Jul. 1956): 4–5; Clyde W. Park, ed., *Milk Packaging for Retail Distribution: Report of a Controlled Experiment* (Cincinnati: A. H. Pugh, 1956), 62.

3. Gus Rothe, "Bottle Recovery Drive," *MD* (Jan. 1945): 30–31, 68; A. Maurice Davis et al., "Packaging," *MD* (Jul. 1962): 39–40.

4. Hugh L. Cook, *Paper Packaged Milk in Wisconsin: Its Part in Expanding Distribution Areas* (Madison: University of Wisconsin Agricultural Experiment Station, 1953), 24.

5. Cook, *Paper Packaged Milk,* 3, 7, 10–17; "Meeting Competition with Paper," *MD* (Jan. 1954): 68, 90; Faye Henle, "Diversified Dairies: The Search for Greener Pastures Is Paying Off," *Barron's,* Apr. 22, 1957, 11–13; Golden Guernsey Dairy Cooperative, "The Heart of Golden Guernsey Dairy Cooperative" n.d. (1960s), 4, box 1, folder 1, GG.

6. J. C. Winter to B. A. Holt, "Submission of Progress Report and Proposal," Sep. 9, 1957, box 1, folder 8, entry 42, AMSR; "Progress Report on Research and Related Services Applicable to Dairy," Oct. 1957, 125–26, ibid.; Budd A. Holt to W. C. Crow, W. H. Elliott, R. W. Hoecker, and J. C. Winter, "Priorities on Branch Proposals by Dairy Research and Marketing Advisory Committee," Feb. 13, 1957, ibid.

7. A. N. Jarrell, "Milk-Dealer Industry: Earnings in Late 1951 and Early 1952," *MLR* 75 (Oct. 1952): 422–23; C. G. McBride, "Can We Hold War Time Marketing Gains in Post War Adjustments?" *MD* (Jan. 1945): 33–34, 94–95; Officers and Directors of the Bowman Dairy Company to Members of the Bowman Team, "The Five-Day Week in the Milk Business," Oct. 4, 1951, box 30, folder 6, series II, subseries 4, BDC; Golden Guernsey Dairy Cooperative, *Annual Report,* 1957, and *Annual Report,* 1969, box 1, folder 6, GM; Williams et al., *Organization and Competition,* 33; Wisconsin Division of Economic Practices, "Retail Store Handling," *MD* (Oct. 1963): 14.

8. Central Conference of Teamsters, Minutes of Dairy Division Meeting, Sep. 23, 1958, Chicago, Nov. 5, 1959, Detroit, MI, box 4, folder 10, IBT 695; Edward Thom, "What about Dock Delivery?" *MD* (Apr. 1959): 46–47, 54–58; "Trend toward Wholesale," *MD* (Jun. 1955): 18; Frank J. Gillespie to Hoffa, "Committee on Wholesale Fluid Milk Chain Store Warehouse Delivery," Feb. 20, 1959, box 12, folder 8, IBT 695; Abraham Weiss to Teamster Locals Having Contracts in the Fluid Milk Industry, "Provisions in Teamster Dairy Contracts Dealing with Dock Delivery or Platform Pick-Up," Jan. 1962, box 28, folder 8, ibid.; Donald E. Hirsch, "Ways of Lowering Milk Distribution Costs," *MD* (Jul. 1953): 65–72; "Pay Cuts of up to $10,000 per Year," *MD* (Dec. 1960): 6; Fred De Armond, "Salesmen and/or Teamsters," *MD* (Jul. 1956): 54, 86–94; Hoffa to All Central Conference of Teamsters Local Unions, Jul. 16, 1959, box 70, folder 19, IBT 695; "The New York Milk Strike: A Study in Futility," *MD* (Feb. 1962): 44, 74; *NYT*, Oct. 26, 1961, 1.

9. Cook, *Paper Packaged Milk*, 6; "Survey Reveals Information on Store Distribution," *MD* (Jul. 1946): 66; "Skimmed from the News," *MD* (May 1954): 30.

10. Anonymous to the Editor, "Store Rebates," *MD* (Dec. 1958): 37; "The Hand that Rocks the Cradle," *MD* (Dec. 1958): 41; A Wisconsin Milk Dealer to the Editor, "Unfair Competition," *MD* (Apr. 1960): 164; Central Conference of Teamsters, Minutes of Dairy Division Meeting, Sep. 23, 1958, Chicago, box 4, folder 10, IBT 695; D. I. Padberg, "Changes in Competition," *MD* (May 1964): 41, 73–74; "Milk Hike Rumpus," *BW*, Jan. 13, 1951, 52–54; "Milk Pricing: Housewives Pay for Outmoded Controls," *Time*, Dec. 13, 1954, 88; "Milk Marketing," *Consumer Reports*, Aug. 1955, 381–83.

11. Don Merlin, "The Milk Industry Rides a Tiger," *MD* (Dec. 1960): 24–25, 69; "Bowman Chain Store Marketing Organization," Feb. 1, 1960, box 30, folder 6, series II, subseries 4, BDC.

12. Charles E. Miller, "Hauling Memories Recalled," *MMH* (Jul. 1968): 14–15; Douglas Harper, *Changing Works: Visions of a Lost Agriculture* (Chicago: University of Chicago Press, 2001), 236–37; E. J. Finneran, "From Cow to Kitchen," *Nation's Business*, Jun. 1937, 24–26, 169–72; John Schultz, Milk Hauling Contract, Feb. 25, 1931, box 1, folder 5, AMPI; Donald B. Agnew, *How Bulk Assembly Changes Milk Marketing Costs* (Washington: Agricultural Marketing Service, 1957).

13. Advertisement for Heil Co., "Everybody Profits with Direct Farm-to-Dairy Bulk Pick-Up," *MD* (Jul. 1953): 48; Kenneth Sanders, "What's the Outlook for the Bulk Tank Pick-Up System?" *MD* (Aug. 1953): 38; Joseph M. Cowden, *Comparing Bulk and Can Milk Hauling Costs* (Washington: Farmer Cooperative Service, 1956); "Progress Report on Research and Related Services Applicable to Dairy," Oct. 1957, 120–21, box 1, folder 8, entry 42, AMSR; D. Hanson, "Less Work, More Profits with Milk Tanks," *SF* (Aug. 1952): 46–47, 76, 78, 80–81; Advertisement for Mojonnier Bulk Milk System, "All about Bulk Milk," *MD* (Jun. 1953): 35; Minutes, Board of Directors Meeting, Dec. 14, 1956, reel 2, CBC.

14. Dennis H. Murphy, "Around Chicago, Milk's Going Bulk," *MD* (Aug. 1956): 44–45, 57–58; "Selling Producers on the Farm Bulk Tank System," *MD* (Jan. 1954): 58–61, 86; "Will a Bulk Tank Pay?" *FJ* (Oct. 1955): 60–62; Harper, *Changing Works*, 216–19; Kendra Smith-Howard, "Perfecting Nature's Food: An Environmental and Cultural History of U.S.

Dairy Production and Consumption, 1900–1975" (Ph.D. diss., University of Wisconsin-Madison, 2006); "Bulk Tank Milk Now 45% of Milwaukee Market," *MD* (Jun. 1956): 148.

15. Minutes, Special Board of Directors Meeting, Wisconsin Cooperative Creamery Association, Jul. 22, 1954, box 5, folder 1, WDC; Karl Shoemaker, Wisconsin Dairy Marketing Specialist Annual Report, 1953, box 454, Marketing Folder, FES; Hugh Moore, Wisconsin Dairy Marketing Specialist Annual Report, 1957, box 427, Marketing Folder, ibid.; Minutes, Board of Directors Meeting, Apr. 2, 1954, Sep. 7, 1954, reel 2, CBC; "Farm Bulk Tanks Featured at Wisconsin State Fair," *MD* (Aug. 1956): 112; "Farm Bulk Milk Tank Cooling Expanding Fast, Survey Shows," *MD* (May 1956): 164–5; "Farm Tank Installations up 30% over 1958," *MD* (Aug. 1959): 44.

16. "History of Hillpoint Co-Operative Dairies," in Hillpoint Co-Operative Dairies, Financial and Operating Statement, 1953, box 3, folder 3, WDC. On Rochdale-inspired European agricultural cooperatives and their influence on U.S. agrarian progressives, see Rodgers, *Atlantic Crossings,* 326–43.

17. Truman Graf, Wisconsin Dairy Marketing Specialist Annual Report, 1956, FES, box 423, marketing folder, 2–3; Truman Graf, "Bulk Tanks Bring Long Term Benefits," *Wisconsin Agriculturist and Farmer* (Mar. 7, 1959); Karl Shoemaker, Wisconsin Dairy Marketing Specialist Annual Report, 1954, box 539, marketing folder, FES; Truman F. Graf, "Implications of Milk Supply Situation in the Chicago Milk Shed on Organization of Dairy Cooperatives," in *Proceedings of Proposals for Reorganization of Dairy Cooperatives,* University of Wisconsin, Madison, Feb. 11, 1967, box 2, folder 9, AMPI; Minutes, Membership Meeting, Wisconsin Cooperative Creamery Association, Jan. 26, 1956, box 5, folder 2, WDC; Truman F. Graf, Wisconsin Dairy Marketing Specialist Annual Report, 1958, box 411, marketing folder, FES; Gale L. VandeBerg, Wisconsin Annual Narrative Report, Project IV, Marketing and Utilization, Dec. 31, 1962, box 30, project IV folder, FES.

18. Minutes, Board of Directors Meeting, Hillpoint Cooperative Dairies, Apr. 7, 1955, box 2, folder 7, WDC; G. G. Schuette, Speech at Annual Meeting of Hillpoint Cooperative Dairies, n.d. [1960?]), box 3, folder 5, ibid.; Minutes, Board of Directors Meeting, Hillpoint Cooperative Dairies, May 8, 1958, WDC, box 2, folder 8; "Southwest Wisconsin Marketing Agreement," 1966, box 2, folder 9, AMPI; "History behind W. D. C," *Wisconsin Dairies Co-op News,* May 1963, 3, box 1, folder 1, WDC; Minutes, Board of Directors Meeting, Hillpoint Cooperative Dairies, Apr. 15, 1967, box 3, folder 1, ibid.; Minutes of Social Meeting of Consolidated Badger Cooperative, Sep. 7, 1950, reel 2, CBC.

19. Minutes of Resolutions Committee Meeting of Consolidated Badger Cooperative, Apr. 15, 1958, reel 2, CBC; Torgerson, *Building Markets,* 102–3; Williams et al., *Organization and Competition,* 31–32.

20. "Wisconsin Ships Record Milk Volume," *MD* (Apr. 1966): 30; "Milk Transfer Station Dedicated," *MMH* (Sep. 1966): 8–9; "The Move to Tank-to-Tank Transfer," *MD* (May 1960): 32–33, 118; William T. Butz, *Long-Distance Shipment of Market Milk* (Washington: Economic Research Service, 1964).

21. "New Era in Chicago Milk Marketing," *MD* (Jun. 1966): 22; Madison Milk Producers Cooperative Dairy, Press release, Nov. 10, 1967, box 2, folder 10, AMPI; Harold S.

Nelson to Lyman D. McKee, "Proposal to Provide a Standby Fluid Milk Supply for Markets of the Midwest and Southwest," Aug. 3, 1966, ibid.; E. Dale Odom, "Associated Milk Producers, Incorporated: Testing the Limits of Capper-Volstead," *AH* 59 (Jan. 1985): 40–55; Truman F. Graf et al., "Memorial Resolution of the Faculty of the University of Wisconsin on the Death of Emeritus Professor Hugh L. Cook," May 2, 1983, Faculty Biographical Files, UWA; Minutes of Meeting, Apr. 17, 1967, box 2, folder 9, AMPI; "AMPI News," Oct. 4, 1969, folder 10, ibid.; Norm Reeder, "Operating Co-Ops, Let's Unite Now!" *FJ* (Jan. 1970): 29, 61.

22. Percy S. Hardiman, interview by Dale Trelevan, Aug. 3, 1976, WHS, tape 3, side 1; "Objectives and Purposes of Suggested Reorganization," 1969, box 2, folder 9, AMPI.

23. "Average Bulk Milk Hauler," *MMH* (Apr. 1963), 13; Fred F. Schwenn, "Wisconsin Hauler Likes His Work," *MMH* (May 1965): 5; "Good Way of Life Based on Modern Hauling Business," *MMH* (Aug. 1961): 3–4; Fred Schwenn, "Pick Ups," *MHFT* (Sep. 1973): 3. On unpaid women's work masking labor costs in dairy farming, see Jess Gilbert and Raymond Akor, "Increasing Structural Divergence in United States Dairying: California and Wisconsin since 1950," *Rural Sociology* 53 (Spring 1988): 56–72; Joan M. Jensen, "Dairying and Changing Patterns of Family Labor in Rural New Mexico," *New Mexico Historical Review* 75 (Apr. 2000): 157–94.

24. Fred Schwenn, "Pick Ups," *MHFT* (May 1973): 3; "We Salute You, Modern Milk Haulers of America," *MMH* (Oct. 1960): 5; Myron P. Dean, *10 Steps in Bulk Milk Pick-Up* (Madison: University of Wisconsin Extension Service, August 1961), box 60, marketing-dairy folder, FES; "Milk Hauler Key to Quality Control," *MHFT* (Jul. 1973): 17.

25. "Commission Says 'No' to Regulation of Hauling Rates," *MMH* (Mar. 1964): 6; Jim McKee, "Milk Hauler Group Favors Rate Rules," *MMH* (May 1961): 7 (emphasis in original); "No Exceptions—Every Producer on Every-Other-Day Pickup," *MHFT* (Feb. 1973): 4–5; "Producers Say Most Haulers Are Neat, Prompt, Accurate," *MHFT* (Mar. 1973): 9; Minutes, Board of Directors Meeting, Nov. 2, 1951, reel 2, CBC; Minutes, Board of Directors Meeting, Wisconsin Creamery Company Cooperative, Feb. 3, 1958, Feb. 5, 1958, Jan. 15, 1959, box 4, folder 5, WDC.

26. John J. Keller, "On the Firing Line," *MMH* (Jun. 1962): 10–11; Dan E. Sauve, "Why Hauling Regulations?" *MMH* (Nov. 1962): 10; John J. Keller, "On the Firing Line," *MMH* (Jul. 1962): 10; W. M. Roberts, "Technology Department: Hauling Charges," *MD* (Oct. 1959): 144–46; Minutes, Board of Directors Meeting, Wisconsin Cooperative Creamery Association, Mar. 3, 1955, box 5, folder 1, WDC.

27. "Employers Signed to the State Milk Tank Agreement by Local 695," Sep. 9, 1954, box 14, folder 12, IBT 695; David Gourlie, Complaint to Wisconsin Joint State Milk Tank Area Committee, Oct. 11, 1956, box 32, folder 3, ibid.; Allan Torhorst to John Picago, Aug. 8, 1945, ibid.; Minutes, Milk Tank Meeting, Madison, May 8, 1953, box 18, folder 5, ibid.

28. Minutes, Milk Tank Meeting, Madison, May 8, 1953, box 18, folder 5, IBT 695; Minutes, Meeting between Local Unions and Milk Tank Operators, Milwaukee, Aug. 7, 1957, box 79, folder 7, ibid.; Minutes, Wisconsin Teamsters Joint Council, Milk Tank Committee Meeting, Jul. 24, 1959, box 21, folder 6, ibid.; Minutes, Wisconsin Teamsters Joint Council No. 39, Milk Tank Negotiations, Milwaukee, Sep. 7, 1961, ibid.; National Labor

Relations Board, International Brotherhood of Teamsters et al. and Rudolph Schroeder and Randy Schroeder, Case No. 13-CB-518, *Decision and Order,* May 16, 1958, ibid.; Ross M. Madden to Lester M. White, "Schroeder and Son," Sep. 4, 1957, ibid.; Clem Gerstner (Teamsters Local 75) to Frank Gillespie, Thomas Hagerty, and Stanley Baumann, Mar. 8, 1960, box 21, folder 6, ibid.

29. Fred Schwenn, "Pick Ups," *MHFT* (Jan. 1974): 3; Sanders, *Roots of Reform,* 413–16; Saloutos and Hicks, *Twentieth-Century Populism;* "Lewis in the Milkshed," *NW,* Apr. 27, 1942, 48; Dale Kramer, "John L. Lewis: Last Bid?" *Harper's,* Aug. 1942, 275–83; Jim McKee, "Milk Hauler Group Favors Rate Rules," *MMH* (May 1961): 7; "Milk Haulers' Round Table," *MMH* (May 1961): 12–13, 23; "Teamsters, Farmers Feuding," *MD* (Feb. 1963): 24; "Driver Labor Standards," *MMH* (Oct. 1960): 8; Minutes, Wisconsin Teamsters Joint Council, Milk Tank Committee Meeting, Jul. 24, 1959, box 21, folder 6, IBT 695.

30. Public Service Commission of Wisconsin, "Petition of the Wisconsin Milk Haulers Association, Inc., for an Investigation of Rates and Charges for Milk Haulers and the Establishment of Minimum Rates, Hearings," Feb. 17, 1961, box 18, folder 5, IBT 695; Myron P. Dean, Wisconsin Dairy Marketing Specialists' Annual Report, 1961, box 60, marketing-dairy folder, FES; John J. Keller, "On the Firing Line," *MMH* (Dec. 1963): 10–11.

31. James R. McKee, "Why Our Milk Haulers Association Asks for Rate Regulations," *MMH* (Mar. 1961): 4–5; "Difference in Hauling Rates," *MMH* (May 1962): 6–10; Public Service Commission of Wisconsin, "Petition of the Wisconsin Milk Haulers Association"; "When Milk Haulers Meet," *MMH* (Jul. 1961): 4–5; "Rate Hearings Is Hot Issue," *MMH* (Mar. 1962): 6, 12; Minutes, Board of Directors Meeting, Aug. 7, 1959, reel 2, CBC; C. T. McCleery, "Madison, Wisconsin Milk Marketing Area, Federal Order No. 51, Annual Report," 1963, 38, box 30, entry 26, AMSR; "Commission Says 'No' to Regulation of Hauling Rates," *MMH* (Mar. 1964): 6.

32. Williams et al., *Organization and Competition,* 8; *NYT,* Mar. 23, 1967, 22.

33. *NYT,* Mar. 16, 1967, 22; *NYT,* Mar. 18, 1967, 33; *NYT,* Mar. 23, 1967, 22; *NYT,* Mar. 25, 1967, 10; *NYT,* Mar. 26, 1967, 147; *NYT,* Mar. 30, 1967, 1; *NYT,* Aug. 14, 1967, 1; *NYT,* Mar. 21, 1967, 22; *NYT,* Mar. 30, 1967, 1, 54; *NYT,* Apr. 9, 1967, 46; Norm Reeder, "NFO Milk Contracts Worry Big Co-Ops," *FJ* (Feb. 1970): 71; "Truckers Provide 'Market on Wheels' for NFO Milk," *MHFT* (Dec. 1973): 6.

CHAPTER SEVEN: AGRARIAN TRUCKING CULTURE
AND DEREGULATORY CAPITALISM, 1960–80

1. "Overdrive Dissects Mike Parkhurst," *OD* (Sep. 1971): 8–9, 10, 13; "Who We Are, Why We Are, Where We Are," *OD* (Feb. 1962): 25; "Truckin' with OD," *Time,* Sep. 1, 1975, 56; Harry Crews, "The Trucker Militant," *Esquire,* Aug. 1977, 146.

2. Anne B. W. Effland, "When Rural Does not Equal Agricultural," *AH* 74 (Spring 2000): 489–501. Key texts on the agrarian myth include: Richard Hofstadter, *The Age of Reform: From Bryan to F. D. R.* (New York: Vintage Books, 1955); Leo Marx, *The Machine in the Garden: Technology and the Pastoral Ideal in America,* 2nd ed. (New York: Oxford Uni-

versity Press, 2000 [1964]), esp. 97–100, 125–28; Henry Nash Smith, *Virgin Land: The American West as Symbol and Myth* (Cambridge, MA: Harvard University Press, 1950), esp. 123–32; Tamara Plakins Thornton, *Cultivating Gentlemen: The Meaning of Country Life among the Boston Elite, 1785–1860* (New Haven, CT: Yale University Press, 1989). The use of the word "men" is quite intentional, as the agrarian myth was strictly gendered from its inception; see Fink, *Agrarian Women;* Jensen, *With These Hands;* Jon Gjerde, *The Minds of the West: Patterns of Ethnocultural Evolution in the Rural Middle West, 1830–1917* (Chapel Hill: University of North Carolina Press, 1997); Sonya Salamon, *Prairie Patrimony: Family, Farming, and Community in the Midwest* (Chapel Hill: University of North Carolina Press, 1992). The Supreme Court cases were *Wesberry v. Sanders,* 376 U.S. 1 (1964) and *Reynolds v. Sims,* 377 U.S. 533 (1964). See Michael L. Balinski and H. Peyton Young, *Fair Representation: Meeting the Ideal of One Man, One Vote* (New Haven, CT: Yale University Press, 1982).

3. Jack Temple Kirby, *The Countercultural South* (Athens: University of Georgia Press, 1995).

4. Axel Madsen, *Open Road: Truckin' on the Biting Edge* (San Diego: Harcourt, Brace, 1982), 134; Hank Miller to the Editor, *OD* (Jan. 1963): 5; Otto Riemer, *Hammer Down* (Winona, MN: Apollo Books, 1985), 23.

5. Interstate Commerce Commission, *The Independent Trucker: Nationwide Survey of Owner-Operators* (Washington: ICC Bureau of Economics, 1978), 5; Frederic Will, *Big Rig Souls: Truckers in America's Heartland* (West Bloomfield, MI: A & M, 1992), 129.

6. "The Gold Guitars," *NW,* Apr. 4, 1966, 96; Paul Hemphill, *The Nashville Sound: Bright Lights and Country Music* (New York: Simon and Schuster, 1970); Steve Waksman, *Instruments of Desire: The Electric Guitar and the Shaping of Musical Experience* (Cambridge, MA: Harvard University Press, 1999), 75–112; Bill C. Malone, *Country Music U.S.A.,* rev. ed. (Austin: University of Texas Press, 1985), 256–58; "Country Music Snaps Its Regional Bounds," *BW,* Mar. 19, 1966, 96; George O. Carney, "Spatial Diffusion of the All-Country Music Radio Stations in the United States, 1971–74," *JEMF Quarterly* 13 (Summer 1977): 58–66; "C&W Pulse Published for 24 U.S. Markets," *CMA Close-Up* (Sep. 1965): 1.

7. *NYT,* Dec. 4, 1966, D33; Fodor, "Truck Song," 19; Dixie Deen, "Six Days on the Road Puts Ravin' Dave Dudley on Country Music Map," *MCN* 4 (July 1966): 11.

8. Horstman, *Sing Your Heart Out,* 321.

9. "Starday's Unique Concept: A Country Label Exclusively," *Billboard* (Nov. 2, 1963): 73; Dixie Deen, "Don Pierce of Starday," *MCN* (Jan. 1967): 9; Fodor, "Truck Song," 20; Atlas Artist Bureau press release, "The Willis Brothers," October 1978, CMHF, Vic Willis File; Starday/Gusto Records press release, "Red Sovine," October 1978, CMHF, Red Sovine File; Jack Hurst, "Red Sovine: Teller of Sad Tales," *Macon (Georgia) Telegraph,* Aug. 2, 1976, 5B.

10. Haslam, *Workin' Man Blue;* "Profiles: Ken Nelson," *CMA Close-Up* (Oct. 1964): 1–2; Dave Hoekstra, "Major Nelson," *Chicago Sun-Times,* Nov. 30, 1997, CMHF, Ken Nelson File; Jeremy Tepper, Liner notes to *The Best of Red Simpson: Country Western Truck Drivin' Singer,* [audio compact disc] (New York: Razor and Tie / Diesel Only Records, 1999); Bill C. Malone and Judith McCulloh, eds., *Stars of Country Music: Uncle Dave Macon to Johnny Rodriguez* (Urbana: University of Illinois Press, 1975), 326–39; Malone, *Don't Get above Your Raisin',* 137–39.

11. Kenneth W. Fitzgerald, "The Trucker's Balladeer," *ORPD,* Apr. 1977, 44; Malone, *Country Music U.S.A.*, 320.

12. Fitzgerald, "The Trucker's Balladeer," 44; C. O. Bruce, Jr. to the Editor, *OD* (Aug. 1966): 7–8; Raymond, "Hitch Your Truck to a Country Star," 179; "Truckers Everywhere Love Country Music," *ORPD,* Sep. 1978, 30.

13. Virginia Alderman, "Truckers Jamboree," *Country Song Roundup,* May 1975, CMHF, Dick Curless File; Ted Gioia, *Work Songs* (Durham, NC: Duke University Press, 2006), 35–62, 169–81.

14. Malone, *Don't Get above Your Raisin',* 117–48, 53–88; Cecilia Tichi, *High Lonesome: The American Culture of Country Music* (Chapel Hill: University of North Carolina Press, 1994), 19–78; Charles Fields, James Kirchstein, and Donald Riis, "Big Rig Rollin' Man," performed by Johnny Dollar, Chart Records 1057; Tommy Collins, "Roll, Truck, Roll," performed by Red Simpson, Capitol ST 2468.

15. Geoff Mack, "I've Been Everywhere," performed by Asleep at the Wheel, United Artists UA-LA038-F; Roy Baham, "Rollin' Rig," performed by Dave Dudley, United Artists / Rice RR-5064; Abner Buford, "Long White Line," performed by Charlie Moore and Bill Napier, King 45–6004; Merle Haggard, "White Line Fever," Capitol ST 384; Robert Krueger, *A Gypsy on 18 Wheels: A Trucker's Tale* (London: Praeger, 1975), 13; Mrs. Wilfred Abernathy to the Editor, *OD* (Jan. 1965): 6; Madsen, *Open Road,* 17.

16. Fink, *Agrarian Women;* Neth, *Preserving the Family Farm;* Jane Adams, *The Transformation of Rural Life: Southern Illinois, 1890–1990* (Chapel Hill: University of North Carolina Press, 1994); Rebecca Sharpless, *Fertile Ground, Narrow Choices: Women on Texas Cotton Farms, 1900–1940* (Chapel Hill: University of North Carolina Press, 1999).

17. Don Q. Crowther and Mortier W. LaFever, "Wages and Hours of Labor in the Intercity Motor Bus and Truck Transportation Industries, July 1933," *MLR* 38 (Jun. 1934): 1433; "Trucker's Wife Shares Long-Haul Distance Driving," *PW* (Mar. 1955): 14; D. Daryl Wyckoff, *Truck Drivers in America* (Lexington: Lexington Books, 1979), 77; Leah F. Vosko and David Witwer, "'Not a Man's Union': Women Teamsters in the United States during the 1940s and 1950s," *Journal of Women's History* 13 (Fall 2001): 169–92; Kessler-Harris, *In Pursuit of Equity,* 239–89.

18. Linda Buis to the Editor, *OD* (Sep. 1964): 15–16; Krueger, *Gypsy on 18 Wheels,* 74–75; *NYT,* Nov. 10, 1975, 58; Chris Darrell Roberts, Jim Thornton, and Scott Turner, "Little Pink Mack," performed by Kay Adams, Tower 269.

19. Marcella Hurley Koch, "Her Producers Accept and Respect This Lady Hauler," *MMH* (Oct. 1962): 16; *NYT,* Nov. 10, 1975, 58; "'Westward the Women' Had Nothing on the Jones Gals Who Run Trucks," *KT* (Jan. 1954): 12.

20. John Krill, "The Trucker Wore Pink," *OD* (Dec. 1965): 39; "Overdrive Dissects Mike Parkhurst," 18; Pam Pantelis to the Editor, *OD* (Sep. 1967): 7; Guy Willis and William Brown Ellis IV, "Wheels A-Turning," performed by the Willis Brothers, Starday / Nashville NLP-2052; Dixie Deen and Ray King, "Truck Driving Son of a Gun," performed by Dave Dudley, Mercury 72442; Jim Nesbitt, "Truck Drivin' Cat with Nine Wives," Chart Records 1018; Cal Martin, "Diesel Smoke, Dangerous Curves," performed by Doye O'Dell, Intro Records RR-1867.

21. *NYT,* Nov. 10, 1975, 58; Runcie, "Social Group Formation," 215; Red Sovine and Gordon Clifford Grills, "Woman behind the Man behind the Wheel," performed by Red Sovine, Starday Gusto 169; Tommy Hill and Red Sovine, "Giddy-Up Go," performed by Red Sovine, Starday 737; Dixie Deen, "Red Sovine: 'I Didn't Jump the Fence,'" *MCN* (Jun. 1967): 3–4; Dave Dudley, Interview by Daniel Zwerdling, on National Public Radio's *All Things Considered,* Aug. 30, 1997, transcript, 3, Dave Dudley File, CMHF; Earl Greene, Carl Montgomery, and Earl Montgomery, "Six Days Awaiting," performed by Kay Adams, Tower ST 5033.

22. Merle Haggard, "Movin' On," Capitol 4085.

23. Richard Ramsey, "The People versus Smokey Bear," *Journal of Popular Culture* 13: 2 (1979): 338–44; Riemer, *Hammer Down,* 10; Studs Terkel, *Working: People Talk about What They Do All Day and How They Feel about What They Do* (New York: Pantheon Books, 1974), 209; A Trucker in Vietnam to the Editor, *OD* (May 1967): 18.

24. *WSJ,* Nov. 28, 1951, 1, 11; *WSJ,* Oct. 26, 1964, 1, 8; John A. Jakle and Keith A. Sculle, *The Gas Station in America* (Baltimore: Johns Hopkins University Press, 1994), 72, 75; Anne Constable, "In Georgia: Footnotes from a Trucker's Heaven," *Time,* Feb. 19, 1979, 6–7; Kirk Slack to the Editor, *OD* (Jul. 1965): 10–11; R. M. (Johnnie) Johnson to the Editor, *OD* (Dec. 1961): 4; "Overdrive Truck Stop Recommendations," *OD* (Oct. 1961): 13; "Thumbs Down on the Following Truck Stops," *OD* (Apr. 1963): 16; "Memoirs of Emily Viparina," Woods Highway Truck Library, No. 17.

25. John J. Harris to the Editor, *OD* (Nov. 1963): 11–12.

26. Leone, *Negro in the Trucking Industry;* Russell, *Out of the Jungle,* 121–22; House Small Business Committee, *Regulatory Problems of the Independent Owner-Operator in the Nation's Trucking Industry, Part 1, Hearings,* 94th Cong., 2nd sess., May 19, 20, 26, Jun. 5, 1976, 275; *WSJ,* Nov. 9, 1966, 32.

27. *Teamsters v. United States,* 431 U.S. 324 (1977). On the "wages of whiteness" in industries other than trucking in the mid-twentieth century see Nelson, *Divided We Stand;* Brattain, *Politics of Whiteness;* Dana Frank, "White Working Class Women and the Race Question," *International Labor and Working-Class History* 54 (Fall 1998): 80–102.

28. House Small Business Committee, *Regulatory Problems of the Independent Owner-Operator, Part 1,* 266, 270, 284; Robert E. Weems, Jr., and Lewis A. Randolph, "The National Response to Richard M. Nixon's Black Capitalism Initiative: The Success of Domestic Détente," *Journal of Black Studies* 32 (Sep. 2001): 66–83; Senate Commerce, Science, and Transportation Committee, *Economic Regulation of the Trucking Industry, Part 2, Hearings,* 96th Cong., 1st sess., Jun. 26, 27, 1979, 552.

29. George Lipsitz, *The Possessive Investment in Whiteness: How White People Profit from Identity Politics,* rev. ed. (Philadelphia: Temple University Press, 2006); Leone, *Negro in the Trucking Industry,* 39; U.S. Commission on Civil Rights, *The Federal Civil Rights Enforcement Effort-1974,* vol. 1 (Washington: U.S. Commission on Civil Rights, 1974), 174.

30. On Populism and neopopulism, see Goodwyn, *Populist Moment;* John D. Hicks, *The Populist Revolt: A History of the Farmers' Alliance and the People's Party* (Lincoln: University of Nebraska Press, 1961 [1931]); Robert C. McMath, Jr., *American Populism: A Social History, 1877–1898* (New York: Hill and Wang, 1993); Sanders, *Roots of Reform;* Michael

Kazin, *A Godly Hero: The Life of William Jennings Bryan* (New York: Knopf, 2006); Horowitz, *Beyond Left and Right;* Kazin, *Populist Persuasion.*

31. Russell, *Out of the Jungle,* 213–26; Witwer, *Corruption and Reform,* 141–45.

32. "A Big Union that's Haunted by Its Own Success," *USNWR,* Aug. 8, 1977, 75; Russell, *Out of the Jungle,* 213–26; James and James, *Hoffa and the Teamster;* Levinson et al., *Collective Bargaining and Technological Change,* 19–20; Charles R. Perry, *Deregulation and the Decline of the Unionized Trucking Industry* (Philadelphia: Wharton School, University of Pennsylvania, 1986), 35, 110; Harold M. Levinson, "Trucking," in *Collective Bargaining: Contemporary American Experience,* ed. Gerald G. Somers (Madison, WI: Industrial Relations Research Association, 1980), 135; Verla Bullard, "Social Status of the Truck Driver," *OD* (Feb. 1971): 55–56.

33. Jean A. Briggs, "Put that Hammer Down, Good Buddy!" *Forbes,* Sep. 1, 1980, 118–20; Merrill, *Forty-Six Years a Truckman,* 23–24; "From One Secondhand Truck to a Giant Truckline," *Nation's Business,* Jul. 1978, 44; *NYT,* Nov. 22, 1961, 66. On welfare capitalism, see David Brody, *Workers in Industrial America: Essays on the Twentieth Century Struggle,* 2nd ed. (New York: Oxford University Press, 1993), 48–81; Cohen, *Making a New Deal,* 159–83; Sanford M. Jacoby, *Modern Manors: Welfare Capitalism since the New Deal* (Princeton, NJ: Princeton University Press, 1997).

34. Wyckoff, *Truck Drivers,* 4; U.S. General Accounting Office, "Effects of Regulatory Reform on Unemployment in the Trucking Industry," Report to the Honorable Dennis DeConcini, U.S. Senate (Washington: General Accounting Office, 1982), 13; Bureau of the Census, *1972 Census of Transportation, Selected Service Industries, S-7: Nonregulated Motor Carriers and Public Warehousing* (Washington: Bureau of the Census, 1974–75), 22; House Public Works and Transportation Committee, *Regulation of Carriers Subject to the Interstate Commerce Act, Hearings,* 94th Cong., 2nd sess., Sep. 14, 28, 1976, 165–66; Perry, *Deregulation and the Decline of the Unionized Trucking Industry,* 62; Interstate Commerce Commission, *Independent Trucker,* 17.

35. Terkel, *Working,* 211–12; *NYT,* May 25, 1970, 43; *NYT,* Apr. 14, 1970, 29; *NYT,* Jul. 4, 1970, 1, 19; *NYT,* Jan. 18, 1976, 1, 34; *NYT,* Apr. 3, 1976, 1, 13; *NYT,* Jun. 13, 1976, 28; *WSJ,* Jun. 15, 1976, 5; "Overdrive Dissects Mike Parkhurst," 9–10; Mike Parkhurst, "Overdrive Editor Pledges All-Out Organizing and Financing Effort," *OD* (Nov. 1974): 33; Homer Hanna to the Editor, *OD* (Sep. 1966): 13–14. On Teamster dissidents, see Samuel R. Friedman, *Teamster Rank and File: Power, Bureaucracy, and Rebellion at Work and in a Union* (New York: Columbia University Press, 1982); Kenneth C. Crowe, *Collision: How the Rank and File Took back the Teamsters* (New York: Scribner's, 1993).

36. "Trade Barriers," *Motor Carrier* (Jan. 1940): 17; Clarence Neuendorf to All Company Drivers, "Scaling Loads to Conform to State Axle Limits and Overweight Tickets," May 14, 1958, box 13, folder 14, IBT 695; H. S. Norton, *Highway Transportation Barriers in 20 States* (Washington: Agricultural Marketing Service, 1957); Lawrence J. Ouellet, *Pedal to the Metal: The Work Lives of Truckers* (Philadelphia: Temple University Press, 1994), 156–63; Michael Agar, *Independents Declared: The Dilemmas of Independent Trucking* (Washington: Smithsonian Institution Press, 1986), 121–38; Jack Cady, "Kansas 5 A.M.," *Rolling Stone,* Nov. 22, 1973, 62.

37. Riemer, *Hammer Down,* 52, 55; "How the Octopustic ICC Strangles Free Enterprise," *OD* (Jul. 1966): 46; Robert Fellmeth et al., *The Interstate Commerce Omission: The Public Interest and the ICC* (New York: Grossman, 1970); "Famed Economist Speaks to Truckers," *OD* (Mar. 1973): 60–61; "New Attack on Old Walrus—Senator James McClure Introduces Bill to Abolish ICC," *OD* (May 1975): 48. See Gabriel Kolko, *The Triumph of Conservatism: A Reinterpretation of American History, 1900–1916* (New York: Free Press, 1963) and *Railroads and Regulation, 1877–1916* (Princeton, NJ: Princeton University Press, 1965).

38. Brian Balogh, "Integrating the Sixties: The Origins, Structures, and Legitimacy of Public Policy in a Turbulent Decade," *Journal of Policy History* 8:1 (1996): 1–34; Douglas Rossinow, *The Politics of Authenticity: Liberalism, Christianity, and the New Left in America* (New York: Columbia University Press, 1998); Maurice Isserman and Michael Kazin, *America Divided: The Civil War of the 1960s,* 3rd ed. (New York: Oxford University Press, 2008); John A. Andrew III, *The Other Side of the Sixties: Young Americans for Freedom and the Rise of Conservative Politics* (New Brunswick, NJ: Rutgers University Press, 1997); McGirr, *Suburban Warriors.*

39. Terkel, *Working,* 210; "Overdrive Dissects Mike Parkhurst," 21.

40. Clearly George Wallace's racial demagoguery and Richard Nixon's "southern strategy" shaped the politics of the period, as many whites came to resent forced busing and affirmative action. Nonetheless I contend that pocketbook politics remained a durable component of white working-class disillusionment in the 1970s, and that racial demagoguery was not the sole, factor in the rightward shift in 1970s U.S. political culture. Key works on both sides of this debate include: Edsall and Edsall, *Chain Reaction;* Dan T. Carter, *The Politics of Rage: George Wallace, the Origins of the New Conservatism, and the Transformation of American Politics* (New York: Simon and Schuster, 1995); Ronald P. Formisano, *Boston against Busing: Race, Class, and Ethnicity in the 1960s and 1970s,* rev. ed. (Chapel Hill: University of North Carolina Press, 2004); Lassiter, *Silent Majority;* Kruse, *White Flight;* Crespino, *In Search of Another Country.* Historians are increasingly moving beyond "backlash" theories to explain the rise of conservatism in the 1970s; see, especially, Bruce Schulman and Julian Zelizer, eds., *Rightward Bound: Making America Conservative in the 1970s* (Cambridge, MA: Harvard University Press, 2008).

41. J. Gonzalez to the Editor, "Flexibility," *OD* (Jan. 1973): 18; M. P. Funkhouser to the Editor, "Trucker Urges Nationwide Shutdown," *OD* (Sep. 1973): 13.

42. Harry Maurer, "Organizing the 'Gypsies,'" *Nation,* Jan. 11, 1975, 11; *NYT,* Dec. 5, 1973, 34; "The Shutdown," *OD* (Jan. 1974): 40; *NYT,* Dec. 6, 1973, 1; *NYT,* Dec. 15, 1973, 70; *NYT,* Dec. 6, 1973, 46; *NYT,* Dec. 17, 1973, 43.

43. *NYT,* Jan. 21, 1974, 14; *NYT,* Jan. 25, 1974, 12; Wyckoff and Maister, *Owner-Operator,* 58–59; *NYT,* Jan. 28, 1974, 19; *NYT,* Feb. 4, 1974, 1, 22.

44. *NYT,* Jan. 27, 1974, 34; *NYT,* Feb. 1, 1974, 58; *NYT,* Feb. 6, 1974, 20; *NYT,* Feb. 8, 1974, 65; *NYT,* Feb. 9, 1974, 1, 14; *NYT,* Feb. 12, 1974, 69; *NYT,* Apr. 2, 1974, 7; *NYT,* May 14, 1974, 75; Maurer, "Organizing the 'Gypsies,'" 14.

45. *NYT,* Dec. 14, 1973, 18; Dee Jackson to the Editor, "As Long as It Takes," *OD* (Jun. 1974): 5; Richard O. Dewey to the Editor, "The Price of 55 MPH," *OD* (Jun. 1974): 13–14; *NYT,* Dec. 6, 1973, 41; *WP,* Dec. 1, 1979, 1, 4; Richard M. Nixon, "Radio Address about Pro-

posed Transportation Legislation", Feb. 9, 1974, *Public Papers of the Presidents of the United States* (Washington: GPO, 1975), 150; "The Second Shutdown—What Really Happened," *OD* (Mar. 1974): 50; "112 Phantom Truckers Picket Washington," *OD* (Jul. 1974): 79.

46. *NYT,* Jan. 31, 1974, 19; Maurer, "Organizing the 'Gypsies,'" 15; Charles Bisanz, "The Anatomy of a Mass Public Protest Action: A Shutdown by Independent Truck Drivers," *Human Organization* 36, no. 1 (1977): 63–69; "The Shutdown," *OD,* 40.

47. Jane Stern, *Trucker: A Portrait of the Last American Cowboy* (New York: McGraw-Hill, 1975), 13; John P. Stevenson to the Editor, *OD* (Aug. 1964): 13–16; Bruce J. Schulman, *The Seventies: The Great Shift in American Culture, Society, and Politics* (New York: Free Press, 2001), 102–20; James C. Cobb, "From Muskogee to Luckenbach: Country Music and the 'Southernization' of America," in *Redefining Southern Culture* (Athens: University of Georgia Press, 1999), 78–91; Malone, *Don't Get above Your Raisin',* 136–44.

48. *Smokey and the Bandit,* dir. Hal Needham, 97 min., Universal Studios, 1977, digital video disc. The selection of Coors beer as a plot device was appropriate, insofar as the Coors company at the time marketed its beer only in western states, giving it an image as an antieastern working-man's brew. Furthermore the company's owner, Joseph Coors, was a right-wing politician famous for his opposition to hippies, the federal government, the "liberal establishment," birth control, and labor unions. See Grace Lichtenstein, "Rocky Mountain High," *NYT Magazine,* Dec. 28, 1975, 14–16.

49. *NYT,* Aug. 9, 1977, 27; *Convoy,* dir. Sam Peckinpah, 110 min., EMI Films, 1978, videocassette.

50. McCall quoted in Kenneth L. Woodward, Peter S. Greenberg, and Susan Malsch, "The Trucker Mystique," *NW,* Jan. 26, 1976, 44; *NYT,* Jun. 28, 1978, C17; Frank Rich, "Duck Soup," *Time,* Jul. 10, 1978, 78; Will, *Big Rig Souls,* 84.

51. Franklin Tugwell, *The Energy Crisis and the American Political Economy: Politics and Markets in the Management of Natural Resources* (Stanford, CA: Stanford University Press, 1988), 118–27; David Farber, *Taken Hostage: The Iran Hostage Crisis and America's First Encounter with Radical Islam* (Princeton, NJ: Princeton University Press, 2004); *NYT,* Jun. 5, 1979, 18; *NYT,* Jun. 8, 1979, 14; *NYT,* Jun. 9, 1979, 8; *NYT,* Jun. 11, 1979, 16; *NYT,* Jun. 14, 1979, 16; *NYT,* Jun. 19, 1979, 18; Bonventre et al., "Truckers in Revolt," 45; Tom Morgenthau et al., "The Energy Plague," *NW,* Jul. 2, 1979, 22; "When Truckers Threatened the Nation," *USNWR,* Jun. 25, 1979, 10.

52. "One Hellacious Uproar," 22; *NYT,* Jun. 15, 1979, 1; *NYT,* Jun. 15, 1979, 1; *NYT,* Jun. 17, 1979, 22; *NYT,* Jun. 20, 1979, 1; "Spreading Toll of Truckers' Strike," *USNWR,* Jul. 2, 1979, 4; *NYT,* Jun. 22, 1979, B4; Bonventre et al., "Truckers in Revolt," 45.

53. Dorothy Robyn, *Braking the Special Interests: Trucking Deregulation and the Politics of Policy Reform* (Chicago: University of Chicago Press, 1987); Martha Derthick and Paul J. Quirk, *The Politics of Deregulation* (Washington: Brookings Institution, 1985); Rothenberg, *Regulation, Organizations, and Politics,* 221–43. While political scientists have generally focused on Congress as the locus of deregulatory politics, several historians have argued that presidential administrations were the driving force; see Rose, Seely, Barrett, *Best Transportation System in the World;* McCraw, *Prophets of Regulation;* W. Carl Biven, *Jimmy Carter's Economy: Policy in an Age of Limits* (Chapel Hill: University of North Carolina Press, 2003).

54. Richard N. Farmer, "The Case for Unregulated Truck Transportation," *JFE* 46 (May 1964): 408.

55. Senate Agriculture Committee, *Agricultural Transportation Problems, Part 2, Hearings,* 95th Cong., 1st sesss., Sep. 27, 28, 1977, 2; Senate Commerce, Science, and Transportation Committee, *Economic Regulation of the Trucking Industry, Part 1, Hearings,* 96th Cong., 1st sess., Mar. 28, 1979, 187, 192, 191; Mike Parkhurst, "H. R. 2777-Not Deregulation, but Reregulation," *OD* (Apr. 1979): 38, 40, 41.

56. Robyn, *Braking the Special Interests,* 37–38, 97, 218; *WP,* Jan. 23, 1979, D7–8; Cohen, *Consumers' Republic;* Collins, *More;* Alan Wolfe, *America's Impasse: The Rise and Fall of the Politics of Growth* (New York: Pantheon Books, 1981); Allen J. Matusow, *The Unraveling of America: A History of Liberalism in the 1960s* (New York: Harper and Row, 1984).

57. Senate Commerce, Science, and Transportation Committee, *Economic Regulation of the Trucking Industry, Part 2, Hearings,* 96th Cong., 1st sess., Jun. 26, 27, 1979, 378–79, 359, 377.

58. Ibid., 528; ibid., *Part 3,* 96th Cong., 1st sess., Sep. 6, 7, Oct. 2, 1979, 922–23; ibid., *Part 5,* 96th Cong., 2nd sess., Feb. 21, 26, 27, 1980, 1773–74.

59. House Public Works and Transportation Committee, *Motor Carrier Act of 1980,* H. Rpt. 96–1069, 96th Cong., 2nd sess., Jun. 3, 1980, 1, 7, 10, 20.

60. Schwartz, *J. B. Hunt;* Perry, *Deregulation and the Decline of the Unionized Trucking Industry,* 103, 110; Cynthia Engel, "Competition Drives the Trucking Industry," *MLR* 121 (Apr. 1998): 34–41; Michael H. Belzer, *Sweatshops on Wheels: Winners and Losers in Trucking Deregulation* (New York: Oxford University Press, 2000); John S. Heywood and James H. Peoples, "Deregulation and the Prevalence of Black Truck Drivers," *Journal of Law and Economics* 37 (Apr. 1994): 150.

61. Maurer, "Organizing the Gypsies," 12.

Conclusion

1. "Tell Overdrive: Ronald Reagan," *OD* (Jan. 1981): 30–31.

2. Gil Troy, *Morning in America: How Ronald Reagan Invented the 1980s* (Princeton, NJ: Princeton University Press, 2005); John W. Sloan, "The Economic Costs of Reagan Mythology," in *Deconstructing Reagan: Conservative Mythology and America's Fortieth President,* by Kyle Longley et al. (Armonk, NY: M. E. Sharp, 2007), 41–69; Barbara Ehrenreich, *Nickel and Dimed: On (Not) Getting by in America* (New York: Metropolitan Books, 2001); Hodgson, *More Equal than Others;* Schertz and Doering, *Making of the 1996 Farm Act;* Jane Adams, ed., *Fighting for the Farm: Rural America Transformed* (Philadelphia: University of Pennsylvania Press, 2003).

3. *NYT,* Feb. 11, 1983, 27; Keeshin, *No Fears,* 33; *NYT,* May 1, 1982, 12; *NYT,* Jan. 8, 1983, 8; *NYT,* Jan. 31, 1983, 8; *NYT,* Feb. 2, 1983, B20; *NYT,* Feb. 3, 1983, 1, 16; *NYT,* Feb. 4, 1983, 1, 10; *NYT,* Feb. 5, 1983, 1, 28; *NYT,* Feb. 6, 1983, NJ25; *NYT,* Feb. 11, 1983, 13.

4. Daniel Madar, *Heavy Traffic: Deregulation, Trade, and Transformation in North American Trucking* (Vancouver: University of British Columbia Press, 2000), 65–197, 171; Alejandro Diaz Landero, "An Economic Appraisal of the Deregulation Process in the Mexican

Transport Market," *Journal of the Transportation Research Forum* vol. 31, no. 1 (1990): 101–8; Rosario Espinal, "Development, Neoliberalism, and Electoral Politics in Latin America," *Development and Change* vol. 23, no. 4 (1992): 38–39; Mark Eric Williams, *Market Reforms in Mexico: Coalitions, Institutions, and the Politics of Policy Change* (Lanham, MD: Rowman and Littlefield, 2001), 111–32; Robert R. Alvarez and George A. Collier, "The Long Haul in Mexican Trucking: Traversing the Borderlands of the North and the South," *American Ethnologist* 21 (Aug. 1994): 606–27.

5. John T. Jones, *The Economic Impact of Transborder Trucking Regulations* (New York: Garland, 1999), 40–44; *NYT*, Feb. 24, 2007; James P. Hoffa, "Trucks Not Ready for Our Roads," *WP*, Mar. 15, 2007, 18; *WSJ*, Mar. 3, 2007, B5; Phyllis Schlafly, "President Opens Border to Mexican Trucks and Drivers," Townhall.com, Mar. 12, 2007.

6. Kathryn Marie Dudley, *Debt and Dispossession: Farm Loss in America's Heartland* (Chicago: University of Chicago Press, 2000); Peggy F. Barlett, *American Dreams, Rural Realities: Family Farms in Crisis* (Chapel Hill: University of North Carolina Press, 1993); Jim Hightower, *Hard Tomatoes, Hard Times: The Failure of the Land Grant College Complex* (Washington: Agribusiness Accountability Project, 1972); Fink, *Cutting into the Meatpacking Line;* Wilson J. Warren, *Tied to the Great Packing Machine: The Midwest and Meatpacking* (Iowa City: University of Iowa Press, 2007), 66–72; Leon Fink, *The Maya of Morganton: Work and Community in the Nuevo New South* (Chapel Hill: University of North Carolina Press, 2003); Lichtenstein, ed., *Wal-Mart*.

Appendix A: Note on Quantitative Data Sources

1. George Delahanty and D. K. Patton, *Manpower Profiles, Manpower Allocation and Labor Relations in Transportation, with Special Reference to the Trucking Industry* (Evanston, IL: Northwestern University Press, 1965), 42; House Public Works and Transportation Committee, *Regulation of Carriers Subject to the Interstate Commerce Act, Hearings,* 94th Cong., 2nd sess., Sep. 14, 28, 1976, 165.

POLITICS AND SOCIETY IN TWENTIETH-CENTURY AMERICA